THE COMPLETE BACKYARD BIRDWATCHER'S HOME COMPANION

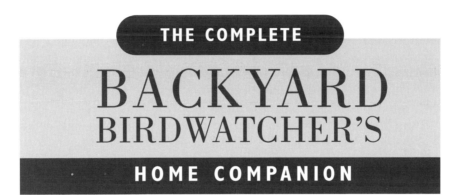

THE COMPLETE BACKYARD BIRDWATCHER'S HOME COMPANION

Donald S. Heintzelman

Ragged Mountain Press / McGraw-Hill

Camden, Maine • New York • San Francisco • Washington, D.C. • Auckland • Bogotá • Caracas • Lisbon • London • Madrid • Mexico City • Milan • Montreal • New Delhi • San Juan • Singapore • Sydney • Tokyo • Toronto

Ragged Mountain Press
A Division of The McGraw-Hill Companies

10 9 8 7 6 5 4 3 2

Library of Congress Cataloging-in-Publication Data
Heintzelman, Donald S.
The complete backyard birdwatcher's home companion / Donald S. Heintzelman.
p. cm.
Includes bibliographical references and index (p.).
ISBN 0-07-134520-5 (alk. paper)
1. Bird watching. 2. Bird attracting. I. Title.
QL677.5.H435 2000
598'.07'234—dc21 00-042537

Questions regarding the content of this book should be addressed to
Ragged Mountain Press
P.O. Box 220
Camden, ME 04843
www.raggedmountainpress.com

Questions regarding the ordering of this book should be addressed to
The McGraw-Hill Companies
Customer Service Department
P.O. Box 547
Blacklick, OH 43004
Retail customers: 1-800-262-4729
Bookstores: 1-800-722-4726

This book is printed on 70# Citation by Quebecor Printing Co., Fairfield, PA
Design by Carol Inouye, Inkstone Communications Design
Production management by Janet Robbins
Page layout by Deborah Evans
Edited by Tom McCarthy, Alex Barnett, and Constance Burt

Photographs by Donald S. Heintzelman unless otherwise credited.
Chapter opener illustrations by Elayne Sears.

Color insert credits: All photos by the author except for the following: Page 1: Black-chinned Hummingbird by Richard Holmes; Common Flicker by Greg Oskay. Pages 2–3: Gambel's Quail, Inca Dove, Black-chinned Hummingbird, Cactus Wren, Curve-billed Thrasher by Richard Holmes; Gila Woodpecker by William Paff/ Cornell Laboratory of Ornithology. Pages 4–5: House Finch by Del McNew; Tuffted Titmouse by Annemarie Nelson. Page 8: Golden-fronted Woodpecker by Richard Holmes; Puple Martin by Purple Martin Conservation Association; Northern Mockingbird, Baltimore Oriole by Annemarie Nelson. Landscape paintings by Elayne Sears.

To the memory of Roger Tory Peterson

(1908–1996),

valued colleague and friend,

who launched the Age of Birdwatching.

CONTENTS

A color insert may be found after page 134

ACKNOWLEDGMENTS

During the research and writing of this book, many people, agencies, and organizations in the United States and Canada provided assistance. It's a great pleasure to acknowledge them here.

The staff of the National Wildlife Federation—in particular, President Mark Van Putten and Backyard Wildlife Habitat Program Manager Heather Carskaddan—were exceptionally cooperative and helpful. Heather obtained for me the names and addresses of selected participants in the Federation's Backyard Wildlife Habitat Program and provided newsletters, references, and updated information on certified habitats in each state.

The Canadian Wildlife Federation and Backyard Habitat Programs Coordinator Maria MacRae provided books and helpful information about its Backyard Habitat for Canada's Wildlife and Golden Gardens programs.

The Purple Martin Conservation Association and Director-Founder James R. Hill III provided much valuable Purple Martin information, plus permission to redraw and reproduce its Purple Martin Range and Migration Map, and a color photograph of a Purple Martin and a SuperGourd.

Wild Ones–Natural Landscapers, Ltd., and President Bret Rappaport provided helpful information pertaining to that organization's website and innovative activities.

Jane Crowley and Kimberly Hope from the national offices of Wild Bird Centers of America, Inc., and Alicia Craig-Lich from the national offices of Wild Birds Unlimited, Inc., also provided selected lists of storeowners in their respective companies. Several backyard habitats discussed in this book resulted from these recommendations.

Numerous nonprofit organizations in the United States and Canada provided additional information, literature, and photographs. They include the Alliance for the Chesapeake Bay and its BayScapes program, the American Bird Conservancy and its Cats Indoors! The Campaign for Safer Birds and Cats, the American Bird Conservation Association for details about the organization and excellent Purple Martin housing photographs, and the American Birding Association for copies of its *Code of Birding Ethics*. The North American Nature Photography Association also provided permission to reprint its code of ethics, *Principles of Ethical Field Practices*.

The Cornell Laboratory of Ornithology provided information about its backyard bird programs, as did the North American Bluebird Society about the needs of Eastern, Mountain, and Western Bluebirds, with permission to redraw and reproduce designs for bluebird nest boxes.

Other nonprofit organizations providing helpful information include Chicago Audubon Society; Colorado Bird Observatory; Conservancy Purple Martin Society;

Florida Audubon Society; Historic Bartram's Gardens; Hummer/Bird Study Group; Hummingbird Society; Los Angeles Audubon Society; Maryland Ornithological Society; National Bird-Feeding Society; National WildBird Refuge, Inc.; Native Plant Society of Texas; Nature Society; National Audubon Society of New York State; North American Nature Photography Association; Ottawa Field-Naturalists' Club; Pennsylvania Audubon Society; Roger Tory Peterson Institute of Natural History; Purple Martin Society, N.A.; Red Deer River Naturalists and the Federation of Alberta Naturalists; George Miksch Sutton Avian Research Center; Wildlife Information Center, Inc.; and WindStar Wildlife Institute.

It's especially pleasant to acknowledge the cooperation of several bird photographers whose outstanding photographs add immeasurably to the appearance and value of this book. They are James R. Hill III, Richard Holmes, Lindsay Kirk, Del McNew, Jerry Pavia, and Eleanor Solberg. To each I extend my sincere appreciation.

Some outstanding backyard wildlife habitat owners also allowed their photographs to be published here for the first time, adding to the book's attractiveness and value. They are John Boyer, Barbara Feldt, Sandy Fliniau, Amy Ginsbach, Eve Heidtmann, Evelyn Helm, Mary C. Jackson, Annemarie Nelson, Greg Oskay, Kay Packard, Mary Plimpton for Beth H. Smith, and Chris J. Slabaugh Sr.

Sources for product photographs and/or drawings include Arundale Products; Bushnell Sports Optics; Celestron International; Droll Yankees, Inc.; Heath Manufacturing Co.; Invisible Fence Co., Inc.; Leica Camera, Inc.; Mirador Optical Corporation; Nikon Sports Optics; Pentax Corporation; Questar Corporation; Swarovski Optik, N.A.; Swift Instruments, Inc.; Water Resources Design, Inc.; and Carl Zeiss Optical, Inc.

Paul Hess spent nearly two weeks searching the World Wide Web for websites pertaining to birds, backyard birding, and birding in general, and then compiled the information into a mini-report that became the starting point for preparing appendix 3, Birding on the Internet. Other folks who provided helpful information include Tina Bailey, Nick Barber and his mother Kathleen A. Barber, Fritz Brock, Joyce Gilmore, and John and Peggy Leahy.

Backyard habitat owners who also provided information and assistance early in this book's development include Pat Adams, Ray Congdon, Lee Duer, Crystal and Frank Ortmann, and Connie Redak. My sincere appreciation is extended to all of these people.

Donald S. Heintzelman
Allentown, Pennsylvania

1 Basic Birdwatching

Summer flower garden near the entrance to David and Arlene Koch's backyard habitat.

It was mid-May in Bethlehem, a small historic city in eastern Pennsylvania. The caress of a gentle spring breeze and the fragrance of flowers were welcome to long-time birdwatcher Catherine Barlieb early that morning. The day promised nothing extraordinary; she had previously seen the birds she expected to see today. But Catherine Barlieb, an elementary schoolteacher and an outstanding birdwatcher, retains the sense of wonder that is evident in young children. With steady hands and observational skills developed over decades of birding, she spotted movement among the leaves as she trained her well-worn binoculars on the crown of a big oak tree. Roughly the size of an American Robin, the bird moved sluggishly from branch to branch, mostly hidden among the vegetation. At moments it revealed the astonishingly vivid red of its body, which contrasted boldly with its deep black wings and tail. Few North American birds equal the spectacular beauty of the spring coat of an adult male Scarlet Tanager. Catherine watched the gorgeous bird feeding on insects until it finally flew out of sight.

Arlene Koch is another avid birdwatcher. She and her husband David live in a rural valley two miles from the Delaware River near Easton, Pennsylvania. Over the past decade, they have converted their 15 acres of yard and farmland into a fascinating haven for the birds that now abound there. They delight in watching a steady movement of birds visiting their many feeders, small waterfall and pool, and adjacent fields. The enhanced habitat that David and Arlene have created is vivid testimony to what can be done—on a variety of scales—to provide the food, shelter, water, and nesting sites that birds and other wildlife require and seek out.

BIRDWATCHING AS A HOBBY

When backyard birdwatchers engage in their hobby, they're participating in an activity enjoyed by tens of millions of people in North America and elsewhere. Birdwatching provides a relaxing and educational diversion from the stress of life and work. Unlike many hobbies, backyard birdwatching combines indoor and outdoor recreation. The outside component consists of creating a backyard habitat that will attract birds and encourage them to nest and raise their young. The indoor component includes educating oneself about the habits and natural history of birds, compiling lists of birds sighted, listening to recordings of birdsongs, watching videos and television programs on birding topics, and sampling the world of resources available to birders on the Internet. For modern backyard birdwatchers, nature and high technology combine to expand the pursuit in ways inconceivable even a decade ago.

Birdwatching is what you want it to be: it can be a meditative, solitary experience or a richly social activity. Many group birdwatching activities are organized by local chapters of the National Audubon Society or state-level Audubon societies. Other wildlife conservation organizations, usually nonprofit groups, offer birding trips to parks and other sites. The Wildlife Information Center, Inc., for example, occasionally does this, as well as the Sierra Club and Nature Conservancy groups, nature centers, and similar organizations. Birdwatching programs are also organized by some birding equipment and supply stores, such as the nationwide chains Wild Bird Centers and Wild Birds Unlimited.

I highly recommend group outings, which can be great fun. Beginning birdwatchers can greatly enhance their early experiences and probably avoid some confusion by associating with experienced birders. Group birding allows novices to sharpen their birding techniques and identification skills in the company of experts. But beginning birders shouldn't be intimidated by the pace of some field

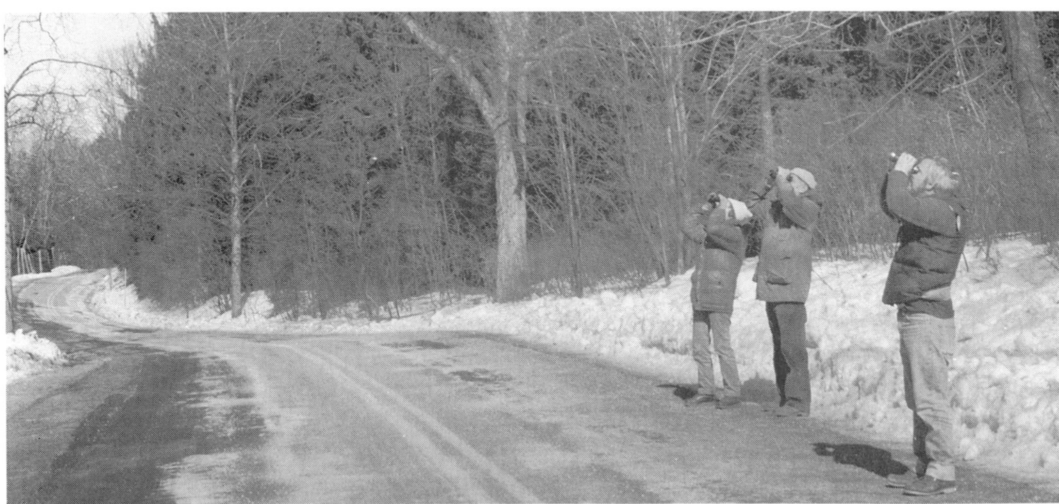

Birders enjoying a winter field trip along a rural road in the Pocono Mountains, Pennsylvania.

trips or the sophisticated language and attitudes exhibited by some field-trip leaders. Ask questions! Experienced birders were at one time beginners themselves, so answering questions from eager beginning birders is an obligation shared by all field-trip leaders.

WHO IS A BACKYARD BIRDWATCHER?

The world of birdwatching at the beginning of the twenty-first century is very different from what it was a hundred years ago. With many millions of active participants, backyard birdwatching is birding's primary activity. It is difficult to define precisely what a backyard birdwatcher or any other kind of birder is. They are people who enjoy watching birds such as Northern Cardinals, Rose-breasted Grosbeaks, House Finches, and Black-capped Chickadees coming to feeders in their yards. Later in this chapter, I discuss some other branches of birding.

Backyard birdwatchers also take joy in providing secure housing for nesting House Wrens, bluebirds, Tree Swallows, and Purple Martins, who will return season after season to the apartment-style dwellings they favor. Just ask Chris Slabaugh of Nappanee, Indiana, who heads the American Bird Conservation Association and manages a sprawling Purple Martin colony of numerous martin houses on his farm. He's the "landlord," as Purple Martin colony owners like to refer to themselves.

And backyard birdwatchers are captivated watching birds like American Robins, Gray Catbirds, Brown Thrashers, and Northern Cardinals enjoying a bath in cool, fresh water on a hot summer day—and increasingly during winter, for more backyard birdwatchers are discovering how much birds enjoy heated water in northern winters. John and Nancy Boyer of Allentown, Pennsylvania, for example, heat water in winter in a birdbath in their beautifully landscaped backyard habitat, which has resulted in many birds visiting their yard during winter for refreshing baths.

Experienced backyard birdwatchers know that this hobby is a state of mind, and devotees derive great pleasure simply from observing birds, their splendid colors, and fascinating behavior. They delight in adding native flowers, shrubs, and trees to their property to create a habitat attractive and hospitable to birds and other wildlife. Backyard birders represent all

BIRDER VERSUS BIRDWATCHER

The definitions of a "birder" and a "birdwatcher" vary from person to person. Many birders and some magazines use the terms interchangeably. That's what I do, although I now tend to use "birder" more frequently than "birdwatcher." Some think of birders as those who put their main emphasis on bird listing and compiling large life lists, whereas birdwatchers are people who take more time to carefully observe, study, and enjoy wild birds.

Chris J. Slabaugh Sr./American Bird Conservation Association

Purple Martin houses on the farm headquarters of the American Bird Conservation Association near Nappanee, Indiana.

John Boyer

American Robins enjoying a warm water winter bath in the backyard habitat of John and Nancy Boyer, Allentown, Pennsylvania.

ENHANCING BACKYARD HABITATS

The National Wildlife Federation reports that more than 26,000 backyard habitat improvement projects have been registered as of May 2000. That means that more than 50,000 acres of backyard habitat are preserved for the benefit of birds and other wildlife in the United States and Canada. Nearly all of these registered habitats, and thousands more that are not registered, serve as excellent backyard birdwatching locations for their owners, friends, and guests.

walks of life—doctors, lawyers, teachers, business people, factory workers, homemakers, and students. They range in age from toddlers to folks a hundred years old—ordinary people who recognize the connection between birding and conservation. They have taken practical action to preserve the habitats that birds and other wildlife depend on at a time when essential habitats are being degraded or destroyed across the United States.

Increasingly, informed gardeners and landscapers are emphasizing the use of native trees, shrubs, and wildflowers to enhance backyard habitats. That's an excellent approach because these species are well adapted to the areas in which they are being returned, and produce fruits, berries, and flowers that birds are equally well adapted to using for food, shelter, and nesting.

Although there are other branches of birding, backyard birdwatching attracts the largest audience. There are tens of millions of participants. The American Birding Association (ABA), for example, has among its members the world's most avid general birders and bird listers, yet 80 percent of ABA members also consider themselves backyard birders.

If you are a beginning backyard birder, start by considering potential birding sites in your own backyard. How productive your yard is—how many species and individual birds it hosts—depends on geographic location, time of the year, degree of habitat enhancement, characteristics of adjacent areas, and human activities nearby. Over the span of an entire year, a typical backyard with a reasonable amount of habitat diversity—such as a few trees and shrubs, some flowers, and water in the form of a simple birdbath—likely will host at least a dozen resident or migratory birds. Often the number of species present is much larger.

Birds that typically visit North American backyard feeders in winter include doves, woodpeckers, nuthatches, jays, finches, juncos, and sparrows. During spring or autumn, birds likely to appear in the same backyard include thrushes, vireos, and wood warblers. And, during the spring and summer breeding season, doves, wrens, thrushes, finches, and sparrows raise their young while taking advantage of a yard's shrubs and trees, food (natural and at feeders), and water.

Levels of Involvement

From its humble beginning early in the twentieth century, birding has grown and diversified to at least four levels of involvement in backyard birdwatching; however, where each begins and ends cannot be clearly defined. Many backyard birders gradually slip from one category into the next.

In recent years, there has been an explosion of casual interest in backyard birdwatching. Millions of folks with limited knowledge of birds represent the beginning ranks of backyard birdwatchers. Although many eventually move on to more advanced birding stages, many other beginning birders are satisfied to remain at the entry level.

Serious backyard birdwatchers comprise another category in the collective world of birding—the millions of avid backyard birders who greatly enjoy having birds visit feeders, encourage birds to nest in birdhouses, and can recognize and identify common and some rarer birds in their yards. Many of these people are also seriously involved in improving their backyard wildlife habitats.

So-called general birdwatchers typically develop from the ranks of serious backyard birders. To enjoy the full scope of their birding hobby, general birders leave their backyards and frequently visit local parks, nature centers, wetlands, cemeteries, state parks, and wildlife refuges.

Sometimes they even travel much farther afield, especially during vacations or on long weekends, to visit national parks and national wildlife refuges in nearby states, as well as elsewhere across the nation or in Canada. In making these birding trips, general birders seek as many new species of birds for their life lists as possible.

Finally, there are highly experienced, sophisticated, advanced birdwatchers who spend hours carefully observing birds at feeders, birdbaths, and other backyard areas, keeping careful, detailed, written notes on their observations.

These folks also frequently travel across the nation, sometimes even overseas, to observe, study, photograph, videotape, and add more species of birds to their life lists. Some advanced birders also conduct detailed field studies of selected bird species and publish their original research findings in state or national ornithological journals.

Special Branches of Birdwatching

Other special branches of birdwatching also are growing rapidly, including some of the most exciting types of birding.

Pelagic birding—looking for oceanic birds on the high seas—is one of the smaller special categories of birdwatching, but its followers are devoted. Several companies and birding organizations now offer pelagic birding trips off the Atlantic, Gulf, and Pacific coastlines of the United States. Sometimes ocean trips combine pelagic birding with whalewatching.

Hawk watching is particularly popular. Thousands of hawk watchers visit mountaintops, coastal and Great Lakes shorelines, and other areas in autumn or spring to see flights of migrating hawks, ospreys, eagles, falcons, and other raptors.

Venturing outside at night to find, listen to, or see owls is another special branch of birdwatching. Some state parks, nature centers, and wildlife refuges schedule "owl prowls" for birders and the general public.

Other popular branches of birdwatching include watching waterfowl, shorebirds, hummingbirds, wood warblers, finches, and sparrows, and species such as Purple Martins and Eastern, Mountain, and Western Bluebirds.

Birding as a Competitive Sport

The competitive sport of birding, which emphasizes the compiling of the longest world list of bird species seen, is a popular twist on birdwatching. The ABA is a leader in this activity.

Although some life-listers have seen more than half of the world's 9,700 or more species of birds, nobody has seen all of them—nor is it likely they will. Some are so rare or little known they have been seen only a few times since their discovery. Others, such as the Bachman's Warbler, may be extinct.

However, some birds still are being discovered and are described as new to science; for example, in Ecuadorian and Peruvian Amazonia and the Philippines. Newly discovered species, therefore, are special new attractions for bird listers.

Another complication in seeing all the world's birds is that new scientific studies sometimes split long-recognized species into two or more new species. The reverse also happens, as when certain former oriole species are grouped together and recognized as the Baltimore Oriole.

On the other hand, not all serious birdwatchers are bird listers; in fact, some have no interest in listing at all. Still, anyone can maintain life lists, including

Canada Geese landing at Lake Muhlenberg, Allentown, Pennsylvania. Local parks are often good locations to enjoy birding.

backyard bird lists, as a means of enjoyment. Many backyard birders enjoy reviewing notes of their past observations. It costs nothing and adds another worthwhile dimension to backyard birding.

BENEFITS (AND DELIGHTS) OF BACKYARD BIRDING

If you've spent time observing birds in a backyard habitat, you've probably discovered some of the benefits. Let's look at some.

Aesthetic Pleasure

The vivid colors of many birds begin to explain why sixty million people in the United States alone feed and house and watch birds in specially created habitats just outside their windows. Few are unmoved by the gorgeous metallic colors of male hummingbirds in North America—Ruby-throated in the East and Allen's, Rufous, Calliope, Broad-tailed, Black-chinned, Blue-throated, Magnificent, and Lucifer in the West. And why should it be otherwise? These tiny bundles of energy, packaged in dazzling metallic coats of many colors, strafe the garden, hover at the feeder, and sometimes even briefly fly backward.

Or consider the colors of male Red-headed Woodpeckers, Red-bellied Woodpeckers, or northern and southern forms of Red-breasted Sapsuckers. Who can deny their aesthetic appeal? These are magnificent birds, wonders of color and form, animated before our very eyes.

Then come the wood warblers, a New World family of birds with wonderful patterns of yellow, black, gray, and other hues including chestnut, orange, and even red, such as in male Painted Redstarts and Red-faced Warblers. Nor should we omit the impressively colored plumages of grosbeaks, finches, male Red Crossbills, and White-winged Crossbills, with their lovely red colors, and male Painted Buntings.

Other birds, especially raptors, provide aesthetic attractions in their splendid powers of flight, regal appearance, and spirit. Peregrine Falcons, for example, have been famous for centuries in America, Europe, and the Middle East for their spectacular stoops (i.e., fast dives) at prey.

To color and flight we must add song. Is there a birdwatcher anywhere in the eastern United States who does not thrill at the clear whistle of a male Northern Cardinal? Or the sweet, thin, "Old Sam Peabody, Old Sam Peabody" notes of the lovely White-throated Sparrow stopping briefly to rest in a backyard as it migrates northward in

Richard Holmes

A female Broad-billed hummingbird feeding at a red yucca flower.

spring? Yet, of all the delightful avian singers that frequent North American backyards, none can match the mellow, flute-like notes of a Wood Thrush. Slow and liquid, the songs of these magnificent singers are most impressive in early morning, at dusk, and sometimes on cloudy days.

Environmentally Friendly

Backyard birdwatching fosters strong support for conservation and preservation of birdlife in backyards and far beyond. As more of the continental United States falls victim to urban and suburban sprawl, the fifty thousand acres of enhanced backyard habitats scattered across America and Canada play an increasingly important role in offsetting the loss of wild habitat. Many common resident songbirds, as well as migrants, are responding by using these small havens of shelter and protection. As even more backyard habitats are improved, the conservation and protection benefits will continue to increase.

By birdwatching in your backyard, you also save gasoline and reduce air pollution and wear on vehicles and tires. This may sound trivial, but when millions of backyard birders each save a few gallons of gasoline by birding at home, the annual savings becomes significant. (Or, better yet, try biking when you leave your own yard for local birdwatching destinations—you'll benefit both the environment and yourself.)

Saves Travel Time

Americans are very busy, mobile people, rushing from one place to the next as if their very lives depended on it. By simply looking out a kitchen or dining-room window, however, backyard birdwatchers can instantly participate in their hobby—often while enjoying a meal. For millions of backyard birdwatchers, there is no need for hours of travel to a birding destination, which gives them more time to enjoy birds visiting feeders, raising their young in birdhouses, resting on perches, or relishing the refreshing waters of birdbaths.

You'll have more time available as a backyard birder to really watch birds carefully. That's another important benefit—deeper insight into the lives of wild birds.

Kinship with Nature

Backyard birdwatchers develop an enhanced kinship with nature over time as they watch doves, woodpeckers, sparrows, and other species selecting and using feeders. You soon begin to appreciate that birds are not resources or products, but rather living, breathing animals. They have many of the same needs as people—food, water, shelter, habitat for rest and sleep, and places to raise their young. They share our world and landscape. Perhaps that's why many backyard birdwatchers very quickly develop an emotional bond with "their birds" that visit or live in their yards.

As birders gain experience, they recognize that birds exhibit a range of emotions including fear, trust, and even some degree of pleasure, although it's not always possible to evaluate the presence of the latter with cold, scientific objectivity.

Consider birdsong. Ornithologists long have known that one of the major functions of birdsong is to enable males of many species to attract a mate during the breeding season, as well as to establish and defend a nesting territory. However, there also may be other reasons why birds sing. I've noted on some occasions how readily some birds, such as House Finches, respond to the sounds of music by Mozart, Beethoven, and other classical composers. Can it be that a House Finch singing along with such music is doing so for the pure joy of singing?

For city dwellers, kinship with nature in some form is very important if they are to regain their awareness that we are all part of nature—and bound by basic, natural ecological and environmental laws and restrictions. The sunflower seeds in plastic bags purchased at a supermarket by an urban birdwatcher did not naturally come that way. They were grown on farms, processed, packaged in a grain or feed mill, and then shipped to the store where they were purchased. When an urban birder watches a bird take those seeds from a feeder, she is in a small but important way reminded of her basic kinship with nature.

KIDS AND FAMILIES

Birdwatching offers great benefits specifically to families with children. Over the breakfast table, children and parents can share the sight of birds visiting backyard feeders, nesting in birdhouses, and bathing in birdbaths. An interest in birds and nature developed at home can reform a child's entire education. Children will have excellent opportunities to use birds as the subjects of school reports for classes in biology, ecology, environmental science, or conservation. Young birdwatchers have the opportunity to connect their academic work to the fascinating activities of birds in their own backyards, and their schoolwork may well reflect that enhanced curiosity and immediacy.

Birdwatching as a family activity commonly centers on birds in backyards, but it need not always be confined there. Many families also enjoy watching birds on vacations. Take Lance Beeny, for example. He introduced his three children, ages three, ten, and eleven, to birding at Bear River Migratory Bird Refuge in Utah—one of our nation's truly superb birding sites. Using as a guide a free Children's Bird List obtained at the refuge's information box, the kids saw nearly every bird on the list—including Western Grebes, White-faced Ibises, Canada Geese, Ring-necked Pheasants, Black-necked Stilts, Killdeer, and Ruddy Ducks. They also identified some rarer species not on the children's list. The result was a successful field trip—and exposure of

A Gray Catbird removing a fecal sac from a nestling.

THE FATHER OF MODERN BIRDWATCHING

The most famous and honored of all twentieth-century birders, Roger Tory Peterson, began his extraordinary lifetime adventure with birds and birdwatching in 1920, as a seventh-grade student. He was a problem child, however, and credits his teacher, birds, and birding as the attraction that steered him into an amazingly productive and rewarding lifetime of adventure. With the 1934 publication of A Field Guide to the Birds, *Peterson showed everyone how to watch and appreciate birds with a brilliance unequaled in the twentieth century—and matched only once before, in the nineteenth century, when John James Audubon produced his monumental* The Birds of America.

The Roger Tory Peterson Institute of Natural History in Jamestown, New York, carries forward the work of its famous namesake. It has a wide range of training workshops, courses, and other programs for prekindergarten through twelfth-grade teachers. In training teachers, the Institute provides another means for Roger Tory Peterson's love of birds and other wild things to spread throughout the United States and beyond.

the children to a worthwhile, wildlife-related family activity.

Camps dedicated to birding offer an excellent way to encourage a child's interest in nature and birds. For example, in 1986, Victor Emanuel—avid birder and founder of Victor Emanuel Nature Tours—provided a special opportunity for teenage children interested in birds. He established Camp Chiricahua, a two-week adventure for a select group of children from across the United States, who learned birding from experts including Roger Tory Peterson, Kenn Kaufman, and Emanuel.

Emanuel's original vision lives on. In 1998, for example, the ABA offered six summer camps, with need-based financial aid, in cooperation with the Institute of Field Ornithology in Maine, Colorado Bird Observatory, and Victor Emanuel Nature Tours.

The Colorado Bird Observatory, a nonprofit bird conservation organization, is one of the oldest of its kind in the western United States. Its primary focus is conservation of the rich diversity of birds of the Rocky Mountains and Great Plains. It accomplishes these objectives by conducting projects and programs in scientific research and public education. The observatory also hosts summer camps for students aged eleven to eighteen. The names and themes of each year's camps change, but birds are at the core. The camps are a blend of education, public outreach, and research designed to meet the needs of children of different ages. These camp programs continue to provide outstanding bird-related experiences for all participants—the types of experiences that someday could direct a student into a professional career in ornithology, ecology, biology, or teaching.

BIRDING CODE OF ETHICS

As tens of millions of Americans participate in backyard and other forms of birdwatching, there is concern about the effects of people on birds. Are birders approaching a feeding American Oystercatcher too closely, causing needless stress on the bird—and thereby causing it to stop feeding and fly away? Is a female Song Sparrow forced to stop incubating her eggs and flee her nest because a photographer is trying to take close-ups of the bird on the nest, disrupting her behavior? Is a migrating Black-throated Green Warbler, perched on a tree branch in an extremely exhausted condition, forced to exert its remaining energy reserves to fly away because a birdwatcher noticed the bird's seemingly "tame" behavior and walked much too close to it? These are a few examples of situations in which "birding ethics" should be foremost in the birder's mind.

In extreme cases of very bad birder judgment and clear exhibition of unethical birding behavior, state and federal bird-protection laws potentially can be used to arrest and prosecute birdwatchers, bird photographers, or other people causing disturbance, injury, or death to birds. On a much less restrictive plane, however, basic ethical guidelines can be used to assure that birdwatchers and bird photographers do not threaten or harm birds.

Bird photographer Arthur Morris, for example, writing in *Bird Watcher's Digest*, proposed some guidelines as an elementary form of birding ethics. His guidelines include being considerate of other birdwatchers and bird photographers, avoiding chasing a bird to secure better views or photographs, refraining from disturbing flocks of feeding or roosting birds, ensuring that fragile habitats are not damaged or destroyed by wandering off marked paths or trails, and obeying posted rules established for regulated areas such as wildlife sanctuaries.

In addition to these informal ideas regarding a code of ethics for birdwatchers, several organizations in North America have developed formal birding codes.

American Birding Association's Code of Ethics

The ABA established a formal, detailed code of birding ethics, which all of its members are expected to observe. With so many people now involved in birding, and the increasing possibility that birds can be harmed due to inappropriate (even if unintentional) birder behavior, I recommend that all birdwatchers adopt and adhere to this code of ethics. Here's a condensed version of the code:

1. Respect wildlife, its environment, and the rights of others.

2. Promote the welfare of birds and their environment.
   - Support the protection of important bird habitat.
   - Avoid stressing birds or exposing them to danger.
   - Remain well back from nests, roosts, display areas, and feeding sites.

3. Respect the law and the rights of others.

4. Ensure that feeders, nesting structures, and other artificial bird environments are safe.
   - Maintain and clean feeders and nesting structures regularly.
   - Keep birds safe from predation by cats and other domestic animals.

5. Give special care to group birding, whether organized or impromptu.
   - Respect fellow birders. Share your knowledge, especially with beginners.

- Document unethical birding behavior, intervene if prudent, and notify appropriate individuals or organizations.
- Teach ethics through word and example of leaders.
- Limit group impact on birds and their environment, and others using the same area.

Backyard birders who want to read the full text of the ABA's Code of Ethics may request a copy by contacting the American Birding Association (see contact information in appendix 1, Birding and Habitat Enhancement Organizations).

Other Birding Codes of Ethics

Several other birding organizations have developed their own ethical birding codes, usually partly based on the ABA code.

The Brookline Bird Club, founded in 1913 in Brookline, Massachusetts, is one of the oldest and largest birding organizations in Massachusetts. It has its own code of ethics, adapted from that published by the ABA. Similarly, the birding code of ethics adopted by the New Hampshire Audubon Society is based on the ABA code.

Regardless of slight variations in each code, the purpose of each is to assure that birders inflict no injury or damage to birds or birding sites, and respect each other as they participate in the hobby of birdwatching.

In addition to millions of people who participate in birdwatching, a growing number of people include bird and environmental photography among their wildlife-related activities. It's important that bird photographers also obey an ethical code to assure the protection of birds, other wildlife, wild plants, and habitats that are the subjects of their photography.

Aware of the need for such an ethical code, the North American Nature Photography Association (NANPA) developed its own ethical code, Principles of Ethical Field Practices, excerpted here.

- Learn patterns of animal behavior.
- Know when not to interfere with animals' life cycles.
- If an animal shows stress, move back and use a longer lens.
- Acquaint yourself with the fragility of the ecosystem.
- Stay on trails that are intended to lessen impact.
- When appropriate, inform managers or other authorities of your presence and purpose.
- Learn the rules and laws of the location.
- If minimum distances exist for approaching wildlife, follow them.
- Ask before joining others already photographing in an area.

Backyard bird photographers wishing to learn more about Principles of Ethical Field Practices or the NANPA may contact the organization directly (see appendix 1).

2 The Natural History of Birds

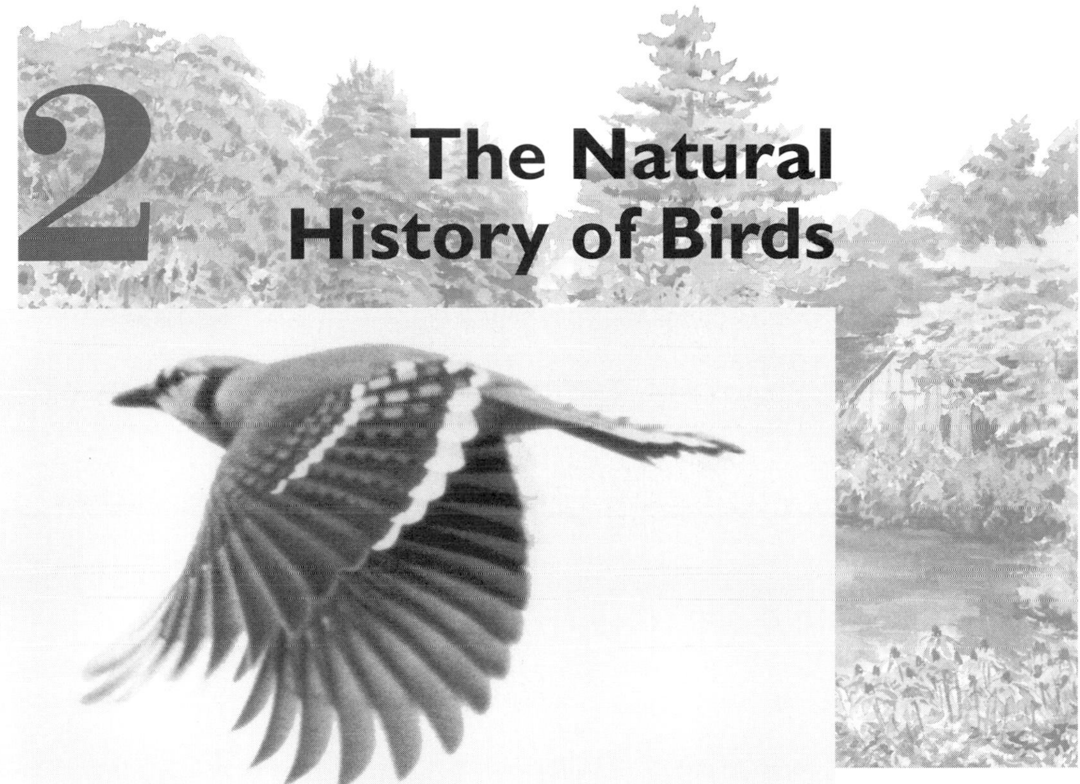

A Blue Jay in flight. Feathers are the unique features that define birds.

There are more than 9,700 species of birds distributed throughout the globe. What do birds like Black-capped Chickadees, White-breasted Nuthatches, and American Robins have in common?

The answer to this question, and many others, can be found in the increasing number of books dealing with all aspects of birds and their lives. Appendix 6 contains a representative sample of such books. Do read some of them.

DEFINING BIRDS

The most obvious characteristics of birds are feathers and, for most birds, the ability to fly. Zoologists classify birds as warm-blooded animals with backbones, in the Class Aves. However, that's too complicated to interest many backyard birdwatchers; so, let's consider a less complicated definition. Fortunately, it's possible to find one that's both simple and unique: a bird is any (adult) animal that is covered with feathers. No animals other than birds have feathers; in addition, no modern birds have teeth.

When some birds, such as American Robins, are newly hatched, they don't yet have feathers covering their bodies. They enter the world completely naked and totally dependent on their parents for food, shelter, and protection. But within a few days of hatching, young American Robins and other birds like them are growing down feathers. By the time they're approximately ten days old, many more feathers are visible. American Robins very quickly develop a protective coat of feathers.

Not all birds are naked as newly hatched nestlings. Some already are covered with down feathers when they hatch, such as Canada Geese and other waterfowl, and are also quickly able to walk (and, in some cases, swim) as soon as their down is dry. While these birds still depend on their parents for protection, remaining very close to them for weeks to learn how to find food, they have a head start on exploring the world compared with birds like American Robins, American Goldfinches, and Song Sparrows.

The next obvious question is: How do birds compare with other animals that also have backbones? Birds and mammals—such as humans, dogs, and cows—are warm-blooded animals with backbones. Because mammals are featherless, by definition they are not birds. Instead, they have hair or fur that covers them and mammary glands, which birds lack. Fish, amphibians, and reptiles also have backbones, but they are cold-blooded and also lack feathers.

WHERE DID BIRDS COME FROM?

The birds backyard birdwatchers see today are the products of millions of years of evolution. They differ considerably from the first known birds that appeared on the earth, about 140 million years ago, in a geologic age called the Jurassic Period. Let's examine that period more closely.

The first known fossil bird species, *Archaeopteryx lithographica*, had feathers. It was therefore a bird, but it was not capable of the powerful, muscle-driven flight we see in most modern birds. Instead, this ancient bird glided downward from a higher perch to a lower one, then climbed again to another higher perch, and repeated the process.

Archaeopteryx differed in other significant ways from modern birds. For example, it had teeth (which perhaps explains the expression "rare as hen's teeth"). Imagine that—a bird with teeth!

But nothing on our planet stands still. Constant change—sometimes so very slow we can't see it by ordinary means—always is in progress. Thus, as many millions of years passed, the ancestors of modern birds we see and enjoy today in our backyards and elsewhere evolved into their current forms. It's a remarkable event, this slow and never-ending alteration of what life on earth looks like, and it's one of nature's truly wonderful phenomena of our world! But there's more to it than that.

Not only did birds—and other animals, plants, and even the earth itself—change many times over vast periods of geologic time, birds also did something else nearly as interesting and remarkable: they spread into nearly every region and habitat of the world. Is that so unusual? Birds do have wings, after all, and most species can fly. They can move around with relative ease compared with mammals, reptiles, and amphibians. Some species, like Arctic Terns, travel great distances every year. Indeed, birds are probably the most perfectly designed animals to disperse across landscapes—even continents and oceans—and take up residence in many different types of habitats. Scientists call this process "adaptive radiation."

Over millions of years, as these marvelous events were happening, the physical appearance of the continents changed dramatically. Some species of birds—as well as other animals and plants—were able to adapt successfully in response, and eventually transformed themselves into new species. Others could not and became extinct. If their skeletons—and, in rare cases, feathers—were preserved as impressions in stone, they became fossils. Thousands of extinct birds already are known to scientists as fossils, and more continue to be discovered every year. However, we can infer that there are many gaps in the fossil record, and it's unlikely that scientists will ever find fossils of every species of extinct birds.

Why many species of birds, as well as other animals and plants, became extinct differs from species to species. Habitat loss is a prime cause of extinction: birds were unable to change their behavior and adapt to changing conditions when some habitats vanished or became scarce. In this way, the current unrestrained expansion of human civilization also has been responsible for the modern extinction of many species.

Some bird species became too specialized in their food habits and were unable to adapt when changing environmental conditions eliminated their food supply. The Ivory-billed Woodpecker is a good example (see sidebar, page 16). But while many species vanished over millions of years, many new bird species evolved in a process that still continues. In the Galapagos Islands, 600 miles off the coast of Ecuador, and in a much more disrupted manner in the Hawaiian Islands, it's possible to see evolution progressing among closely related species and subspecies of birds living on specific islands in both archipelagoes.

In 1835, Charles Darwin discovered this evolutionary process when he visited the Galapagos Islands during the voyage of HMS *Beagle*. His observations and study of Galapagos birds and other animals—significantly augmented with similar evolutionary ideas presented by naturalist Alfred Russell Wallace—led to the classic foundation of evolutionary theory.

It's important not to equate the process of natural extinction, which typically occurred at a glacial pace over thousands or millions of years, with the abruptness of human-caused extinctions in previous centuries or decades. Until we came on the scene, environmental change generally proceeded so slowly that endangered species had time to adapt. That's not the case now.

UNDERSTANDING BIRD NAMES

What's in a name? Backyard birdwatchers may be surprised to discover that there is a great deal more to bird names than is immediately obvious. There are two basic types of bird names: common (or vernacular) and scientific. Backyard birders almost always use the former, but rarely or never use the scientific names, which are composed of two and sometimes three Latin or Latinized names.

Several books have been devoted to bird names and how they were selected. Perhaps the best is the revised edition of *The Dictionary of American Bird Names* by Ernest Choate. The stories of how some bird names came into being are fascinating. Let's explore the matter more fully.

THE IVORY-BILLED WOODPECKER

The Ivory-billed Woodpecker was a magnificent creature that only a handful of aged ornithologists remember seeing alive in certain swamps of Louisiana and elsewhere in the South. It was so specialized in its food habits—certain kinds of bark beetles of mature trees—it could not survive when tracts of old-growth trees were cut. It's tragic that this spectacular woodpecker has probably become extinct. It has not positively been sighted or heard for many years in the United States. Recently, however, a few Ivory-billed Woodpeckers were reported in the mountains of Cuba.

Fortunately, we know a great deal about this wonderful bird. In the 1930s, ornithologists were aware of the plight of Ivory-billed Woodpeckers and were able to learn much about these big, wonderful woodchoppers.

Cornell University graduate student James T. Tanner was asked in 1935 by Cornell's famous ornithology professor, Arthur A. Allen, to join an expedition to the swamps of Louisiana in search of rapidly disappearing Ivory-billed Woodpeckers. Tanner eagerly joined the expedition and quickly proved his worth as a field ornithologist. Several birds were beautifully photographed by Dr. Allen, and their unique voices were recorded. Those priceless photographs and sound recordings are all that exist today.

After returning from the successful expedition, Tanner was selected as the first recipient of a newly established Audubon Ivory-billed Woodpecker Fellowship. The results of that collaboration and vital field research were published by the National Audubon Society in October 1942 as The Ivory-Billed Woodpecker.

Every ornithologist and hopefully every birdwatcher feels sadness at the sight of Allen's wonderful black-and-white photographs of Ivory-billed Woodpeckers taken in 1935, and George Miksch Sutton's painting of a pair of Ivory-bills in Tanner's report. The fate of North America's largest woodpecker—and the second largest in the world—reminds us that birds and other wildlife and plants can become extinct when their habitats are not protected and preserved.

Common Names

When a backyard birdwatcher talks about a Blue Jay or Wilson's Warbler, that birder is using common bird names. Every species of bird in North America, as well as Europe and most other parts of the world, has at least one common name. Sometimes species have several common names, which can cause a great deal of confusion among scientists and backyard birders, especially beginners. However, international efforts seek to select only one acceptable English name for each of the more than 9,700 species of birds. What's clear as we enter the twenty-first century is that a final acceptable list of English names for all the birds in the world remains some distance in the future—and perhaps never will be completely achieved.

Common names have come about in various ways. In the case of the Blue Jay, for example, "blue" describes the color of the bird; however, the origin of "jay" is unknown. Choate and Paynter speculate that it came from a Roman name of certain pets or that it was selected to mean bright (gay) feathers. In the case of Wilson's Warbler, the common name is easier to trace. It honors Alexander Wilson (1766–1813), the father of American ornithology. In addition to the Wilson's Warbler, a species of the storm petrel, plover, and the warbler genus *Wilsonia* also honor his name.

Common names are used almost exclusively by backyard

birdwatchers. However, I've also heard some of the world's leading ornithologists, such as the late Alexander Wetmore, a former Secretary of the Smithsonian Institution and one of the twentieth century's great ornithologists, use common bird names in ordinary conversations with professional colleagues, as well as when discussing some research. Indeed, most professional ornithologists do so frequently, especially in everyday conversation.

But it is not long before beginning backyard birdwatchers discover that some birds have several common names—depending on which field guide is used and/or when the guide was published. Why is a Dark-eyed Junco sometimes called a Slate-colored Junco? And why is a Northern Cardinal not always called just that instead of simply a cardinal?

In North America, the American Ornithologists' Union (AOU) is charged with proposing and accepting one standard common name for each species of living bird on this continent. It does so via the deliberations of a small committee of ornithologists responsible for preparing new editions of the *Check-List of North American Birds*. This book is not a publication that backyard birdwatchers will want to look at very long or attempt to study. Rather, it's a basic technical reference globally accepted by ornithologists and other scientists as the standard reference for names (common and scientific) and other information pertaining to North American birds.

In 1998, the seventh edition of this book was published. Although it contains current thinking regarding common bird names, readers of the new checklist will quickly discover that several common bird names are different than those used in the sixth edition or the much-beloved fifth edition. For example, in 1957, a Northern Cardinal in eastern North America was called "Cardinal"; however, by 1983, the sixth edition changed the name to "Northern Cardinal," which remains intact in the seventh edition.

Despite the worthwhile objective of establishing standard English names for North American birds, many birders and ornithologists are unhappy that it seems to have backfired and caused confusion. For example, whenever a common name is changed by the AOU, every field guide and other printed document using the former name or names become outdated. The same applies to information on computer files and disks, audio recordings of birdsongs, and numerous other documents.

That's why backyard birdwatchers using older editions of Peterson or other field guides find obsolete names for some species. Newer editions use names updated to conform to current AOU standards. In some cases, like the Baltimore Oriole, the original name was changed, then changed back to its original version: Baltimore Oriole.

There is also a checklist of North American birds published by the ABA. It doesn't always conform to the AOU list, both in terms of common bird names and species accepted as valid records for North America. However, the AOU list prevails in scientific (and, hopefully, birding) circles.

The ABA also publishes a useful series of ten regional bird checklists for North America, which make it possible to add recently accepted species to particular regions without reprinting an entire book.

Scientific Names

The scientific name of a bird is composed of two and sometimes three Latin or Latinized words. For example, the scientific name of one of the North American subspecies of the American Robin is *Turdus migratorius migratorius*. In this example, *Turdus* is the genus. In many cases, a genus contains more than one species. For example, *Turdus* contains sixty-five different species of thrushes.

The second part of the scientific name, *migratorius*, is the species name; only the American Robin has *Turdus migratorius* as its species name. However, American Robins have evolved several subspecies, or geographic races. The third name, *Turdus migratorius migratorius* is the subspecies; another subspecies name is *Turdus migratorius confinis*. Because this thrush has subspecies, it's called a "polytypic species." A species without subspecies is called a "monotypic species."

Scientists who select Latin names for birds are called "taxonomists." They may or may not have discovered new species, but in naming them, they are bound by international rules. Sometimes the Latin names describe the physical appearance of a species or subspecies. In other cases, the names refer to the bird's behavior or where it lives, or even honor a person by including his or her first or last name as part of the scientific name.

Although backyard birdwatchers are not likely to use scientific names, it's good to be aware of them and the reasons for their existence.

Classification and Bird Names

A look at any field guide for bird identification quickly reveals that birds are not classified and arranged alphabetically. In more traditional field guides, such as the Peterson and Golden guides, the classification or arrangement of birds more or less follows the scientific system used by ornithologists. Essentially, the classification attempts to show an evolutionary progression of various species, with the most primitive birds appearing first and the most advanced appearing at the end of the book.

While the evolution of birds is best represented as a tree with many branches extending in various directions, it's not a practical way to present it in a book; therefore, a linear arrangement is used. The sequence used in the scientific classification of birds moves from the general to the specific.

There are numerous higher categories also used by taxonomists in the full classification of birds, of interest only to professional ornithologists, which are not included in the simplified classification that follows. Here's an example of how a common backyard bird, the Gray Catbird, is classified:

Class Aves: Birds

Order *Passeriformes*: Perching Birds

Family *Mimidae*: Mockingbirds and Thrashers

Genus: *Dumetella*

Species: *carolinensis*

HOW MANY BIRD SPECIES ARE THERE?

Odd as it may seem, the number of living species of birds varies over time as new species are discovered and other species become extinct. But it is still possible to arrive at a reasonable estimate.

When I began studying ornithology in the 1950s, I learned that about 5,600 species of living birds existed in the world. Today, more than 9,700 species are known to exist. The reasons for the increase are varied, but include the discovery of dozens of species new to science—particularly in tropical areas such as Amazonia—and the use of sophisticated new analytical methods to further evaluate some "species" already recognized.

Among the new research techniques are DNA analysis and comparative behavior of birds. Thus, even in areas known as well as North America, some long-established "species" are split into new species because DNA or other analyses demonstrate that a former "species" actually is two or more different species.

This process of discovering new species and redefining older ones will continue far into the twenty-first century. Even then, the number of living bird species recognized by ornithologists may never finally be settled because a small number of bird specimens housed in the world's research collections resist categorization. Unless status can be determined once and for all, it will be impossible to arrive at the final number of extant bird species.

North America

When Alexander Wilson, the father of American ornithology, and his rival, John James Audubon, explored the North American wilderness early in the nineteenth century, they discovered several strange wood warblers nobody has ever seen since. Perhaps they were odd variations of known species or rare hybrids between two species. Or they may actually have been the last remaining individuals of a species very nearly extinct even in Wilson's and Audubon's time. Whatever these birds were, they remain ornithological enigmas.

One of these odd birds was called the "Blue Mountain Warbler" by Wilson, who secured two specimens near Blue Mountain in Pennsylvania. He painted and described the birds in 1812 in his pioneering *American Ornithology*. Later, Audubon also painted the bird and included it in his monumental *Birds of America*.

However, it's important to remember that Wilson and Audubon experienced the unrepeatable opportunity of exploring the American wilderness before it suffered the widespread destruction we know today. They had opportunities to discover and observe birds, other wildlife, and flora in settings we will never know and can't fully appreciate. It's entirely possible that these two pioneers of American ornithology did indeed witness a few species of birds no longer in existence.

However, in North America—which the AOU defines in its 1998 edition of the *Check-List of North American Birds* as including Canada, the United States, Central America, the West Indies, and the Hawaiian Islands—there are 2,008 species of birds currently recognized. That number will increase slightly in time as other vagrants reach the list's coverage area.

Typical States

On a state-by-state basis, the number of bird species known to occur varies considerably. Factors include geographic ranges of different birds, number of habitat types in the state, the state's location relative to the Atlantic or Pacific Ocean or the Gulf of Mexico, whether major migration routes are located within the state, and the number of skilled birders active in the state. Texas, for example, currently leads the list with 618 validated bird species reported within its borders. New York State has 451 species on its list. In Utah, 408 species of birds have been reported; in Kentucky, 345 species are on the official list.

County and Local Areas

In addition to state bird lists, there is considerable interest in lists of birds validated as occurring in various counties in states across the nation. In my home state of Pennsylvania, for example, several excellent county lists have been published in recent years. The best is William Uhrich's *A Century of Bird Life in Berks County, Pennsylvania*, published in 1997 by the Reading Public Museum, which lists 330 bird species. It could easily serve as a model for the preparation and publication of lists for other counties and states.

Most beginning backyard birdwatchers in North America have probably never heard of county, state, or national bird lists. Nevertheless, there are times when unusual or rare birds appear at feeders, and that's when a wider familiarity with Class Aves is helpful. Indeed, when rare or unusual birds appear, a backyard birdwatcher may have the opportunity to contribute to ornithological knowledge by adding a new species to a county, state, or (very rarely) national bird list. At such times, several experienced birders try to visit the places where rare birds appear, which gives a backyard birder the chance to learn about the wider world of birding beyond backyard habitats.

ADAPTATIONS

Because so many different habitats exist in the world, it's not surprising that many birds developed specialized bills, feet, body shapes, and colors to aid in securing food, other necessities of life, and even survival. Let's look at body parts more closely to see how they help different birds live in the habitats they occupy.

Bills

It does not take long for even the newest backyard birdwatchers to notice that different species of birds have bills strikingly different in appearance. Several bill shapes have evolved on birds we see in North America, usually reflecting the types of food they eat.

Examples of adaptations in bird bills include hooked bills on hawks for tearing prey apart, long bills on hummingbirds for probing flowers to extract nectar, chisel-like bills on woodpeckers for drilling holes in wood to obtain food and construct nesting cavities, flattened and notched mandibles on flycatchers for capturing insects, small and fine bills on vireos and wood warblers, and strong robust bills on grosbeaks and other finches for cracking seeds.

ACCIDENTAL SIGHTINGS

As the name suggests, an accidental is a bird sighted in an unexpected location. Sometimes, as in the case of some accidental seabird sightings, a bird may be thousands of miles from its normal geographic range. One never knows when a species from another area—or even another continent—will unexpectedly appear thousands of miles from where it should be. These birds add real excitement and spice to birding. Moreover, it is not too unusual to discover accidental birds appearing at backyard bird-feeding stations.

Accidental bird sightings at feeding stations might include anything from hummingbirds to thrushes, tanagers, grosbeaks, or sparrows. When backyard birdwatchers see an unfamiliar bird visiting feeders, they should take two steps. First, with binoculars and a guide book, check it very carefully to try to determine its correct identity. Second, if the bird's identity remains questionable or is tentatively determined to be a very unusual species, immediately contact more experienced birders or bird photographers to verify the identification. When very rare or accidental birds appear at bird feeders, the birding and ornithological communities require satisfactory documentation. For more on documenting accidentals, see chapter 10, The Active Birder.

Not all records of accidental birds occur at backyard bird-feeding stations. One accidental I documented in October 1959, at Hawk Mountain in eastern Pennsylvania, appeared after the remnants of a hurricane passed through the area. It was a seabird called a Kermadec Petrel (see photo page (242), which normally lives in the subtropical zone of the South Pacific Ocean. My 16 mm motion pictures of the bird circling the North Lookout represent the only record for the species in North America. Observing and filming that bird are among the highlights of my professional ornithological career. It was only in 1998, after decades of critical review, that the record was accepted and the bird was placed on the main North American bird list in the seventh edition of the AOU's Check-List of North American Birds. *Very few accidental bird records ever receive as intense or prolonged an evaluation period!*

Because the bills of different species have evolved to help birds fill different ecological niches, backyard birdwatchers must use different types of feeders when they establish feeding stations. That's why birding equipment and supply stores sell so many different types of feeders. As we see in chapter 6, Bird Feeders, hummingbirds, chickadees, woodpeckers, and seed-eating birds like finches and sparrows all require different feeder designs.

Feet

Birds display the same variety of adaptation in feet as in bills. The webbed toes of a Canada Goose or Mallard, for example, allow the bird to swim very effectively. Birds of prey like Red-tailed Hawks evolved very strong legs and toes, plus sharp talons (i.e., claws) for grasping and killing prey. On the other hand, the reversed outer, or fourth, toes on the feet of a woodpecker allow it to climb and cling to trees. In comparison, many birds visiting backyard wildlife habitats are passerines (the largest group of birds in the world), like American Robins, which have long hind toes designed for perching on objects such as tree limbs, fences, and wires.

Occasionally, odd things happen at backyard bird-feeding stations. For example, an injured bird may try to adapt to a feeder or food source that it normally would ignore. This happened one January with a Red-tailed Hawk with an injured foot that appeared at the feeders maintained by Betsy and Karl Rogers in western Washington. To the astonishment of the Rogers, the hawk was seen at a feeder tray eating suet, which is normally eaten by woodpeckers. Unable to capture its normal prey (mice and rats) because of its injury, the hawk was apparently so hungry that it changed its diet entirely, demonstrating a fair degree of intelligence in the process.

Noting the hawk's predicament, the Rogers provided an improved food supply, consisting of more meat and occasional rodents, on a modified feeder so the hawk could obtain the food more easily. As a result, the bird remained in the area until spring. Another Red-tailed Hawk then appeared and apparently bonded with the injured hawk. Both birds then disappeared, but the next November, a Red-tail again was seen in the Rogers' woods. When more raptor food was placed in the previous year's special hawk feeder, the Red-tail flew in and ate it. Probably the bird was the same Red-tail that arrived unexpectedly the previous winter. The hawk visited the special feeder for the duration of the second winter.

In September 1998, at the backyard feeders of John and Nancy Boyer in Pennsylvania, I saw another example of an injured bird. A male Northern Cardinal that had more than three-quarters of its upper bill broken off continued visiting a sunflower-seed tray feeder, picking up seeds with some difficulty and cracking them open as best it could. The Boyers told me the bird survived at least one winter in this condition, so the bird might live a reasonably normal life span despite its seriously damaged bill.

Situations such as these are abnormal, but they permit fascinating insights into the abilities of some birds to make radical changes in feeding behavior in order to survive. It's anybody's guess how much intelligence is involved when injured birds improvise, but I suspect that birds and other wild animals are more intelligent than people generally recognize.

Body Shape

Bills and feet are not the only parts of birds that evolved over millions of years. Basic body shapes also evolved, as evidenced by backyard birdwatchers when birds are observed at feeders, birdhouses, or elsewhere in a backyard habitat. A House Finch, for example, is very different in body shape than a Mourning Dove, which in turn is shaped differently than a Blue Jay. The sleek Peregrine Falcon looks nothing like a Wild Turkey in body type.

To a considerable extent, body shape among birds reflects life styles of the particular species and habitats in which they live. A Song Sparrow is well suited for living in open areas containing brush, shrubs, and trees such as roadsides, or in gardens and yards, where it feeds on seeds. A Peregrine Falcon is designed for very fast aerial movement, and lives in open areas such as river valleys or coastal, mountain, and tundra settings, where its food supply of waterfowl, shorebirds, and other birds can be readily seen and captured.

Colors

Birds, of course, come in a great variety of colors. Insofar as North American birds are concerned, any birder easily can see the range of colors among different species by looking at color plates in a bird identification field guide, such as Peterson's *A Field Guide to the Birds*.

A charming little Black-capped Chickadee, for instance, is mainly black, grayish, and white, whereas an American Robin shows vivid colors such as its bright brick-red breast (which varies in shade between sexes and subspecies). Even more colorful are Yellow Warblers and Yellow-breasted Chats. A male Northern Cardinal is strikingly more colorful (some individuals are much brighter red than others) than a female Northern Cardinal, and the same applies to male and female Baltimore Orioles. In the case of these two species and many others, the marked difference in coloration is called "sexual dimorphism." Other common examples that backyard birdwatchers are likely to see include Ruby-throated Hummingbirds, House Finches and Purple Finches, and Indigo Buntings. In the case of Belted Kingfishers, however, the situation is reversed: the females are more colorful than the males.

Quite a few birds are drably colored. Many sparrows are shades of brown, with that color appearing as spots, streaks, lines, and other markings on their sides and upper parts. Similarly, many thrushes and wrens have a good deal of brown in their plumage, especially on their sides and upper parts.

Protective coloration—camouflage—is another reason why many birds are colored as they are. If you look at Peterson's color plates of brown thrushes, for instance, all are one shade of brown on their backs and heads, and most have varying degrees of spots on their light-colored underparts, called "counter-shading." These color combinations help the birds blend into their surroundings and escape predators and other danger. That's why many female birds wear duller colors than males—to avoid predators by being less conspicuous, especially when they're incubating eggs or brooding young, when they don't flee as quickly as during other times of the year. The white rump patch on Northern Flickers is also a type of protective coloration, directing the attention of a predator to a less vulnerable part of the bird's body, perhaps saving the flicker's life.

The actual colors one sees in feathers are formed by either chemical compounds or the physical structure of feathers. Let's look more closely at some of these colors.

Among colors in feathers formed by pigments, what ornithologists call "biochromes"—red, yellow, and orange—are produced by so-called "carotenoids." Furthermore, these colors are linked to the types of plant food certain birds eat, and are products of a bird's digestive process. On the other hand, dark pigments called "melanins" cause feathers to appear brown, brownish-yellow, or black.

Nevertheless, on very rare occasions, it's possible to see black feathers appear white for a brief moment, depending on how light hits the feathers and the position of the observer. I've seen this several times in American Crows. However, the white feathers on the head of some individual waterfowl, like Tundra Swans and Snow

Geese, sometimes are stained a brownish-orange color due to iron in the mud and water. This coloration, therefore, has nothing to do with pigments in feathers or structural coloration; it's merely an external stain on the white feathers, which can disappear when old feathers are molted and new feathers are grown.

Green, on the other hand, is more complicated. It can result from certain pigments or their combinations, as well as the physical structure of feathers. The idea that the physical structure of feathers can cause them to appear as different colors is remarkable. In birds, structural coloration is represented by blue, white, and certain noniridescent greens. Thus, Blue Jays and Eastern Bluebirds appear blue due to the way light is reflected off the physical structure of their feathers rather than from the presence of any blue pigment. However, the spectacular iridescent colors seen in some birds, such as hummingbirds, are the result of how the barbules of feathers are connected together and how they absorb or reflect light. Certain pigments, particularly some types of melanins, also are contained in the barbules of some birds with iridescent colors.

BIRD HABITATS

Birds are not distributed uniformly throughout the world. Some species are found on certain continents but not on others. Within continents, some birds live in some regions but are absent elsewhere. This difference in geographic distribution adds significantly to the appeal of birding. The distribution of the world's 9,700 or more species of birds is controlled to a great extent by ecological factors, particularly habitat type.

Nothing is more important to the survival of birds than correct habitat. Gray Catbirds typically are found in gardens and brushy areas with dense undergrowth, Mallards in ponds and around their edges, and Wood Thrushes in woodlands and woodlots. Each bird requires a different habitat type. The same is true for birds visiting backyard habitats. In subsequent chapters, I'll show you how to create a backyard habitat to attract and sustain birds through gardening, landscaping, and the use of feeders, baths, and nest boxes. But let's look briefly at common bird habitats.

Habitat Types

Throughout North America, there are numerous distinct habitat types occupied by different species of birds, which are described in many bird identification field guides and other references. John Farrand Jr.'s *How to Identify Birds* is an excellent reference. Farrand identifies eighteen different habitat types of interest to birders in North America. (For a detailed review of his habitat categories, see chapter 4, Bird Identification and Field Guides.)

Some habitats are of particular interest to backyard birdwatchers because small examples can be replicated in backyards, including freshwater marshes, ponds, brooks, wooded swamps, bogs, woodlots, pine barrens, streamside forests, thickets, prairies, deserts, and alpine meadows. Which of these can be created or enhanced in a particular backyard depends, of course, on the composition of the yard and the region where it's located.

In some cases, such as alpine meadows, the elevation of the site is critical. Backyard birdwatchers living high in the Colorado Rocky Mountains might be able to develop a small alpine meadow, but one could not expect to establish the same along the New Jersey seashore.

It is possible to restore a small patch of prairie in a backyard on the Great Plains. This is being done regularly by some members of the Wild Ones–Natural Landscapers, Ltd., a nonprofit organization devoted to gardening and landscaping with native plants. Some federal agencies, such as Region 5 of the U.S. Environmental Protection Agency (EPA), also promote preservation or restoration of prairies using native plant species that originally were present in these habitats. The EPA has useful information on its website, in brochures, and in its *Source Book on Natural Landscaping for Local Officials* (see appendix 2). Similarly, the Division of Natural Heritage of the Illinois Department of Natural Resources published *Prairie Establishment and Landscaping* to assist people wanting to restore small patches of prairie on their properties using appropriate native plants. In Arizona, the Arizona Game and Fish Department published *Landscaping for Desert Wildlife*, which provides detailed recommendations on native trees, shrubs, cacti, succulents, flowers, and grasses for landscaping purposes.

However, many essential bird habitats are virtually impossible to replicate, including rocky shorelines and coastal cliffs, beaches and dunes, mudflats and tidal shallows, large saltwater marshes, rivers and lakes, large blocks of old-growth forest, mountain cliffs, gorges, mesas, and tundra.

Habitat Loss and Preservation

Wildlife habitat loss in the United States is the single-most important factor responsible for the extinction of birds and other wild species, and for drastic reductions in populations of many other species. There are many reasons for habitat loss, but ignorance and human greed are responsible for much of it.

Housing developments, such as this near Lehigh Gap, Pennsylvania, seriously degrade, or destroy, important bird habitat for resident and migratory birds.

The development of millions of acres of farmland and other open spaces accounts for an appalling amount of habitat loss. The loss of wetlands habitat in the United States is a disaster, due in large part to ignorance of the special ecological importance of wetlands.

Wildlife conservationists are continually seeking better and more effective ways to preserve

America's vital, remaining wildlife habitat—and to restore degraded or lost acres insofar as it's possible. Backyard birdwatchers can help by creating or improving wildlife habitat in their backyards.

Certain aspects of this general habitat loss are of critical importance to birds. One looming crisis concerns stopover habitats for migratory songbirds flying north across the Gulf of Mexico during spring. This problem has not gotten much publicity, but thanks to a few ecologists working in a fairly new research discipline, called stopover ecology, these appalling losses are being recognized. These losses extend up to fifty miles inland, along a three-hundred-mile front on the northern shoreline of the Gulf of Mexico in southern Texas, Louisiana, and Mississippi.

These stopover habitats are old beach ridges, called "cheniers," that extend inland some twelve miles from the coast, parallelling the coastal shoreline. They contain wooded upland oak, hackberry, honey locusts, and red mulberries—trees and shrubs providing essential food for as many as forty-five million northward-bound, nearly exhausted migratory songbirds that hit the Gulf Coast after hours of flying across the Gulf of Mexico. Tragically, many cheniers are targeted for landscape development. Indeed, these habitat losses are very serious and, by 2010, could spell doom for at least sixty-three species of migratory neotropical songbirds—birds like Wood Thrushes and many wood warblers that breed in North America but winter in Latin America or the West Indies.

Many private owners of cheniers allow cattle-grazing, other agricultural activities, land development for homes and industry, and gas and oil exploration on their property. These uses degrade the ecological value of stopover habitats, which means migrants like Gray Catbirds, Canada Warblers, Ovenbirds, and thrushes have no place to forage for badly needed food.

It remains to be seen whether The Nature Conservancy and other nonprofit organizations can work out effective protection agreements with private owners of critical cheniers. The long-term future of birdwatching as a hobby is partly dependent on these conservation efforts. Backyard birdwatchers living in these critical areas also can assist by creating or enhancing their backyard habitats with the native trees, shrubs, and wildflowers that migratory songbirds need for resting and feeding. In Rhode Island, for example, backyard birders can include pokeweed, bayberry, and northern arrowwood. In general, the more native-food-producing trees and shrubs planted for the benefit of migratory and other birds, the better. It will be impossible to completely compensate for all destroyed bird habitats, but a degree of restoration is certainly possible. Backyard birdwatchers, even beginners, can lead this conservation effort.

Loss of stopover habitat is not restricted to coastal areas. The Kittatinny Raptor Corridor in Pennsylvania is also being degraded. It includes the famous Kittatinny Ridge, along which tens of thousands of migratory birds of prey and other migratory songbirds travel every autumn. While most of the mountain is owned by federal, state, and local governmental agencies and a few private conservation organizations, it is not true for farmland, woodlots, wetlands, and other habitats extending out five miles from the north and south bases of the ridge. Development there is continuing—sometimes with the support of local governmental officials.

To help to deal with this problem, the Wildlife Information Center developed its Kittatinny Raptor Corridor Project, which seeks to preserve important wildlife habitat within the Raptor Corridor.

If backyard birdwatching is to thrive through the twenty-first century, habitat preservation is the single-most vital, long-term action birdwatchers and other wildlife conservationists can take to preserve the birdlife of North America.

ECOLOGICAL NICHE

Now that we have a sense of what "habitat" means, what is meant by "niche"? Habitat is the home area where individuals of a particular species live. American Robins live in gardens or yards with lawns and other trees, shrubs, and flowers. However, their relatives, the Wood Thrushes, live in forests or large woodlots. Both birds are thrushes, but they occupy different habitats. When ecologists talk about "niche," they are referring to the type of "work" that individuals of a particular species perform—how and where birds go about finding food and the types of food they select. Birds of related species can coexist in the same habitat without serious interference or competition because they occupy different ecological niches.

Now let's look at some related birds living in the same habitat and consider their ecological niches. Wood warblers provide some excellent examples. Studies of wood warblers show that different species forage for food at different elevations, ranging from ground level to the tops of tall trees. For instance, Canada, Kentucky, and Worm-eating Warblers seek food low to the ground, whereas Black-and-White, Black-throated Blue, and American Redstart warblers forage at medium heights. On the other hand, Blackburnian and Cerulean Warblers seek food high overhead in the tops of tall trees or within a forest canopy.

As detailed as that might sound, these wood-warbler foraging heights are only general indications of where the birds find food. More sophisticated ecological studies of warbler foraging behavior have revealed still more detailed information, such as where on specific trees certain wood warblers search for food—high or low on the tree, on the trunk, thick limbs, thin limbs, and so on.

In addition, slightly different types of food are captured and eaten. Thus, wood warblers and other birds depend on niche partitioning to sort themselves out when related species live in the same habitats. While the same habitat may be occupied, the birds do not seriously compete with each other for the same food. Scientists refer to this niche partitioning as the principle of competitive exclusion.

Of course, the danger of two or more species occupying the same niche within a particular habitat does not apply to completely different birds needing different types of food. For example, a pair of American Kestrels nesting in a box placed along the edge of an old field will capture mostly voles, some insects, and an occasional small bird. However, Red-tailed Hawks hunting over an old field also may capture voles, but they use different hunting methods and nest in different settings, such as in trees in woodlots adjacent to the fields, near the edge of a woodland, or even on exposed utility towers. The two raptors are not competing for nesting sites

BIRD BEHAVIOR

With more than 9,700 species of birds in the world, it is not surprising that birds exhibit many variations and types of behavior. Backyard birdwatchers should have no problem observing some of the more common behavior traits related, for example, to nesting and mating, or visiting feeders and birdbaths. A few examples include singing, bathing, and preening feathers. Several good books are available that provide an introduction to bird behavior, such as the three volumes of A Guide to Bird Behavior *by Donald and Lillian Stokes. They discuss selected traits and behavior patterns of numerous species. For the Black-capped Chickadee, for example, the Stokeses discuss signature visual displays, such as head-forward and wing-quiver. For auditory displays, they include the well-known Fee-Bee-Song and Chickadeedee-Call, as well as less common displays. They provide further information on courtship, breeding, nest-building, plumage, seasonal movements, and social behavior. All of this information is presented in a simple, accessible style that the layperson can follow.*

and the food they utilize tends to be common to abundant.

FOOD REQUIREMENTS

Birds of various species eat different kinds of food throughout the year. Learning about these dietary habits is one of the fascinating parts of backyard birdwatching. An excellent source is *American Wildlife and Plants: A Guide to Wildlife Food Habits* by Alexander Martin et al.

Applied to backyard habitats, different types of bird feeders and foods are needed to satisfy requirements of feeder birds. Moreover, food consumed during winter may be different from the dietary habits of the same birds during other seasons.

For example, Downy Woodpeckers searching for food away from feeding stations eat adult beetles, some beetle and moth larvae, and ant heads, as well as scale insects and aphids, caterpillars, spiders, and snails. They also eat the fruits of dogwood, poison ivy, Virginia creeper, and serviceberry—plus corn and acorns. However, at backyard feeders, their diet consists of suet, nutmeats, occasional sunflower seeds, and corn—foods that can be provided conveniently.

Hairy Woodpeckers, larger versions of Downy Woodpeckers, eat ants, adult beetles and their larvae, caterpillars, millipedes, and aphids. Plant food includes the fruits of poison ivy, pokeweed, cherry, dogwood, and Virginia creeper. Some corn and apple is also consumed. However, at backyard feeders, Hairy Woodpeckers eat suet, sunflower seeds, peanut butter, nuts, and pieces of apples and bananas.

Red-bellied Woodpeckers, in comparison, eat insects like larvae of wood-boring beetles, ants, crickets, grasshoppers, caterpillars, and occasionally small lizards or tree frogs. Acorns, fruits, and berries of many plants are also eaten—oaks, corn, grapes, cherry, mulberry, Virginia creeper, pine, hickory, bayberry, and poison ivy. The fruits of beech, dogwood, black gum, hazelnut, elderberry, and palmetto also are consumed. Red-bellied Woodpeckers visiting backyard bird feeders, however, eat suet, sunflower seeds, and even pieces of apples and oranges. Sometimes they even store acorns and cracked corn—making them different from Downy and Hairy Woodpeckers.

On the other hand, Purple Finches provide an example of seasonal variation in diet. During warmer seasons, they typically eat plant seeds, fruits, and buds, resulting in a diet nearly 100 percent plant matter. Preferred foods are elm and apple buds and seeds; buds and fruits of cherry and peach trees; and fruits, berries, and seeds of dogwood, sweet gum, honeysuckle, grape, and poison ivy. In winter, however, Purple Finches visit backyard bird feeders to eat sunflower and niger seeds. Seed trays and other types of feeders, such as the popular Droll Yankees, all are visited. Occasionally, they'll even fly to the ground to pick up seeds.

Regional populations of the same species may develop different feeding habits as well. House Finches, with native populations in western North America and an introduced, migratory population in eastern North America, have different feeding habits. In the West, they often live near farms or in orchards. In California, they take cultivated fruits and other crops, although seeds remain primary items in their diet. Other important plant foods include filaree, turkey mullein, mustard, knotweed, prune, fig, and pigweed. At western feeding stations, House Finches are omnivorous—they'll eat seeds, grains, pieces of apples and oranges, and other items offered on tray, hanging, and ground feeders. In the East, House Finches eagerly eat niger and sunflower seeds in tube feeders.

White-crowned Sparrows are mostly western and southern birds—the relatives of White-throated Sparrows of the East—although some White-crowns also occur in the East. Their food consists of plant matter plus a few insects and spiders. In the Northeast, seeds of oats, bristlegrass, smartweed, and panicgrass are important dietary items. However, on the prairies, ragweed seeds and the seeds of sunflowers, goosefoot, pigweed, and oats are food items. In the western mountains and deserts, White-crowned Sparrows eat sunflower, pigweed, goosefoot, and knotweed seeds; on the Pacific Coast, particularly California, oats and the seeds of pigweed, mayweed, and chickweed are mainstay food items.

At backyard feeders, White-crowned Sparrows commonly eat sunflower seeds on low tray feeders or scattered on the ground. This preference is not surprising because their bills are designed for cracking seeds.

White-throated Sparrows are lovely birds that feed on smartweed and ragweed seeds, as well as ants, beetles, caterpillars, millipedes, spiders, and snails. At backyard feeders, however, sunflower seeds are relished, either scattered on the ground or also offered in feeding trays.

NESTING REQUIREMENTS

As we've already seen, birds don't nest any place they happen to be. Some species tolerate a wide range of nesting sites, others are very specific in their requirements. Let's look at a few examples.

Ospreys are fish-eating raptors. They select nesting sites near rivers, lakes, seashores, and other large bodies of water, and they construct impressive nests on various supporting structures, such as dead trees, utility poles, towers, roofs of houses, and platforms erected for their use. The Osprey nest shown on the next page, for example, was built in a dead red cedar tree along coastal New Jersey. The size of the man checking the nest shows how large some Osprey nests are.

An impressive Osprey nest along coastal New Jersey. This Osprey researcher is gathering data and preparing to band nestlings.

Before Peregrine Falcons were nearly extirpated in North America by DDT pollution after World War II, most eastern Peregrines nested on cliffs overlooking river systems. Ornithologist Joseph J. Hickey studied these sites, referring to them as "ecological magnets" because generations of Peregrines returned to the same cliffs and ledges to nest. For these falcons, nesting requirements were very specific. If a cliff did not meet the exact needs of these birds, the site was rejected.

Belted Kingfishers require riverbanks where soil is adequately soft to allow the birds to excavate a burrow in which the eggs are deposited and incubated and the nestlings are raised.

Song Sparrows like open areas, often near water, with shrubs and brush in which to build their nests. Given those requirements, they nest in backyards, parks, farms, gardens, and many other places.

Other birds prefer specific habitat types, elevations above the ground, or other requirements to build their nests and raise a family. That's why conservation biologists insist that it's vital to preserve as much habitat and ecosystem diversity as possible. It is the only way to ensure as many species as possible in backyard habitats and other areas.

BIRD MIGRATION

For as long as people have lived and noticed their surroundings, they've been aware of bird migration. The seasonal comings and goings of birds are hard to overlook.

What is bird migration? Put simply, it is the periodic movement of birds traveling from one geographic location to another. We immediately think of seasonal migration, but even the daily movement of many birds is a kind of migration. We know a lot about bird migration, but much remains to be learned, and thousands of ornithologists and birders continue to study migrating birds. To these people, this study is one of the most fascinating, enjoyable, and informative aspects of birdwatching.

A BAN ON DDT

After the end of World War II, a chemical called DDT became the most widely used pesticide in the United States and elsewhere in the world. One of a group of chlorinated hydrocarbon compounds, it is deadly to many species of insects.

Unfortunately, DDT accumulates in the fat of birds, other wildlife, and people. It is this tendency of sublethal amounts of DDT to be stored in animal fat, undergoing biomagnification, that made the pesticide so dangerous.

As more DDT accumulated in the fat of larger birds associated with wetlands—Bald Eagles, Ospreys, Peregrine Falcons, Brown Pelicans, and dozens of other species—evidence of unexpected biochemical reactions appeared in them. Their eggshells became thin, and broke while being incubated, leading to dramatic losses of young birds—so much so that these species became endangered and nearly extinct.

Aware of this wildlife crisis, biologist and celebrated author Rachel Carson (1907–1964) published Silent Spring *in 1962 to warn of the dangers of uncontrolled and indiscriminate uses of biocides in agriculture, forestry, horticulture, and the general environment. Despite vicious attacks on her book—and herself—Carson defended its vital message in the same quiet, gentle way she wrote her books and conducted her life.*

As a result of Silent Spring, *as well as other new information, in 1972, DDT was banned in the United States; Canada and western Europe also banned it. Since then, as the result of millions of dollars spent on endangered-species management, populations of some birds once decimated by DDT have recovered. The Peregrine Falcon is no longer listed as endangered by the U.S. Fish and Wildlife Service and, as this book goes to press, efforts are also being made to remove the Bald Eagle from the federally endangered species list. Ospreys and Brown Pelicans have also recovered well.*

However, DDT is still exported to some nonindustrialized nations. That means some migratory birds that breed in North America and winter in Latin America may still be exposed to DDT—among other powerful pesticides—on their wintering grounds or during migration. Many other biocides also are used widely in the United States and elsewhere without complete knowledge of their long-term effects on birds, wildlife, and people. However, the environmental movement launched in 1962 by Rachel Carson is working to achieve environmentally sound public policies for all biocide uses in the United States and the world.

In recognition of the worldwide impact of Silent Spring *on governmental policies and the widespread view that Carson was a most important founding voice of the modern environmental movement in America, she was posthumously awarded the Presidential Medal of Freedom—our nation's highest civilian decoration—in 1980 by then-President Jimmy Carter.*

When a Ruby-throated Hummingbird appears in May at a sugar-water feeder in a backyard in Massachusetts, that bird has completed an exhausting, dangerous, nonstop flight across the Gulf of Mexico from its wintering grounds in Mexico or Central America. It has performed an extraordinary feat of navigation, strength, endurance, and survival. Yet, to the hummingbird, it's only one part of an annual cycle that thousands of earlier generations also completed successfully.

Similarly, when backyard birdwatchers notice unusual birds in their yards during spring or autumn—perhaps Cape May Warblers, Black-throated Green Warblers, Blackpoll Warblers, or Wilson's Warblers—it may not be apparent that they are migrants; if they disappear within a few hours or days, they probably are.

What is important for backyard birdwatchers to understand is that both migratory birds and nonmigratory residents appear in backyards. For migrants, the quality of the backyard habitat—especially protective cover, food, and water—is of major importance. In fact, the number of high-quality backyard habitats may make the difference between life and death for some birds—especially those located at stopover locations along the Gulf of Mexico, the Atlantic and Pacific coastlines, and other locations.

Backyard birdwatchers need not be experts about bird migrations, but it's worthwhile to learn some basics; for example, knowing which species are most likely to appear during seasonal migrations. That adds extra excitement to backyard birdwatching when an unusual or rare bird appears. See appendix 6, Further Reading, for excellent sources about bird migration, such as my *The Migrations of Hawks*, Jean Dorst's *The Migrations of Birds*, and Scott Weidensaul's *Living on the Wind: Across the Hemisphere with Migratory Birds*.

It does not take long for backyard birdwatchers to discover that there are two basic types of bird migration: daily and seasonal. Let's look at each.

Types of Migration

Daily bird migrations are exactly what the name suggests. They are flights of birds, like American Crows and European Starlings, from a roost (i.e., a sleeping location) to another location (e.g., a backyard habitat), then returning in the evening to the roost. As backyard birdwatchers become aware of daily migrations, they soon notice local examples. In some parts of North America, local populations of Canada Geese engage in daily migrations.

Daily bird migrations need not involve large numbers of birds. (Technically, even one bird can demonstrate daily migration.) However, some roosts contain thousands, sometimes even millions, of American Crows or mixed flocks of European Starlings, Red-winged Blackbirds, Common Grackles, and other species. Roosts begin forming in autumn, continue through winter, and gradually break up in spring.

Many North American birds undertake seasonal migrations twice each year, during spring and autumn; these are the migrations normally thought of by birdwatchers. Migratory birds include waterfowl, hawks and other birds of prey, shorebirds, some owls, thrushes, wood warblers, grosbeaks, finches, and some sparrows. During spring and autumn, backyard birdwatchers try to maintain a particularly careful watch for unusual birds appearing in their yards or flying overhead.

Why do birds like American Robins, Gray Catbirds, vireos, wood warblers, and Baltimore Orioles migrate? There is no single answer. Each migratory species, and sometimes even certain populations of some species, migrates for different reasons. There are two basic reasons, however, why birds engage in seasonal migrations: to escape harsh or severe winter weather conditions, spending the winter months in warmer and more hospitable climates and habitats; and to have access to food. Insectivorous vireos and wood warblers are good examples of birds that must migrate to warmer climates during winter to obtain insects, their main food supply. These birds would starve if they remained in colder sections of North America during winter when insects are not available. Sometimes these two factors work in concert.

On the other hand, birds such as Wild Turkeys, Northern Bobwhites, and Ring-necked Pheasants do not migrate; they remain in the same habitat year-round. They are able to find enough food and shelter to survive—even during hard winters; therefore, there is no advantage in migrating.

What about some finches? They do not migrate southward every year. Rather, they engage in periodic migrations, or invasions, particularly when natural food supplies such as plant seeds are temporarily in short supply and inadequate to support them on their northern breeding grounds. When this happens, birdwatchers enjoy unusual opportunities to see the so-called "finch" species—Common Redpolls, Pine Siskins, Pine Grosbeaks, and crossbills—at backyard feeders. Many beginning birders have added these birds to their life lists during "finch years."

In some parts of the United States, certain species of birds may exhibit both daily and seasonal migration simultaneously for short periods; Tundra Swans provide a good example. In eastern Pennsylvania, in February and March, large flocks of migratory swans stop during their long-distance migrations to spend a few weeks resting and feeding in stopover staging areas along the Susquehanna River. During these staging stops, the swans spend nights on the river, safe from predators. Early each morning, they fly to farm fields several miles inland, returning after feeding to the river for the night.

Tundra Swans on a spring migratory staging area on the Susquehanna River near Washington Boro, Pennsylvania.

After several weeks, the swans leave the staging area and continue their long-distance migrations to the Arctic, where they nest. Backyard birdwatchers who live in the migration route have a good opportunity to observe a very beautiful example of daily bird migration interlinked with seasonal migration.

Seasonal migrations or occasional wanderings by individual birds are the reasons why birds such as cormorants, eagles, and gulls, which might otherwise not be expected, appear on a backyard birdwatcher's life list.

Time of Migrations

Migrating birds undertake seasonal migrations at different times during a twenty-four-hour period. Many migratory neotropical songbirds—birds like thrushes and wood warblers that breed in North America but winter in Latin America or the West Indies—migrate at night. Therefore, the best time to see some of these birds is just after sunrise, when they land in backyard habitats to rest and feed before continuing their travels.

An immature Broad-winged Hawk migrating south to its wintering grounds in South America.

Other long-distance migrants, such as Ospreys, Broad-winged Hawks, and Peregrine Falcons, are diurnal (i.e., daytime) migrants. They use conspicuous landmarks as navigational aids. These birds are best seen during their autumn migrations at more than a thousand locations in North America, including Mounts Tom and Wachusett in Massachusetts, Bake Oven Knob and Hawk Mountain in Pennsylvania, Cape May Point in New Jersey, Hawk Ridge in Minnesota, Bentsen-Rio Grande Valley State Park and Santa Ana National Wildlife Refuge in Texas, and Point Diablo in California.

Some migratory birds, such as Canada Geese, migrate at night and during the day. In October, it's fun to watch wedges of migrating geese flying southward high overhead. Many backyard birdwatchers add this species to their life lists merely by looking up as the noisy birds appear overhead.

Routes

The U.S. Fish and Wildlife Service publishes a little book titled *Migration of Birds* that explains and maps migration routes used by Red-eyed Vireos, Connecticut Warblers, American Redstarts, Scarlet Tanagers, Western Tanagers, Rose-breasted Grosbeaks, Bobolinks, and Harris's Sparrows. These maps give birdwatchers a better appreciation of an important part of the lives of some birds that visit bird feeders and use nesting houses in backyard habitats. Indeed, much is known about North American bird migration routes, flyways, and corridors.

Many years ago, W. W. Cook was one of the first ornithologists to identify generalized routes used by migratory birds flying from the continental United States to wintering grounds in the West Indies and Latin America. Many routes include long, over-the-water flights—a dangerous, sometimes lethal, undertaking—although an adequate number of birds use these routes successfully.

The most perilous is the nearly continuous, over-the-water Atlantic Ocean route taken by shorebirds such as American Golden Plovers. They begin on the coasts of Labrador and Nova Scotia, reaching landfall again in the Lesser Antilles; then they continue to the South American coast. Birds not in peak physical condition or not having full fat reserves that are converted into energy are likely to fall into the ocean and perish. While some other migration routes also involve over-the-water flights, none are so long or exhausting as the route from Maritime Canada to

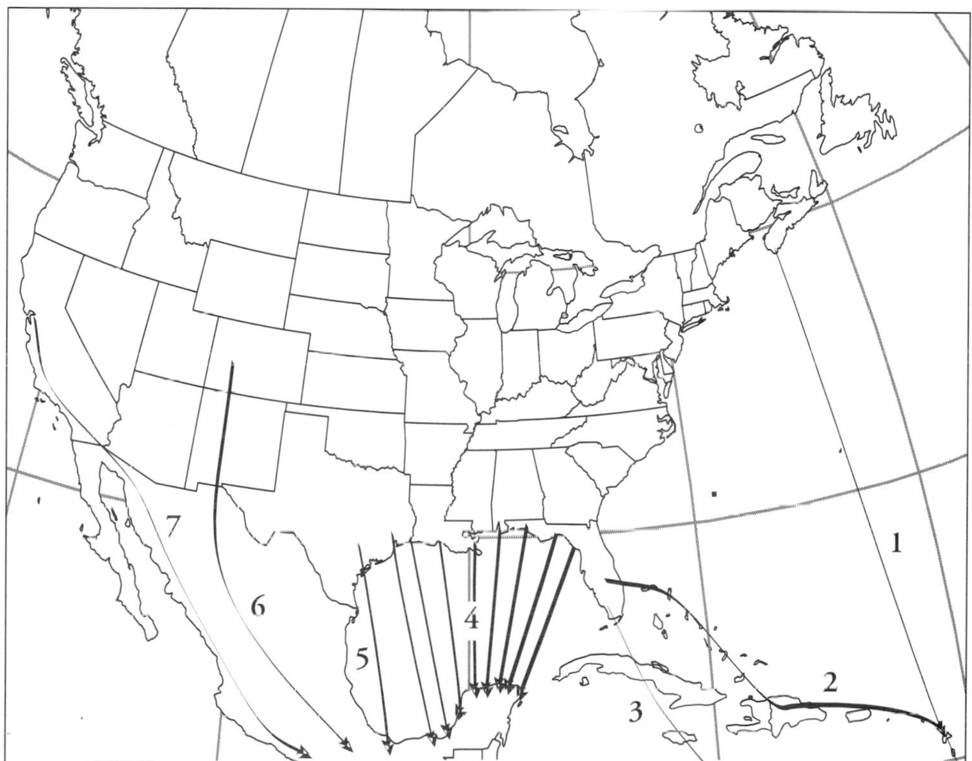

Principal bird migration routes used by North American migratory birds. Redrawn from Frederick C. Lincoln and Steven R. Peterson in *Migration of Birds*.

the Lesser Antilles. Many migratory neotropical songbirds use shorter routes, such as across the Gulf of Mexico. Let's look more closely at some major groups of birds and their migrations.

Waterfowl are economically important game birds, so their migrations are studied intensely by U.S. Fish and Wildlife Service biologists. Based on studies in which birds were marked (i.e., banded) and tracked, a model of waterfowl migration was developed with four major migration routes, or flyways, in North America: Atlantic, Mississippi, Central, and Pacific. More recent research, however, shows numerous waterfowl-migration corridors and flightlines across the North American continent. Nevertheless, the four original waterfowl flyways remain useful for administrative purposes, and give beginners a good general picture of the migration routes used by North American ducks, geese, and swans.

Spring and autumn hawk migrations in North America are spectacular. Thousands of hawks, eagles, falcons, and other species migrate across a broad front, flying to or from their breeding grounds. Autumn hawk migrations are well studied. I've documented in *The Migrations of Hawks* some 2,000 or more locations where migrating hawks can be observed, and new sites are being discovered—especially in western North America. The Hawk Migration Association of North America is deeply involved in studying these migrations.

Where major geographic features form migration barriers—especially large water barriers like the Great Lakes—most migrating raptors avoid crossing them and follow shorelines. Other landscape features, such as mountains, also divert raptor migrations along their flanks.

During spring, several major concentration areas are known along the Great Lakes shorelines. In New York State, Braddock Bay and Derby Hill are famous. Whitefish Point in Michigan's Upper Peninsula is another raptor and songbird concentration area.

In North America, several major migration routes are used in autumn by migrating hawks: the Atlantic Coastline; the Piedmont, inland from the coastline; the Kittatinny Ridge or Blue Mountains and ridges north of the Kittatinny in Pennsylvania; the northern and western shorelines of the Great Lakes; the Great Plains; the Rocky Mountains; parts of the Gulf Coast; and the Pacific Coast.

Some songbirds, however, use different migration routes. Harris's Sparrows, for example, use a narrow migration route from northern breeding grounds southward to the central part of the continental United States. In the United States, the Harris's Sparrow's migration belt is only about 500 miles wide, narrowing in eastern Texas to a width of about 150 miles (see map page 38).

Rose-breasted Grosbeaks are lovely birds that nest in some backyard habitats in the northern United States and southern Canada—a breeding area 2,500 miles wide. However, when these birds migrate southward in autumn, their migratory path is only about 1,000 miles wide. Grosbeaks from some of the western populations fly through central Texas into Mexico, with some birds continuing to northern South America. However, many Rose-breasted Grosbeaks from the East follow the Atlantic Coast into northern Florida, then fly over the ocean, cross The Bahamas

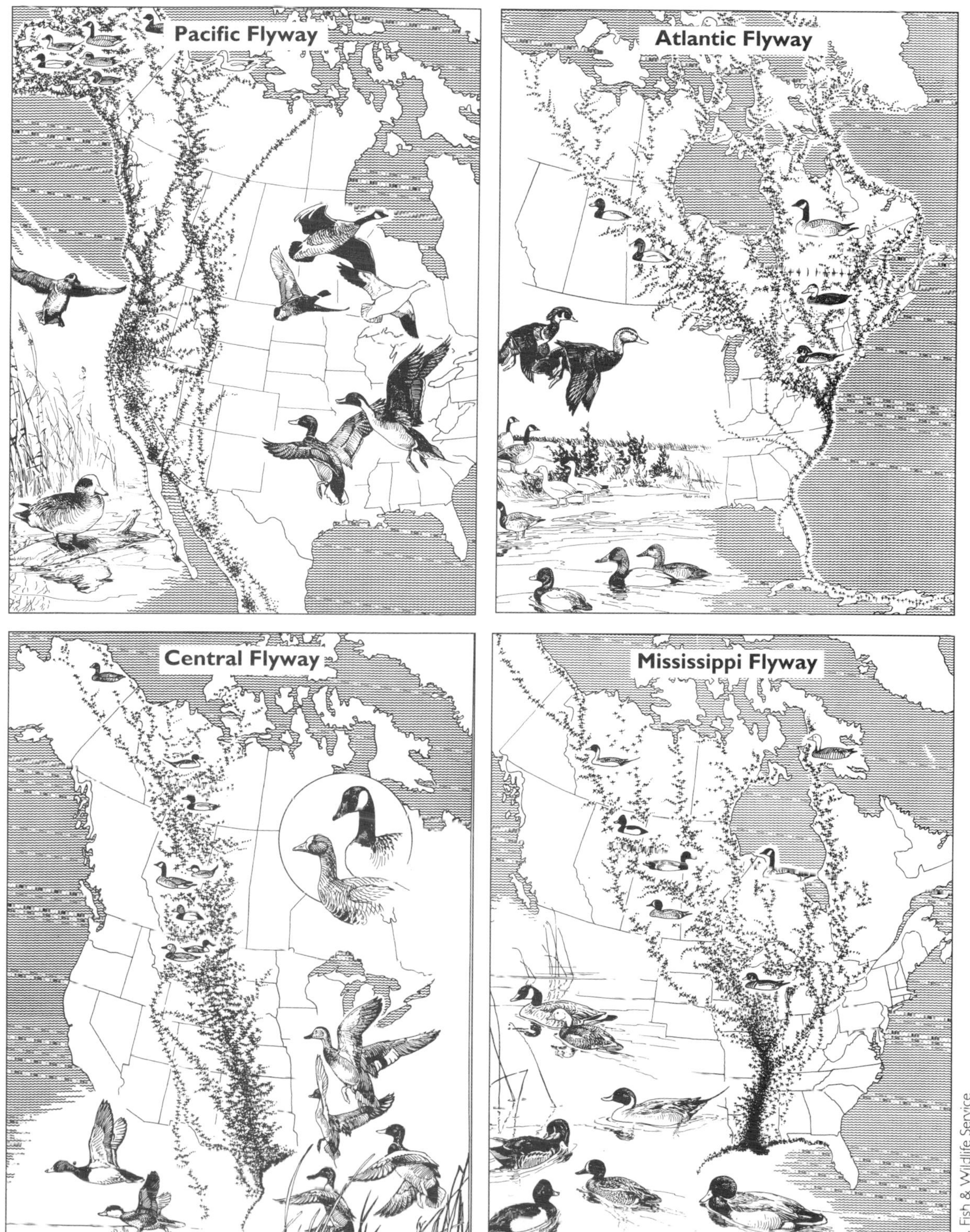

U.S. Fish & Wildlife Service

Waterfowl flyways now used by the U.S. Fish & Wildlife Service to administer waterfowl management in the United States.

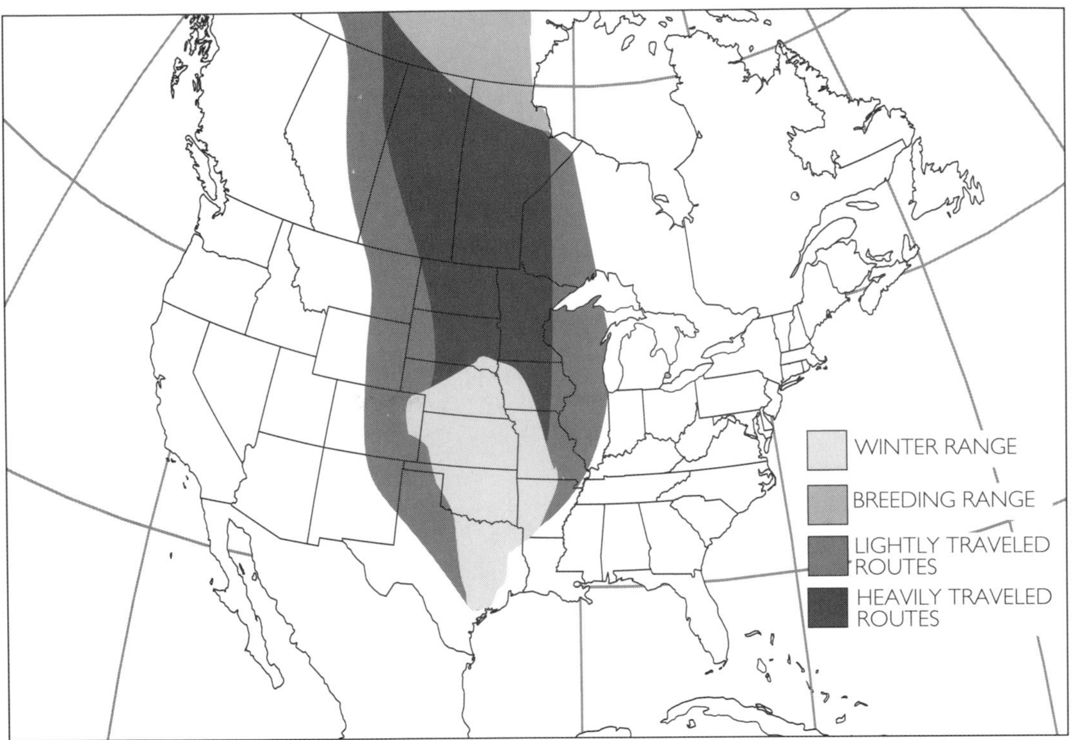

The migration and distribution of the Harris's Sparrow in North America. Redrawn from Frederick C. Lincoln and Steven R. Peterson in *Migration of Birds*.

and part of Cuba's eastern end, and continue across the Caribbean Sea to northeastern Colombia and Venezuela.

Scarlet Tanagers also nest in some northern backyard habitats. At the northern end of the breeding range, they occupy an area some 1,500 miles wide; however, their wintering grounds in South America are only about 500 miles wide.

During autumn, migrating Scarlet Tanagers use stopover resting and feeding areas as far south as Virginia, the southern Appalachian mountain areas, and the eastern Great Plains states. However, tanager migration routes are different for birds from the western side of the breeding range. Those birds fly across eastern Texas and the Gulf of Mexico to the Yucatan Peninsula. They then continue through Central America and over the Pacific Ocean from the western side of Costa Rica and northern Panama to their wintering grounds in western Colombia, Ecuador, and northern Peru.

Meanwhile, eastern tanagers fly to the vicinity of the Chesapeake Bay and continue over the Atlantic Ocean to the Bahamas. They then continue across the eastern end of Cuba, across the Caribbean Sea, and reach landfall in northern Colombia, where they head inland to their wintering grounds.

After spending months on their wintering grounds in the West Indies, Central America, and South America, some migratory neotropical songbirds return to their North American breeding grounds using roughly the same migration routes taken in autumn. However, many other species use different spring migration routes to return to North America. Some routes are shaped like a loop or an ellipse. American Golden Plovers and Connecticut Warblers use migration loops; Short-tailed Shearwaters also use a gigantic migration loop.

Other migratory birds use dogleg migration routes—pathways that have conspicuous bends or twists in them. Tundra Swans and California Gulls are examples.

The migration routes of some birds show leap-frog patterns: one population or subspecies may leapfrog over the geographic range of another population or subspecies during spring and autumn migrations; for example, Canada Geese, Peregrine Falcons, and Fox Sparrows.

This discussion barely scratches the surface of what is now known about bird migration. For beginning backyard birdwatchers, however, simply learning which species might stop for a few hours or days in a backyard habitat greatly increases the enjoyment of birdwatching.

Although maps in field guides show breeding and wintering ranges and, in some cases, areas through which birds migrate, the actual migration flyways and corridors are not plotted on those maps. However, backyard birdwatchers can refer to bird checklists for specific geographic areas to determine which birds are known to occur locally. Some areas also have detailed and comprehensive books documenting the status of local birds. Two excellent examples are Allan and Helen Cruickshank's *The Birds of Brevard County, Florida*, and William Uhrich's *A Century of Bird Life in Berks County, Pennsylvania*.

Backyard birdwatchers can easily find out from their public library if checklists or more elaborate books about birds of their area are published. The local National Audubon Society chapter or birding club will know where these references are available.

Distances

The distances traveled by birds during seasonal migrations vary with each species. Some birds migrate remarkably long distances between North American nesting grounds and South American wintering grounds. For example, one Peregrine Falcon, banded as a nestling in the Northwest Territories in Canada, migrated 9,000 miles to Argentina, where it was recovered four months later! Similarly, Ospreys raised along the Atlantic Coast of North America routinely migrate to the West Indies, Central America, and even Amazonia, where they spend the first two years of their life, later returning to North America to nest. Likewise, Broad-winged Hawks and Swainson's Hawks migrate thousands of miles to wintering grounds deep in South America. Most impressive is the Arctic Tern's 22,000-mile migration to the Antarctic, then back to the Arctic.

Species better known to backyard birdwatchers also make annual migrations covering thousands of miles from North America to Brazil, including Common Nighthawks, Cliff Swallows, some Barn Swallows, and certain thrushes. Bobolinks annually fly from the northern United States and southern Canada to the center of South America.

However, not all birds are long-distance migrants. Some only fly to the southern United States to spend the winter. For example, American Robins that nest in

Alaska and Canada migrate to the South, where they sometimes share habitat with southern relatives. Rock Wrens, Pine Warblers, Field Sparrows, and Black-headed Grosbeaks have extensive summer breeding ranges in North America, but also winter in the ranges of southern cousins.

Eastern Bluebirds, Common Grackles, Red-winged Blackbirds, and Chipping Sparrows also migrate southward during autumn—but only as far as the Gulf of Mexico. In fact, during very mild winters, some remain in suitable locations with acceptable temperatures, habitat, and food supplies.

Finally, some birds seen at backyard feeding stations do not engage in seasonal migrations, or do so only sporadically. Northern Bobwhites, Wild Turkeys, and Song Sparrows do not migrate in winter. Similarly, Black-capped Chickadees often do not migrate, but sometimes gather in wandering groups in late summer and autumn; at other times, they do migrate. White-breasted Nuthatches sometimes engage in autumn migrations involving dozens or even hundreds of birds.

On the other hand, Red-breasted Nuthatches routinely engage in periodic autumn migrations as food supplies in their northern summering grounds dwindle and the birds seek food farther south. That's one of the reasons why these lovely nuthatches are more plentiful at backyard feeding stations during some winters than in others.

Dangers

Seasonal migrations are times of great danger for birds. Millions perish due to predation, exhaustion, disease, starvation, and accidents, such as collisions. Humans are indirectly or directly responsible for many of these losses. However, by enhancing backyard habitats in critical locations with native trees, shrubs, and wildflowers, birdwatchers can compensate for some loss of habitat and give migrating birds some of the food they need for survival when reaching landfall. Backyard birdwatchers should not overlook the important roles they can play in conservation.

Nevertheless, mortality is a natural part of the ecological balance in which birds participate. Predation, disease, and accidents during migration naturally control the population of species of birds that might otherwise increase at a disruptive and unsustainable rate. Thus, migration can contribute to the so-called "balance of nature." Of course, this balance never is static. Bird populations constantly undergo numerical changes. That's why many advanced birders and ornithologists find the study of bird populations so interesting. Roger Tory Peterson, the greatest and most famous of all birders, was deeply interested in bird population dynamics.

Navigation during Migration

Among the most fascinating aspects of bird migration are the methods by which migrating birds navigate to reach their summering or wintering grounds. How do migrating birds navigate? We have yet to answer that question fully, but we have learned a lot by banding and even by tracking individual birds with radio transmitters, satellites, and radar. For example, we can study migration and navigation by placing tiny radio transmitters on hawks and various other birds, and having the radio signals received and recorded on satellites for later downloading to receivers on earth.

LONGEVITY OF NORTH AMERICAN BIRDS

How long do wild birds live? Because of the banding of birds and records maintained by the Bird Banding Laboratory at the Patuxent Wildlife Research Center in Laurel, Maryland, ornithologists have detailed information about bird longevity. The eleven longest-living birds are listed as follows, with life spans provided:

- *Laysan Albatross: 42 years, 5 months*
- *Black-footed Albatross: 40 years, 8 months*
- *White Tern: 35 years, 11 months*
- *Sooty Tern: 35 years, 10 months*
- *Wandering Albatross: 34 years, 7 months*
- *Arctic Tern: 34 years*
- *Great Frigatebird: 33 years, 7 months*
- *Black-browed Albatross: 32 years, 5 months*
- *Caspian Tern: 29 years, 6 months*
- *Red-tailed Tropicbird: 28 years, 6 months*
- *Brant: 28 years, 6 months*

Here is a sampling of the life spans of other North American birds based on information provided by the Bird Banding Laboratory. The birds are listed in AOU sequence.

- *Canada Goose: 28 years, 5 months*
- *Wood Duck: 22 years, 6 months*
- *Sharp-shinned Hawk: 11 years, 6 months*
- *Red-tailed Hawk: 25 years, 9 months*
- *Peregrine Falcon: 16 years, 10 months*
- *Wild Turkey: 12 years, 6 months*
- *California Quail: 6 years, 11 months*
- *Northern Bobwhite: 6 years, 5 months*
- *Mourning Dove: 27 years, 3 months*
- *Greater Roadrunner: 3 years, 9 months*
- *Great Horned Owl: 27 years, 7 months*
- *Elf Owl: 4 years, 11 months*
- *Lucifer Hummingbird: 4 years, 1 month*
- *Golden-fronted Woodpecker: 5 years, 8 months*
- *Hairy Woodpecker: 15 years, 10 months*
- *Great Crested Flycatcher: 13 years, 11 months*
- *Blue Jay: 17 years, 6 months*
- *Barn Swallow: 8 years, 1 month*
- *Tufted Titmouse: 13 years, 3 months*
- *White-breasted Nuthatch: 9 years, 10 months*
- *Brown-headed Nuthatch: 5 years, 9 months*
- *Brown Creeper: 4 years, 7 months*
- *House Wren: 9 years*
- *Eastern Bluebird: 8 years*
- *Western Bluebird: 5 years, 1 month*
- *American Robin: 13 years, 11 months*
- *Cedar Waxwing: 8 years, 2 months*
- *Scarlet Tanager: 10 years, 1 month*
- *Song Sparrow: 11 years, 4 months*
- *Rose-breasted Grosbeak: 12 years, 11 months*
- *Brown-headed Cowbird: 16 years, 10 months*
- *Cassin's Finch: 7 years*
- *House Sparrow: 13 years, 4 months*

Ospreys, Broad-winged Hawks, Swainson's Hawks, and tundra Peregrine Falcons travel thousands of miles from one continent to another probably by following landmarks such as mountain ranges, shorelines of the Great Lakes, ocean and bay shorelines, and other landscape features. In addition to keen eyesight, raptors would seem to need extremely retentive memories to recognize conspicuous landmarks along the entire migration route. Still, recognition of landmarks does not by itself explain how immature birds locate navigational landmarks on their first migration.

What about the millions of songbirds that migrate at night? Because they can't see conspicuous geographic landmarks, how do they navigate? These birds recognize stars and navigate by their relative orientation to the night sky. It appears that many birds inherit genetically programmed star maps. Some birds also may use a keen sensitivity to electromagnetic fields.

There is still so much to be learned about the methods migratory birds use to navigate during their seasonal migrations, however, that current knowledge of bird navigation remains in a relatively primitive state.

3 Equipment for Birdwatching

Bushnell Sport Optics

The Bushnell 8 x 42 Natureview Binoculars, one of many models manufactured by this company, are popular among birdwatchers.

Backyard birdwatching does not require a great deal of equipment; in fact, the closest thing to standard birdwatching equipment is a decent pair of binoculars. Many birdwatchers also use spotting scopes or telescopes and photographic or video equipment, along with many smaller items. This equipment is available in a wide range of prices and quality, so backyard birdwatchers have many choices. To enjoy backyard birdwatching fully, it's necessary to use birding equipment correctly, so each equipment section contains use and care pointers.

BINOCULARS

If you are like most beginning backyard birdwatchers, you enjoy excellent views of chickadees, nuthatches, woodpeckers, finches, and other birds that visit feeders, especially those positioned close to a kitchen or dining-room window. Eventually, however, you'll probably want binoculars to view birds perched on shrubs or trees, or using feeders or birdbaths farther away.

Binocular Basics

When looking at a pair of binoculars, you will see an engraved set of numbers somewhere on the instrument—most common are 7 x 35, 7 x 50, and 8 x 42. What do they mean? The first number indicates the amount of magnification, or how many times the image seen through the binoculars is enlarged. For example, in 7 x 50, the magnification is seven times. The second number indicates the diameter in millimeters of each of the objective (i.e., front) lenses on the binoculars; in our example, 50 mm. This size determines how much light the binoculars can gather.

Brightness

The brightness of an object viewed through binoculars—and the degree to which binoculars are effective in low light—depends on the quality of the optics and exit pupil size, which is the ratio of magnification to objective lens size. To determine the exit pupil size of a pair of binoculars, divide the diameter of the objective lens by the magnification of the glasses. Binoculars with the most light-gathering capability have the largest exit pupil sizes and front lenses.

A pair of 7 x 50 binoculars, for example, has exit pupils of 7.14 mm, 7 x 35 binoculars have exit pupils of 5 mm, and 8 x 42 binoculars have exit pupils of 5.25 mm. Up to about 7 mm, the larger the exit pupil size and the larger objective lens size, the brighter the image seen through binoculars. As a matter of practical use, backyard birding binoculars should not have exit pupil sizes smaller than 4 mm.

Another factor affecting image brightness is lens coating. Both outside lenses and those inside the binoculars should be coated to reduce glare and optical distortion and to increase image brightness. Cheaper binoculars do not have coated internal lenses; avoid them.

Magnification and Field-of-View

The magnification that binoculars provide is one of the major features to consider. Magnifications range from 3x to 20x; I recommend 7x or 8x for birdwatching. The Bushnell Natureview 8 x 42, for example, provides adequate magnification and a relatively wide field-of-view. All major binocular manufacturers make at least one model with 8x magnification.

"Field-of-view" refers to the width of the area you see at a range of 1,000 yards when you look through the binoculars. A 375- or 400-foot field-of-view at 1,000 yards is typical. Backyard birdwatchers should select binoculars with a relatively wide field-of-view because it will be easier to locate birds.

Resolution

When birders talk about "resolution," they're discussing the sharpness of images seen through binoculars. The best (and most expensive) binoculars deliver razor-sharp images throughout the entire viewing field, including the outer edges. Their lenses are made from the finest optical glass ground to exacting standards, and they are fully coated on outside and inside surfaces.

In *The Audubon Society Handbook for Birders*, ornithologist Stephen Kress suggests this simple test of binocular resolution. Put a road map or newspaper on a wall, stand 25 feet away, then look through your binoculars to see if the edges of the field-of-view are sharp enough to read the print. If the image is sharp throughout the entire field-of-view, the binoculars are of high quality and very satisfactory for birding.

Weight and Feel

The weight of binoculars may not leap to mind as a factor, but it is an important consideration for birdwatchers, who hold binoculars to their faces for extended periods. Weights range from about 7 ounces for some mini-binoculars to 58 ounces for a few models. Other factors being equal, such as the weight of the metal and glass used, weight goes up with objective lens size—7 x 50 binoculars weigh more than 7 x 35 binoculars. Backyard birdwatching binoculars fall in the range of 19 to 30 ounces, although some folks prefer even lighter models.

Likewise, the ergonomics of a pair of binoculars—how they fit and feel in a backyard birdwatcher's hands—is of considerable importance to some folks. To evaluate the ergonomics of binoculars, spend time handling various brands and models.

Eye Relief

Eye relief, measured in millimeters, refers to the maximum distance a viewer can hold his or her eyes from the eyepieces and still see a full picture. Eye relief is important to people who wear eyeglasses, and should be "long" (between 14 and 20 mm). If you wear eyeglasses, be sure to ask the salesperson about eye relief, or check the manual that comes with the binoculars, and look through binoculars to actually check eye relief.

Image Stabilization

Technological advances have made it possible to improve how steady a birder can hold binoculars. Canon, for example, borrowing from its video-camera technology, makes Image Stabilizer binoculars (e.g., 10 x 30, 12 x 36, and 15 x 54) that dampen unwanted motion, thus permitting use of higher magnifications that were previously impossible without a tripod. A combination of a special liquid-filled prism, electronic sensors, and a microprocessor comprise Canon's Image Stabilizer technology. Zeiss uses mechanical image-stabilization technology on its 20 x 60 BS binoculars.

Most backyard birdwatchers do not use binoculars with such high magnification, but for anyone whose hands are somewhat unsteady, it is a welcome product.

Focus

Modern binoculars have a center focus wheel. When turned, it focuses both barrels (i.e., sides) of the binoculars simultaneously. (The eyepiece on one of the barrels must be adjusted first to accommodate your individual eye.) Birdwatchers should buy only binoculars with the center-focus feature.

Binocular Prisms: Roof and Porro

There are two basic designs of binoculars. Most of the finest binoculars—Leica, Swarovski, and Zeiss—are roof-prism design. Through outstanding engineering, they have two straight barrels that allow the necessary lenses, prisms, and other mechanical parts to be neatly placed inside. All inside parts are sealed from dust, grit, and moisture. Some models are filled with nitrogen gas to prevent fogging in very humid weather. Roof-prism binoculars are more compact and lighter in weight than Porro binoculars. Although roof-prism binoculars have less depth-of-field than is found in Porro binoculars, this does not tip the balance for experienced birders. The best are superb optical instruments that last a lifetime if handled properly. Bushnell, Pentax, Swift, and a few other companies also sell roof-prism models. Their prices are on the order of several hundred dollars.

Binoculars that incorporate the standard Porro design, named for a nineteenth-century Italian telescope designer, are not straight-barreled and are widely used by birders. Prior to the 1960s, when the roof-prism design was introduced, all birding binoculars were Porro prism glasses.

Many models of Porro prism binoculars—manufactured by Bushnell, Celestron, Fujinon, Kowa, Minolta, Nikon, Olympus, Optolyth, Pentax, and Swift—are adequate for beginning backyard birders.

Mini-Binoculars

Many optical-equipment manufacturers make palm-size or mini-binoculars that are very light in weight. Are they useful for backyard birding? The answer generally is yes. The most expensive brands and models have high-quality optics.

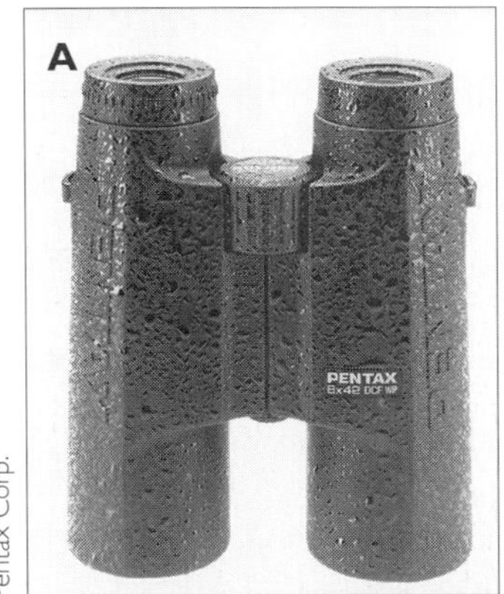

Pentax Corp.

Swift Instruments, Inc.

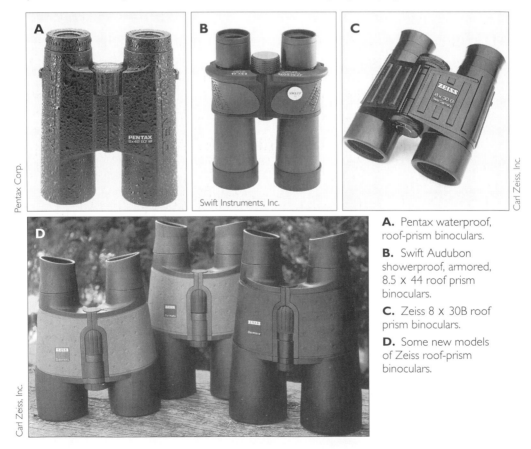

Carl Zeiss, Inc.

Carl Zeiss, Inc.

A. Pentax waterproof, roof-prism binoculars.

B. Swift Audubon showerproof, armored, 8.5 x 44 roof prism binoculars.

C. Zeiss 8 x 30B roof prism binoculars.

D. Some new models of Zeiss roof-prism binoculars.

Swift Instruments, Inc.

Swift Porro prism 8 x 40 binoculars.

Nikon, Inc.

Nikon Porro prism binoculars.

Experienced birders do not use mini-binoculars as their main instrument, however, because of their poorer light-gathering capacity. Nevertheless, many carry them on nonbirding trips so they're able to observe unusual birds that happen to appear unexpectedly. Because of their small size, mini-binoculars can be carried in a handbag, briefcase, pocket, or the glove compartment. (However, no binoculars should ever be left in a sweltering vehicle in summer.)

Shopping for Binoculars

Selecting birding binoculars can be daunting. At least twenty-four manufacturers offer binoculars, although far fewer are well known. Which brands are used widely by birdwatchers? Leica, Swarovski, and Zeiss are the finest on the market—and very expensive. Good midpriced binoculars suitable for backyard birding are made by Bushnell, Canon, Celestron, Fujinon, Kowa, Minolta, Mirador, Nikon, Olympus, Pentax, Steiner, and Swift.

Beginning backyard birdwatchers should select models with the most light-gathering capability. Whether to select roof-prism or Porro design binoculars is a matter of individual choice; I prefer the roof-prism design. Not long ago, the finest roof-prism binoculars cost between $1,000 and $1,500, depending on the manufacturer, model, and magnification. Recently, however, Leica reduced its prices, and Zeiss introduced a less expensive line. That's good news because more birders can afford these instruments. Porro design binoculars are more bulky than roof-prism models,

Miracor Optical Corp.

Examples of Mirador binoculars. Birdwatchers use several of the available models.

but millions of backyard birdwatchers use them. Many styles with this design are available from most binocular manufacturers.

There is a tremendous range in binocular prices: $25 to $6,000. However, as the owner of one birding equipment and supply store noted, most binoculars he sells to backyard birders fall into the lower-end price range, roughly $39 to $150. In general, you get what you pay for with binoculars. That's an important point to remember.

Leica, Swarovski, and Zeiss are very expensive because they're superb optical instruments, manufactured to extremely exacting standards of quality, materials, design, and production. My preference is Leica, but all are superlative. Indeed, one birding friend is wildly enthusiastic about his new Swarovski EL binoculars.

On the other hand, you don't have to spend a thousand dollars for binoculars in order to enjoy fine birdwatching. So, what do satisfactory binoculars cost?

Good glasses are available within the $100 to $500 range, which is what I recommend for beginning backyard birdwatchers. Avoid binoculars that sell for less than about $40; they usually have inferior design, components, and construction—and can't withstand the rough treatment birders unavoidably inflict on binoculars. Sometimes cheaper binoculars are actually worse than having none because they do not provide crisp, sharp images or images with accurate colors. They also may cause serious eyestrain during prolonged use.

There are many places to purchase binoculars. The national chains of birding equipment and supply stores—individual store franchises operating under the name of Wild Bird Center or Wild Birds Unlimited—routinely sell midpriced binoculars, but can order more expensive models not on display.

Some mail-order discount companies catering to birders offer many brands and models of binoculars, with prices well below suggested retail. When dealing with these companies, know exactly which brand and model you want to purchase. With research, you can purchase higher-end binoculars at lower prices.

Leica Camera, Inc.

One of several models of Leica binoculars.

Some larger nature centers, wildlife refuges, state and local Audubon societies, and birding organizations sell binoculars in their shops. In addition, organizations such as the ABA select and sell binoculars well suited to the needs of birders. When you purchase binoculars from nonprofit organizations, you're also helping their funding needs.

Discount merchandise stores and sporting goods stores also sell low- and mid-priced binoculars. Many photographic equipment and supply stores, too, have limited selections of binoculars—in some cases, Leica, Swarovski, and Zeiss. Prices at these stores vary considerably. For example, in New York City, B & H Photo-Video-Pro Audio stocks a wide range of binocular brands and models at very competitive prices, including

(continued on page 52)

USE AND CARE: BINOCULARS

Over the past forty-five years, I've seen many beginning birders fail to get the most from backyard birdwatching because of damaged binoculars, improperly adjusted binoculars, and difficulty using eyeglasses with binoculars. Without proper adjustment, for example, binoculars can be a liability rather than an essential tool.

Handle with Care

Some years ago, a local birdwatcher I know loaned an expensive pair of Leica binoculars to a friend for a few days (not a good idea). When they were returned, without apology, the instrument's lenses were cracked. The binoculars had been dropped on a concrete driveway! Even the world's best binoculars are not indestructible and can be ruined if used carelessly and irresponsibly. Binoculars are delicate, precision optical instruments. Handle them carefully and gently, and you'll get years of service. Specifically:

- *Avoid leaving binoculars in the glove compartment of a locked vehicle on hot summer days. Temperatures can become nearly oven-hot, seriously damaging optical components including lens coatings and the lenses themselves. In addition, anyone breaking into a vehicle is likely to steal anything of value, including binoculars.*
- *Avoid dropping or banging binoculars on hard surfaces such as concrete or rocks.*
- *As a precaution when climbing or engaged in other vigorous activities, tuck binoculars inside your coat or jacket or hold onto them with one hand to avoid having them hit a hard surface.*

The Eyeglass Problem

Anyone who wears eyeglasses knows it's not easy to use binoculars, because eyeglasses prevent the user from putting his or her eyes close to the eyepieces. The unfortunate result is that a substantial part of the field-of-view is reduced. This situation is not conducive to good birding because it prevents easy scanning of treetops for vireos, wood warblers, and other birds, and it increases the difficulty of following birds engaged in rapid movement, such as Sharp-shinned Hawks flying at close range. Fortunately, many modern binoculars come equipped with rubber eyecups that can be rolled down, screwed closer to the eyepieces, or removed. This allows the eyeglass wearer to bring the eyepieces closer to the eyes, increasing some of the otherwise reduced field-of-view.

While some birders who wear eyeglasses are satisfied with this partial solution, I am not. I remove the rubber eyecups from my binoculars, then take off my eyeglasses each time I use them—an inconvenience to which I long ago grew accustomed. However, I receive an unexpected benefit: by putting my eyes so close to the eyepieces, the field-of-view of my 10X binoculars becomes much wider than if the eyecups were kept in place (even in a rolled-down position).

(continued next page)

USE AND CARE: BINOCULARS

(continued from previous page)

If you wear eyeglasses, tell the salesperson, who may suggest certain brands or models to accommodate the problem. The first thing to consider is eye relief—the maximum distance a viewer can hold a pair of binoculars away from her eyes and still see a full view. People who wear glasses should buy binoculars with long eye relief (usually between 14 and 20 mm).

Finally, a word of caution: if you use binoculars while wearing eyeglasses, be certain that the eyecups are made of rubber or some other material that will not scratch eyeglasses.

Adjusting Eyepieces

Eyepieces should be adjusted to accommodate each person's individual eyesight requirements. This essential adjustment takes only a few seconds.

On Porro binoculars, one of the eyepieces is engraved with lines or numbers, and can be turned. That's the side of the binoculars that needs adjustment. To adjust your binoculars for your eyes, stand about 30 feet away from an object with sharp markings. Next, follow these instructions:

1. *Close your eye on the side of the binoculars with the adjustable eyepiece (usually the right side).*
2. *Looking only through your left eye, turn the center focusing wheel or knob—located somewhere between the two barrels—until the object you are looking at becomes clear and as sharp as possible.*
3. *Now, without moving the center focusing wheel or knob again, close your left eye and open your right eye—the one on the side with the adjustable eyepiece.*
4. *Using only your right eye, look at the same object, and turn the adjustable eyepiece until you can see it as clearly and sharply through the right barrel as on the already correctly focused left side.*
5. *Make a mental note of the setting on the right eyepiece so you can immediately return it to that position without repeating the entire set-up process. This is a useful trick used by experienced birders if they accidentally move the eyepiece setting.*

Focusing

Because birds frequently move rapidly, birders must be able to adjust the focus of their binoculars quickly. From this point on, only the center focusing wheel or knob between the two barrels should be turned to keep both barrels in sharp focus.

However, binoculars have a minimum distance for which they can be focused. This varies with different brands and models, but new birding binoculars allow focusing for distances of 10 to 13 feet.

Cleaning

Because you'll use binoculars in all sorts of weather and habitats, a certain amount of dirt collects on lenses and other parts. Your binoculars should be cleaned when necessary to provide the best possible service.

Cleaning binoculars should be limited only to external surfaces. In the unlikely event that dirt gets inside the binoculars, they should be sent back to the manufacturer or another authorized repair service, where they can be properly cleaned and reassembled by qualified technicians. Never attempt to take binoculars apart and clean the inside yourself.

Any birder can clean the outside surfaces of a pair of binoculars. For nonoptical metal parts, simply wipe surfaces clean with a soft cloth that, if necessary, can be slightly dampened with warm water.

The optical lenses of binoculars, however, must be cleaned in an entirely different way. Dirt on lenses should first be gently brushed away by using a soft lens brush, or blown away by using air from a pressurized container.

If fingerprints or other oily smudges are on the lenses, put a drop of lens-cleaning solution onto a folded piece of lens-cleaning tissue. Then, gently *wipe the lens surface in a circular pattern until the lens is clean. The same process is used for spotting scopes and camera lenses.*

Some new binoculars come with lens-cleaning materials. Otherwise, lens-cleaning solution, tissue, and pressurized cans of air can be purchased at camera and photographic supply stores. These items, and a soft lens cleaning brush, should be part of a birder's standard field equipment.

Emergency Care

It's amazing what can happen to birdwatching binoculars. Aside from a collision with a rock, water is probably the most serious threat. That's less true, of course, for rubber-coated, waterproof models.

It's important that water never be allowed to seep into the internal mechanisms of binoculars. Therefore, it's best not to expose them to drizzle or rain, even when so-called rainguards are placed over the eyepieces. Just tuck the binoculars inside your shirt, jacket, or into a waterproof backpack. However, if a tiny amount of moisture does get inside, they can be put in a dry, warm location for several days to dry out. If that does not work, send them to the manufacturer for repairs.

Dealing with binoculars that have been dropped into water is another matter. If they are inexpensive, discard them and buy a new pair. However, if they are expensive binoculars, try to salvage them. Professional cleaning of binoculars retrieved from fresh water must be done promptly. If the binoculars were dropped into salt water, rinse them thoroughly in fresh water, seal them in a plastic bag, and send them immediately to the manufacturer by next-day delivery service. Immediate repairs might be able to restore the damaged instruments. It's a good idea, however, to ask for a telephone quote for the repair cost. If it's too expensive, discard them and buy a new pair.

(continued from page 48)
Bushnell, Canon, Leica, Minolta, Nikon, Pentax, Swarovski, and Zeiss. I recommend this company's free product catalog (see appendix 4).

There is one more way of obtaining binoculars: ask for the binoculars of your dreams as a gift! They make excellent gifts, so don't hesitate to drop plenty of hints.

SPOTTING SCOPES

To a backyard birdwatcher accustomed to viewing birds at window feeders, the idea of using a spotting scope may sound ridiculous. Binoculars, after all, provide magnification of seven times or more. Nevertheless, many backyard birdwatchers have discovered how exciting it is to see birds very close up with a spotting scope that provides magnification of twenty times or more. Many backyard birdwatchers swear by these instruments. Let's discuss the features of spotting scopes and then consider models for backyard birdwatching.

Focal Length

The first consideration when selecting a spotting scope is the focal length of the lenses. Expressed in millimeters, this is the distance between the lenses and the plane where the image produced by the lens is formed. For our purposes, the longer the focal length of the lenses, the bigger the image of the bird that's produced.

Aperture

The next consideration is aperture. When birders use this term in reference to spotting scopes, they mean the diameter of the front lens of a scope, expressed in millimeters. Aperture size is important because a large aperture produces a brighter image than a smaller size. Generally, large-aperture lenses also produce greater (higher) resolution than smaller ones.

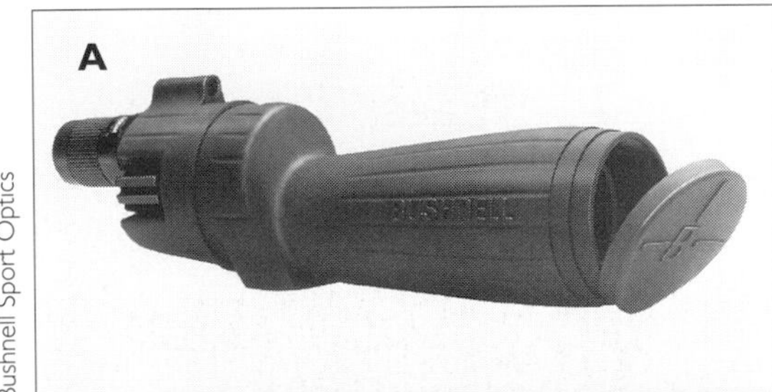

Bushnell Sport Optics

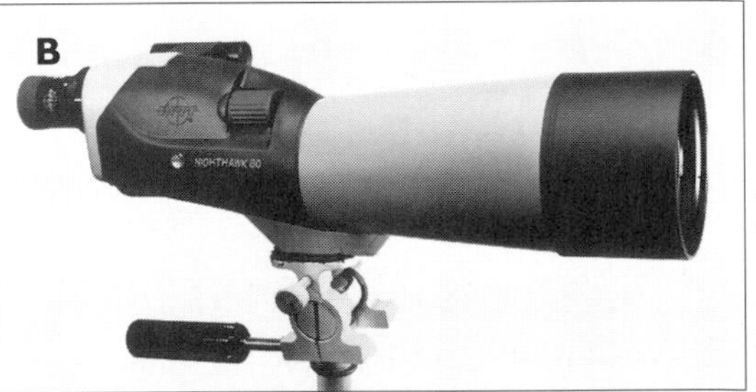

Swift Instruments, Inc.

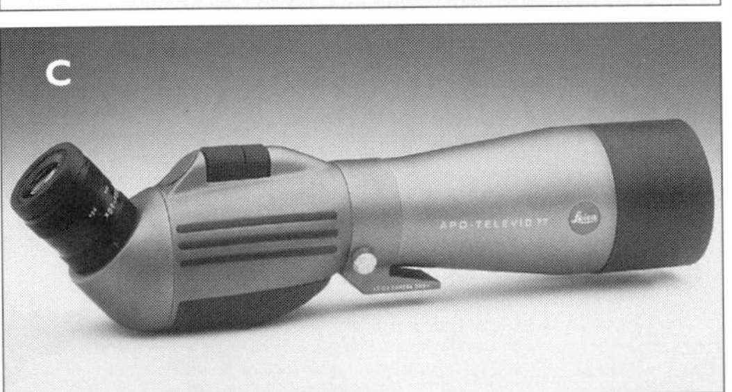

Leica Camera, Inc.

A. A Bushnell 15–45x zoom Spacemaster spotting scope.

B. A Swift 80 mm 849 Nighthawk spotting scope.

C. The Leica APO-Televid 77 spotting scope. These are superb optical instruments highly prized by experienced birdwatchers.

A lens with a 60 mm aperture is typical, such as on the Bushnell Spacemaster spotting scope. Spotting scopes equipped with 80 mm aperture lenses give birders even brighter images in dim light, even at higher levels of magnification, but 80 mm instruments are expensive. However, manufacturers such as Nikon and Kowa produce expensive, top-of-the-line 60 mm aperture spotting scopes with special optical glass; these instruments almost equal the performance of the larger 80 mm aperture spotting scopes.

Special lenses called "apochromatic lenses," or APOs, are used in the best spotting scopes, such as the Leica Televid 77 APO. APO lenses produce better color rendition and sharper images at higher magnifications.

Eyepieces

The eyepiece of a spotting scope—the section closest to the viewer's eye—gives the image additional magnification. Eyepieces are made in fixed and zoom styles. Fixed eyepieces come in magnifications of 15x, 20x, 30x, 45x, and 60x, and so on. As the name implies, a fixed eyepiece has an inherent magnification, such as 20x. If you want more magnification, you must change eyepieces. A zoom eyepiece allows a birder to change the amount of magnification without switching eyepieces. Although some older zoom eyepieces are inferior, newer models (e.g., Leica, Nikon, and Swarovski) are excellent. As a rule, though, fixed magnification eyepieces deliver better images.

Some spotting-scope manufacturers give birders the option of having the eyepiece either in a straight line behind the scope or positioned at a 45-degree angle; the latter type is better suited to situations when several people of different heights use one scope. Kowa, Nikon, and Swarovski have designed their 45-degree eyepiece mount so that it can be turned to the side.

Reflecting Telescopes

Some birders use a reflecting telescope, which has a mirror rather than special lenses for focusing. This produces extraordinarily sharp, brilliant images with every detail visible. The Questar Birder 3.5-inch is the standard against which all reflecting telescopes (and spotting scopes) are measured. Celestron sells a less expensive model.

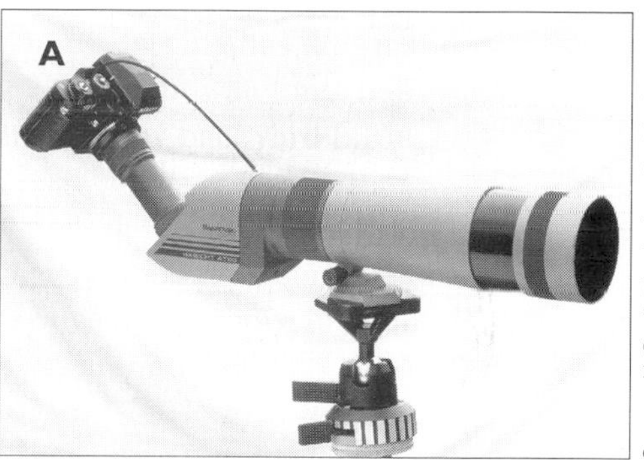

Swarovski Optik North America Limited

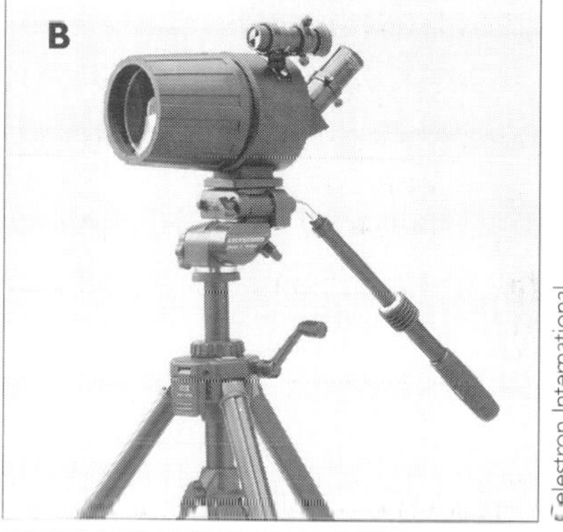

Celestron International

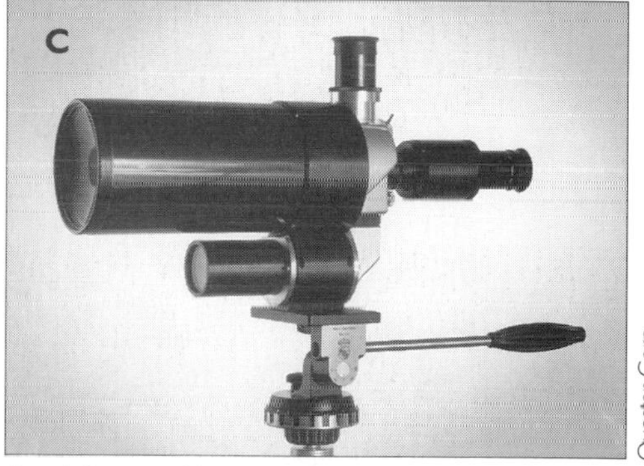

Questar Corp.

A. A Swarovski spotting scope.

B. A Celestron telescope.

C. A Questar Birder telescope.

USE AND CARE: SPOTTING SCOPES AND REFLECTING TELESCOPES

It's necessary to use spotting scopes and reflecting telescopes correctly to derive maximum birdwatching benefits. Here are some helpful hints.

Wearing Eyeglasses

I've already discussed using eyeglasses with binoculars; eyeglass wearers also may have difficulty using spotting scopes or reflecting telescopes. For some people, the solution is simple—take the eyeglasses off. However, other folks can't do that, so using an eyepiece with long eye relief is important. This allows you to keep you eye back slightly from the eyepiece, and still see the whole image. If possible, look through a long-eye-relief eyepiece with your glasses on before making your purchase.

Cleaning

Spotting scopes and reflecting telescopes require the same careful cleaning that binoculars do, and the same methods are used. Clean only external lens surfaces. If any cleaning of internal areas is necessary, send the instrument to the manufacturer for expert maintenance.

Shopping for Scopes and Telescopes

Which spotting scope or reflecting telescope is right for a birder? Dave Ross, from the Cornell Laboratory of Ornithology, and birder and optical specialist Michael Porter evaluated numerous models with the concerns of the birdwatcher in mind. They tried out scopes and telescopes made by several manufacturers, including Bushnell, Celestron, Fujinon, Kowa, Leica, Nikon, Optolyth, Questar, Swarovski, Swift, Televue, and VENONscope.

The Cornell evaluations rated Questar's Birder the finest reflecting telescope in the world. If you want something extraordinary, buy it. Not far behind were three exceptional spotting scopes: the Kowa TSN-824, the Swarovski ST-80 HD, and the sleek Leica APO Televid 77 mm.

Another way you can evaluate spotting scopes or reflecting telescopes is on birding field trips or at birding festivals, where you can compare and try different models. Some birding equipment and supply stores also allow you to try out different models. Surveys in birding magazines that evaluate and rate popular models are also helpful.

How much should you spend on a spotting scope or reflecting telescope for backyard birdwatching? Simply put, spend as much as possible: the higher the price, the better the instrument.

For a good spotting scope, spend between $500 and $1,000; certainly not less than about $250. Reflecting telescopes are even more expensive. The Questar Birder 3.5-inch costs from $3,100 to $3,700. Celestron and some other brands are less expensive. Spotting scopes and telescopes also can be bought at discount prices from mail-order companies catering to birdwatchers.

USE OF TRIPODS

Tripods are used by backyard birdwatchers to support spotting scopes, reflecting telescopes, cameras with 400 mm telephoto lenses, and video cameras. If a tripod is selected carefully, it can be used to satisfactorily support all of this equipment. Alternatively, buy two tripods so two pieces of equipment can be used simultaneously.

I recommend using a video camera tripod head onto which a spotting scope, reflecting telescope, camera lens, or video camera is mounted for a smoother pan (i.e., turn) than when an ordinary camera head is used.

Birdwatchers also can use two different types of tripod-head couplings. The standard one has a threaded post that screws into the bottom of the scope, telescope, camera lens, or video camera. Alternatively, a quick-release coupling, available in various models, allows a scope, telescope, camera lens, or video camera to be quickly attached or removed from the tripod. Bogan, Gitzo, and some other companies make quick-release couplings.

If you use a quick-release coupling, you must put a mounting plate (part of the coupling), which costs a few dollars, on the bottom of each piece of equipment. A photographic equipment and supply store will have different models and types of quick-release couplings and mounting plates.

Many tripods have a center post that can be elevated. I recommend that it not be extended fully because some movement, perhaps caused by wind, can be present when you look through a spotting scope, reflecting telescope, or camera lens. Rather, extend the tripod legs to the appropriate height needed to provide a more solid base for whatever is mounted on the tripod.

TRIPODS

Because spotting scopes, reflecting telescopes, and cameras with telephoto lenses greatly magnify images of birds, they must be firmly supported; the slightest motion resembles an earthquake to the viewer. A tripod will support the equipment and is especially useful when looking at or photographing birds that are perched, floating on water, or moving slowly.

Two popular tripod brands are Bogan and Gitzo. Buy one that's slightly more robust than necessary to be certain it provides rock-solid support for all your optical and camera equipment. Good tripods are expensive; be prepared to pay between $150 and $200.

Some photographic equipment stores also have a selection of tripods and necessary heads. The ABA sells selected models for use with spotting scopes, as do some birding equipment and supply stores.

CAMERAS AND FILM

For many backyard birders, bird photography is an important part of their pastime. Fascinating as it is to observe birds, many find it even more enjoyable to capture on film close-up images of birds visiting feeding stations, birdbaths, and nest boxes. With birding photography, the observer contributes to the final image by manipulating photographic variables, such as composition, lighting, film, and exposure. The result is an image that reflects a photographer's own distinctive style.

It isn't possible to survey the world of photography, but let's touch on topics and equipment of special interest to bird photographers.

PETERSON'S PHOTOGRAPHY

Roger Tory Peterson, who published the landmark A Field Guide to the Birds *in 1934, was also an avid bird photographer, taking outstanding photographs of countless species all over the world. These photographs not only illustrated his books and articles, but also contributed to his bird paintings because they documented behavior patterns, habitats, and subtle variations in plumage. Peterson also shot miles of 16 mm motion-picture film and incorporated his outstanding footage in lectures given across the nation and overseas.*

35 mm Single-Lens Reflex Cameras

The basic tool of the bird photographer is a 35 mm single-lens reflex (SLR) camera that uses interchangeable lenses. These cameras enable a photographer to look directly through the lens to see exactly what's being photographed. That's essential, especially when using 400 mm telephoto lenses that magnify images eight times. Most 35 mm SLR cameras have excellent built-in light meters that automatically adjust to light conditions and the speed (i.e., light sensitivity) of the film.

You most likely will use a lens made by the camera's manufacturer because the lens and camera are sold as a package. For example, I often use a Nikkor 35–80 mm autofocus zoom lens that came with my Nikon N-70. You don't need to purchase camera and lens from the same company, however; Sigma makes high-quality lenses that are less expensive than those made by Nikon. In either case, the flexibility of a 35 mm SLR camera is critical—it allows the bird photographer to change lenses on a moment's notice.

Shopping for Cameras and Lenses

There is so much excellent photographic equipment now available that the best purchase may require some research. Although price is generally a good indicator of quality in photographic cameras and lenses, it does not mean that backyard bird photographers with limited budgets can't buy good cameras and lenses—especially when buying equipment through discount channels. The key is research and price comparison. Here are my hints and suggestions.

Cameras

The 35 mm SLR camera I like is a Nikon N-70, which has sophisticated features, including accurate exposure metering and sharp autofocusing. Likewise, Contax, Leica, and Canon (upper-end models) also make superb cameras; in the mid-range, Canon (the less costly models), Minolta, Olympus, Pentax, and Yashica are all popular.

How much should you spend on a camera? Be prepared to pay between $450 and $600 for a 35 mm camera and a lens (preferably zoom) for general photographic purposes.

Lenses

Lenses for 35 mm SLR cameras come in many focal lengths, models, and prices. A Nikkor zoom lens (30–80 mm) purchased separately costs between $100 and $300, depending on the model. A 400 mm telephoto lens can cost between $250 and $1,300 or more, depending on the manufacturer, model, and speed. Still, bargains can be found; I have a 400 mm autofocus Sigma telephoto lens that cost $275 and produces sharp, crisp photographs.

Finally, telephoto lenses for 35 mm cameras on the order of 500, 600, 800, or 1,000 mm can cost from $1,000 to $10,000, depending on the manufacturer, model, focal length, and speed of the lens. These lenses are usually owned by professional photographers.

Film

Backyard bird photographers taking slides for projection can do no better than Kodachrome, long the standard against which all other color films are compared. Kodachrome 64 has enough speed for most bird photography and produces crisp slides; Kodachrome 200 is more light sensitive. The color dyes used in Kodachrome are extremely stable and don't change over long time periods. Fuji is another popular manufacturer of film; Fujichrome 50, 100, 200, and 400 are all widely used for color slides.

Kodak, Fuji, and other companies also make many types of color print film. Select one with a speed of 100 or 200 for ordinary backyard bird photography. Kodak Tri-X is an excellent film for taking black-and-white bird photographs. In all film, the higher the speed number, the greater the sensitivity to dim light.

Medium-Format Cameras

Medium-format cameras are the alternative to 35 mm SLR cameras favored by professional photographers. They use a larger film size (120 or 220) and produce 2¼- by 2¼-inch negatives or color transparencies. When film of this size is combined with some of the very finest photographic lenses available—30 mm wide angle to 500 mm telephoto—images of superb sharpness are possible. My preference is Hasselblad, but other brands include Bronica, Contax, Mamiya, Pentax, and Rollei.

Why are medium-format cameras not used by most backyard bird photographers? The primary reason is their extremely high cost. A Hasselblad 501-CM body without a lens costs at least $1,600; other models cost up to $7,000. Lenses are also very expensive: between $1,800 and $7,000, depending on the model, focal length, and speed. Medium-format cameras also weigh more than 35 mm SLR cameras, and film costs are slightly higher because of their larger size.

Nevertheless, the larger format of medium-format cameras is a world apart from 35 mm photography. If a backyard bird photographer wants a medium-format camera, I recommend Hasselblad. It's the choice of NASA and the most demanding medium-format photographers. My Hasselblad equipment—a twenty-five-year-old camera body, 80 mm Zeiss Planar lens for general photography, and 500 mm Zeiss Tele-Tessar telephoto lens for photographing birds—is exceptional.

A particularly useful feature of Hasselblad and other medium-format cameras is their interchangeable film magazines. They allow a partly exposed roll of film to be removed from the camera and a different film magazine to be put on the camera. Basic models use either twelve or twenty-four exposures. Hasselblad film magazines cost between $700 and $950. Color films are available for taking color prints or transparencies; Kodak Tri-X is just one of the black-and-white films available.

USE AND CARE: PHOTOGRAPHIC CAMERAS AND LENSES

Photographing birds in your backyard involves the same basic techniques as any other type of photography—with a few exceptions.

- *It's desirable to have the image of the bird fill as much of the color slide or print as possible. That means getting close to the subject by either using a 400 mm telephoto lens, placing the camera one or two feet from a window feeding tray, or hiding in a photographic blind (basically a small tent) near a feeder, birdbath, or nest box.*
- *If using a camera with adjustable shutter speeds, use as fast (rapid) a shutter speed as possible to freeze quick movements of the bird you are photographing. Shutter speeds of at least 1/500 second are desirable.*
- *Try to use as high an f-stop number as possible, especially for a 400 mm telephoto lens. The higher the f-stop number, the smaller the aperture. The smaller the aperture, the more depth-of-field in the photograph. This is especially important when photographing small birds that require getting the camera close to them. There will always be a tradeoff between a high f-stop number and a fast shutter speed. For example, a combination set at f:16 and 1/1000 second changes to f:11 at 1/2000 second.*

To take good photographs, it's critical that photographic lenses are kept clean. Also, avoid exposing photographic equipment to direct sunlight for many hours. On extremely hot days, the equipment and film can be damaged. The combination of extended use and heat can deplete the power in the batteries that run modern 35 mm single-lens reflex and medium-format cameras. Check the batteries regularly when on an extended outing.

Storing Photographic Film

Professional photographers store large amounts of fresh film for extended periods by putting the packaged film in a deep freezer; this significantly extends its useful life. When you need film, remove it from the freezer twenty-four hours before use.

Process exposed film as quickly as possible. After 35 mm slides or prints are returned from processing, store them in archival-quality slide or print preserver sheets available at camera stores. PrintFile Archival Preservers is a popular brand, and these sheets can be placed in a three-ring notebook binder.

Digital Cameras

Digital cameras electronically record images instead of using photographic film. These images can be transferred from the camera onto a computer hard drive for permanent storage. In most cases, 3x is the maximum optical magnification for zoom lenses on digital cameras. (Much more costly professional digital cameras, however, such as some Kodak models built with a Nikon camera body, will accept autofocus Nikkor lenses, including telephotos 400 mm or longer.)

An important advantage of digital photography over conventional photographic film is that digital pictures can be viewed immediately after being taken, then edited and manipulated on computers. A picture taken with a digital camera can be inserted directly into a layout program and used in a birding newsletter or student report. It also can be printed out as a high-quality image suitable for framing and display. Birdwatchers will surely think of countless uses as the technology becomes more popular.

Agfa, Canon, Epson, Fujifilm, Kodak, Minolta, Nikon, Olympus, Panasonic, Sanyo, and Sony all make "point-and-shoot" digital cameras in the $350-to-$1,000 price range. None of these models is capable of using interchangeable telephoto lenses. The highest optical magnification they provide is 3x enlargement. These cameras are useful for general and scenic photography—ducks and geese in local parks—but are not well suited for taking pictures of small wild birds, unless you have a bird feeder tray outside a window two or three feet from the camera.

The more expensive professional digital cameras by Fujifilm, Kodak, Minolta, Nikon, and Sony, priced from $1,500 to $20,000, accept a full range of interchangeable lenses, including essential 400 mm or longer telephotos necessary for photography at bird feeders, nest boxes, and birdbaths. Examples include the Canon EOS-2000; Kodak DCS-315, DCS-520, and DCS-560; Minolta RD-175; Nikon E3/E3S; Fujifilm DS560/DS565; and Sony MVC-FD91 and DSC-D700.

VIDEO

In the mid-twentieth century, backyard birdwatchers commonly took 8 and 16 mm motion pictures of birds. I remember my old birding friend and Audubon wildlife warden Theodore R. Hake showing me his 8 mm home movies of nesting shorebirds on the tundra around Churchill, Manitoba, in Canada. They were wonderful pictures that brought back to him many memorable birding days in one of North America's most famous shorebird nesting locations. Today, video has completely replaced film among amateurs and there are dozens of models from which to choose. Canon, Hitachi, JVC, Panasonic, Sharp, and Sony all offer models costing less than $1,000, often between $400 and $750.

There are many advantages in using video cameras. They provide automatic exposure metering and the camera's zoom lens will usually magnify at least eight to twelve times. For birdwatchers, I recommend a video camera with a 12x or more zoom lens, comparable to a 600 mm telephoto lens on a 35 mm camera. A synchronized soundtrack accompanies the video, and videotape is inexpensive. Most importantly, a bird photographer can replay videotapes immediately after taking them—and redo scenes that need improvement.

8 mm Format

One popular type of video camera uses 8 mm videotape format to record images. Canon, Hitachi, JVC, Panasonic, Sharp, Sony, and others make cameras using this format. They are compact, lightweight, and some have lenses that zoom from 8 to 72x magnification—more than adequate for taking closeups of birds at backyard feeders, birdbaths, and birdhouses.

Hi8 Format

Hi8 is another videotape format that produces amazingly high-quality images (thus the "*Hi*8") and stereo sound recordings. These cameras have a zoom lens providing a maximum of 12x or higher magnification. Many use analog technology, but a new version (Sony DCR-VX 1000) uses digital recording technology. Canon, JVC, Panasonic, and most other manufacturers also make Hi8 video cameras.

USE AND CARE: VIDEO CAMERAS

Using video cameras to make videos of backyard birds is a wonderful way to enhance birdwatching and preserve delightful experiences. Perhaps that's why bird videography is so popular with many birders.

Maintain a video camera as you would a photographic camera. Clean external lens surfaces, and be sure fresh or fully charged batteries are in the video camera. It's wise to recharge batteries after each videotaping session, paying careful attention to the instruction manual.

After securing raw videotape, it's necessary to edit it so the best scenes are woven into a polished production. Unfortunately, that is one of the difficulties of home videography. However, with an Apple computer and an excellent videotape editing application like Avid Cinema, backyard bird videographers can easily produce very sophisticated shows. The digital, nonlinear editing capability of Avid Cinema allows scenes to be moved around quickly—each scene is cut to an appropriate length and placed where the editor wants it. Music, bird sounds, and narration soundtracks can be added exactly as desired, and special effects such as titles, fade-outs, and wipes are readily available.

Moreover, if old 8 or 16 mm home movies of birds taken years ago are transferred to videotape (at a local camera shop), that videotape footage can be included in home videotape productions.

Because original analog videotape scenes are input to the computer directly from a VCR or video camera (preferably using an S-video connection), then edited digitally and output again in analog format, little loss of original quality occurs, resulting in completed productions that are crisp and bright. However, editing videotape with Avid Cinema requires at least 96 MB of RAM and massive hard-drive capacity—not less than 4.0 GB and preferably 9 GB or more. With this computer setup, Avid Cinema allows you to make excellent twelve-minute home videotapes, adding a new and creative dimension to the hobby of backyard birdwatching.

VHS Format

These analog video cameras use standard consumer-size videotape cassettes, larger than 8 mm and Hi8 cassettes, which makes it very convenient to purchase videotape. Moreover, original VHS videotapes are of good quality; however, as with all analog videotape, editing and making copies results in decreased sharpness and color quality on the copies. Most VCRs use VHS format, so it's easy to play homemade or commercially produced VHS videotapes on standard VCRs.

Super-VHS

Another version of VHS is called Super-VHS (or S-VHS). Like Hi8, Super-VHS video cameras greatly improve image sharpness and color quality compared with the VHS format. Many standard video camera manufacturers make this format, which uses analog technology to record.

ANALOG OR DIGITAL?

Video-recording technology is progressing rapidly. Currently, two recording systems are used in home video cameras: analog and digital. Analog is the older system, and many existing video cameras use this method. The main drawback of analog is loss of image sharpness and color quality when copies are made. In a digital recording, picture and sound are broken down and stored as digital information. The newer digital video cameras produce very sharp video images and superb soundtracks. Digital recording also means there's no loss of video or sound quality when videotape is edited, regardless of how many copies are made.

Digital Video Cameras

Canon, JVC, Panasonic, Sony, and other manufacturers also make video cameras using digital recording technology. Examples include Sony's DCR-VX 1000 3-CCD Digital Camcorder and Canon's XL-1, which allow the use of interchangeable lenses.

Although these video cameras cost many thousands of dollars, other models satisfactory for backyard bird photography can be purchased for about $1,000.

BirdCam

A small video camera called BirdCam is now available to fasten onto or near a bird feeder, nest box, birdbath, or other places that birds visit. It has a 12-inch flexible gooseneck that allows the camera to be exactly mounted and positioned to secure close views of birds in action. The camera is put in a special durable case to protect it from all types of weather. A mounting shoe allows the BirdCam to be removed quickly. A 50 to 250-foot connecting cable runs from the camera to your television or VCR, where the audio and video signals are received. Backyard birdwatchers can use this device to take close-up videos of birds living their lives as naturally as possible. Some birding equipment and supply stores sell these cameras.

AUDIO RECORDING

Some backyard birdwatchers use portable tape recorders to make recordings of bird sounds. Most of these recordings are for personal use and aren't intended to achieve professional recording quality. If professional quality recordings are desired, more sophisticated and expensive tape recorders and microphones are necessary.

Specialized Recording Equipment

Many portable tape recorders are available, but none costing less than $400 is suitable for high-quality bird-sound recording. A brief list of satisfactory brands and models follows.

Among monaural cassette tape recorders, the one recommended for beginning recordists is the Marantz Corporation Model PMD-222. It has a third playback-monitor head used for monitoring recording quality with headphones; uses tape types I, II, and IV; has a good VU meter; has a three-pin XLR style connector for its microphone input; and has RCA phonograph pin jacks for output connections. It is responsive to frequencies up to 14.5 kHz and has an internal playback speaker. It costs $415.

MICROCASSETTE RECORDERS

Using microcassette tape recorders, which are small, compact, and lightweight, for dictating notes and observations of birds is another simple and effective way that birders can make good use of tape recorders. Many birders find it's easier to dictate notes and observations into a microcassette recorder than to write in a notebook. Examples include the Olympus Pearlcorder S950 and Pearlcorder S700, Panasonic Microcassette Recorder, and Sony Pressman and Memopack, which are battery-powered and use tiny microcassettes. Digital microrecorders, such as the Olympus D-1000 Digital Recorder, Panasonic Digital Recorder, and Sony Digital Recorder, eliminate the use of tapes entirely.

Among stereo cassette tape recorders suitable for beginning recordists, either Marantz Corporation's model PMD-430 or Sony's model TCD5 Pro II is acceptable. The Marantz PMD-430 ($525) has a third playback-monitor head, a very useful feature. While the Sony TCD5 Pro II (costing $1,125) lacks a third head, it is very well constructed and offers professional cannon-style microphone inputs, excellent speed stability, and superior frequency response. It is arguably the best portable cassette recorder available.

Among open-reel monaural tape recorders, the Nagra 4.2 (costing $6,500 new or $2,500 in good used condition) is highly desirable but no longer made. If money is no object, the Nagra IV-S ($14,000) is the stereo open-reel tape recorder of choice. Nagra tape recorders are heavier than other brands. However, experts in the Library of Natural Sounds at the Cornell Laboratory of Ornithology consider these recorders the most durable available, proclaiming they "do not fail."

Microphones

For professional-quality bird-sound recording, two basic types of microphones are used: parabolic reflector microphones and shotgun microphones. Several satisfactory parabolic reflectors are available, including several models of the 22-inch Telinga Pro parabolic reflector; some are equipped with microphones and others can accept microphones made by other companies. The Dan Gibson 18-inch parabolic reflector microphone is also used by some bird-sound recordists, although it uses dated technology. Experts at the Cornell Laboratory of Ornithology recommend the Mineroff Electronics SME-PR-1000 18-inch epoxy-coated aluminum reflector as a good, low-budget starter system when it is equipped with an inexpensive microphone, such as the Audio Technica AT10A condenser omnidirectional microphone (costing about $210). The Sennheiser ME-66/K6/MZW66 system (about $470) is recommended as a good shotgun microphone for general use.

Bird-Sounds Recording Workshop

Backyard birdwatchers with a serious interest in recording bird sounds can receive expert instruction and field experience by attending a week-long workshop on this subject, offered by the Library of Natural Sounds at the Cornell Laboratory of Ornithology. Expert instructors from the library lead the workshops, which include daily hands-on field recording sessions. For more details, check the Cornell Laboratory of Ornithology website (see appendix 3).

Commercial Recordings of Bird Sounds

Commercial recordings of bird sounds are made by trained ornithologists or advanced birders using sophisticated equipment. There are many recordings of birdsongs and sounds available as vinyl records, tape cassettes, and CDs. (Some specialized recordings are only available as vinyl records.) Several bird-sound recordings also deal with specific groups of birds, such as wood warblers or other common backyard species. Listening to bird-sound recordings can be a great educational tool for beginning birdwatchers, giving them an opportunity to hear and memorize the sounds of common backyard species. Of course, for other birdwatchers, simply listening to birdsongs is a pleasure.

Backyard BirdSong by Richard Walton and Robert Lawson, in the Peterson Field Guide Series, is a particularly helpful audio cassette. It groups twenty-eight common birdsongs according to similar sounds, and points out what birdwatchers should listen for to differentiate one bird's song

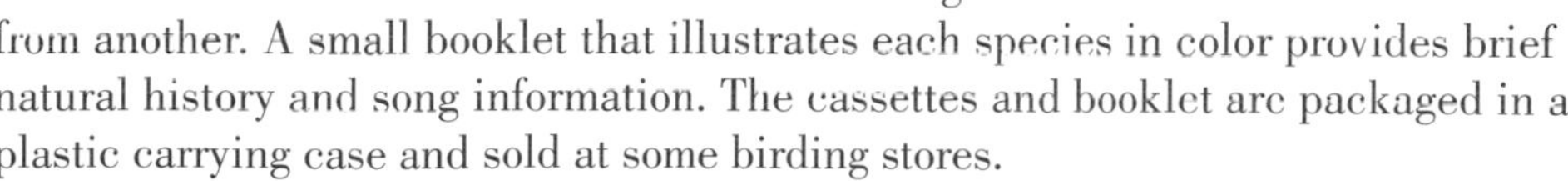

from another. A small booklet that illustrates each species in color provides brief natural history and song information. The cassettes and booklet are packaged in a plastic carrying case and sold at some birding stores.

THE CORNELL LIBRARY OF NATURAL SOUNDS

The most famous collection of bird-sound recordings is in the Library of Natural Sounds at the Cornell Laboratory of Ornithology in Ithaca, New York. It contains more than 140,000 recordings of more than 6,000 species of birds, as well as other wildlife. This collection is used for scientific research, conservation, and educational purposes. For example, the Library of Natural Sounds provided recordings for thirty-one records, CDs, and cassettes, including sounds of birds issued by the National Geographic Society and the Peterson Field Guide Series.

More comprehensive in species coverage are the various *Birding by Ear* guides to birdsong identification by Richard Walton and Robert Lawson; Roger

Tory Peterson's *Field Guide to Birdsongs: Eastern/Central North America* is equally helpful. Each is available in cassette or CD format, available in some birding stores.

Most recordings of backyard bird sounds cost about $35 for cassettes and $40 for CDs, and can be purchased at birding equipment and supply stores, as well as from the ABA. Some recordings are also available by mail order from sources advertised in national birding magazines.

Similarly, professionally produced videotapes of birds such as raptors and hummingbirds are growing in popularity. These videos give beginning backyard birdwatchers excellent close-up views of birds engaged in a range of activities. They are both a pleasure to view and an effective way to improve identification skills from your armchair. Most bird videotapes cost about $40. Birding equipment and supply stores stock bird videotapes, the ABA also sells them, and others are advertised in national birding magazines and sold by mail order. I encourage birdwatchers to take advantage of these products. They can enhance their knowledge of birds, identification skills, and enjoyment of their hobby.

SOME EARLY BIRD-SOUND RECORDINGS

The first bird-sound recording was made in 1889 in Germany by Ludwig Koch. A captive Common Shama's voice was inscribed on an Edison wax cylinder. Sometime around 1899 in North America, a Brown Thrasher's song was recorded on a gramophone, and in 1900 in England, Cherry Kearton made the first recordings of wild bird sounds—a Song Thrush and a Nightingale—on a wax cylinder.

In 1929, Arthur A. Allen and Peter Paul Kellogg from Cornell University recorded House Wren, Rose-breasted Grosbeak, and Song Sparrow sounds on optical sound film synchronized with action film. From those pioneering efforts have evolved high-quality bird-sound recordings used by millions of backyard birdwatchers.

MISCELLANEOUS BIRDING EQUIPMENT

Here are some suggestions for miscellaneous birding equipment that's useful to backyard birders.

Audubon Bird Call

The Audubon Bird Call produces a squeak when the metal part of the device is turned within the wooden part. That squeak is extremely interesting to many songbirds and some raptors, and attracts small birds hiding in protective cover. The Audubon Bird Call is sold in birding equipment and supply stores for about $6, and I recommend it to every backyard birdwatcher.

Field Guide Carrying Cases

Many birding equipment and supply stores sell carrying cases in which field guides can be conveniently carried. They either fasten via loops or some other arrangement to a person's belt or have a detachable shoulder strap. They are very useful when a birder needs a field guide, notebook, and pen, but also for keeping arms and hands free to use binoculars.

Birder's Vests

Birder's vests are designed with as many as eighteen pockets in which field guides, notebooks, food, and other gear can be carried—keeping arms and hands free to use binoculars. They are advertised in national birding magazines and sold by the ABA.

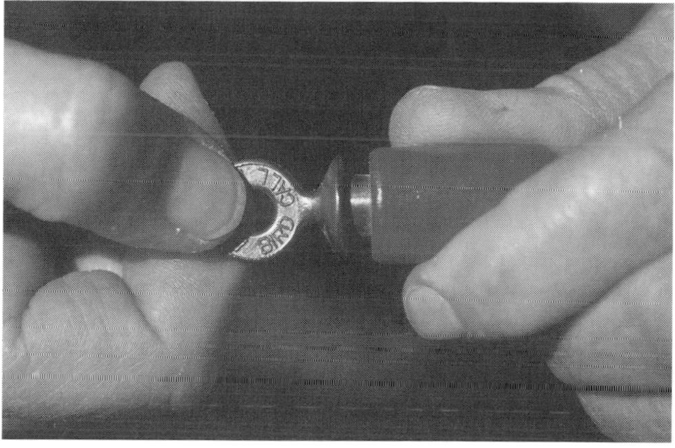

A birder using an Audubon Bird Call.

Hats and Sunscreen

When birding in areas exposed to sunlight, birders should wear a protective hat and apply sunscreen to face, arms, and legs. These measures can help prevent serious sunburn and provide shade for the eyes. A hat also may help prevent injury from birds, such as an Eastern or Western Screech-Owl defending its nesting territory.

Pen and Notebook

Many birdwatchers carry a pen and small notebook to make notes (or they dictate notes into a microcassette tape recorder). Reading them years after they were written can bring back memories of enjoyable bird observations. Always include the complete date and location where observations were made. A minimal entry also includes habitat, species seen, and their numbers.

For scientifically inclined backyard birdwatchers, information preserved in field notebooks has permanent value when articles are prepared for publication in newsletters, scientific journals, and other documents, as well as the local historical record. The information may have far more long-term historical value than you realize. To ensure that valuable birding field notes become part of the local historical record, you can provide in your will for the disposition of your notes. If they are to contribute to our understanding of birds, it's essential that they be placed in an appropriate institution, such as a county historical society, state museum, wildlife research library, or college or university library or archives where professional curators or archivists handle and store such documents.

Embroidered Patches

Many birders put embroidered bird-organization patches from local bird clubs, state chapters or the National Audubon Society, or birding hotspots on hats, jackets, backpacks, and birding vests. Some patches are very colorful—and rare. The head of an Atlantic Puffin on Machias's Seal Island off the Maine coast is one of the rarer patches. Some birdwatchers collect embroidered bird patches as an extension of their hobby.

4 Bird Identification and Field Guides

An American Black Duck swimming.

Learning to identify birds is one of the first challenges that beginning birdwatchers face. Without mastering the basic skills, it is impossible to become involved in birdwatching in a meaningful way. In this chapter, we look at bird identification through the lens of the two major approaches, the Peterson method and the Farrand method.

In 1934, Roger Tory Peterson published his landmark work, *A Field Guide to the Birds*, the first modern field guide. Peterson demonstrated that each bird has unique field marks, distinctive markings that separate it from all other species. By telling people exactly what to look for, Peterson helped millions see birds more clearly. It is no exaggeration to say that Peterson's method launched the modern era of birdwatching by consolidating a large amount of detailed information into the most concise form possible.

In 1988, John Farrand published *An Audubon Handbook: How to Identify Birds*. Instead of the evolution-based organization (most primitive to most advanced birds) of the Peterson and later guides, Farrand's method groups birds according to easily discernible characteristics, such as shape, color, and habitat. The birder then uses subcategories to refine the identification. This involves more information than the Peterson method.

It is important to remember the difference between a field guide and an identification method (a sequence of steps one takes to identify a bird). A number of excellent field guides are available, and we will consider them. You may prefer the Peterson guide or use a field guide by another author (indeed, most popular guides are indebted to some degree to the Peterson method). However, Peterson and Farrand represent the two major approaches to bird identification. Their books stand apart for their effectiveness and coherence as methods. Each approach has its advantages, and it remains for birdwatchers to decide which is best for them. I recommend the Peterson guide and method for the beginner

PETERSON FIELD GUIDE SERIES

Every backyard birdwatcher in North America should own Roger Tory Peterson's field guide to eastern or western birds. When Peterson burst upon the scene in 1934, he sparked a major leap forward in the conception and design of a field guide. A Field Guide to the Birds, *now in its fourth edition, has been a faithful companion to millions of North American birders. It contains comparative color illustrations of the species normally found in eastern and central North America. (In the first edition, most plates were in black and white.) Peterson's innovative features include*

- *arrows on the color plates indicate key field marks on each species*
- *succinct descriptive write-ups focus only on the most obvious and important field marks*
- *a brief list of similar species*
- *brief notes on voice*
- *distribution maps*
- *habitat information*

In 1941, Peterson also produced A Field Guide to Western Birds. *A completely revised and enlarged third edition of the western guide is now available, covering all birds found north of Mexico and west of the one-hundredth meridian in North America. The entire text is new and 700 species are illustrated in 165 color pictures, with more than 1,000 postures depicted. In the back of the book are 441 species-distribution maps.*

Texans like to say they do everything in a big way, and that certainly applies to the state's avifauna—618 species are on record. It is not surprising, therefore, that Texas is the only state with its own field guide; Roger Tory Peterson published A Field Guide to the Birds of Texas *in 1960 at the request of the Texas Game and Fish Commission. The book is out of print, but it can be found in the used-book market.*

One more Peterson field guide is of particular value to beginning backyard birdwatchers. Peterson First Guide to Birds of North America *includes the 188 most common and conspicuous North American birds. It is illustrated in color and has brief species accounts but no distribution maps. Anyone who wants to become a backyard birdwatcher or introduce children to birding will find this guide the ideal place to start.*

The Peterson System now consists of more than fifty additional field guides, among them his own bird guides to western North American, Texas, Mexico, Great Britain, and Europe, as well as guides written by other authors to animals, plants, rocks and minerals, and stars. Together, they form the Peterson Field Guide Series.

for several reasons, not the least of which is because it uses arrows pointing to key field marks for each species. However, the two approaches complement and illuminate one another, and I encourage the student of one to try the other. The ultimate aim is to identify birds quickly and accurately.

PETERSON BIRD IDENTIFICATION METHOD

Peterson's method of identifying birds is fully covered in his landmark *A Field Guide to the Birds* and *A Field Guide to Western Birds*. Although the system includes species and groups that do not normally appear in backyards, I urge beginners to learn to use it—especially if they plan to venture beyond their own yards.

Eight Kinds of Birds

The Peterson identification method recognizes eight major categories of birds, organized around visual (easily discernible) physical traits.

Swimmers

Most beginning birdwatchers can recognize members of this group because of their distinctive shapes when swimming, standing on land, or flying. Clearly, a Canada Goose, American Black Duck, or Mallard does not look like a Gray Catbird or a White-crowned Sparrow.

Some backyard birdwatchers have swimmers living on or near their property. Depending on their location, birders with ponds in their backyard habitat may receive seasonal visits from Canada Geese and several other types of waterfowl. Mallards are fairly common, nesting under protective shrubs near houses or other buildings.

REED'S GUIDES

Some important guides to bird identification were published prior to 1934, particularly those written beginning in 1905 by Chester Reed from Worcester, Massachusetts. Reed's guides were approximately checkbook-size and easy to carry on field trips. They contained basic information about each species, including name, description, song, nest, distribution, and a good color painting.

Reed's guides helped hundreds of thousands of Americans identify birds in their backyards and local parks. For their time, they were remarkably advanced. Any backyard birdwatcher using one today should be able to identify most of the birds visiting bird feeders.

Chester Reed died in 1912, in his mid-thirties, and with his passing went any possible revisions, updates, or other improvements to his guides. The Reed era of bird field guides was over, although his books continued to be published long after his death. The first field guide I used was a Reed guide.

Aerialists

Birds that Peterson places in this group spend a lot of time in flight, and have distinctive shapes or silhouettes. They include seabirds, pelicans, frigatebirds, gannets and boobies, tropicbirds, jaegers and skuas, gulls and terns, and skimmers. A Herring Gull, for example, does not look like an American Robin. Beginning backyard birdwatchers should not have difficulty learning to recognize some aerialists, such as pelicans and gulls.

While many backyard birdwatchers may never see aerialists in their yard, others will have gulls and terns flying overhead or even perching on trees or other objects in their backyard habitat. People living in coastal areas may even have gulls or terns nesting in their backyard.

Long-Legged Waders

This group includes herons, ibises, cranes, and other related birds. A novice might have trouble distinguishing certain members of this group—a Great Blue Heron resembles a Sandhill Crane, for example. However, the overall shape of long-legged wading birds is so different from other birds that they are hard to mistake as a category.

Smaller Waders

Depending on your backyard habitat, you may see examples of this group, which includes rails, plovers, sandpipers, and snipe. It's possible that shorebirds like Killdeer and Spotted Sandpipers will visit and even nest in a backyard habitat.

Fowl-Like Birds

Many backyards will never host fowl-like birds such as quail, turkeys, grouse, or pheasants. However, in some eastern United States backyards, Northern Bobwhites occasionally appear. Elsewhere, particularly in the West, quail may appear more frequently in backyard habitats. Look for California Quail in West Coast backyards and Gambel's Quail in American Southwest backyards; delight in observing these birds and adding them to your life list.

GOLDEN GUIDE

In 1966, Golden Press published A Guide to Field Identification: Birds of North America *by Chandler Robbins, Bertal Bruun, and Herbert Zim. For the first time, birders had access to all North American bird species in a single compact volume (Peterson divided the continent in half and treated Texas separately). The guide offers illustrations by bird artist Arthur Singer, distribution maps, concise species write-ups, and the novel use of sonograms (i.e., graphical representations of bird sounds). The guide employs an innovative spread-based organization, allowing the reader to take in at a glance all the relevant information about a group of birds. Singer's wonderful color paintings also illustrate distinctive behavior for some species, particularly waterbirds.*

The "Golden Guide" became an instant classic among birdwatchers, and millions of copies are used by North America's birders. In 1983, an expanded and revised edition was published. Most birders who own Peterson guides also own the Golden Guide and use both, but many new birders seem unaware of its availability.

A Spotted Sandpiper incubating eggs.

Birds of Prey

Birds of prey, or raptors, are spectacular birds, including hawks, eagles, falcons, and owls. Vultures no longer are included in this category (Peterson considered them raptors) because they are related to storks; for ordinary birding purposes, however, regard them as raptors.

No matter where a backyard habitat is located, a raptor may appear near feeders. Backyard birdwatchers should not be distressed if an occasional hawk or owl surprises a finch or sparrow at the feeder. Predators evolved to capture, kill, and eat other wildlife—and help maintain the ecological balance of nature.

Certain other raptors—Red-shouldered and Red-tailed Hawks, American Kestrels, and Merlins, as well as certain owls—also may discover feeding stations, particularly during winter, and capture an occasional bird.

Nonpasserine Land Birds

Nonpasserine land birds include doves, cuckoos, hummingbirds, swifts, nighthawks, kingfishers, and woodpeckers. Some of these—doves, hummingbirds, and woodpeckers—are birds that beginning birdwatchers should be able to recognize.

ACCIPITERS

Accipiters are hawks that belong to the genus Accipiter. *There are forty-nine species found throughout the world, but only three occur in North America: Northern Goshawks, Cooper's Hawks, and Sharp-shinned Hawks. All three feed largely on small- and medium-sized birds, which is why they are referred to as "bird hawks." Cooper's Hawks and Sharp-shinned Hawks are most likely to visit backyard feeders during autumn, winter, and early spring because they are attracted by the concentrations of birds.*

If a hawk appears at your feeding station, watch it carefully and try to learn how these predators interact with prey. If you actually see a bird captured and eaten by the hawk, do not be distressed—you've just seen a dramatic part of the balance of nature in action, something even raptor experts rarely witness. Remember that federal (and most state) wildlife laws fully protect all birds of prey; it's illegal to injure or kill them.

A

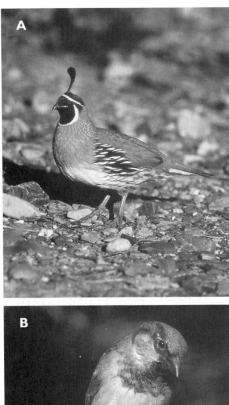

Richard Holmes

Del McNew

A. A Gambel's Quail in Arizona.
B. House Sparrow

These species are more primitive than groups like thrushes and sparrows.

Passerine Birds

The passerine, or perching, birds include flycatchers, vireos, jays, swallows, chickadees and titmice, wrens, kinglets, thrushes, thrashers, wood warblers, tanagers, finches and sparrows, blackbirds and orioles, and some other groups. Although many species are in this category, most beginning birdwatchers can recognize a sparrow and a wren. However, it's doubtful if beginners will recognize vireos or wood warblers. That's why field guides were invented: to help people quickly recognize and identify unfamiliar birds.

A. Perched profile of an *Accipiter*, as sometimes seen in backyard habitats.

B. An Eastern Screech Owl. These birds sometimes visit, or live in, backyard habitats.

Additional Traits

Once a bird has been placed in one of Peterson's eight basic categories, it's time to consider sixteen additional physical features or behavioral traits that help birdwatchers identify birds. In each additional category, common species are used as benchmarks against which other birds can be compared.

Size

Birds occur in a wide range of sizes in North America. Ruby-throated Hummingbirds and Winter Wrens are very small; Ospreys and Bald Eagles are very large—between them are hundreds of species. It is useful to familiarize yourself completely with certain common birds, and then use their size as a comparative reference to describe an unidentified bird. Rock Doves (pigeons), American Robins, and House Sparrows are all common birds that work well for comparison.

Body Shape

What is the shape of a bird when it's perching or standing? Do Belted Kingfishers look like wrens, or hawks like owls? Do

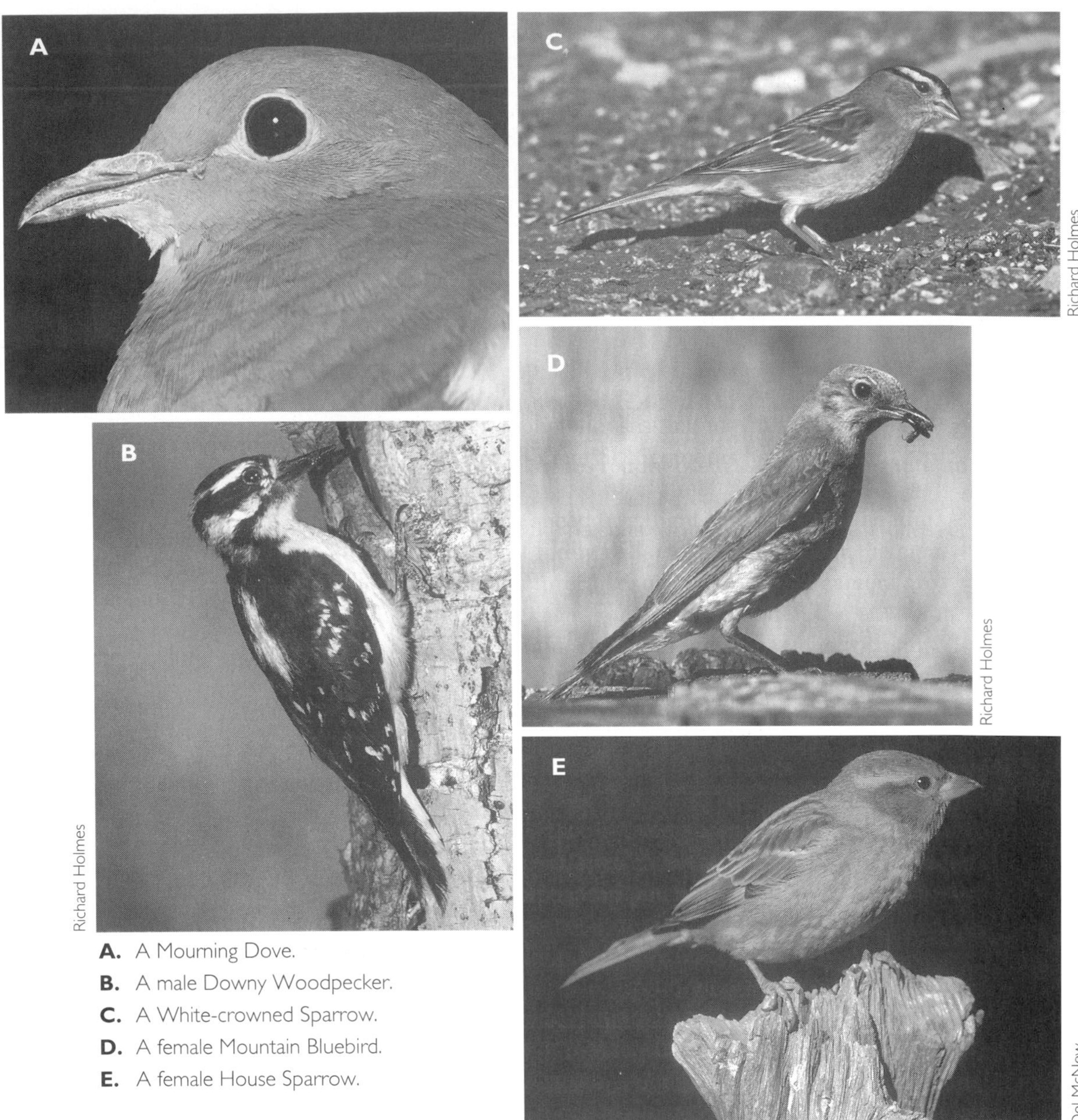

A. A Mourning Dove.
B. A male Downy Woodpecker.
C. A White-crowned Sparrow.
D. A female Mountain Bluebird.
E. A female House Sparrow.

woodpeckers look like sparrows, or gulls like jays? Two birds that Peterson uses as benchmarks for body shape are European Starlings and cuckoos.

The point in making comparisons is to instill in the minds of beginning birdwatchers the fact that not all birds look alike, and that differences in shape are helpful when trying to identify birds. Experienced birdwatchers automatically use shape as a field mark. Beginning birdwatchers can become familiar with shapes of bird groups by paging through color plates in field guides. Peterson's field guides are particularly useful because several related species are shown on each plate. It won't take long to learn them, and then put the new knowledge to use in the field.

Richard Holmes

Del McNew

A. A Northern Flicker showing typical woodpecker profile.

B. This Song Sparrow's profile is very different from that of a woodpecker.

Wing Shape

The wing shapes of certain birds in flight are important field marks. Two species that Peterson uses for examples are the Northern Bobwhite and the Barn Swallow: the latter's wings are pointed, whereas the former's are rounded. A Sharp-shinned Hawk's wings are short and rounded, while those of an American Kestrel are long and pointed. Recognizing field marks like these can lead quickly to correct identification. Wing shape is crucial in the identification of birds such as accipiters, buteos, falcons, shorebirds, and swallows.

Tail Shape

The shape of a bird's tail also can be a helpful field mark for Swallow-tailed Kites, Mourning Doves, and Barn Swallows. For example, is the tail unusually long or short? Is the tip squared, notched, rounded, or deeply forked? To get a feel for how the shapes of bird tails vary, study the pictures in the field guides.

Bill Shape and Size

You will see a remarkable diversity of bill shapes and sizes among backyard birds. The shape and size of a bird's bill can reveal something about its feeding habits and help with identification.

The short, stout bills of sparrows and finches are well adapted to cracking open sunflower and other types of seeds. Some examples in the East are Fox Sparrows, Song Sparrows, White-throated Sparrows, and Northern Cardinals. In the West, examples include White-crowned Sparrows, Golden-crowned Sparrows, and House Finches.

Vireos and wood warblers have small, fine bills optimized for picking up and eating small insects or larvae. Some examples in the East are Yellow-throated Vireos, Black-throated Green Warblers, and Worm-eating Warblers. In the West, examples include Gray Vireos, Lucy's Warblers, and Black-throated Gray Warblers.

Long, dagger-like bills look markedly different from the two previous types, and are seen in birds like terns that feed on fish. Common Terns and Elegant Terns are good examples.

A hook-tipped bill is designed to enable a raptor to tear apart flesh. Birds having this type of bill include Ospreys, Red-tailed Hawks, and Peregrine Falcons.

The most unusual bills seen in a North American backyard are on Red Crossbills and White-winged Crossbills. As the name suggests, the mandibles are crossed—a unique adaptation for cracking open and extracting seeds from pine cones.

Eye-Stripes and Eye-Rings

An eye-stripe is a noticeably dark or light line running near or through a bird's eye. Similarly, an eye-ring is a conspicuous light ring around a bird's eyes. Both are valuable field marks.

Among raptors, adult and immature Northern Goshawks have a bold white eye-stripe above each eye. Northern Bobwhites, particularly males, also have bold white eye-stripes. Among birds seen at feeders, Red-breasted Nuthatches have a white eye-stripe above the eye and another black eye-stripe through the eye; Carolina Wrens have a bold white eyebrow stripe; Red-eyed Vireos have a white eye-stripe bordered with black; and breeding Chipping Sparrows have a bold white eyebrow stripe and a black eye-stripe through the eye.

Ruby-crowned Kinglets have broken white eye-rings and Townsend's Solitaires, gray birds found in the West, have conspicuous white eye-rings. Nashville and Connecticut Warblers also have conspicuous white eye-rings.

Striped Crowns, Crown Patches, and Caps

Certain birds have striped crowns (i.e., the top of the head), crown patches (i.e., an area of contrasting color on top of the head), or caps (i.e., a solid area of contrasting

A. The bill of this Osprey is designed to tear flesh.

B. A Northern Bobwhite showing its bold, white eyebrow.

color, generally smaller than a crown patch, on top of the head) that serve as field marks.

Among birds with conspicuously striped crowns are Black-and-white Warblers, Clay-colored Sparrows, Savannah Sparrows, White-throated Sparrows, and White-crowned Sparrows. At least two species, White-throated Sparrows in the East and White-crowned Sparrows in the West, are backyard-feeder birds.

Examples of birds with crown patches include White-crowned Pigeons, male Ruby-crowned Kinglets, Golden-crowned Kinglets, Chestnut-sided Warblers, Swainson's Warblers, and McCown's Longspurs.

Some North American birds have caps—the color of which varies for each species—as part of their field marks. However, there's overlap in the use of the terms "crown patch" and "cap." Birds with caps include male Black-backed Woodpeckers, Carolina Chickadees, Black-capped Chickadees, Boreal Chickadees, Brown-headed Nuthatches, Gray Catbirds, Chipping Sparrows, Swamp Sparrows, and Common Redpolls.

NATIONAL AUDUBON SOCIETY GUIDES

The National Audubon Society endorses two field guides that are popular among backyard birdwatchers. The National Audubon Society Field Guide to North American Birds: Eastern Region *was written by John Bull and John Farrand Jr. (Later, Farrand would develop his own field guides and the novel approach to bird identification reviewed earlier in this chapter.) The companion volume for the western regions was written by Miklos Udvardy.*

Both guides illustrate species with color photography grouped together at the front of the book. A bird's name and size are indicated with the image, and the reader is referred to supporting text in later pages. The arrangement looks great, but it can be cumbersome to page back and forth between image and text. The Audubon guides also don't use Peterson-style arrows to indicate key field marks.

Crests and Hoods

Permanent or adjustable *crests* (i.e., peaked feathers on top of the head) are field marks for some species. Examples include male Wood Ducks, Hooded Mergansers (the males are spectacular with their fan-shaped white crests open), Red-breasted Mergansers, Belted Kingfishers, Greater Roadrunners, Pileated Woodpeckers, Steller's Jays, Blue Jays, Bridled Titmice, Tufted Titmice, Cedar Waxwings, Northern Cardinals, and Phainopeplas.

Some birds have hoods as field marks—uniformly and distinctly colored feathers covering the whole head and sometimes part or all of the neck (the terms "hood" and "crest" are occasionally interchanged). Examples include male Hooded Warblers, male Connecticut Warblers, and Mourning Warblers.

A male Hooded Merganser with hood raised.

NATIONAL GEOGRAPHIC SOCIETY GUIDE

Despite a crowded and impressive field, the National Geographic Society entered the market in 1983 with the National Geographic Field Guide to the Birds of North America. *Combining an excellent text and illustrations (prepared by various bird artists), the book is well thought of by birdwatchers. Specifically, the guide is distinguished by its attention—both in text and illustrations—to variations in plumage that are important field marks for immature birds.*

In 1999, Jon Dunn edited a third edition. Published in a larger format than the Peterson or Golden field guides, this one won't fit in a pocket, although that's not so important to backyard birdwatchers. Its updated information is helpful, but it does not include all species on the AOU checklist's main list.

A Turkey Vulture in flight showing the two-toned underwing pattern.

Wing Bars, Patches, and Patterns

Some birds display wing bars, patches on their wings, or other distinctive wing patterns, which can be important field marks.

Wing bars occur when distinctively colored feathers form lines or bars on the wings of birds. Birds with wing bars include White-winged Crossbills, Pine Grosbeaks, Pine Siskins, Blue Grosbeaks, and Lazuli Buntings.

Likewise, quite a few birds have conspicuous patches on their wings, including Red-headed Woodpeckers, Acorn Woodpeckers, and Red-winged Blackbirds.

There are also birds that have other distinctive wing patterns. A few examples include Snow Geese with black wingtips, male Common Mergansers with extensive white wing areas, Turkey Vultures with a two-toned blackish-and-whitish underwing pattern, and adult male Northern Harriers with black wingtips.

Rump Patches

A few birds have distinctive rump patches that serve as field marks that are often visible when the birds are in flight. Examples are a white rump on the Northern Harrier and Northern Flicker, a rusty rump on the Cliff Swallow, and a yellow rump on the Yellow-rumped Warbler.

Tail Markings and Patterns

Tail markings and patterns can serve as field marks and are helpful in identifying some birds. Eastern Kingbirds have white tips on their tails. A Bewick's Wren's long tail has white corners, whereas Rock Wrens have buffy tail corners.

Blue-gray Gnatcatchers have long black and white tails, which are often held in a cocked position not unlike a wren's tail. Yellow Warblers have yellow tail spots and

American Redstarts have bright orange areas on their tails. Cedar Waxwings and Bohemian Waxwings have yellow tips on their tails. Dark-eyed Juncos have white outer tail feathers and Lark Sparrows have black tails with conspicuous white corners. Vesper Sparrows also have white outer tail feathers.

Behavior

Sometimes birds exhibit distinctive behavior that serves as an important identification clue. Wrens cock their tails. Many flycatchers perch on exposed utility wires or dead twigs, from which they dart out to capture insects and then return. Eastern Phoebes bob their tails when perched. Spotted Sandpipers teeter up and down when running along a shoreline.

Tree-Climbing

With certain birds, climbing and descending trees, and even tree-climbing style, represents an essential behavior pattern. Hairy Woodpeckers climb tree trunks in jerks, and slightly smaller Downy Woodpeckers behave similarly on smaller tree

STOKES GUIDES

Despite the availability of a large number of field guides to bird identification, Donald and Lillian Stokes entered the arena in 1996 with Stokes Field Guide to Birds: Eastern Region *and* Stokes Field Guide to Birds: Western Region, *published by Little, Brown.*

Like the Audubon and Farrand field guides, the Stokes guides use color photographs to illustrate birds. Basic information is provided for each species: common name, scientific name, identification, habitat, voice, and a distribution map. Stokes guides have several innovative design features helpful to backyard birdwatchers. Each book opens with a Quick Guide, which groups common backyard and feeder birds by colors. Special inserts called Learning Pages provide an overview of key identification categories, such as hawks, shorebirds, gulls, flycatchers, wood warblers, and sparrows. An index to bird groups, based on tabs of different colors, helps birders quickly find the relevant section of the book. The front and back inside covers also have an excellent Quick Alphabetical Index listing page numbers of bird groups. Icons allow readers to identify at a glance species that commonly visit bird feeders or use birdhouses.

Additional innovations include brief behavior information, feeding and nesting data, brief habitat information, voice descriptions, and the conservation status of each species via arrows pointing up or down to indicate increasing or declining populations.

Stokes field guides set forth a "three-dimensional birding" concept. They aim to develop a well-rounded understanding of species identification, bird behavior, and conservation, including habitat enhancement in backyards and national and local land preservation efforts. They also encourage birders to support conservation organizations.

The Stokeses also published A Guide to Bird Behavior, *a field guide to bird behavior in three volumes, each covering the behavior of twenty-five species. Drawings illustrate many types of behavior.*

branches. Brown Creepers circle trees while moving upward. More curious and fascinating is the behavior of Red-breasted and White-breasted Nuthatches. These characters typically descend headfirst down a tree trunk, sometimes stopping to look around or to search for food among crevices in the bark—a most unusual and distinctive behavior that immediately identifies nuthatches.

Backyard birdwatchers can depend on types of tree-climbing behavior as a major aid in sorting out woodpeckers, creepers, and nuthatches.

Flight Style

Not surprisingly, one important behavior of some birds is their flight style. Sharp-shinned Hawks, Cooper's Hawks, and Northern Goshawks flap their wings several times, glide, and then return to flapping. Northern Flickers and American Goldfinches display an undulating flight. Mourning Doves fly in straight lines. Belted Kingfishers hover over a river or creek, then drop down to capture a fish. Most remarkable are the Ruby-throated Hummingbirds and western hummingbirds, which hover in front of backyard feeders or flowers. Using their bills and tongues, they explore for sugar water, nectar, and tiny insects. Then, they back away—the only birds capable of flying backward.

Swimming

Because swimming is an essential part of the normal activity of many birds, swimming style can be an important clue to their identification. Common Loons sit very low in the water as they swim. In their search for food, marsh ducks such as American Black Ducks, Mallards, and Blue-winged Teals feed on the surface (dabbling) and poke their head and neck underwater, with their tail pointing skyward (upending).

For ducks like Canvasbacks, Redheads, Ring-necked Ducks, and Common and Barrow's Goldeneyes, diving is an important identification clue. Hooded, Common, and Red-breasted Mergansers also dive underwater to catch fish in bills that are equipped with saw-edged mandibles.

Richard Holmes

A Blue-throated Hummingbird hovering at a hummingbird feeder.

The Mallard is one of a number of waterfowl species called marsh ducks, or dabblers. Mallards are familiar to almost everyone.

Although they are not waterfowl, coots and gallinules also swim and resemble ducks, but hold themselves more upright than ducks and pump their heads. American Coots dive and dabble.

Wading

Quite a few waterbirds wade in search of food. Long-legged waders including Great Blue Herons, Great Egrets, and Snowy Egrets are especially distinctive. With their long legs, they're able to wade into moderately deep water to search for fish. Other birds that wade to secure food include bitterns, storks, cranes, and shorebirds, such as American Avocets, Greater Yellowlegs, and Willets.

Final Thoughts about the Peterson Method

The Peterson bird identification method is important to backyard birdwatchers because it takes the dizzying variety of colors, shapes, and patterns exhibited by birds and distills them into concise, essential field marks for each species. The innovative little arrows that are Peterson's trademark point only to key field marks. They help beginning birdwatchers focus only on what's important. The result is a quick and accurate method for identifying birds.

FARRAND BIRD IDENTIFICATION METHOD

In 1988, ornithologist John Farrand Jr. presented a new approach to identifying birds in *How to Identify Birds: An Audubon Handbook*, which was written as a

FARRAND GUIDES

John Farrand Jr., skilled birder and ornithologist, spent countless hours observing birds during lazy summer days throughout North America, Latin America, Europe, and Africa. Trained in zoology and a former editor of the periodical American Birds, *he benefited further by working with birders and ornithologists across North America, and having access to birding reports and studies from every part of the continent.*

The upshot of his considerable experience was a revolutionary new approach to identifying birds. In 1988, Farrand published two field guides to North American birds, Eastern Birds: An Audubon Handbook *and* Western Birds: An Audubon Handbook, *which aimed to simplify the identification process by departing from the Peterson guides and the later Golden guides. While Peterson identified birds by pinpointing unique traits, Farrand organizes birds into sixty-two groups based on broad, easily recognizable traits such as shape, color and pattern, and habitat type. The field guides are lavishly illustrated with color photographs and drawings. The liberal use of photography is another departure from the Peterson guides, which rely on bird paintings. A discussion of a single species may include as many as four color photographs—each depicting specific field marks—plus basic species information.*

A companion volume, How to Identify Birds: An Audubon Handbook, *helps birders sharpen their identification skills. In the remainder of this chapter, we consider his identification method as outlined in that book. All three Farrand books are published by McGraw-Hill.*

companion volume to his *Eastern Birds: An Audubon Handbook* and *Western Birds: An Audubon Handbook*. Farrand's method factors in more variables than Peterson's method, which may make it more difficult for the beginning birdwatcher. Nevertheless, the beginner will profit by studying Farrand's revolutionary book.

Farrand identifies birds according to six fundamental categories: habitat, size, behavior, shape and posture, color and pattern, and voice. The intersection of these six basic categories, as refined by the birder, produces an identification.

Habitat

Based only on the fact that you're sitting on a sand dune or sinking into a peat bog, you can make significant inferences about the birds you will encounter before you even lift your binoculars. Thus, for Farrand, habitat becomes an important field mark. Because North America encompasses many habitats, Farrand arranged them into five broad groups: saltwater areas, freshwater areas, forests, open areas, and urban and residential areas. Each broad habitat type is then defined further.

Saltwater Areas

Although few backyards are located in a saltwater habitat, it is a major category from the perspective of general birding. Farrand divides saltwater areas into a number of subgroups, the first of which is open ocean. Oceanic birds include species such as Black-footed Albatrosses, Black-capped Petrels, Audubon's Shearwaters, and Wilson's Storm Petrels. Birders living in a coastal area may occasionally host oceanic birds in a backyard habitat. Storms sometimes carry these birds inland as "storm waifs."

Inshore waters consist of saltwater bays, harbors, tidal inlets, estuaries, and other sheltered saltwater areas. These are good places to find Laughing Gulls, Great Black-backed Gulls, Royal Terns, Forster's Terns, and Black Skimmers.

Farrand further separates inshore waters into groups including rocky shores and coastal cliffs, beaches and coastal dunes, mudflats and tidal shallows, and salt marshes. Each group supports its own birds. Along the northeastern Atlantic coastline, for example, rocky shores and coastal cliffs attract Common Murres, Black Guillemots, Atlantic Puffins, Northern Gannets, and Black-legged Kittiwakes. On the northwestern Pacific coastline, Marbled Murrelets, Cassin's Auklets, Rhinoceros Auklets, and Tufted Puffins occupy rocky shore habitats.

Beaches and coastal dunes attract Herring Gulls, Royal Terns, Ruddy Turnstones, Least Sandpipers, and other shorebirds. Least Terns and Piping Plovers nest on open sand beaches; Willets nest slightly inland, amid or behind primary coastal dunes.

Mudflats and tidal shallows are inshore waters used extensively by shorebirds and gulls. As the tide rises and falls throughout the day, birds advance and retreat with the changing water levels. Birds that feed in this habitat include Laughing Gulls, Clapper Rails, Greater Yellowlegs, Long-billed Dowitchers, and Black-bellied Plovers.

Salt marshes represent Farrand's final saltwater habitat. These ecologically productive wetlands are characterized by marsh grasses and other vegetation.

A. Laughing Gulls along a bay shoreline.

B. Nesting Northern Gannets on Bonaventure Island, Québec, Canada. The birds nest on the ocean-facing cliffs and flat areas at the top of the cliff.

Birds that use them include Snow Geese, Clapper Rails, Snowy Egrets, White-faced Ibises, and Forster's and Black Terns.

Freshwater Areas

Moving inland, freshwater habitats support a wide range of birds. Freshwater marshes provide nesting, resting, and feeding areas for a diverse assortment of birds, including Blue-winged Teals, Northern Shovelers, Northern Pintails, Green-winged Teals, American Bitterns, King Rails, Short-eared Owls, Marsh Wrens, Yellow-headed Blackbirds, and Red-winged Blackbirds.

Lakes, ponds, rivers, and reservoirs attract waterfowl that feed on fish and other aquatic animals and plants. Birds commonly seen in these areas include Canada Geese, American Wigeons, American Black Ducks, Mallards, Northern

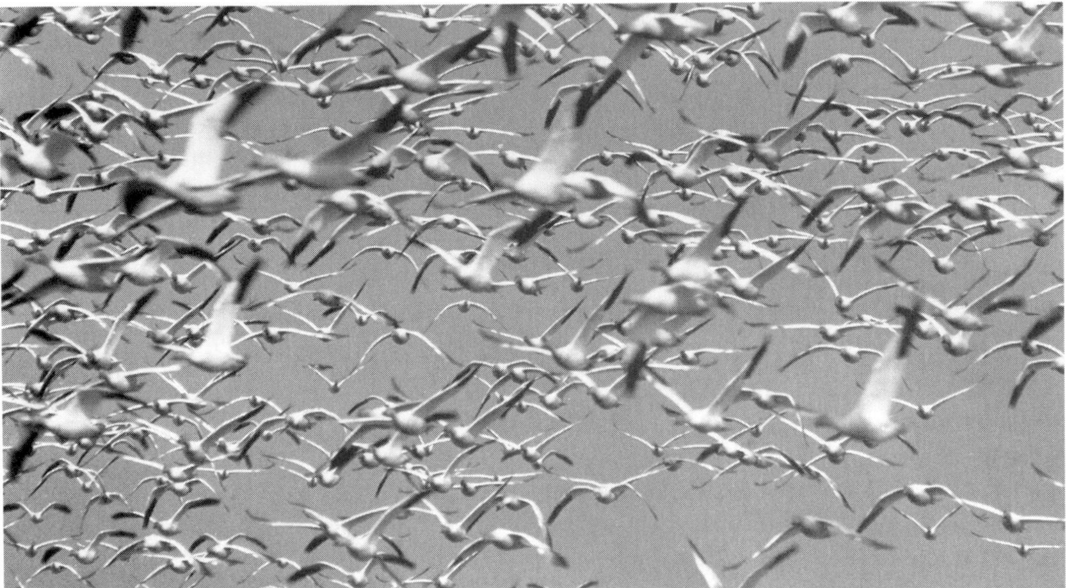

A flock of Snow Geese rising from a New Jersey salt marsh.

Shovelers, Green-winged Teals, Ring-necked Ducks, Barrow's Goldeneyes, and Hooded Mergansers. Fish-eating raptors such as Ospreys and Bald Eagles also use these habitats. During spring migration, Tundra Swans pause on these bodies of water before continuing their migration to tundra nesting grounds.

Freshwater streams and brooks typically flow more rapidly than rivers, often over beds of rocks and pebbles in the mountains. Certain birds rarely leave streams or brooks. Louisiana Water Thrushes are linked to brooks and streams in wooded areas during their breeding season; however, during migration, they occur in swamps and along lake margins. Northern Waterthrushes prefer aquatic areas with slower moving water, such as bogs and northern swamps. When brooks flow across pastures and meadows, an intersection of habitat types is produced and birds from each habitat may be present, such as Red-winged Blackbirds and Vesper Sparrows.

Additional freshwater habitats include coastal mangroves and southern wooded swamps. These are specialized habitats rich in birdlife. Coastal mangroves along parts of coastal Florida are home to large numbers of nesting herons and egrets, and provide shelter for other birds like Brown Pelicans, White Ibises, and Roseate Spoonbills. Mangrove Cuckoos and Black-whiskered Vireos also inhabit coastal mangroves. Southern wooded swamps provide homes for birds like Snowy Egrets, Little Blue Herons, Yellow-crowned Night Herons, Wood Storks, Barred Owls, and Limpkins.

Forests

Forests are major bird habitats. Farrand identifies five basic types as bird habitats: boreal forests; eastern deciduous forests; southeastern pine forests (and pine barrens); western coniferous forests; and dry western woodlands, streamside forests, chaparral, and thickets.

Boreal forests, sometimes called "taiga," consist of spruce, fir, and larch trees. They extend across a large part of the far northern portions of North America from Alaska to northern Québec and Newfoundland, and southward to the United States–Canadian border. Some even reach into northern New England. Boreal forests are also found at high elevations in mountainous areas southward to Georgia, and at high elevations on western mountains.

In general, boreal forests are home to fewer birds than more southern forests because very cold northern winters restrict floral diversity and food supply. However, boreal forests are home to some rarer and more interesting birds; for example, Spruce Grouse, Boreal Owls, Northern Hawk-Owls, Three-toed Woodpeckers, Boreal Chickadees, Cape May Warblers, Red Crossbills, White-winged Crossbills, and Pine Grosbeaks.

The eastern deciduous forest is a broad habitat category that includes mixed deciduous-pine and hemlock forests in northern areas, mixed deciduous forests farther south, and extremely species-rich deciduous forests in the Smoky Mountains. These forests support varied populations of numerous species of birds, including Northern Goshawks, Broad-winged Hawks, Ruffed Grouse, Great Horned Owls, Blue Jays, Black-capped Chickadees, White-breasted Nuthatches, Hairy Woodpeckers, Downy Woodpeckers, Red-bellied Woodpeckers, Eastern Wood Pewees, Wood Thrushes, Ovenbirds, Scarlet Tanagers, and Indigo Buntings.

One subtype of the eastern deciduous forest is the northern wooded swamps, which are wet forests in parts of Canada and the northern United States. They include flooded areas, either seasonal or year-round; alder and maple swamps; river-bottom forests; and bogs. Examples are black-spruce bogs in Maine, cedar bogs and spruce-larch bogs in Minnesota, spruce-fir bogs in New York, red-maple swamps in Massachusetts and New York, and rhododendron swamps in Virginia. Birds typically found in these areas—especially to the north—include Wood Ducks, Red-shouldered Hawks, American Woodcocks, Solitary Sandpipers, Barred Owls, Palm Warblers, Northern Waterthrushes, Connecticut Warblers, Mourning Warblers, Hooded Warblers, Lincoln's Sparrows, and Rusty Blackbirds.

AMERICAN BIRD CONSERVANCY GUIDE

The American Bird Conservancy is an international conservation organization that focuses its bird conservation efforts in the Americas. In 1997, the group produced its own field guide to identification of North American birds, All the Birds of North America. *The book was conceived and designed by Jack Griggs with the input of eleven ornithological consultants and twelve bird artists, who produced the guide's excellent illustrations.*

The guide focuses on bird habitats, field marks, and feeding behavior. In its emphasis on habitat, the guide probably owes a debt to Farrand's system, which categorizes species into thirty-five groups, each with a unique icon. A birder looks at icons on the inside front and back covers, picks one similar to the bird being observed, turns to the appropriate pages, and hopefully can identify the bird by comparing it with the species illustrated. Color illustrations, range maps, and text usually appear together on a page. Limited information is provided on extinct birds as well. The American Bird Conservancy guide is a useful reference.

Moving southward along the coastal plain in the eastern United States, from Delaware to Florida, and then westward to Texas, one encounters extensive southeastern pine forests. Several special birds are found in these habitats, including the endangered Red-cockaded Woodpecker. It lives and nests in mature yellow- and longleaf pine forests containing fungus-infected trees with relatively soft heartwood. Brown-headed Nuthatches also depend on southeastern and Gulf Coast pine forests, from which they rarely stray. Other birds found in southeastern pine forests include Northern Bobwhites, Red-bellied Woodpeckers, Pine Warblers, and Bachman's Sparrows.

Pine barrens in Michigan and those near Albany, New York, on Long Island, New York, and in south-central New Jersey are also included in the southeastern pine forests category. Michigan's pine barrens are home to the endangered Kirtland's Warbler, which requires jack-pine barrens at a specific state of growth in which to nest. Pine barrens are home to many unusual plant species.

Western coniferous forests include a variety of forest types. In the Pacific Northwest there are spectacular wet, lowland, old-growth forests. Sitka spruce, western red cedars, and western hemlocks, as well as an abundant and diverse understory of shrubs and herbaceous plants, grow there. Spotted Owls are characteristic of these forests. Elsewhere in the western United States, many forests are also known collectively as western coniferous forests. Which conifer species produce a particular forest depends on the elevation on a mountain where the trees are growing, compass direction of the slope, amount of rainfall received, and other factors. Birds found in western coniferous forest habitats include Northern Pygmy Owls, Clark's Nutcrackers, Gray Jays, Steller's Jays, White-headed Woodpeckers, Williamson's Sapsuckers, Three-toed Woodpeckers, Red-breasted Nuthatches, Pygmy Nuthatches, Mountain Chickadees, Golden-crowned Kinglets, Varied Thrushes, Townsend's Warblers, Western Tanagers, Evening Grosbeaks, Cassin's Finches, and Red Crossbills.

Richard Holmes

Richard Holmes

A. A Cassin's Finch, typically found in western coniferous forests.

B. A Steller's Jay is another western coniferous forest species.

Farrand's final forest category consists of dry western woodlands, streamside forests, and chaparral areas and thickets. Whiskered Screech-Owls are typical of pinyon-juniper forests; Summer Tanagers are found in oak woodlands; Elegant Trogons (in southeastern Arizona) and Vermilion Flycatchers occur in streamside forests; and White-crowned Sparrows live in chaparral and pine woodlands. Finally, thickets (i.e., dense growths of trees, shrubs, and weeds) provide a home for Mountain Quail, Black-billed Cuckoos, and Lazuli and Painted Buntings.

Open Areas

Under open areas, Farrand recognizes four habitats: open country, grasslands, and groves; deserts and sagebrush plains; mountain cliffs, gorges, mesas, and bare rocky slopes; and alpine tundra and meadows. Each attracts different birds, at least during part of each year.

The open country, grasslands, and groves category includes a wide range of natural and manmade areas. Virgin grasslands and prairies typically are breeding habitats for Mountain Plovers, Upland Sandpipers, Long-billed Curlews, Greater Prairie-Chickens, McCown's Longspurs, and Baird's Sparrows.

Altered open landscapes, such as agricultural fields, pastures, golf courses, and airports, are also part of the open-country category. Birds in these areas include Red-tailed Hawks, Upland Sandpipers, Rock Doves, Burrowing Owls, Eastern or Western Kingbirds, American Crows, Red-winged or Yellow-headed Blackbirds, Eastern or Western Meadowlarks, and House Sparrows.

A third habitat variation, brushy open country, attracts some unusual birds (some only in southern Texas and the American Southwest), such as Common Ground Doves, White-winged Doves, Scaled Quail, Cactus Wrens, Sage Thrashers, Golden-winged Warblers, Chestnut-sided Warblers, Yellow-breasted Chats, Lark Buntings, Sage Sparrows, Black-chinned Sparrows, and Dickcissels.

Deserts and sagebrush plains are two distinct open areas. In the American Southwest, desert flora include

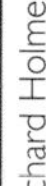

Richard Holmes

Lindsay Kirk

A. Cactus Wrens are American Southwest desert birds.

B. A Black-billed Magpie, found in sagebrush plains.

agave, yucca, shrubs, and cacti and succulents. Birds in these harsh areas include Scaled Quail, Greater Roadrunners, Elf Owls, Costa's Hummingbirds, Cactus Wrens, Bendire's Thrashers, and LeConte's Thrashers. Birds associated with sagebrush plains of the Great Basin include Sage Grouse, Black-billed Magpies, Sage Thrashers, and Brewer's Sparrows.

Mountain cliffs, gorges, mesas, and bare rocky slopes are typical Western habitats characterized by limited vegetation. Birds found in these areas include California Condors, Golden Eagles, Prairie Falcons, Barn Owls, Common Poorwills, White-throated Swifts, and Rock Wrens.

In the East, a small number of Golden Eagles nest on mountain cliffs in Atlantic Canada and perhaps Maine, as do Common Ravens on mountain cliffs in northern Pennsylvania and the Shenandoah National Park in Virginia. It remains to be seen whether Peregrine Falcons will reoccupy hundreds of former nesting ledges and cliffs along major river systems in the East.

Most alpine tundra and meadows occur on very high western mountains in California, Montana, and Washington, where lovely carpets of wildflowers cover grassy meadows and tundra patches at high elevations. Birds living in these habitats include White-tailed Ptarmigan, Rock Ptarmigan, and Rosy Finches.

Urban and Residential Areas

Farrand recognizes urban areas, residential areas, and parks as basic habitats factored into bird identification. Birds typically seen in urban areas (defined as

THE PEREGRINE FALCON IS SAVED

In August 1999, the U.S. Fish and Wildlife Service removed the Peregrine Falcon from the federal endangered species list. Secretary of the Interior Bruce Babbitt called delisting Peregrines one of the most dramatic success stories of the Endangered Species Act.

The world's fastest birds, Peregrines are famous for stooping (i.e., diving) at breathtaking speeds of 175 miles per hour or more. The falcons nearly became extinct in the continental United States after World War II because of DDT pollution. The pesticide caused their eggshells to become thin and break while being incubated. No young were produced.

In 1962, Rachel Carson sounded the alarm with the publication of Silent Spring, *which alerted the public and the federal government to the urgent need to ban DDT. The book sparked a national debate. Emergency conferences, research, and other actions were taken, including experimental captive breeding programs to save Peregrine Falcons (and Bald Eagles) from extinction.*

In 1970, the U.S. Fish and Wildlife Service placed the Peregrine Falcon on the federal endangered species list, and in 1972 the EPA banned the use of DDT in the United States.

These decisions represented the first major steps in a long, controversial, and very costly effort that led to the historic delisting announcement. There are now at least 1,650 Peregrine breeding pairs in the United States and Canada.

densely developed cores of cities) include Rock Doves, Ringed Turtle-doves, Spotted Doves, European Starlings, House Sparrows, and even Peregrine Falcons, which have been introduced into some cities.

In comparison, commonly seen species in many residential areas and parks of North America include Common Nighthawks, Chimney Swifts, Mourning Doves, American Robins, European Starlings, Common Grackles, Black-headed Grosbeaks, House Finches, and House Sparrows.

An American Robin sitting on her nest incubating eggs in a suburban backyard habitat.

Size

As with Peterson's system, a basic field mark in Farrand's method is the size of a bird's body (rather than total length or shape). Farrand selected seven familiar birds as yardsticks against which other birds are measured.

Very Small (3½ to 5 inches)

Rufous Hummingbirds, Brown-breasted Nuthatches, Bushtits, Sedge Wrens, Golden-crowned Kinglets, and Lesser Goldfinches fall into the very small category. Each can fit into the palm of your hand.

Sparrow-Sized (5¼ to 8¼ inches)

Birds included in the sparrow-size category are Black-capped Chickadees, White-breasted Nuthatches, Yellow-rumped Warblers, House Sparrows, and Field Sparrows.

Robin-Sized (9 to 11 inches)

Birds in this category include Mourning Doves, Burrowing Owls, Hairy Woodpeckers, Eastern Kingbirds, Cactus Wrens, Northern Mockingbirds, American Robins, Western Meadowlarks, Red-winged Blackbirds, and Northern Cardinals.

FINCH YEARS

Backyard and other birdwatchers in the continental United States sometimes use "finch" to refer to an assortment of seed-eating birds whose breeding ranges are in the northern parts of North America. They include Evening Grosbeaks, Pine Grosbeaks, Purple Finches, Rosy Finches, Hoary Redpolls, Common Redpolls, Red Crossbills, White-winged Crossbills, and Pine Siskins.

During winters when food is unusually limited on northern breeding grounds, large numbers of these birds undertake southward invasions into the northern United States. Birders refer to these autumn and winter invasions as "finch years." This is an excellent opportunity to see rarer, colorful northern finches at backyard feeders and to add them to your life list.

Pigeon-Sized (13 inches)

Ordinary pigeons, or Rock Doves, represent the fourth size category. Other examples are Eared Grebes, Least Bitterns, Sharp-shinned Hawks, Greater Yellowlegs, Forster's Terns, Black Guillemots, and Clark's Nutcrackers.

Crow- and Raven-Sized (17 to 27 inches)

Birds in this category are fairly large, and include Wood Ducks, Blue-winged Teals, Red-tailed Hawks, Spruce Grouse, Ruffed Grouse, Laughing Gulls, Short-eared Owls, and American Crows.

Goose-Sized (25 to 43 inches)

Birds in this group are large. Examples include Snow Geese, Canada Geese, White Ibises, Anhingas, Tricolored Herons, Little Blue Herons, Roseate Spoonbills, Herring Gulls, and Turkey Vultures.

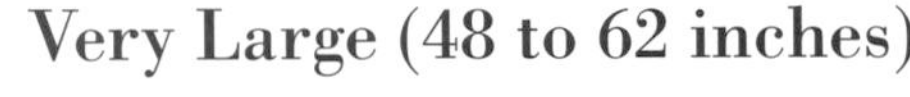

Very Large (48 to 62 inches)

Some North American birds are very large with typically slow wingbeats. Examples include Wild Turkeys, the "Great White Heron" (color morph of Great Blue Herons in southern Florida), Brown Pelicans, White Pelicans, Tundra Swans, and Bald Eagles.

Try comparing the sizes of common birds in your backyard to become familiar with these categories.

A. American Crows are one of Farrand's seven yardstick birds.

B. The Canada Goose is another of the yardstick birds in Farrand's size system.

Behavior

Certain behavior is characteristic of certain birds or bird groups, and can serve as a field mark. Sometimes behavior is closely tied to habitat.

Behavior Associated with Water

Under Farrand's system, waterbirds may show more than twenty distinctive behavior traits. Here are just a few examples.

Swimming is the most obvious behavior associated with water. Tundra Swans, Canada Geese, Wood Ducks, and Mallards are commonly seem swimming on ponds, lakes, rivers, and bays. The technique of sinking is employed by diving waterfowl such as Ruddy Ducks. They tightly compress their feathers against their bodies and gradually sink beneath the surface as air trapped in their plumage is forced out. Grebes and Anhingas swim with only their head and neck poking out of the water.

As the name suggests, diving ducks dive under the water for food. Horned Grebes, Canvasbacks, Redheads, Ring-necked Ducks, Greater and Lesser Scaups, Common and Barrow's Goldeneyes, Buffleheads, and Ruddy Ducks all use diving behavior. Seaducks such as scoters and Oldsquaws also use diving behavior, as do mergansers.

Many waterfowl are surface-feeding, or dabbling, ducks. Mallards, American Black Ducks, Northern Pintails, American Wigeons, and Blue-winged, Green-winged, and Cinnamon Teals are examples. They poke their head underwater to secure food; very large birds like Tundra Swans and Mute Swans put their head and neck entirely underwater. In a quite different approach, Red-necked Phalaropes spin in a circle on the water's surface to stir up aquatic animals upon which they feed.

Related to dabbling is upending, or tipping up, in which the bird reaches for aquatic plants simply by pivoting in the water with its tail pointing up and its head and chest underwater. Mallards, Northern Shovelers, Blue-winged Teals, and many other ducks display this behavior, as do geese and swans.

Wading into shallow water to secure food is another distinctive behavior. This method is used by birds with long legs, such as Great Blue Herons, Great Egrets, other herons and egrets, Wood Storks, and Black-necked Stilts.

Behavior Associated with Land

Owls use head-bobbing to obtain a clearer perception of distance or as a mild form of alarm. Burrowing Owls sometimes use head-bobbing while standing outside their burrows, as do American Kestrels perched on poles and utility wires. Head-bobbing is thus a distinctive behavior and serves as an effective field mark in Farrand's method.

Tree-clinging is common among woodpeckers. The birds cling to tree bark with their feet and toes, and use stiff tail feathers as a prop. Anyone watching a nuthatch for the first time probably questions their own eyes or their sobriety—surely birds do not walk headfirst *down* tree trunks! Nuthatches routinely descend

A. A kettle of migrating Broad-winged Hawks above a Pennsylvania hawkwatching lookout during September.

B. A typical V formation of migrating Canada Geese.

tree trunks by clinging to the bark with their strong legs and toes. Moreover, they act even more gravity-defiant by extending their head outward as they effortlessly climb down, up, or around trees. Red-breasted Nuthatches, White-breasted Nuthatches, Brown-headed Nuthatches (in southeastern U.S. pine forests), and Pygmy Nuthatches (in western U.S. coniferous forests and California's coastal pine forests) are always fun to watch.

Varied Thrushes, American Robins, and Northern Mockingbirds all use distinctive running-and-stopping behavior when foraging.

Wing-flashing, used by Northern Mockingbirds, happens when a bird stands on the ground, and spreads its wings forward and outward in rapid, jerky motions, making the large white wing patch on each wing conspicuous.

Tail-bobbing is used by Eastern Phoebes, Kirtland's Warblers, Ovenbirds, and Water Pitpits. The reason for this behavior is not known, but it is a field mark for these birds.

Flight Style

As we've seen, the flight style of an individual bird can hasten identification—the hovering of a hummingbird or the undulating flight of woodpeckers. Beginning birdwatchers should learn to recognize distinctive group formations as well. Most people are familiar with the V formations or arcs of migrating Canada Geese during spring and autumn. The formation changes as one bird, then another, assumes the point position, but the basic shape more or less is maintained—an excellent field mark. Tundra Swans, Snow Geese, and Sandhill Cranes also fly in wedge or V formations, but their colors and sounds are different from Canada Geese.

European Starlings, Red-winged Blackbirds, and other so-called blackbirds fly in compact formations and maneuver with amazing precision, as if on cue. Look for this behavior in autumn and winter when the birds leave or return to their roosts.

Shape and Posture

As discussed in Peterson's method, the shape and posture of birds' bodies can be critical field marks. Tufted Titmice have pointed crests that can be elevated at will. Swans have a distinctive arched neck. Together, these attributes comprise the fourth component of Farrand's method.

Plumes and Tufts

Some birds, like Great Horned Owls, Eastern and Western Screech-Owls, and certain other owls have ear tufts that they raise or lower. They are not ears and have nothing to do with hearing. Game birds like Gambel's Quail, California Quail, and Mountain Quail also have a permanent plume extending upward above the bird's head. In combination with other field marks, these head decorations can determine identity.

An adult Turkey Vulture standing on the ground. The relatively small head is naked or unfeathered.

Bills

As we saw in Peterson's method, the size and shape of bird bills reflect their feeding habits and serve as field marks. Farrand divides the variety of bills with great precision.

The bills of waterbirds vary enormously: some are long and stout, as on Brown Pelicans; others are slightly downcurved, as on Wood

Storks; and others are strongly downcurved, as on White Ibises. Some waterbirds have long and slim bills, like Long-billed Dowitchers. Common and other terns have pointed bills. Wilson's and Northern Phalaropes have needle-like bills, whereas Stilt Sandpipers, Curlew Sandpipers, and Dunlin have slightly downcurved bills. Other waterbirds have flat bills, such as the knobbed bills of Surf Scoters, the shovel-shaped bills of Northern Shovelers, and the spoon-shaped bills of Roseate Spoonbills.

Among land birds, the variety is no less. Common Nighthawks and Whippoorwills have very small bills. Bobolinks have conical bills. Hummingbirds have very long bills designed to penetrate flowers to secure nectar and tiny insects. Raptors have hooked bills to tear flesh. Red-winged Crossbills and White-winged Crossbills have specialized crossed bills for extracting seeds from pine cones.

Richard Holmes

A. A Brown Pelican's bill is long and stout.

B. Atlantic Puffins have colorful, parrot-like bills.

C. Curve-billed Thrashers have strongly downcurved bills.

D. An immature Bald Eagle. The large, powerful bill is designed for ripping apart the flesh of its prey.

Wings and Tails in Flight

The size and shape of wings and tails are helpful in identifying birds in flight—and sometimes they are primary field marks. Some birds have long and narrow wings. Albatrosses are classic examples, but most other seabirds, gulls, terns, Ospreys, and falcons all have rather long and narrow wings. (Ospreys sometimes pull their long wings into a crooked position when using updrafts along mountains, which provides an excellent field mark.)

Northern Harriers also have somewhat long wings, although the tips are rounded under certain flight conditions. These birds can adjust their shape so they appear long and pointed—sometimes deceptively similar to Peregrine Falcon wings.

Rough-legged Hawks have both broad and rather long wings with somewhat rounded wingtips. The wings of Red-tailed, Red-shouldered, and Broad-winged Hawks are proportionally not quite as long.

As with wings, the size and shape of tails can be distinctive. Herring Gulls, for example, have short fan-shaped tails, whereas Gull-billed, Caspian, Royal, Sandwich, and other terns have shallowly forked tails. The short tails of Northern Gannets are pointed; Sharp-shinned and Cooper's Hawks have long plank-like tails.

Tails of Birds Standing, Perched, or Swimming

The tails of certain birds when they are standing, perched, or swimming also can aid identification. Pied-billed Grebes have tails so short that they're not visible when the birds are swimming. American Coots, however, have very short tails that are slightly visible.

Brown Thrashers and other thrashers have long tails. Ring-necked Pheasants also have very long pointed tails, whereas male Northern Pintails have long central tail feathers.

The tails of Pine Siskins and some Sharp-shinned Hawks have distinctly notched tips. There are also species with a squared tip, such as some Sharp-shinned Hawks. The tip of a Cooper's Hawk's tail, however, is very rounded—an important field mark.

An accipiter in flight. All accipiters more or less have this shape in flight, with subtle variations separating the different species.

American Coots have short tails.

Color and Pattern

Color and pattern are Farrand's fifth major category. The colors of many birds are vibrant and beautiful and, in some cases, are important field marks.

Blue

Although some North American birds are blue, there is no blue pigment in bird feathers. The impression of blue is caused by the physical structures of feathers and the way they reflect light. Several birds have deep blue plumage. Painted Buntings have blue heads. Blue Grosbeaks are almost entirely deep blue, except for rufous wingbars. Indigo Buntings are also blue, although they may appear black in poor light. Blue Jays, Pinyon Jays, and Mountain Bluebirds are entirely blue. Eastern Bluebirds, Western Bluebirds, and Lazuli Buntings have color patterns of blue with a rufous breast. Steller's Jays have black heads but blue wings, undersides, rumps, and tail feathers.

Black

Quite a few birds are partly or entirely black. The Phainopepla (with red eyes) and Rusty Blackbirds (with yellow eyes) are both black and robin-sized. Larger black birds include American Crows, Northwestern Crows, Fish Crows, and Common Ravens.

Some birds are black with iridescent green or purple hues when seen in sunlight, including Brewer's Blackbirds, Boat-tailed Grackles, and Great-tailed Grackles. On other birds, black combines with other colors to produce distinctive patterns. Bobolinks have pale yellow napes with a white rump and scapulars. Red-winged Blackbirds have vivid red shoulders. Yellow-headed Blackbirds have vivid orange-yellow heads and breasts, and white wing patches.

Yellow

Many birds have some yellow in their plumage. The Yellow Warbler is mostly yellow. Prothonotary Warblers and Yellow-headed Blackbirds have yellow on their head and breast. American Goldfinches, Evening Grosbeaks, and Scott's Orioles all display bold yellow patterns.

In some species, such as American Goldfinches and Evening Grosbeaks, the vivid patterns of birds in breeding plumage change greatly when they are in winter plumage. The bright yellow body and black wings of male American Goldfinches in breeding plumage change to a drab olive-yellow for both sexes during winter. It's not hard to confuse American Goldfinches in winter with larger and somewhat differently patterned Evening Grosbeaks. Using your field guide, compare the illustrations of the two species.

Red

Red is a favorite color of many birdwatchers, and indeed some birds wear spectacular red plumage. Males of some finch species such as Purple and House Finches have lovely rosy colors, whereas a more pinkish-red hue is found on Common Redpolls, Pine Grosbeaks, and White-winged Crossbills. Some of the most vividly colored birds are those with bright red-and-black combinations; for example, male Northern Cardinals, Scarlet Tanagers, and Vermilion Flycatchers. You will not soon forget the sight of a Scarlet Tanager against green foliage or a Northern Cardinal on snow.

Other major colors in Farrand's organization are olive, gray, and brown.

Sounds

The last of Farrand's major categories in bird identification is sounds made by birds. It sometimes comes as a surprise to beginning birdwatchers to learn that many experienced birders do a good deal of their birding by sound rather than sight. The reason is simple: each species has one or more distinctive sounds. The more bird sounds you learn, the easier it is to identify birds. That's especially true of vireos and wood warblers, which are often heard but are difficult to see among leaves high in trees. It's even possible to drive along a quiet road and identify birds only by hearing their sounds.

Farrand organizes bird sounds in three basic categories: simple sounds, patterns of notes, and varied or repeated phrases.

Simple Sounds

A number of sounds fall into this category. The most common are lisps, such as the single lisp used by Brown Creepers, two lisps by Golden-crowned Kinglets, and repeated lisps by Cedar Waxwings. Chipping Sparrows, Orange-crowned Warblers, and Dark-eyed Juncos use distinctive trills. Grasshopper Sparrows, Clay-colored Sparrows, and Savannah Sparrows use an insect-like buzz. Pigeons and doves, such as Rock Doves and Mourning Doves, make a cooing sound.

Patterns of Notes

Some bird sounds are patterns of notes. For example, White-throated Sparrows make distinctive clear whistles, whereas Eastern Meadowlarks and Field Sparrows produce slurred whistles. Western Meadowlarks have flute-like notes. Some birds also use distinctive melodic or musical warbles, such as Purple, Cassin's, and House Finches.

Birds such as Yellow Warblers, Black-throated Green Warblers, and Blackburnian Warblers use high-pitched, patterned songs, whereas Horned Larks, Marsh Wrens, and House Wrens use distinctive songs lacking clear-cut but very rapid phrases.

Varied or Repeated Phrases

This category contains complex bird sounds. The sounds of Wood Thrushes, Hermit Thrushes, Swainson's Thrushes, and Western Meadowlarks resemble a flute's tones. Some bird sounds consist of repeated phrases, such as those of Common Yellowthroats, Northern Cardinals, and Steller's Jays. Other bird sounds consist of varied phrases; for example, Rose-breasted Grosbeaks, Summer Tanagers, and Western Tanagers. Northern Mockingbirds, Curve-billed Thrashers, and Indigo Buntings produce a combination of varied and repeated phrases, in which a phrase is repeated several times and then a different phrase is introduced and repeated.

Learning Bird Songs

Some people, including those with musical backgrounds, learn bird sounds easily; others find it more challenging and limit their knowledge to those sounds that are common or distinctive.

Professional recordings of bird songs are available as aids to learning bird sounds. Those in the Peterson Field Guide Series are especially helpful (see chapter 3).

Final Thoughts about the Farrand Method

The Farrand bird identification method is a detailed and comprehensive program. I encourage all birdwatchers to explore its full possibilities. As discussed previously, the Peterson and Farrand identification methods complement one another. Whichever method you prefer, you will benefit by studying the other.

5 Creating a Backyard Habitat

Kay Packard

Part of Kay Packard's enhanced backyard habitat in Chamblee, Georgia.

Kay Packard's one-third-acre lot in Georgia is a botanical paradise with eight species of trees, twenty-eight different shrubs, twenty-one species of vines, more than eighty species or varieties of perennials, and eight different ferns. With such a great variety of vegetation carefully planted in a small area, it's no surprise that birds abound in her backyard—Mourning Doves, Ruby-throated Hummingbirds, Blue Jays, Brown-headed Nuthatches, Carolina Wrens, Red-bellied Woodpeckers, Gray Catbirds, Brown Thrashers, Chipping Sparrows, and many more. Between residents, migrants, and oddballs—such as a juvenile Black-crowned Night-Heron that once showed up—no fewer than forty-seven species are now on her backyard bird list.

Likewise, when White-crowned Sparrows, Pine Siskins, Pine Grosbeaks, and Evening Grosbeaks take seeds from the thirteen backyard feeders that Charlie and Sandy Fliniau maintain over the winter at their home high in the Rocky Mountains of Colorado, these birds appear because their basic requirements are being met. Sometimes the Fliniaus enjoy the sight of dozens of rare and lovely Rosy-Finches, both Gray-crowned and Black, that feed on seeds scattered on their deck and perch in a nearby fir tree—a remarkable birdwatching spectacle.

If you want to attract birds to your yard, it's necessary to create or enhance a habitat that provides birds with basic living conditions. A backyard habitat should offer birds several features: vegetation that provides food, protective cover, and nesting sites; bird feeders to supplement natural food sources; nest boxes for species that use them; fresh water for drinking and bathing; and additional landscaping elements such as brush piles to provide cover. If you provide these ingredients, birds will flock to your yard.

In addition, well-planned gardening and landscaping projects add color and beauty to your property, reduce the amount of pesticides and herbicides in use, moderate the summer heat, and increase property value by as much as 10 percent. Of course, gardening and landscaping are pleasurable hobbies in their own right.

In this chapter, we look at how to create an attractive and productive backyard habitat through gardening. Following a general overview of wildlife gardening and the resources available, we survey regions of the United States and southern Canada to highlight particularly good matches between native plant and bird species that no backyard birder should overlook. In a few cases, such as Texas, individual states contain so much ecological diversity that they warrant separate treatment. There is some overlap between the northern regions of the United States and the southern Canadian provinces they border—much of what I say, for instance, about the Pacific Northwest also applies to British Columbia. As a result, the coverage of southern Canada is more selective and focuses on the differences with adjoining U.S. regions.

Chapters 6, 7, and 8 address the other essential elements of the enhanced backyard habitat—bird feeders, nest boxes, and water and shelter.

GARDENING BASICS

The kinds of gardening and landscaping improvements needed to draw birds to a backyard habitat depend on where you live and, in particular, the plants and animals that naturally occur in your geographic area. See the color illustrations between pages 134 and 135 for regional examples of backyard habitats.

A summer garden in Pennsylvania created by Bill Masters. Ruby-throated Hummingbirds are among the wildlife that visit these colorful backyard habitats.

Hardiness

Each section of the country has its own climate, soil, and plant requirements. Most species of trees, shrubs, and flowers occurring in an Arizona desert or along the Pacific Coast are not seen in Maine. Your goal is to select botanical species that are native to your part of the country and its climate and soil conditions. The U.S. Department of Agriculture (USDA) plant hardiness zone map is a crucial tool in selecting a greater variety or number of appropriate trees, shrubs, and flowers for planting in backyard habitats. This is especially true in the eastern half of the United States.

The 1990 revised edition of the USDA plant hardiness zone map is used widely and is included in most catalogs published by seed, flower, tree, and shrub companies and nurseries. The catalogs indicate which zones are best for each species—a great help when selecting the best climatically adapted plants for your habitat.

Simply match the hardiness zone in which your backyard habitat is located with the zones that a seed grower, nursery, or other plant source indicates for flora offered for sale. Those whose ratings include the zone in which your backyard is

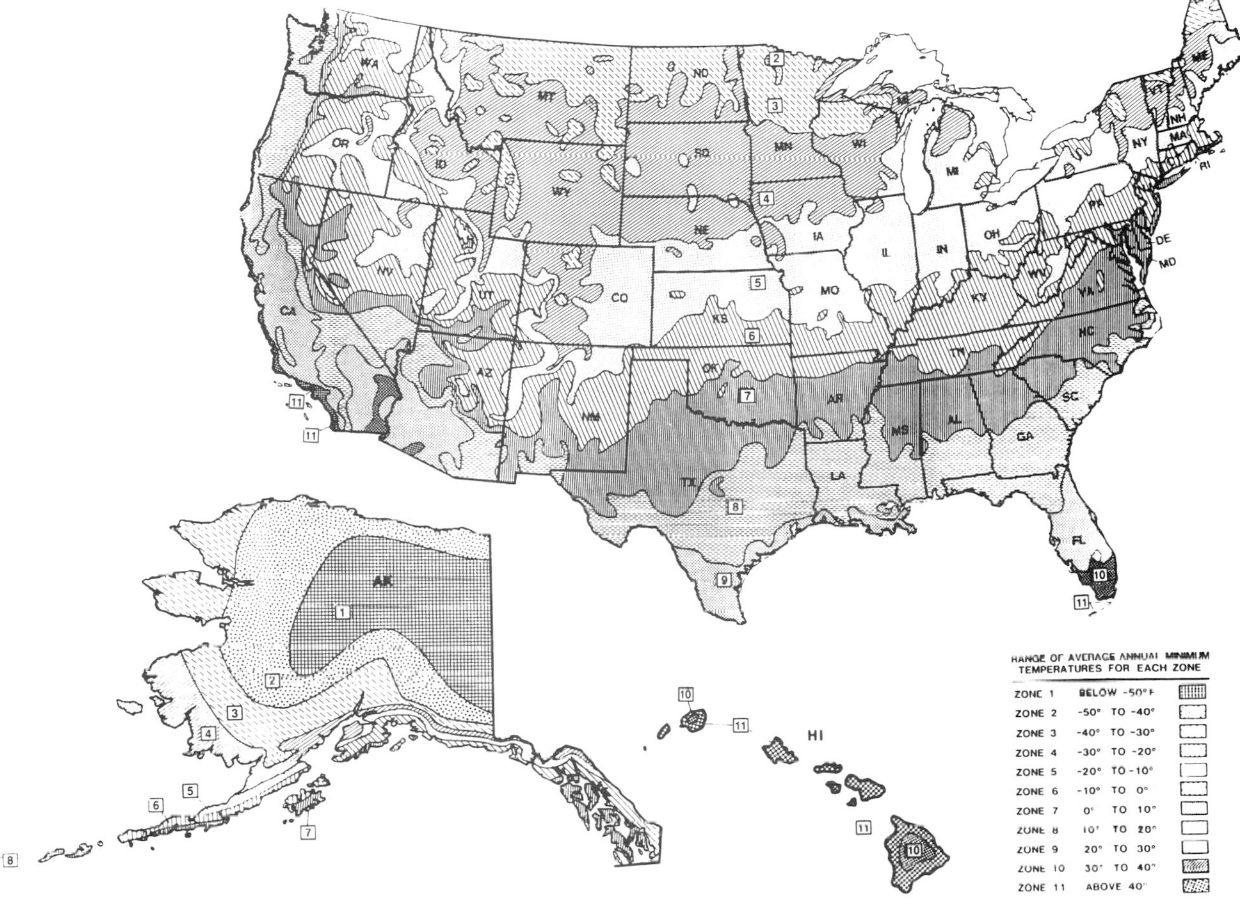

The USDA Plant Hardiness Zone Map. Map courtesy of the Agricultural Research Service, U.S. Department of Agriculture.

located are the most appropriate choices. Other factors in the selection process include soil type, the amount of light and shade present in sections of the backyard habitat, and species of trees and shrubs already growing there.

Your county agricultural agent is also an excellent professional source of gardening, landscaping, and horticultural information. He or she knows local growing conditions and has plenty of literature (much of it free) about trees, shrubs, and plants suitable for local conditions. Be sure to mention that you want information about native plant species. Check your telephone book under County Extension Service or ask your public library for the agent's telephone number.

Selection

How to choose? So many species and varieties of trees, shrubs, and flowers are sold in the United States and Canada that the backyard birder may feel overwhelmed. Do not despair—help is available.

To determine which trees, shrubs, and flowers provide food for birds, go first to a classic of wildlife biology: *American Wildlife and Plants: A Guide to Wildlife Food Habits* by Alexander Martin, Herbert Zim, and Arnold Nelson. Organized by wildlife and plant species, it allows you to work either way in selecting appropriate trees, shrubs, and other vegetation. For example, to find out what Song Sparrows eat, look up that species. Or to learn which birds eat fruits of specific trees or shrubs, turn to their section. The U.S. regional information is especially useful in this book.

Field guides to trees, shrubs, wildflowers, ferns, and other plants, such as the Peterson and National Audubon Society field guides, are also essential references. The National Audubon Society's excellent regional guides to New England, Mid-Atlantic States, Southeastern States, Florida, Rocky Mountain States, Southwestern States, California, and the Pacific Northwest are very informative and illustrated with more than a thousand color photographs, maps, drawings, and other graphics.

Some state wildlife agencies publish books and other literature dealing with selections of trees, shrubs, wildflowers, grasses, and other plants. For example, the South Dakota Department of Game, Fish and Parks published *Sharing Your Space: A Homeowner's Guide to Attracting Backyard Wildlife*, which lists and discusses numerous plants and other components of backyard habitats. The Florida Game and Freshwater Fish Commission offers *Planting a Refuge for Wildlife*, and the Illinois Department of Natural Resources has available *Prairie Establishment and Landscaping* and *Landscaping for Wildlife*.

A Song Sparrow on its nest.

Other states that offer residents helpful publications about gardening and landscaping for habitat enhancement include Idaho, Iowa, Kansas, Kentucky, Maine, Maryland, Michigan, Minnesota, Nebraska, New Hampshire (schoolyard habitats), New Jersey, Oklahoma, Oregon, Pennsylvania, South Carolina, Texas, Vermont, and Washington (see appendix 2 for more information about these state programs).

Michael Dirr's important *Dirr's Hardy Trees and Shrubs: An Illustrated Encyclopedia* is another helpful reference when you're trying to identify native and introduced horticultural species. *Eyewitness Garden Handbooks: Garden Trees*, edited by Francis Ritter, is a photographic guide to more than 450 species and varieties of ornamental trees from many parts of the world. Likewise, *Eyewitness Handbooks: Trees* by Allen Coombes is a visual guide to five hundred tree species, many from around the world.

Using Native Plants

There is a growing movement in the United States away from exotic or introduced (and often invasive) trees, shrubs, and flowers. The celebrated Brooklyn Botanical Garden, a major botanical research center, recommends that all nonnative, invasive species be removed from backyard habitats to prevent or at least slow their spread across the landscape. In other words, avoid planting exotics, regardless of their beauty or hardiness.

Research which native trees, shrubs, and wildflowers you need to enhance your particular backyard habitat. Then purchase those species, and explain to the store manager or owner why you're avoiding nonnative species. When enough peo-

DO IT YOURSELF?

There are two basic ways to create an enhanced backyard habitat: do it yourself, or hire experienced landscapers or wildlife habitat consultants.

You don't have to be an expert to create an excellent habitat. Most people fall somewhere between experts and novices, learning as they create their projects. Doing your own gardening and landscaping usually takes longer, sometimes years longer, than hiring a professional. Most backyard habitats are in a continual process of modification, alteration, and improvement. The key to success is doing the necessary research and then planning carefully before breaking ground. Know what you want to do.

A good starting point is The National Wildlife Federation's Guide to Gardening for Wildlife, *written by Craig Tufts of the National Wildlife Federation's Backyard Wildlife Habitat Program and Peter Loewer.*

Other backyard birders hire professional landscapers to plan their habitats, select trees, shrubs, and flowers, and plant them. Because water is crucial to a successful habitat, some also hire landscape professionals to design and build pools, waterfalls, and similar structures. The results can be stunning, but the cost can be high. If you go this route, you won't be alone—so great is the demand for backyard habitat enhancement that a whole new profession has evolved to provide consulting, design, and installation services.

ple take similar action, owners or managers of garden stores and nurseries will see the light. Indeed, they'll even encourage customers to purchase native species, thereby adding more emphasis to the trend.

Seasonal Considerations

Backyard birders should also pay attention to the seasons in which trees and shrubs produce fruits eaten by birds. Trees, shrubs, and other plants that produce fruit during summer include blackberry, blueberry, cherry, elderberry, mulberry, and serviceberry. In contrast, those producing fruit during autumn include arrowwood, bayberry, dogwood, hackberry, various native honeysuckles, mountain ash, pokeweed, spicebush, and winterberry. Those retaining fruit through much of the winter include bittersweet, chokeberry, crabapple, hawthorn, holly, juniper, poison ivy, snowberry, sumacs, and Virginia creeper.

SOME UNEXPECTED BENEFITS

A restored backyard habitat that plays host to a rich variety of native birds and wildlife is its own reward. Still, there are often unexpected, additional benefits of keeping a wildlife-friendly backyard. Let's look at a few.

Nontoxic Insect Control

Residential gardeners and landscapers pour huge amounts of chemicals into the environment. It's estimated that some homeowners put as much as ten times more toxic chemicals per acre on lawns than farmers use on agricultural fields! That's unfortunate because pollution is a widespread problem of great public concern—especially to folks who know from backyard habitat experiences that birds, other wildlife, and some plants are sensitive to toxic chemicals. Concern has been growing since the early 1960s, when Rachel Carson's *Silent Spring* and Robert Rudd's *Pesticides and the Living Landscape* exposed the dangers of biocides to wildlife and people.

At the same time, people have begun to appreciate how certain birds reduce the numbers of insects. Purple Martins, for example, feed on large numbers of insects, and are lovely birds with which to share a backyard. However, contrary to some claims, mosquitos are not part of their diet.

A female Eastern Bluebird bringing food to its nestlings in an old fence post beside a rural road. When Eastern Bluebirds feed on insects, they provide nonpolluting, nontoxic insect control.

Similarly, encouraging Eastern, Mountain, and Western Bluebirds to use nest boxes in larger backyards (and along bluebird trails) is desirable

WEED LAWS AND THE LIKE

Throughout the United States, many municipalities have enacted so-called weed laws which can ban wildflowers growing too high, too close to roads, or even prohibit some species on properties. Most, if not all, are ecologically unsound, tending to promote expanses of green lawns—which are maintained only through the use of artificial fertilizers and toxic chemicals—rather than backyard habitats containing a diversity of native trees, shrubs, and wildflowers that benefit birds and other wildlife.

Sometimes, these situations produce neighbor conflicts, or even legal disputes with municipal zoning or public-health officials, who think only manicured green lawns are appropriate for yards. Fortunately, people are becoming aware of the problem and are trying to correct it. Attitudes are changing when it comes to weed laws, and lots of trees, shrubs, and wildflowers are now allowed. Brush piles can also be contentious: they're desirable in a backyard habitat because they provide additional protective cover for birds. However, some local health departments may object to them, claiming they harbor rats. So, keep areas around them tidy even when trees, shrubs, and wildflowers grow nearby.

If possible, introduce the changes to your backyard habitat gradually—in most cases, they occur gradually whether you like it or not. That way, you will most likely reduce resistance from neighbors and avoid conflicts with local ordinances, because people tend not to object to landscape changes that slowly change the appearance of an area.

An excellent source of information about local weed- or vegetation-control ordinances is provided on the Wild Ones–Natural Landscapers, Ltd., website (see appendix 3). If you are a backyard birdwatcher having difficulty with governmental officials about weed or other vegetation control, you should carefully read the excellent information provided at that site. It does not provide legal advice but has excellent background information.

and productive. Bluebirds are also lovely birds and a delight to see. The North American Bluebird Society provides information about bluebirds to the public and encourages widespread use of correctly sized and constructed bluebird nest boxes in appropriate locations.

Backyard birdwatchers should remember: every insect that's captured and eaten by a bird represents natural, nonpoisonous, ecologically sound insect control at work.

Energy Conservation

Landscaping for birds and other wildlife also can benefit the property owner directly by saving energy. When deciduous shade trees are located on the southern and western sides of a house, they cool the area during hot weather, thus conserving electrical energy that might be spent on air conditioning. In winter, these same trees without their leaves enable sunlight to reach a house and warm it. Shade trees, of course, add charm and provide nesting and resting places for some backyard birds.

Evergreen windbreaks greatly reduce wind velocity in winter. Properly placed, they simultaneously reduce heating costs and shelter backyard birds. Some birds also nest in windbreaks. A good windbreak design is to stagger pines and cedar trees in two rows, about 150 feet to the west and north of the place needing protection. If this is not possible, as in subdivisions, even one row of conifers acts as a windbreak. (Always keep in mind the height that a mature tree will reach. Be very careful, for example, not to plant species that exceed 15 feet under powerlines.)

RESOURCES FOR HABITAT ENHANCEMENT

Backyard birders quickly discover there's an immense amount of information available about backyard habitat enhancement. Most birding equipment and supply stores stock items needed to enhance backyards for birds. For instance, Wild Birds Unlimited stores sell National Wildlife Federation Backyard Wildlife Habitat Program kits that include everything necessary to plan, design, and register your habitat with the Federation. Several backyard habitat certification programs have been developed by nonprofit organizations. The largest and oldest is operated by the National Wildlife Federation, but others exist, such as the programs offered by Wild Ones–Natural Landscapers, Ltd., Alliance for the Chesapeake Bay, and Windstar Wildlife Institute. Some state wildlife and natural resource agencies also operate backyard habitat certification programs. Following are a few outstanding examples of habitat-enhancement programs; appendix 1 lists many more.

Nonprofit Backyard Habitat Certification Programs

National Wildlife Federation's Backyard Wildlife Habitat Program

In wildlife conservation, few programs are as successful as the Backyard Wildlife Habitat Program. Launched in 1973, both people and wildlife responded quickly, bringing increased species diversity to areas where little wildlife previously existed—and great pleasure to people whose commitment to birds, butterflies, and other wild creatures made this happen.

The program's original selling point was that property owners could create and have certified a wildlife-friendly backyard habitat for about $200. The public loved the idea and immediately began converting lawns into wildlife habitats for bird and other wildlife by planting trees, shrubs, and flowers. Birdbaths and pools provided essential water. Bird feeders and birdhouses were also installed. Then brush piles were added, allowing birds and other small animals to find shelter when hawks, domestic house cats, or other predators appeared.

Urban and suburban areas across the United States and Canada began to welcome back wildlife whose habitat had gradually disappeared. Having passed its twenty-fifth anniversary in 1998, the program continues to expand. The Federation is working to extend the program into more than a thousand schoolyards, public places, business and industrial properties, and even entire communities, such as Alpine, California; Greater Zionsville, Indiana; and Reston, Virginia. Conservationists in Puerto Rico, Switzerland, and Peru even participate in the program. As

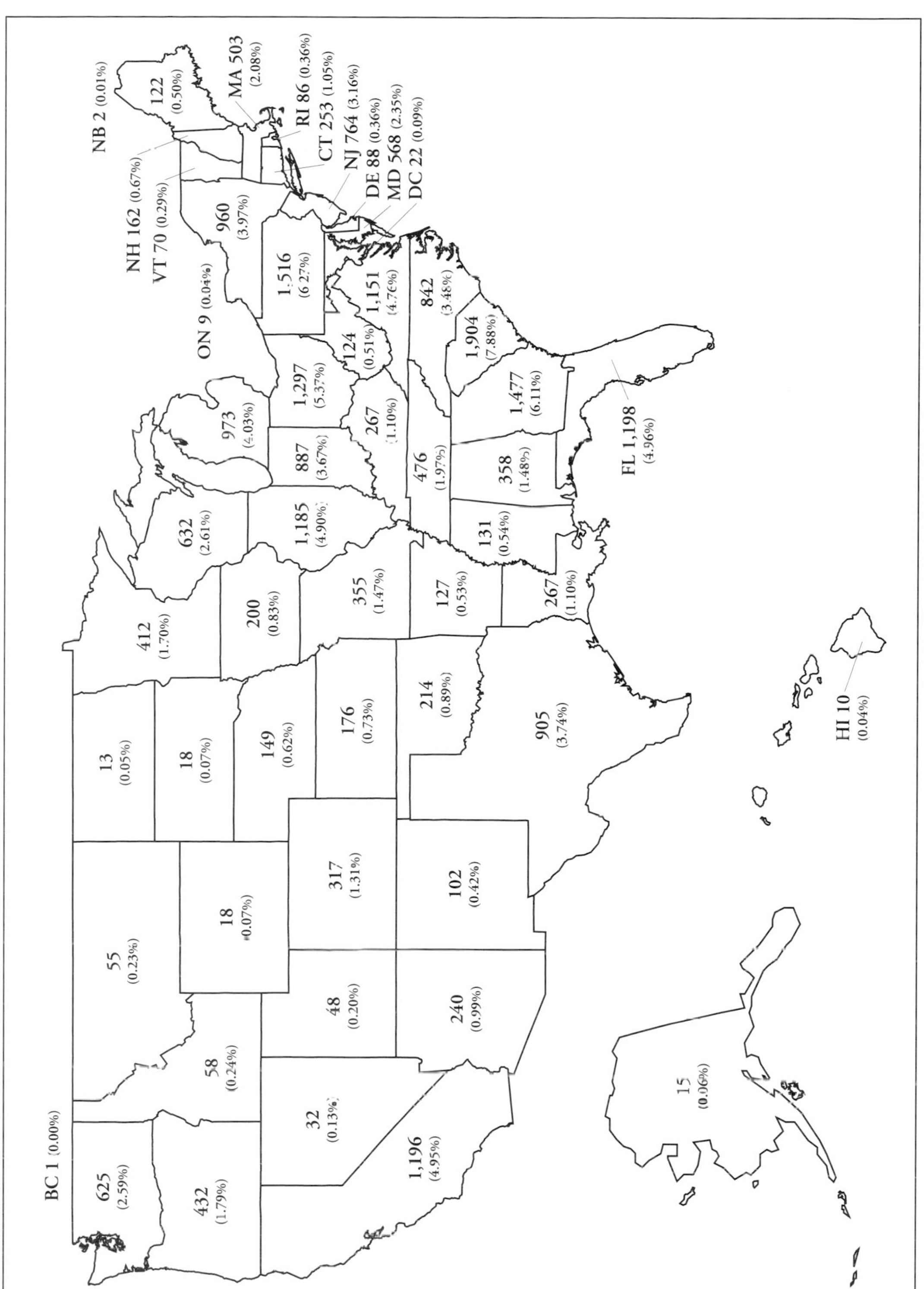

May 2000 distribution of backyard habitats in the United States, as certified by the National Wildlife Federation's Backyard Wildlife Habitat Program.

of May 2000, 26,000 backyard wildlife habitats have been certified, together comprising some 50,000 acres of improved wildlife habitat in urban and suburban areas. The map shows the number of backyard habitats certified in each state. It is a significant conservation achievement. Birdwatchers who want to participate in the Backyard Wildlife Habitat Program should contact the National Wildlife Federation (see appendix 1).

Canadian Wildlife Federation

The Canadian Wildlife Federation also advocates the enhancement of backyard habitats with native trees, shrubs, vines, wildflowers, and other plants for the benefit of birds and other wildlife. The Federation's book, *Backyard Habitat for Canada's Wildlife* by Luba Mycio-Mommers and Susan Fisher, contains comprehensive information about how Canadians can make their backyards more wildlife friendly—thus helping preserve Canada's biological diversity. Included are lists of native plants that provide food and shelter for birds and other wildlife in various Canadian ecozones.

The Canadian Wildlife Federation also operates Golden Gardens, a wildlife gardening program for seniors that encourages these folks to become actively involved in providing enhanced bird and wildlife habitats. Golden Gardens has a registration component for individuals and organizations in Canada. Organizations can apply for grants of up to $100 for the purchase of trees, shrubs, and other plants, as well as related items such as soil, lumber, and rental equipment. Larger grants of $500 are also available to Canadian organizations that match that sum.

Wild Ones–Natural Landscapers, Ltd.

Wild Ones–Natural Landscapers, Ltd., is a nonprofit organization whose goals are to preserve biodiversity in natural landscapes and to promote natural landscaping with native trees, shrubs, and wildflowers and environmentally sound methods.

Wild Ones has chapters in Illinois, Iowa, Kansas, Kentucky, Michigan, Minnesota, Missouri, New York, Ohio, Oklahoma, and Wisconsin. Each chapter has its own officers, agenda of local projects and programs, newsletters, and related materials.

Wild Ones publishes a bimonthly newsletter, the *Wild Ones Journal*, packed with useful articles, features, and advertisements from related companies. Computer users should visit their website (see appendix 1).

Government Backyard Habitat Certification Programs

Many state agencies also operate backyard habitat certification programs. A few examples are described in the following sections; check appendix 2 for your home state.

Maryland Wild Acres Program

The Maryland Department of Natural Resources operates the Wild Acres Program to encourage backyard birdwatchers and wildlife enthusiasts to tailor backyards,

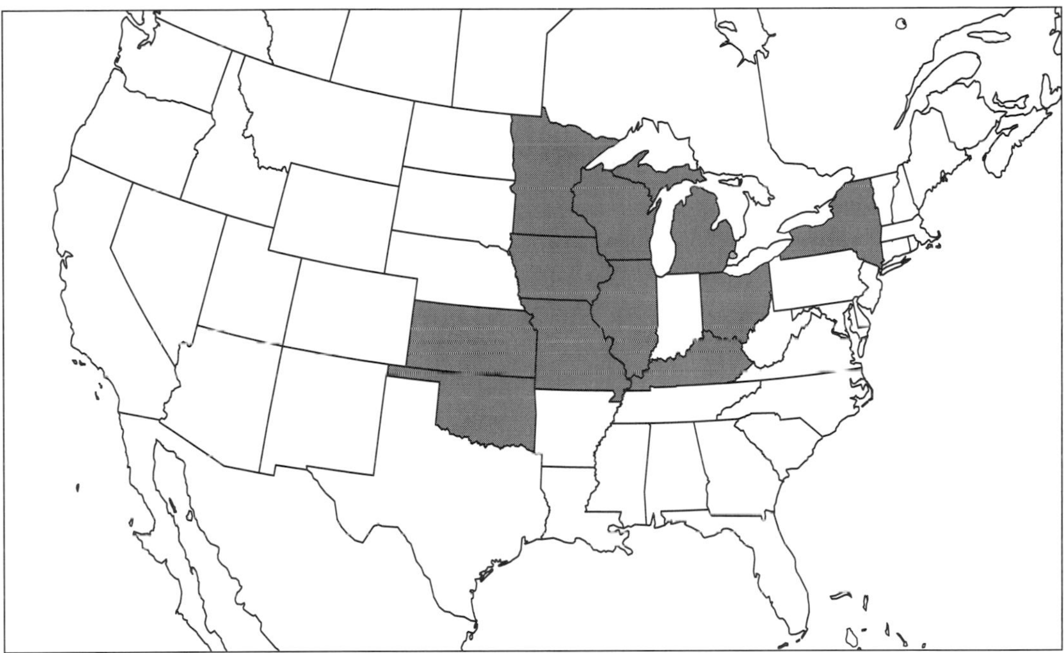

State distribution of chapters of Wild Ones—Natural Landscapers, Ltd.

farms, common open spaces, and other properties for wildlife habitat. By 1998, more than 3,700 properties were participating as certified habitats. Wild Acres information and certification are free.

Most Wild Acres participants find out about the program through birding and gardening stores. When contacted, the Department sends a packet of materials on wildlife gardening, including fifteen project sheets (e.g., how to attract Northern Cardinals or build nest boxes for wrens) and an application for certification. Applications are reviewed by biologists at the Maryland Department of Natural Resources. Certified properties receive a certificate and, for a ten dollar donation, a sturdy outdoor sign identifying the site as part of the Wild Acres Program. To receive information and an application to participate in Maryland's Wild Acres program, see the contact information in appendix 2.

The sign that's available for use in backyards enrolled in the Maryland Wild Acres program.

Oklahoma Wildscapes Certification Program

Oklahoma's program offers two levels of certification of a yard as a wildlife habitat. People who enhance less than 50 percent of their property are said to have a "Wildlife Garden"; those who improve more than 50 percent may certify their property as a "Wildlife Habitat." To get certified (for a modest fee) at either level, request an Oklahoma Wildscapes Certification Packet from the Oklahoma Department of Natural Resources (see appendix 2).

Included are many brochures and a twenty-page booklet, *Attracting Birds*, detailed recommendations and guidelines, plus an application for Wildscapes certification. When applications are received at the Oklahoma Department of Natural Resources, a wildlife biologist reviews them and makes recommendations for further habitat enhancement. Properties meeting acceptable standards are issued a certificate and added to the Oklahoma Wildscapes Registry. A sign indicating that the property is part of the Oklahoma Wildscapes Program is also included.

The sign that's available for use in backyards enrolled in the Oklahoma Wildscapes program.

Texas Wildscapes Program

The Texas Wildscapes Program seeks to develop wildlife habitats where residents of the state live or work. These are defined as small habitats providing food, water, and shelter for birds and other wildlife. In addition to backyards, the program also recognizes apartments, business offices, and community parks.

The program distributes handout brochures, lists of native plants recommended for various Texas regions, and a Backyard Wildlife information kit containing all the information needed to plan and implement backyard habitat improvements. A modest fee is charged for the information packet. The program also sells books, such as *Texas Wildscapes: Gardening for Wildlife*. The final result is receipt of a certificate indicating that the habitat is part of the Texas Wildscapes Program (see appendix 2).

ATTRACTING BIRDS WITH NATIVE PLANTS

In the remainder of this chapter, the distinct ecological regions within North America and good matches between native plant and bird species are discussed. Many other productive bird-plant combinations are given in the chart organized by region.

Northeast

Many trees, shrubs, vines, and wildflowers native to the northeastern United States—the six New England states plus New York, New Jersey, Pennsylvania, Maryland, Delaware, Virginia, and West Virginia—are suited for backyard habitat enhancement projects.

White pine *(Pinus strobus)* is one of the most beautiful of our indigenous pines. Plant it in open areas, with exposure to full sunlight and where moist, sandy loam soil is present. Birds nest in this tree, use it for protective cover, and eat its seeds, among them Mourning Doves, Black-capped Chickadees, White-breasted Nuthatches, Pine Warblers, and northern finches, including Pine Siskins, Red Crossbills, and Evening Grosbeaks.

Eastern hemlock *(Tsuga canadensis)*, a handsome evergreen tree, prefers acid soils, cool ravines and valleys, and north-facing slopes. It tolerates shaded areas in backyard habitats. Plant it as part of the yard's background. Black-capped Chickadees, Pine Siskins, Red Crossbills, and White-winged Crossbills eat its seeds in winter. These lovely trees also provide excellent protective cover and/or night roosting places for nearly two dozen bird species.

Eastern white pine is one of the finest of native trees, and highly desirable for use in backyard habitats throughout its native range in North America.

Eastern red cedar *(Juniperus virginiana)* is another widely distributed evergreen in the Northeast. However, because it is an alternate host for cedar-apple rust, it should not be planted close to apple orchards. Northern Flickers, Gray Catbirds, Brown Thrashers, Eastern Bluebirds, American Robins, Cedar Waxwings, White-winged Crossbills, and Purple Finches eat its fruit.

Let's now turn to deciduous trees. Red mulberry *(Morus rubra)*, a tree of moist habitats in eastern woodlands, provides excellent food for birds. Its fruit ripens in late spring and early summer, and is eaten by Blue Jays, Tufted Titmice, Red-headed Woodpeckers, Red-bellied Woodpeckers, Gray Catbirds, Brown Thrashers, American Robins, Cedar Waxwings, Northern Cardinals, Rose-breasted Grosbeaks, Baltimore Orioles, and Orchard Orioles. However, be careful not to plant introduced white mulberry *(Morus alba)* that interbreeds with red mulberry.

Eastern red cedar grows widely in many parts of the United States. It grows naturally in some backyard habitats.

Of the various maples, sugar maple *(Acer saccharum)* is one of the most popular. It wears brilliant red, orange, and yellow autumn colors, and produces rich sap, which can be converted to maple sugar and syrup. It prefers rich, moist soils

(continued on page 114)

NORTHEAST Birds	Red Pine (*Pinus resinosa*)	Pitch Pine (*Pinus rigida*)	Red Spruce (*Picea rubens*)	White Spruce (*Picea glauca*)	Northern Bayberry (*Myrica pensylvanica*)	Yellow Birch (*Betula lutea*)	Gray Birch (*Betula populifolia*)	Beech (*Fagus grandifolia*)	Chestnut Oak (*Quercus prinus*)	Scarlet Oak (*Quercus coccinea*)	Hackberry (*Celtis occidentalis*)	Yellow Poplar (Tulip Tree) (*Liriodendron tulipifera*)	Sweetgum (*Liquidambar styraciflua*)	Black Cherry (*Prunus serotina*)	Fire (Pin) Cherry (*Prunus pensylvanica*)	Allegheny Serviceberry (*Amelanchier laevis*)	Washington Hawthorn (*Crataegus phaenopyrum*)	Staghorn Sumac (*Rhus typhina*)	Winged or Shining Sumac (*Rhus copallina*)	Smooth Sumac (*Rhus glabra*)	Red Maple (*Acer rubrum*)	Silver Maple (*Acer saccharinum*)	Common Winterberry (*Ilex verticillata*)
Trees																							
Mourning Dove																							
Ruby-throated Hummingbird																							
Red-bellied Woodpecker	●	●			●				●	●				●	●								
Downy Woodpecker																●							
Hairy Woodpecker														●	●	●							
Northern Flicker											●			●	●	●		●	●	●			
Blue Jay								●	●	●					●	●							
Carolina Chickadee	●	●			●																●	●	
Black-capped Chickadee	●	●				●	●									●							
Tufted Titmouse								●	●	●						●							
Red-breasted Nuthatch	●	●	●	●																			
White-breasted Nuthatch	●	●							●	●													
Eastern Bluebird					●						●			●	●	●	●	●	●	●			●
American Robin														●	●	●	●	●	●	●			
Gray Catbird														●	●	●		●	●	●			●
Northern Mockingbird																●		●	●	●			●
Brown Thrasher									●	●				●	●	●		●	●	●			●
Cedar Waxwing														●	●	●							●
White-throated Sparrow													●		●	●							
Northern Cardinal																●		●	●	●			
Rose-breasted Grosbeak														●	●	●					●	●	
Orchard Oriole														●	●								
Baltimore Oriole															●	●							
Purple Finch												●	●	●	●						●	●	
House Finch	●	●																					
American Goldfinch	●	●										●	●								●	●	

					Vines & Shrubs												Wildflowers								Cultivated Crop Plants			
Alternate-leaf Dogwood (*Cornus alternifolia*)	Red-osier Dogwood (*Cornus stolonifera*)	Red-panicle Dogwood (*Cornus racemosa*)	Common Elderberry (*Sambucus canadensis*)	Arrowwood (*Viburnum sp.*)	Raspberry (*Rubus sp.*)	Blackberry (*Rubus sp.*)	Virginia Creeper (*Parthenocissus quinquefolia*)	Common Greenbrier (*Smilax rotundifolia*)	Grape (*Vitis sp.*)	Downy Juneberry (*Amelanchier arborea*)	Running Juneberry (*Amelanchier stolonifera*)	Common Spicebush (*Lindera benzoin*)	Common Highbush Blueberry (*Vaccinium corymbosum*)	Late Lowbush Blueberry (*Vaccinium angustifolium*)	Huckleberry (*Gaylussacia sp.*)	Pokeweed (*Phytolacca americana*)	Canada Lily (*Lilium canadense*)	Wood Lily (*Lilium philadelphicum*)	Spotted Touch-Me-Not (*Impatiens capensis*)	Purple Bergamot (*Monarda media*)	Wild Bergamot (*Monarda fistulosa*)	Wild Sweet William (*Phlox maculata*)	Indian Paintbrush (*Castilleja coccinea*)	Small Red Morning Glory (*Ipomoea coccinea*)	Corn (*Zea mays*)	Oats (*Avena sp.*)	Sunflower (*Helianthus sp.*)	Wheat (*Triticum sp.*)
																✓									✓			✓
																	✓	✓	✓	✓	✓	✓	✓	✓				
			✓	✓			✓		✓																			
✓	✓	✓					✓																		✓			
✓	✓	✓					✓			✓	✓					✓									✓			
✓	✓	✓			✓	✓	✓	✓	✓				✓	✓														
					✓	✓			✓				✓	✓											✓			
							✓	✓					✓	✓														
			✓		✓	✓							✓	✓											✓			
			✓				✓																		✓			
			✓			✓	✓		✓							✓												
✓	✓	✓	✓	✓	✓	✓	✓	✓	✓		✓	✓	✓	✓		✓												
✓	✓	✓	✓	✓	✓	✓	✓	✓	✓			✓	✓	✓	✓	✓												
✓							✓	✓	✓							✓												
✓	✓	✓	✓	✓	✓	✓		✓	✓	✓	✓		✓	✓											✓			
✓	✓	✓	✓	✓	✓	✓		✓	✓	✓	✓					✓												
			✓		✓	✓		✓	✓				✓	✓											✓	✓		
✓	✓	✓	✓	✓	✓	✓		✓	✓							✓									✓		✓	
			✓		✓	✓				✓	✓					✓									✓			
									✓				✓	✓	✓													
					✓	✓			✓				✓	✓														
✓	✓	✓							✓	✓	✓																✓	
			✓																						✓		✓	
																											✓	

A PENNSYLVANIA BACKYARD

Robert and Doris Jones have created an exceptional backyard habitat near Allentown, Pennsylvania. The land on which Bob and Doris built their house was farmland converted to upscale housing. That usually means farmland and wildlife habitat are lost and the degradation of the area's natural biodiversity continues. But Bob and Doris did things differently: they preserved as much natural habitat as possible before their house was built, and then invested substantial time, effort, and money in enhancing more of their property as a wildlife habitat. The result is both aesthetically and ecologically powerful.

The Jones's home is located on an acre of land adjoining a tiny wetland and a neighbor's farm, with some three quarters of the property landscaped for the benefit of birds and other wildlife. In 1995, when Bob and Doris purchased the property, Doris traced and retraced the land before building, carefully planning where she would place woodland paths, bedding areas, ponds, and other wildlife-friendly features. She was also determined to preserve the 140 existing deciduous trees and shrubs. From the beginning, Bob and Doris opted to plant some native species of trees, shrubs, flowers, and other plants to enhance diversity. Since then, they have added to that diversity with sixty deciduous trees and shrubs and thirty-five evergreens; in total, fifty species and varieties are represented.

To enhance the natural beauty and preserve a tiny wetland containing a few lovely cattails, Doris and a professional landscaper added cardinal flowers, marsh marigolds, blue irises, arrowhead, and some other species along its edge. Immediately behind the wetland is a dense thicket of inkberry, Virginia creeper, and huckleberry, the fruits of which birds

A. Part of the lovely wildlife habitat created on the property of Bob and Doris Jones of Allentown, Pennsylvania.

B. Part of the wooded area on the north side of the Jones habitat. Numerous wildflowers grow there.

consume. Eastern Bluebirds sometimes visit the small wetland and thicket, and have a nest box on a nearby lawn.

At the front of the house, Doris planted a large bed of black-eyed Susans that add a riot of vivid yellow to the breezy summer scene. A portion of the bed also contains rhododendron and holly. Additional flowerbeds were placed nearby. In an upland outdoor patio, space was allocated for iris, obedient plant, and others. Several bird feeders, including one for hummingbirds, are located near the edge of the patio and flowerbeds.

Nearby, in a shaded wooded area, May-apple, false Solomon's seal, Jack-in-the-pulpit, asters, and spiderworts were already growing. To these, Doris added more native winterberry, mountain laurel, blueberry, bunchberry, inkberry, witch hazel, and ferns.

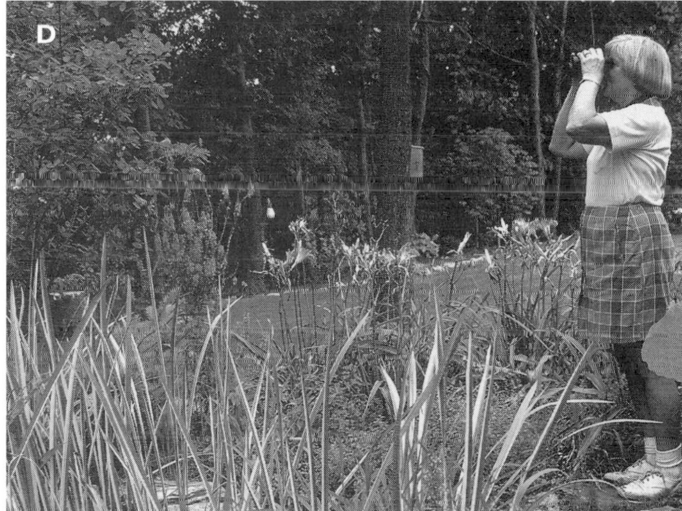

C. The 6,000-gallon pond and waterfall in the Jones backyard.

D. Doris has identified 45 species of birds in this backyard habitat, and the list is growing.

In addition to the tiny natural wetland at the front of the property, a 6,000-gallon pond and waterfall were installed by a professional landscaper. The dramatic visual impact of the pond and waterfall is heightened by substantial vegetation bordering the edges of the pond. Mallards sometimes nest there. Two birdbaths provide more water, and underground plumbing feeds the wetland.

Additional bird-friendly features include a brush pile, log pile, two small rock walls, a meadow area, and ground cover. Bob and Doris maintain twenty-two nest boxes and thirteen feeders.

Doris has forty-five bird species on her backyard list, including Mourning Doves, Downy Woodpeckers, House Wrens, Northern Flickers, Blue Jays, American Robins, Northern Cardinals, House Finches, and American Goldfinches. Some of the more uncommon species include Wild Turkeys, Northern Bobwhites, Red-bellied Woodpeckers, Blue-gray Gnatcatchers, White-crowned Sparrows, White-winged Crossbills, and Evening Grosbeaks.

(continued from page 109)
in uplands and valleys, where it thrives in open areas that receive sunlight. Be careful to plant it far from the reach of road salt.

Sugar maples provide nesting places for American Robins, Red-eyed Vireos, Baltimore Orioles, and Rose-breasted Grosbeaks. When cavities are present, Eastern Screech-Owls, woodpeckers, and other cavity-loving species use them. Evening Grosbeaks eat sugar-maple buds and seeds, and Rose-breasted Grosbeaks, Pine Grosbeaks, and Northern Cardinals eat the seeds. The sweet sap is also eaten by Yellow-bellied Sapsuckers. These birds lap up sap from natural cuts in the trees or drill holes and wait for the sap to flow.

Oaks are divided into the white oak group, which includes chestnut oaks, and the red oak group, which includes willow oaks. White oak *(Quercus alba)* attains heights of 80 to 100 feet, likes moist uplands and well-drained lowlands, and can be used in large backyard habitats.

Although wildlife prefer the white oak group because there is less tannin in the acorns, birdwatchers should not ignore using northern red oak *(Quercus rubra)* as a shade tree.

Acorns (the fruit of oaks) are near the top of the list of preferred wildlife food. Oaks also provide food for Wild Turkeys, Blue Jays, White-breasted Nuthatches, Tufted Titmice, Brown Thrashers, Red-headed Woodpeckers, and Red-bellied Woodpeckers.

Other small trees or shrubs are suitable for use in backyard habitats. Flowering dogwood *(Cornus florida)*, for example, is a common understory tree. In spring, it has lovely white "flowers"; in autumn, its red fruit is eaten by more than a hundred bird species, including Northern Flickers, Downy Woodpeckers, Hairy Woodpeckers, Red-bellied Woodpeckers, Gray Catbirds, Brown Thrashers, Eastern Bluebirds, American Robins, Cedar Waxwings, Northern Cardinals, Purple Finches, Pine Grosbeaks, and Evening Grosbeaks.

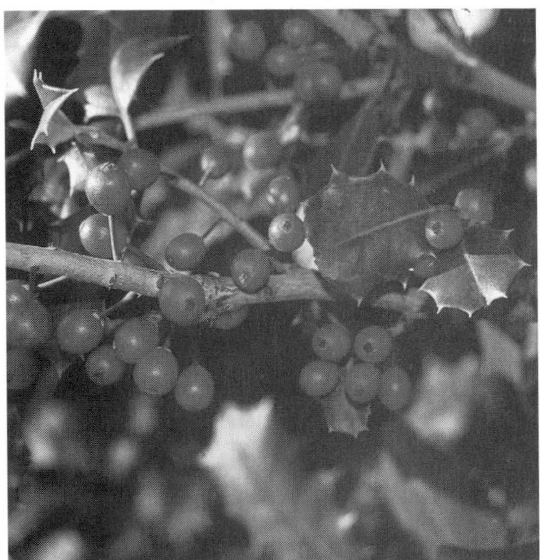
The fruit of American holly is an important food for Eastern Bluebirds and many other species. It's a useful shrub to plant in a backyard habitat within its North American range.

American holly *(Ilex opaca)* can be planted from eastern Massachusetts southward. You'll need to plant male and female hollies close to each other for the red fruits to form. Northern Flickers, Northern Mockingbirds, Gray Catbirds, Eastern Bluebirds, Cedar Waxwings, and White-throated Sparrows eat American holly fruit.

Several juneberry (also called serviceberry or shadbush) species provide nesting sites for birds, who also eat the fruit. Oblong-leaf juneberry *(Amelanchier canadensis)*, for example, produces fruit during June and July that's eaten by Blue Jays, Black-capped Chickadees, Tufted Titmice, Northern Flickers, Downy

A NEW YORK CITY BACKYARD

Between its wilderness areas and suburbs, New York State offers many fine backyard habitats. If you were looking for a model backyard habitat in the Empire State, however, the heart of New York City probably wouldn't be your first stop.

Yet here an exciting habitat flourishes beside a six-story apartment building in Manhattan, three blocks from Times Square. Outside, the din of traffic is unbroken. How could such a place possibly be of value to birds? Nobody would suspect that 1,180 square feet of strikingly beautiful garden and habitat—complete with bird feeders; a variety of trees, shrubs, and flowers; and even a pond—exist behind the building.

Enter Barbara and Fred Feldt. The Feldts and many others who supported the project are people of bold vision, eager to carve out of the middle of Manhattan an unlikely habitat, which now is certified as Number 20,895 by the National Wildlife Federation's Backyard Wildlife Habitat Program.

They began in 1995 with careful plans, $10,000 worth of volunteer labor, and $2,000 of plants and other necessary materials. The garden links semisecluded areas organized around a central focal point, the "dining room by the pond." Once the structure was completed and the soil was in place, the Feldts introduced the initial touches of green by adding ferns, flowers, and vines.

Shrubs and trees also were introduced into the yard, including aspen; dwarf Alberta spruce; Japanese maple; dogwood; lilacs; and variegated, Boston, and English ivy. The many flowers forming part of the yard's plant diversity include lilies, foxgloves, lupines, columbines, roses, violets, mints, and irises. A considerable number of other flowers, including annual vines and native perennials, fill out the plant list.

In terms of wildlife, a few Koi (Japanese carp), Comets (fish), goldfish, and frogs are part of the pond's ecosystem. Birdhouses and feeders are placed in appropriate locations. Seed feeders and suet are stocked from Thanksgiving through Easter, with some seed and suet offered less regularly through the warmer months.

Birds observed using the feeders or appearing in the yard include Rock Doves (pigeons), Black-capped Chickadees, Tufted Titmice, Gray Catbirds, Northern Mockingbirds, White-throated Sparrows, Northern Cardinals, Dark-eyed Juncos, Common Grackles, Baltimore Orioles, and House Finches. In the years to come, it will be fascinating to see which other birds discover this tiny oasis and accept its shelter and food.

All photos by Barbara Feldt

A. Part of the amazing, and very lovely, backyard wildlife habitat of Fred and Barbara Feldt. It's only three blocks from Times Square in Manhattan, and certified by the National Wildlife Federation.

B. Fred Feldt, with BeeBee, a border collie–golden retriever, enjoying the pond in the Feldt's Manhattan backyard habitat.

C. Another section of the Feldts' backyard habitat.

ONTARIO

Birdwatchers in Ontario can visit an outstanding demonstration of backyard habitat enhancement in the center of Ottawa. Fletcher Wildlife Garden seeks to restore and enhance—on a long-term basis—a 16-acre parcel of land containing an old and a new woodlot, a hedgerow, a butterfly meadow, an old field, and an amphibian pond. It adjoins an arboretum and experimental farm.

The Garden was established by the Ottawa Field-Naturalists' Club in cooperation with several other organizations, and is managed by Club volunteers. It is open to the public and easily accessible to Ottawa's urban and suburban residents.

Thus far, the project's results are spectacular. Birds and other wildlife have responded well to this wonderful urban habitat. At last count, 116 bird species have been seen in the garden or flying overhead. Some nest in the garden's varied habitats, whereas others visit for varying periods. Every typical backyard-habitat bird is on the list, including Ruby-throated Hummingbirds, Northern Flickers, Gray Catbirds, and White-throated Sparrows.

The Field-Naturalists' Club has many recommendations for habitat enhancement in southern Ontario. Eastern white pine (Pinus strobus), *red pine* (Pinus resinosa), *white spruce* (Picea glauca), *and northern white cedar* (Thuja occidentalis) *produce fruit eaten by finches and grosbeaks. Among the deciduous trees, excellent additions to a backyard are black walnut* (Juglans nigra), *paper birch* (Betula papyrifera), *northern red oak* (Quercus rubra), *and green ash* (Fraxinus pennsylvanica). *Don't overlook natural colonizer trees such as quaking aspen* (Populus tremuloides), *balsam poplar* (Populus balsamifera), *and yellow birch* (Betula alleghaniensis).

A range of native shrubs is suited for Ontario's climate and produces fruits eaten by many birds. Prime examples that prefer full to partial sunlight are serviceberry (Amelanchier ssp.), *common elderberry* (Sambucus canadensis), *flowering raspberry* (Rubus odoratus), *and pin cherry* (Prunus pensylvanicus). *Good native shrubs that tolerate shade or partial shade include red-berried elder* (Sambucus racemosa), *choke cherry* (Prunus virginiana), *American mountain ash* (Sorbus americana), *and red-osier dogwood* (Cornus stolonifera). *Likewise, vines such as thicket creeper* (Parthenocissus inserta) *can have a place in an enhanced backyard habitat.*

Native wildflowers such as Canada goldenrod (Solidago canadensis), *spotted Joe-pye weed* (Eupatorium maculatum), *and New England aster* (Aster novae-angliae) *produce fruits or seeds eaten by finches, sparrows, and many other birds. Ruby-throated Hummingbirds also relish visiting nectar flowers such as columbine* (Aquilegia canadensis) *and wild bergamot* (Monarda fistulosa).

See appendix 1 for more information about the Fletcher Wildlife Garden and the Ottawa Field-Naturalists' Club.

Woodpeckers, Hairy Woodpeckers, American Robins, Gray Catbirds, Northern Mockingbirds, Brown Thrashers, Cedar Waxwings, Northern Cardinals, Baltimore Orioles, and Rose-breasted Grosbeaks.

Mountain ash *(Sorbus americana)* produces bright reddish-orange fruit—abundantly in alternate years—eaten by Eastern Bluebirds, American Robins, Gray Catbirds, Cedar Waxwings, and other species. In Pennsylvania, I've observed flocks of migrating American Robins stripping bare mountain ash shrubs of their fruit.

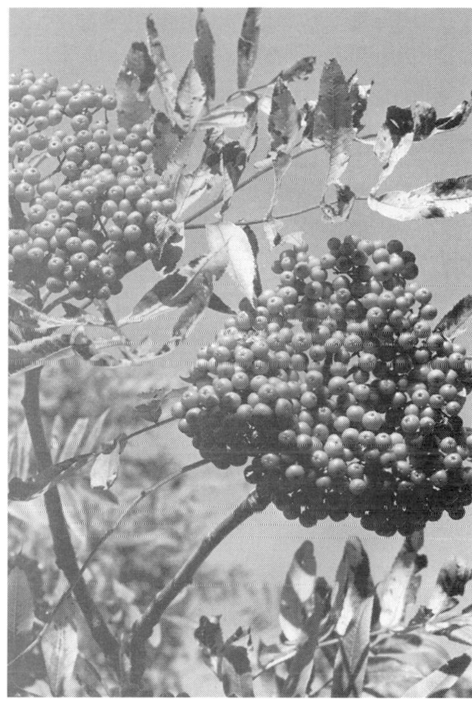

Mountain ash fruit is eaten by many birds, including migrating American Robins.

Vines are also useful in backyard habitats. Since 1736, for example, American bittersweet *(Celastrus scandens)* has been cultivated beside fences, stone walls, and other supports. Male and female plants must be close to each other to promote pollination, which results in orange-colored pods that ripen and break open during autumn to reveal red seed coverings. Birds that eat American bittersweet seeds include Wild Turkeys, Northern Mockingbirds, Eastern Bluebirds, American Robins, and Northern Cardinals.

However, avoid using invasive oriental bittersweet *(Celastrus orbiculatus)*, which grows in more than twenty states and spreads along roadsides, thickets, and woodlands.

The flowers of trumpet creeper *(Campsis radicans)* and trumpet honeysuckle *(Lonicera sempervirens)* are attractive to Ruby-throated Hummingbirds. It's great fun watching these amazing birds feeding on nectar and tiny insects from these plants.

Wildflowers can be included in your backyard habitat, including species attractive to hummingbirds and butterflies. For backyards near wetland areas, cardinal flowers *(Lobelia cardinalis)* attract Ruby-throated Hummingbirds, which visit its red flowers for nectar and tiny insects. Bee balm, or Oswego tea *(Monarda didyma)*, also has spectacular red flowers irresistible to hummingbirds. In other areas, try using fire pink *(Silene virginica)* and eastern columbine *(Aquilegia canadensis)*.

Oriental bittersweet is a nonnative species that should not be used in backyard habitats. Instead, use American bittersweet.

Mary L. Plimpton

Part of the wooded backyard habitat at the home of Beth Smith in Springfield, Virginia.

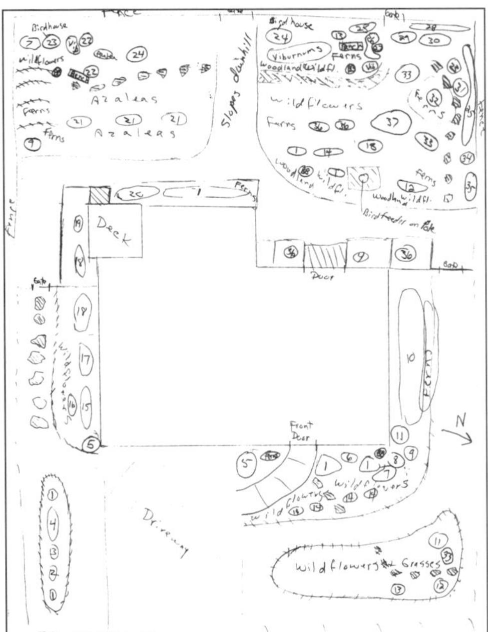

Backyard habitat landscape plan for the property of Beth Smith. You don't have to be an artist to convey all the necessary information: here, numbers refer to a plant list and show relative location and size of plants. Sketch provided by Beth Smith.

A VIRGINIA BACKYARD

Beth Smith is a professional naturalist and landscape consultant in Springfield, Virginia. She enjoys a heavily wooded backyard habitat along the narrow green floodplain of a stream that has resisted development. From a conservation standpoint, the floodplain corridor is particularly valuable as a green link between Huntsman Lake and surrounding natural areas.

Coursing through the green corridor is Cherry Run, a small creek, where beavers build their dams and are seen swimming upstream from the lake in the evening. The corridor is also home to deer, raccoon, red fox, and Red-shouldered Hawks (nesting along the creek). Great Blue Herons and kingfishers fly up and down the creek, and ducks and geese arrive in the fall to rest and feed in the floodplain. This is a very different picture from what the quarter-acre property looked like in 1978, when it was largely an expanse of lawn. Beth quickly recognized the potential of the creek and floodplain and took advantage of it. In her own words, "I am a naturalist by profession and I have always loved plants and animals. Creating a yard with a diversity of life is so much more rewarding than having a typical suburban lot."

Beth has been careful to use native plants. Indigenous trees such as Eastern red cedar, flowering dogwood, red maple, American beech, red oak, tulip poplar, American butternut, and pawpaw provide nesting, resting, and feeding opportunities for birds. Native shrubs were also added, including common winterberry, elderberry, buttonbush, American strawberry bush, coast pepperbush, southern arrowwood, and maple-leaf viburnum.

Many lovely wildflowers grace the yard: Joe-pye weed, New York ironweed, purple coneflower, cardinal flower, aster, goldenrod, and blue lobelia. Native ferns include Christmas, cinnamon, royal, sensitive, and maidenhair.

More than fifty bird species are on Beth's yard list, including Sharp-shinned and Red-shouldered Hawks, Mourning Doves, Ruby-throated Hummingbirds, a number of woodpeckers, Eastern Bluebirds, Wood Thrushes, Gray Catbirds, Northern Mockingbirds, Brown Thrashers, Cedar Waxwings, Chestnut-sided Warblers, American Redstarts, Common Yellowthroats, Eastern Towhees, Northern Cardinals, Fox Sparrows, Dark-eyed Juncos, and Evening Grosbeaks.

Southeast

Let's now look at some native trees, shrubs, vines, and wildflowers appropriate for backyard habitats in the Southeast—Alabama, Arkansas, Georgia, Kentucky, Louisiana, Mississippi, North Carolina, South Carolina, and Tennessee.

I'll start with a small tree or shrub, the Franklin tree *(Franklinia altamaha)*. It's the icing on the tree and shrub selection cake, producing lovely flowers consisting of five large white petals and numerous vivid yellow stamens. *Franklinia* blooms from late July into September. Unfortunately, it needs moist, acid, well-drained soils rich in organic matter; poorly drained soils are deadly to this rare species.

If you want a lovely and historically fascinating small tree or shrub in your backyard habitat—provided it has the correct soil conditions—include *Franklinia* in a border or as an accent species; then challenge your birding friends to recognize it, and relate its history. Or create a unique life list consisting of all birds observed perching or nesting in the *Franklinia*! Much remains to be learned about avian utilization of *Franklinia*.

Longleaf pine *(Pinus palustris)* is suitable for the Piedmont coastal plain and foothills from southeastern Virginia to Florida. Northern Bobwhites, Mourning Doves, Red-bellied Woodpeckers, Carolina Chickadees, Tufted Titmice, Brown-headed Nuthatches, Brown Thrashers, American Goldfinches, Eastern Towhees, and Bachman's Sparrows eat its seeds.

Eastern red cedar *(Juniperus virginiana)* and southern red cedar *(Juniperus silicicola)* can be used in backyards in coastal areas from North Carolina to Florida. However, because they host apple rust, do not plant them near apple,

(continued on page 122)

THE DISCOVERY AND RESCUE OF THE FRANKLIN TREE

The Franklin tree—or Franklinia, *as it's usually called—has a remarkable history. Discovered in 1765 by Philadelphia botanists John Bartram and his son William,* Franklinia *was found growing only within several acres on the banks of Georgia's Altamaha River.*

Determined to save the lovely species, William Bartram returned in 1773 and 1778 to the original Georgia site, gathered seeds, and propagated them in his father's now famous Historic Bartram's Gardens in Philadelphia.

The Bartrams were delighted with their botanical discovery, a species new to science, and named its genus Franklinia *in honor of their distinguished friend and fellow Philadelphia resident, Benjamin Franklin. And* altamaha*? It refers to the Georgia river beside which the tree was discovered.*

But there's more to the story. By 1803, not another Franklinia *was found in the wild—perhaps due to excessive collecting of specimens for London nurseries and natural flooding of the site. It's from the few, rare, historic plants in Bartram's Gardens that every* Franklinia *alive today in North America traces its lineage—a continuing botanical- and genetic-preservation triumph.* Franklinia *fans rejoice!*

SOUTHEAST — Birds / Trees	Short-leaf Pine (*Pinus echinata*)	Loblolly Pine (*Pinus taeda*)	Black Walnut (*Juglans nigra*)	Shagbark Hickory (*Carya ovata*)	Mockernut Hickory (*Carya tomentosa*)	Pignut Hickory (*Carya glabra*)	Butternut Hickory (*Juglans cinerea*)	Pecan (*Carya illinoensis*)	American Beech (*Fagus grandifolia*)	White Oak (*Quercus alba*)	Southern Red Oak (*Quercus falcata*)	Blackjack Oak (*Quercus marilandica*)	Live Oak (*Quercus virginiana*)	Sugarberry (*Celtis laevigata*)	Red Mulberry (*Morus rubra*)	Sassafras (*Sassafras albidum*)	Sweetgum (*Liquidambar styraciflua*)	Black Cherry (*Prunus serotina*)	Yaupon Holly (*Ilex vomitoria*)	Dahoon Holly (*Ilex cassine*)	Red Maple (*Acer rubrum*)	Flowering Dogwood (*Cornus florida*)
Northern Bobwhite	●	●						●		●	●	●	●									●
Mourning Dove	●	●																				
Ruby-throated Hummingbird																						
Red-bellied Woodpecker	●	●	●	●	●	●	●	●	●	●	●	●	●		●			●				●
Downy Woodpecker										●	●	●	●									●
Hairy Woodpecker																		●				●
Northern Flicker														●				●				●
Pileated Woodpecker																●			●	●		●
Blue Jay	●	●						●		●	●	●	●						●	●		
Carolina Chickadee	●	●																			●	
Tufted Titmouse	●	●							●	●	●	●	●	●	●							
Red-breasted Nuthatch	●	●																			●	
White-breasted Nuthatch	●	●		●	●	●	●	●	●	●	●	●	●									
Eastern Bluebird																			●	●		●
American Robin														●	●			●	●	●		●
Gray Catbird														●		●		●	●	●		●
Northern Mockingbird														●	●	●		●	●	●		●
Brown Thrasher	●	●								●	●	●	●	●				●	●	●		●
Cedar Waxwing																			●	●		
Northern Cardinal																		●				●
Blue Grosbeak																						
White-throated Sparrow																		●	●	●		●
Orchard Oriole															●							
Baltimore Oriole															●			●				
House Finch	●	●																				
American Goldfinch	●	●															●				●	

					Vines & Shrubs										Wildflowers										Cultivated Crop Plants			
Alternate-leaf Dogwood (*Cornus alternifolia*)	Black Tupelo or Blackgum (*Nyssa sylvatica*)	Common Persimmon (*Diospyros virginiana*)	American Elder (*Sambucus canadensis*)	Possumhaw Viburnum (*Viburnum nudum*)	Shining Sumac (*Rhus copallina*)	Blackberry (*Rubus sp.*)	Raspberry (*Rubus sp.*)	Huckleberry (*Gaylussacia sp.*)	Common Highbush Blueberry (*Vaccinium corymbosum*)	Late Lowbush Blueberry (*Vaccinium angustifolium*)	Partridgeberry (*Mitchella repens*)	Greenbrier (*Smilax sp.*)	Virginia Creeper (*Parthenocissus quinquefolia*)	Grape (*Vitis sp.*)	Red or Copper Iris (*Iris fulva*)	Eastern Columbine (*Aquilegia canadensis*)	Pokeweed (*Phytolacca americana*)	Panicgrass (*Panicum sp.*)	Bristlegrass (*Setaria sp.*)	Knotweed (*Polygonum sp.*)	Goosegrass (*Chenopodium sp.*)	Beggarweed (*Desmodium sp.*)	Sunflower (*Helianthus sp.*)	Smartweed (*Polygonum sp.*)	Wheat (*Triticum sp.*)	Oats (*Avena sp.*)	Corn (*Zea mays*)	Cowpea (*Vigna sinensis*)
							X															X					X	X
																	X		X						X	X	X	X
															X	X												
X	X		X											X													X	
X													X														X	
X	X												X				X										X	
X	X						X						X														X	
X	X			X								X	X	X														
							X		X	X				X														
																											X	
						X	X		X	X			X															
																									X		X	
			X										X										X		X	X	X	
	X		X		X				X				X				X											
	X	X			X	X	X		X	X		X	X	X													X	
X			X			X	X	X	X	X		X	X	X			X											
X	X		X		X	X	X					X	X	X			X											
			X		X	X			X	X		X	X	X													X	
		X												X														
X						X	X							X					X	X	X			X		X	X	
																		X	X						X			
X			X			X			X	X		X		X				X	X					X		X	X	
						X	X	X		X	X			X														
						X				X	X			X													X	
			X																								X	
			X																									

(continued from page 119)
crabapple, or hawthorn trees. Northern Flickers, Gray Catbirds, Northern Mockingbirds, American Robins, and Cedar Waxwings eat red cedar fruits and use the trees for protective cover and nesting sites.

Live oak *(Quercus virginiana)* often has majestic branches with abundant growths of hanging Spanish moss. It prefers coastal dunes and ridges in proximity to marshes and other sites with sandy soils. Birds that eat live-oak acorns include Northern Bobwhites, Wild Turkeys, Blue Jays, Red-headed Woodpeckers, Red-cockaded Woodpeckers, and Brown Thrashers.

Beautyberry *(Callicarpa americana)* produces colorful violet fruits consumed by Northern Bobwhites, American Robins, Gray Catbirds, Northern Mockingbirds, Brown Thrashers, Eastern Towhees, and Northern Cardinals.

American holly *(Ilex opaca)* produces bright red fruits consumed by Northern Bobwhites, Wild Turkeys, Mourning Doves, Northern Flickers, Eastern Bluebirds, American Robins, Gray Catbirds, Northern Mockingbirds, and Brown Thrashers.

Southern bayberry, or wax myrtle *(Myrica cerifera)*, provides shelter and nesting sites, as well as fruits eaten by Northern Bobwhites, Wild Turkeys, Red-bellied Woodpeckers, Northern Flickers, Eastern Phoebes, Tree Swallows, Carolina Chickadees, Tufted Titmice, Eastern Bluebirds, Gray Catbirds, Northern Mockingbirds, Brown Thrashers, and Carolina Wrens.

The striking flowers of trumpet vine *(Campsis radicans)* and trumpet honeysuckle *(Lonicera sempervirens)* are attractive to Ruby-throated Hummingbirds. The latter's red fruit is also eaten by Wild Turkeys, Northern Bobwhites, American Robins, Purple Finches, and American Goldfinches.

Wildflowers useful for attracting Ruby-throated Hummingbirds include cardinal flower *(Lobelia cardinalis)* and bee balm *(Monarda didyma)*. Other wildflowers such as beach sunflower *(Helianthus debilis)* and narrow-leaved sunflower *(Helianthus angustifolius)* provide seeds eaten by American Goldfinches.

Florida

Southern Florida's climate is subtropical, whereas northern Florida only borders the subtropical. That's why subtropical floral species are included among those recommended for use by birds in enhancing backyard habitats.

The seeds of several tall pines in northern and central Florida, including longleaf pine *(Pinus palustris)* and sand pine *(Pinus clausa)*, provide food for Northern Bobwhites, Mourning Doves, Red-bellied Woodpeckers, Carolina Chickadees, Florida Scrub Jays, Tufted Titmice, Brown-headed Nuthatches, and Brown Thrashers.

There are several oaks suitable for use in backyard habitats in northern and central Florida. Examples include live oak *(Quercus virginiana)* and myrtle oak *(Quercus myrtifolia)*, which yield acorns eaten by Wild Turkeys, Northern Bobwhites, Red-headed Woodpeckers, Blue Jays, Florida Scrub Jays, and Brown Thrashers.

The fruits of pigeon plum *(Coccoloba diversifolia)*—found in hardwood hammocks and willow sloughs, and used as a street tree—are eaten by White-crowned

Pigeons, Pileated Woodpeckers, and Northern Mockingbirds.

American holly *(Ilex opaca)*, useful in backyard habitats in northern and central Florida, yields fruits eaten by Wild Turkeys, Northern Bobwhites, Mourning Doves, Northern Cardinals, Brown Thrashers, and American Robins.

A Great Crested Flycatcher.

Some trees are best suited to southern and semitropical Florida. Coffee colubrina *(Colubrina arborescens)*, adapted to the extreme southern semitropical part of the state, produces green flowers in autumn that are attractive to Eastern Kingbirds, gnatcatchers, vireos, and wood warblers. Ruby-throated Hummingbirds are attracted to orange flowers of the Geiger tree *(Cordia sebestena)*. On barrier islands and coastal areas from central Florida southward, gumbo-limbo *(Bursera simaruba)* trees produce red fruit consumed by Northern Mockingbirds, flycatchers, vireos, and wood warblers. Lancewood *(Nectandra coriacea)* also produces a deep purple fruit eaten by Wood Thrushes and Veeries.

Additional southern and subtropical trees used in backyard habitats include short-leaf fig *(Ficus citrifolia)*, whose fruits are eaten by Cedar Waxwings and other fruit-eating and insectivorous birds. Several stoppers *(Eugenia ssp.)* also provide food for Blue Jays, Northern Mockingbirds, and Brown Thrashers.

Wild tamarind *(Lysiloma latisiliquum)* produces black seeds within pods that are eaten by flycatchers, gnatcatchers, American Redstarts, and other wood warblers.

Various shrubs also can be used in Florida. In the northern and central parts of the state, for example, sassafras *(Sassafras albidum)* fruits are eaten by Pileated Woodpeckers, Northern Flickers, Eastern Kingbirds, Great Crested Flycatchers, Eastern Phoebes, Gray Catbirds, Northern Mockingbirds, and Brown Thrashers.

American beautyberry *(Callicarpa americana)*, useful throughout the state, produces fruit eaten by Northern Bobwhites, Gray Catbirds, Northern Mockingbirds, Brown Thrashers, American Robins, and Eastern Towhees. Wax myrtle, or southern bayberry *(Myrica cerifera)*, fruit is also eaten by Northern Bobwhites, Tree Swallows, Ruby-crowned Kinglets, White-eyed Vireos, and Yellow-rumped Warblers.

Among shrubs suited for southern and semitropical Florida, bird pepper *(Capsicum annum)* produces vivid red peppers from spring to autumn that Gray Catbirds

(continued on page 126)

FLORIDA

Birds	Slash Pine (*Pinus elliottii*)	Loblolly Pine (*Pinus taeda*)	Eastern Red Cedar (*Juniperus virginiana*)	Southern Red Cedar (*Juniperus silicicola*)	Cabbage Palmetto (*Sabal palmetto*)	Everglade Palm (*Acoelorrhaphe wrightii*)	Chapman Oak (*Quercus chapmanii*)	Turkey Oak (*Quercus laevis*)	Bluejack Oak (*Quercus incana*)	Myrtle Oak (*Quercus myrtifolia*)	Water Oak (*Quercus nigra*)	Laurel Oak (*Quercus laurifolia*)	Sugarberry (*Celtis laevigata*)	Red Mulberry (*Morus rubra*)	Southern Magnolia (*Magnolia grandiflora*)	Sweet Bay (*Magnolia virginiana*)	Sweetgum (*Liquidambar styraciflua*)	Black Cherry (*Prunus serotina*)	Eastern Coralbean (*Erythrina herbacea*)
Wild Turkey	●	●					●	●	●	●	●	●							
Northern Bobwhite	●	●					●	●	●	●	●	●					●		
Mourning Dove	●	●																	
Ruby-throated Hummingbird																			●
Red-bellied Woodpecker	●	●			●		●	●	●	●	●	●		●	●	●		●	
Downy Woodpecker							●	●	●	●	●	●							
Hairy Woodpecker																		●	
Pileated Woodpecker					●	●													
Northern Flicker			●	●			●	●	●	●	●	●	●					●	
Florida Scrub Jay	●	●					●	●	●	●	●	●							
Carolina Chickadee	●	●															●		
Tufted Titmouse	●	●					●	●	●	●	●	●	●	●			●		
Eastern Bluebird													●						
American Robin						●								●					
Gray Catbird													●					●	
Northern Mockingbird			●	●	●	●							●	●				●	
Brown Thrasher	●	●					●	●	●	●	●	●	●	●				●	
Cedar Waxwing																			
Northern Cardinal																	●	●	
Blue Grosbeak																			
Painted Bunting																			
Spot-breasted Oriole																			
Baltimore Oriole														●				●	
House Finch	●	●															●		
American Goldfinch	●	●															●		

							Vines & Shrubs									Wildflowers								
Dahoon Holly (*Ilex cassine*)	Yaupon Holly (*Ilex vomitoria*)	Florida Maple (*Acer barbatum*)	Red Maple (*Acer rubrum*)	Flowering Dogwood (*Cornus florida*)	Black Gum or Black Tupelo (*Nyssa sylvatica*)	Common Persimmon (*Diospyros virginiana*)	Blackberry (*Rubus ssp.*)	Firebush or Scarletbush (*Hamelia patens*)	Necklace Pod (*Sophora tomentosa*)	Seven-year Apple (*Casasia clusiifolia*)	Sea Grape (*Coccoloba uvifera*)	Elderberry (*Sambucus canadensis*)	Shining or Winged Sumac (*Rhus copallina*)	Greenbrier (*Smilax ssp.*)	Virginia Creeper (*Parthenocissus quinquefolia*)	Pokeweed (*Phytolacca americana*)	Indian Paintbrush (*Castilleja coccinea*)	Texas Paintbrush (*Castilleja indivisa*)	Showy Partridge Pea (*Chamaecrista fasciculata*)	Beggarweed (*Desmodium ssp.*)	Doveweed (*Croton ssp.*)	Panicgrass (*Panicum ssp.*)	Bristlegrass (*Setaria ssp.*)	Nectar in Feeders and Flowers
	●	●												●										
				●			●												●	●	●			
																●					●		●	
								●	●	●							●	●						
				●	●							●			●									
				●											●									
				●	●										●	●								
●	●			●	●						●			●	●									
●	●			●	●		●						●	●	●									
			●																					
			●																					
							●								●									
●	●			●	●							●	●		●	●								
●	●				●		●						●											
●	●			●			●					●		●	●	●								
●	●			●	●		●				●	●	●	●	●	●								
●	●			●	●		●					●	●	●	●	●								
●	●					●																		
				●			●									●							●	
																						●	●	
																						●	●	
																								●
							●																	
			●																					
			●																					

(continued from page 123)
and Northern Mockingbirds eagerly eat. Tetrazygia *(Tetrazygia bicolor)* produces fruits during summer and autumn eaten by Gray Catbirds, Northern Mockingbirds, Brown Thrashers, and some thrushes. Christmas berry *(Lycium carolinianum)*, an evergreen shrub, also yields red fruit eaten by White-crowned Pigeons, Northern Mockingbirds, and American Robins.

Several vines have colorful flowers providing Ruby-throated Hummingbirds with nectar and tiny insects. They include coral honeysuckle *(Lonicera sempervirens)* and trumpet vine *(Campsis radicans)* in the northern, central, and southern sections of the state, and cross vine *(Bignonia capreolata)* in northern and central Florida.

A few wildflowers that are attractive to Ruby-throated Hummingbirds include cardinal flower *(Lobelia cardinalis)*, Indian pink *(Spigelia marilandica)*, and standing cypress or Spanish larkspur *(Ipomopsis rubra)*.

Midwest

People living in the midwestern states—Illinois, Indiana, Iowa, Ohio, Michigan, Minnesota, Missouri, and Wisconsin—have many choices of native trees, shrubs, vines, wildflowers, and other plants to enhance backyard habitats for the benefit of birds.

Eastern white pine *(Pinus strobus)* is very useful in backyard habitats because it's a beautiful tree that provides food for Black-capped Chickadees, Red-breasted and White-breasted Nuthatches, Brown Creepers, Red and White-winged Crossbills, Pine Siskins, and American Goldfinches. In the Upper Peninsula of Michigan, also try using jack pine *(Pinus banksiana)*, which the same birds will utilize. Endangered Kirtland's Warblers also nest in jack-pine stands of certain age classes.

Eastern red cedar *(Juniperus virginiana)* is another tree whose fruits are eaten by Northern Flickers, Eastern Bluebirds, Gray Catbirds, Cedar Waxwings, White-winged Crossbills, Purple Finches, and Evening Grosbeaks.

Among deciduous trees, American beech *(Fagus grandifolia)* provides food for Ruffed Grouse, Blue Jays, White-breasted Nuthatches, Tufted Titmice, Rose-breasted Grosbeaks, and Purple Finches. White oak *(Quercus alba)* and various other oaks also yield acorns, which are eaten by Ruffed Grouse, Red-headed Woodpeckers, Downy Woodpeckers, Northern Flickers, Blue Jays, Tufted Titmice, White-breasted Nuthatches, and Rose-breasted Grosbeaks.

Hackberry *(Celtis occidentalis)* fruit is consumed by Northern Flickers, Eastern Phoebes, Hermit Thrushes, American Robins, and various other birds. Red mulberry *(Morus rubra)* fruit is also eaten by Red-headed Woodpeckers, Blue Jays, Tufted Titmice, Gray Catbirds, Brown Thrashers, Northern Cardinals, Rose-breasted Grosbeaks, and Orchard Orioles. Sassafras *(Sassafras albidum)* fruit is eaten by Northern Bobwhites, Pileated Woodpeckers, Eastern Phoebes, Great Crested Flycatchers, Eastern Kingbirds, Hermit Thrushes, and Gray Catbirds.

Black cherry *(Prunus serotina)* and pin cherry *(Prunus pensylvanica)* trees also provide food for Wild Turkeys, Northern Bobwhites, Red-headed Woodpeckers, Hairy Woodpeckers, Northern Flickers, Blue Jays, Hermit Thrushes, American Robins, Gray Catbirds, and Evening Grosbeaks.

(continued on page 132)

AN INDIANA BACKYARD

The backyard of Greg and Clare Oskay provides a fine example of what can be done to enhance a midwestern suburban backyard. By profession, Greg helps homeowners create backyard ponds and improve their backyard habitats. When he set about converting his own property, he had a clear idea about the visual effect he wanted to produce, and how the habitat should serve birds and other wildlife.

In 1982, the property was not wildlife-friendly. Greg and Clare faced a one-third-acre open field that was part of a cornfield subdivision. Greg estimated that converting their land into a wildlife-friendly area for birds should not cost any more than seeding their lot with grass. The key to keeping costs within reasonable limits is to select trees, shrubs, and wildflowers that are most attractive and beneficial to birds.

As we've discussed, plant selection is important. At first, the Oskays didn't realize that Amur honeysuckle was an invasive, introduced species that spreads rapidly. Greg has been fighting it ever since—and trying to replace all exotics with native species, including black cherry, eastern red cedar, red oak, sugar maple, tulip poplar, eastern white pine, elderberry, highbush cranberry, red-twig dogwood, winterberry holly, and Washington hawthorn. Purple coneflowers, bee balm,

(continued on page 129)

Greg Oskay

The lovely pond that Greg Oskay designed and constructed in his backyard habitat in Indianapolis, Indiana.

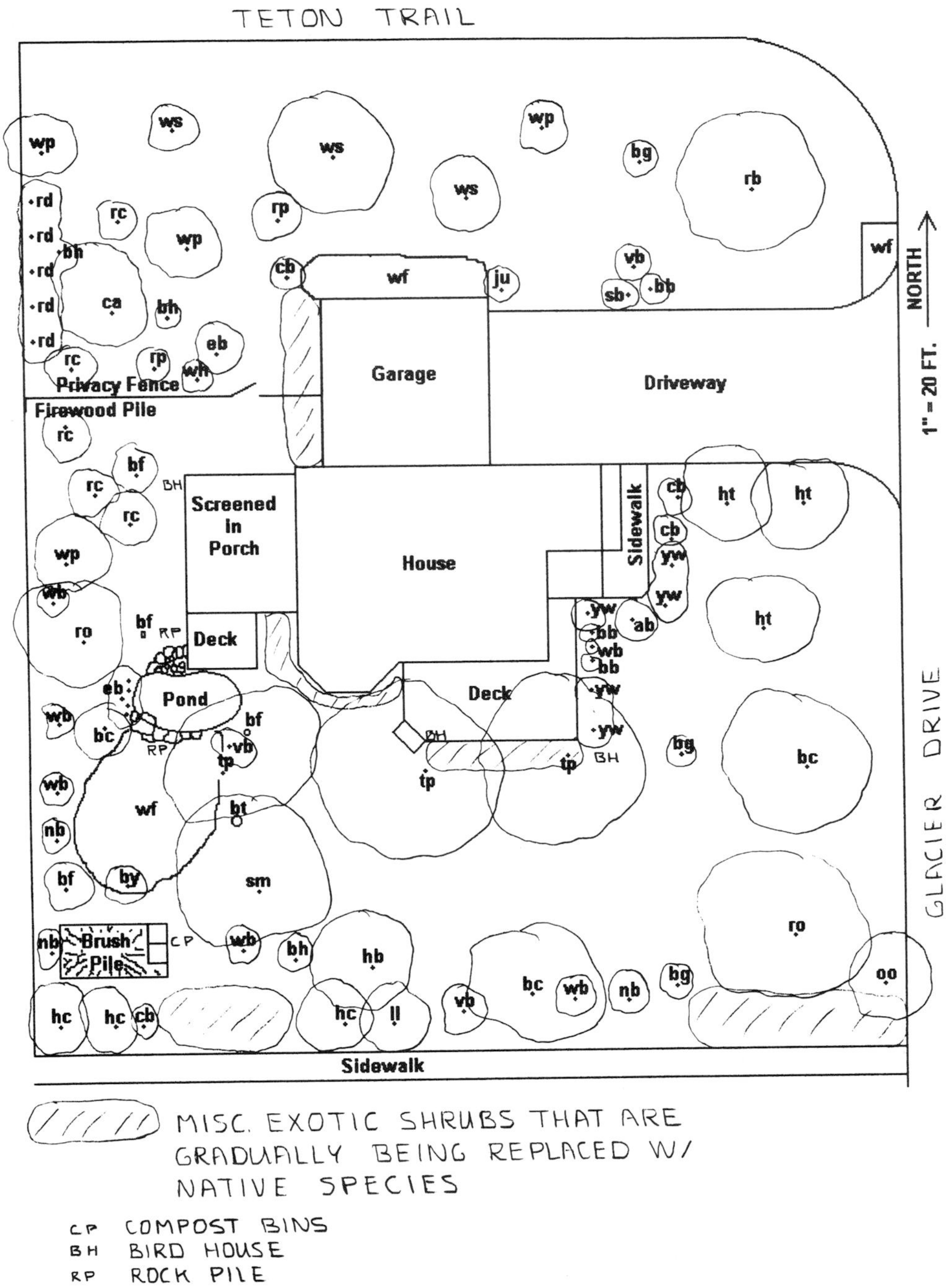

TETON TRAIL

GLACIER DRIVE

NORTH

1" = 20 FT.

Garage

Driveway

Privacy Fence

Firewood Pile

Screened In Porch

House

Sidewalk

Deck

Pond

Deck

Brush Pile

Sidewalk

wp ws ws wp bg rb ws rp rd rc wp rd bh rd ca bh cb wf ju vb sb bb wf rd rd eb rc rp wh rc bf BH rc rc cb ht ht cb yw wp yw wb yw ab ht ro bf RP bb wb bb eb yw wb bc RP bf vb yw BH tp BH bg bc tp tp wb wf bt nb bf by sm ro nb CP wb bh hb oo bg vb bc wb nb hc hc cb hc ll

MISC. EXOTIC SHRUBS THAT ARE GRADUALLY BEING REPLACED W/ NATIVE SPECIES

CP COMPOST BINS
BH BIRD HOUSE
RP ROCK PILE

Greg Oskay's backyard habitat landscape plan. Here, a computer drawing program and two-letter codes are used to show plants and their general sizes and locations.

(continued from page 127)
pokeweed, blue flag iris, fragrant water lily, Joe-pye weed, goldenrod, and butterfly weed are some of the wildflowers on the property.

Birds have responded well to this landscaping; some ninety species are on Greg's backyard tally, with forty to fifty species noted in any given year. On his backyard life list are Sharp-shinned, Cooper's, and Broad-winged Hawks; Black-billed Cuckoos; Eastern Screech-Owls; Ruby-throated Hummingbirds; Red-bellied Woodpeckers; Purple Martins; Carolina Chickadees; Red breasted Nuthatches; Gray-cheeked Thrushes; Philadelphia Vireos; Orange-crowned Warblers; Ovenbirds; Northern Water Thrushes; Connecticut Warblers; Baltimore Orioles; Scarlet Tanagers; Indigo Buntings; Purple Finches; Fox Sparrows; Lincoln's Sparrows; and Swamp Sparrows. Rough-legged Hawks and Yellow-bellied Flycatchers are particularly nice additions on a backyard life list. In 1994, Greg was named Wildlife Conservationist of the Year by the Indiana Wildlife Federation in honor of his work with Backyard Wildlife Habitat Programs.

Greg Oskay

A Mourning Dove dozing on a wood pile during winter temperatures of –20°F. The bird's feathers are fully fluffed up to insulate the bird from the extreme cold.

Greg Oskay

A view of part of Greg Oskay's backyard habitat showing an ecological transition between lawn and wooded habitats. Many songbirds are attracted to these places.

MIDWEST / **Birds**	Red Pine (*Pinus resinosa*)	Pitch Pine (*Pinus rigida*)	Black Spruce (*Picea mariana*)	Eastern Hemlock (*Tsuga canadensis*)	Quaking Aspen (*Populus tremuloides*)	Bigtooth Aspen (*Populus grandidentata*)	Shagbark Hickory (*Carya ovata*)	Shellbark Hickory (*Carya laciniosa*)	Pignut Hickory (*Carya glabra*)	Bitternut Hickory (*Carya cordiformis*)	Eastern Hophornbeam (*Ostrya virginiana*)	Northern Red Oak (*Quercus rubra*)	Black Oak (*Quercus velutina*)	Pin Oak (*Quercus palustris*)	Shingle Oak (*Quercus imbricaria*)	American Elm (*Ulmus americana*)	Slippery Elm (*Ulmus rubra*)	Rock Elm (*Ulmus thomasii*)	Tulip Tree or Yellow Poplar (*Liriodendron tulipifera*)	American Mountain Ash (*Sorbus americana*)	Common Chokecherry (*Prunus virginiana*)
Trees																					
Ring-necked Pheasant																					
Mourning Dove																					
Ruby-throated Hummingbird																			•		
Red-headed Woodpecker												•	•	•	•						
Red-bellied Woodpecker	•	•					•	•	•	•		•	•	•	•						
Downy Woodpecker											•	•	•	•	•						
Hairy Woodpecker																					
Northern Flicker																					
Blue Jay												•	•	•	•						
Black-capped Chickadee	•	•		•																	
Tufted Titmouse												•	•	•	•						
Red-breasted Nuthatch	•	•	•																		
White-breasted Nuthatch	•	•					•	•	•	•		•	•	•	•						
Eastern Bluebird																					
American Robin																					
Gray Catbird																					
Northern Mockingbird																					
Brown Thrasher																					
Cedar Waxwing																					•
Northern Cardinal																					
Rose-breasted Grosbeak							•	•	•	•	•	•	•	•	•	•	•	•			
Baltimore Oriole																					
Purple Finch					•	•					•					•	•	•	•		
American Goldfinch	•	•														•	•	•	•		
Evening Grosbeak																				•	

														Vines		Wildflowers & Weeds							Cultivated Crop Plants				
Allegheny Serviceberry (*Amelanchier laevis*)	Staghorn Sumac (*Rhus typhina*)	Shining Sumac (*Rhus copallina*)	Fragrant Sumac (*Rhus aromatica*)	Smooth Sumac (*Rhus glabra*)	Sugar Maple (*Acer saccharum*)	Black Maple (*Acer nigrum*)	Red Maple (*Acer rubrum*)	Silver Maple (*Acer saccharinum*)	Flowering Dogwood (*Cornus florida*)	Alternate-leaf Dogwood (*Cornus alternifolia*)	Rough-leaf Dogwood (*Cornus drummondii*)	Red-osier Dogwood (*Cornus stolonifera*)	Black Tupelo or Blackgum (*Nyssa aquatica*)	Greenbrier (*Smilax ssp.*)	Grape (*Vitis ssp.*)	Sunflower (*Helianthus ssp.*)	Panicgrass (*Panicum ssp.*)	Bristlegrass (*Setaria ssp.*)	Knotweed (*Polygonum ssp.*)	Pigweed (*Amaranthus ssp.*)0	Doveweed (*Croton ssp.*)	Spurge (*Euphorbia ssp.*)	Wheat (*Triticum aestivum*)	Barley (*Hordeum vulgare*)	Oats (*Avena sativa*)	Corn (*Zea mays*)	Apple (*Malus pumila*)
	●	●	●	●											●								●	●	●	●	●
																●	●	●	●	●	●	●	●			●	
															●											●	●
									●	●	●	●	●		●											●	
									●	●	●	●														●	
									●	●	●	●	●														
									●	●	●	●	●														
●															●								●			●	
●																●											
●															●	●										●	●
					●	●	●	●															●			●	
																●							●		●	●	
	●	●	●	●					●	●	●	●			●												
	●	●	●	●					●	●	●	●		●	●										●	●	●
●	●	●	●	●					●	●	●	●		●	●												
													●	●	●												
									●	●	●	●			●											●	
●									●				●	●	●												
									●	●	●	●			●		●	●	●		●				●	●	
●																				●			●		●	●	
●															●										●	●	
					●	●	●	●	●	●	●	●	●		●												
					●	●	●	●								●											
					●	●	●	●	●	●	●	●															

(continued from page 126)

Blackberry *(Rubus ssp.)* fruits feed many types of wildlife, including Ruffed Grouse, Red-headed Woodpeckers, Northern Flickers, Blue Jays, American Robins, Gray Catbirds, Brown Thrashers, Northern Cardinals, Rose-breasted Grosbeaks, and Orchard Orioles. The fruits of elderberry *(Sambucus canadensis)* are also eaten by many of these same birds.

Common highbush blueberry *(Vaccinium corymbosum)* and its relatives produce fruits eaten by Northern Flickers, Blue Jays, American Robins, Gray Catbirds, Brown Thrashers, and Orchard Orioles.

An attractive vine such as Virginia creeper *(Parthenocissus quinquefolia)* is useful in backyard habitats because its fruit is eaten by many birds, such as woodpeckers (Red-bellied, Downy, Hairy, and Pileated), Northern Flickers, Great Crested Flycatchers, White-breasted Nuthatches, American Robins, Gray Catbirds, and Northern Mockingbirds.

Among wildflowers, Ruby-throated Hummingbirds feed at many species including jewelweed or spotted touch-me-not *(Impatiens capensis)*, bee balm *(Monarda didyma)*, and cardinal flower *(Lobelia cardinalis)*. Other wildflowers also benefit birds; for example, Pine Siskins and American Goldfinches eat seeds, including those of purple coneflowers *(Echinacea purpurea)*.

Great Plains

A smaller range of flora is available for enhancement of backyard habitats in the Great Plains states—Kansas, Nebraska, North Dakota, Oklahoma, and South Dakota.

Eastern red cedar *(Juniperus virginiana)* fruits are eaten by Northern Flickers, Eastern Bluebirds, Gray Catbirds, and Cedar Waxwings. Oaks are much less important on the Great Plains than in the eastern United States, but bur oak *(Quercus macrocarpa)* acorns are eaten by Red-headed Woodpeckers, Downy Woodpeckers, Northern Flickers, and Blue Jays.

Hackberry *(Celtis occidentalis)* and net-leaf hackberry *(Celtis reticulata)* fruits are food sources for Northern Flickers, Eastern Bluebirds, American Robins, Northern Mockingbirds, Brown Thrashers, Cedar Waxwings, and Northern Cardinals.

Common chokecherry *(Prunus virginiana)* fruits, with poisonous stones, are eaten by Red-headed Woodpeckers, Northern Flickers, American Robins, and Gray Catbirds.

Red-osier dogwood *(Cornus stolonifera)* also produces fruits eaten by Downy Woodpeckers, Northern Flickers, American Robins, Gray Catbirds, Brown Thrashers, Cedar Waxwings, and Northern Cardinals.

Smooth sumac *(Rhus glabra)* is another shrub whose fruits provide food for Northern Flickers and American Robins. Virginia creeper *(Parthenocissus quinquefolia)* and thicket creeper *(Parthenocissus inserta)* also produce fruit eaten by Downy Woodpeckers, Hairy Woodpeckers, Northern Flickers, and American Robins.

Among wildflowers, narrow-leaved prairie coneflower *(Echinacea angustifolia)* produces seeds eaten by sparrows and American Goldfinches living in the central and western Great Plains.

MANITOBA

The Naturescape Manitoba program provides information about preservation and habitat enhancement in and around Winnipeg. Summaries of native species are also provided. Naturescape Manitoba does not run a site-certification program, but resources include information on local demonstration sites and how to obtain native plants.

The City of Winnipeg, in cooperation with government agencies and nonprofit organizations, also operates an Urban Habitat Stewardship Resource Network in the city and the surrounding region. Three types of projects are available: restoration, enhancement, and stewardship. Restoration projects attempt to diversify sites with little or no native vegetation.

Enhancement projects repair damaged areas with native vegetation, which might involve planting wildflowers or other small plants under trees where the soil is bare. Stewardship projects entail managing larger natural areas—everything from removing litter to removing invasive weeds to leading tours. The following gardening suggestions are based on successful uses of native species by the Urban Habitat Stewardship Resource Network.

There are five distinct types of habitats in and around Winnipeg: Aspen forest, oak forest, river-bottom forest, prairie, and wetlands. Backyard habitats typically include the first four.

In aspen forests, the dominant tree appropriate for backyard habitat use is quaking, or trembling, aspen (Populus tremuloides). *Additional useable trees providing acorns, fruit, or seeds on which birds dine include balsam poplar* (Populus balsamifera), *bur oak* (Quercus macrocarpa), *green ash* (Fraxinus pensylvanica), *and boxelder, or Manitoba maple* (Acer negundo).

Aspen forest shrubs that produce fruits or seeds consumed by birds include red-osier dogwood (Cornus stolonifera), *pin cherry* (Prunus pensylvanica), *and Saskatoon* (Amelanchier alnifolia).

Trees that produce bird food in oak forests include bur oak (Quercus macrocarpa) *and quaking aspen* (Populus tremuloides). *Similarly, nut- or fruit-producing shrubs attractive to birds include American hazelnut* (Corylus americana) *and pin cherry* (Prunus pensylvanica).

River-floodplain trees and shrubs—called river-bottom forests—that provide food for birds include green ash (Fraxinus pensylvanica), *American basswood* (Tilia americana), *and boxelder, or Manitoba maple* (Acer negundo). *Shrubs used by birds in these forests include American hazelnut* (Corylus americana), *red-osier dogwood* (Cornus stolonifera), *and Saskatoon* (Amelanchier alnifolia).

There were once two kinds of native prairie in Manitoba, tall-grass and mixed-grass; today, much of this habitat is greatly reduced in size or even critically endangered. Nevertheless, it's possible to enhance backyard habitats with native prairie plants that produce seeds or fruits eaten by birds.

For representative tall-grass prairie plants, try using Indian grass (Sorghastrum nutans) *or prairie dropseed* (Sporobolus heterolepis). *Wildflowers include smooth aster* (Aster laevis) *and stiff goldenrod* (Solidago rigida). *Western snowberry, or wolfberry* (Symphoricarpos albus) *and lead plant, or false indigo* (Amorpha canescens) *are representative shrubs.*

Representative mixed-grass prairie species include little bluestem grass (Andropogon scoparius) *and Indian grass* (Sorghastrum nutans). *Wildflowers include dotted blazing star* (Liatris punctata) *and purple coneflower* (Echinacea purpurea)*; sandcherry* (Prunus pumila) *is one of the shrubs that can be used.*

For more information about Naturescape Manitoba and the City of Winnipeg's Urban Habitat Stewardship Resource Network, see appendix 2.

GREAT PLAINS	Vines & Shrubs				Weeds									Cultivated Crop Plants				
Birds	Blackberry (*Rubus ssp.*)	Sugarberry (*Celtis laevigata*)	Alderleaf Juneberry (*Amelanchier alnifolia*)	Grape (*Vitis ssp.*)	Sunflower (*Helianthus ssp.*)	Aster (*Aster ssp.*)	Panicgrass (*Panicum ssp.*)	Bristlegrass (*Setaria ssp.*)	Knotweed (*Polygonum ssp.*)	Goosefoot (*Chenopodium ssp.*)	Pigweed (*Amaranthus ssp.*)	Doveweed (*Croton ssp.*)	Spurge (*Euphorbia ssp.*)	Wheat (*Triticum aestivum*)	Oats (*Avena sativa*)	Corn (*Zea mays*)	Apple (*Malus pumila*)	Soybean (*Glycine max*)
Ring-necked Pheasant			●	●				●						●	●	●		●
Mourning Dove					●		●	●	●		●	●	●	●		●		
Red-headed Woodpecker	●			●											●	●	●	
Downy Woodpecker																●	●	
Hairy Woodpecker																●	●	
Northern Flicker		●	●	●												●		
Blue Jay	●			●										●		●		
Black-billed Magpie														●		●	●	
Black-capped Chickadee					●											●		
Eastern Bluebird	●	●		●														
American Robin	●	●		●											●	●	●	
Gray Catbird	●			●														
Northern Mockingbird	●			●														
Brown Thrasher	●			●												●		
Cedar Waxwing	●			●													●	
Harris's Sparrow					●	●	●	●	●	●				●	●	●		
Northern Cardinal	●	●		●			●	●	●			●			●	●		
Blue Grosbeak								●							●	●		
Orchard Oriole	●																	
American Goldfinch					●													

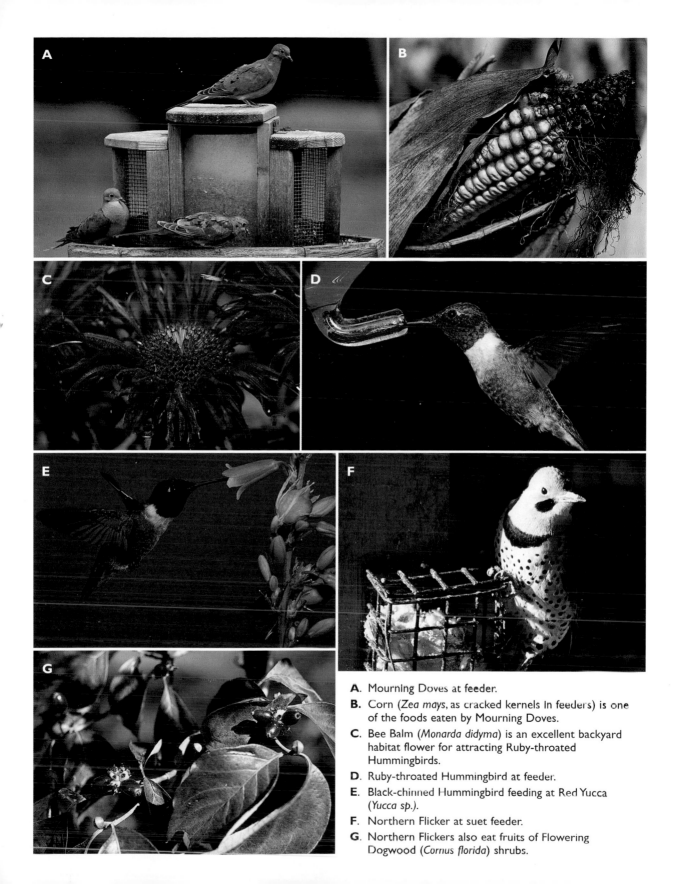

A. Mourning Doves at feeder.

B. Corn (*Zea mays*, as cracked kernels in feeders) is one of the foods eaten by Mourning Doves.

C. Bee Balm (*Monarda didyma*) is an excellent backyard habitat flower for attracting Ruby-throated Hummingbirds.

D. Ruby-throated Hummingbird at feeder.

E. Black-chinned Hummingbird feeding at Red Yucca (*Yucca sp.)*.

F. Northern Flicker at suet feeder.

G. Northern Flickers also eat fruits of Flowering Dogwood (*Cornus florida*) shrubs.

American Southwest Backyard Bird Habitat

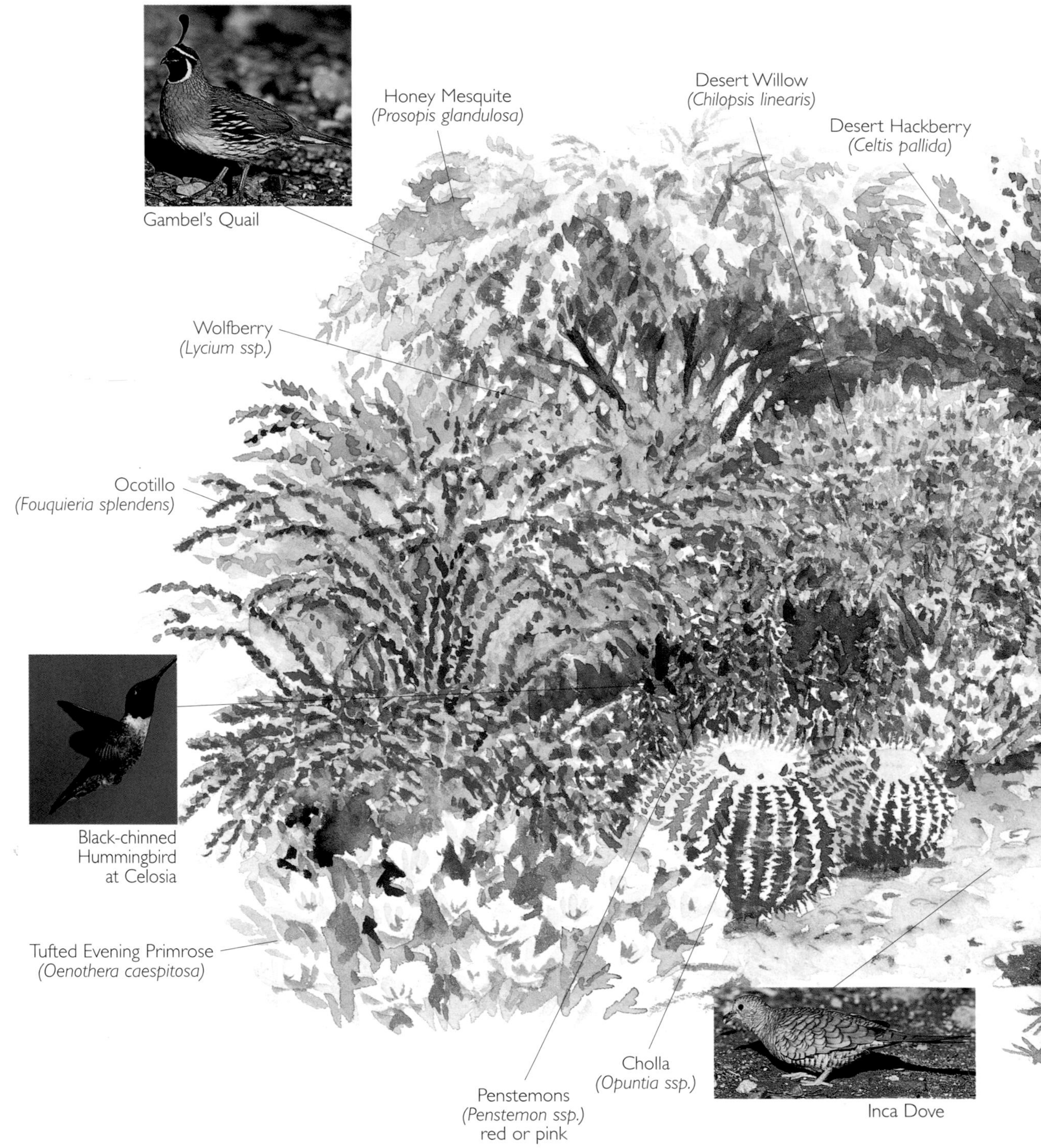

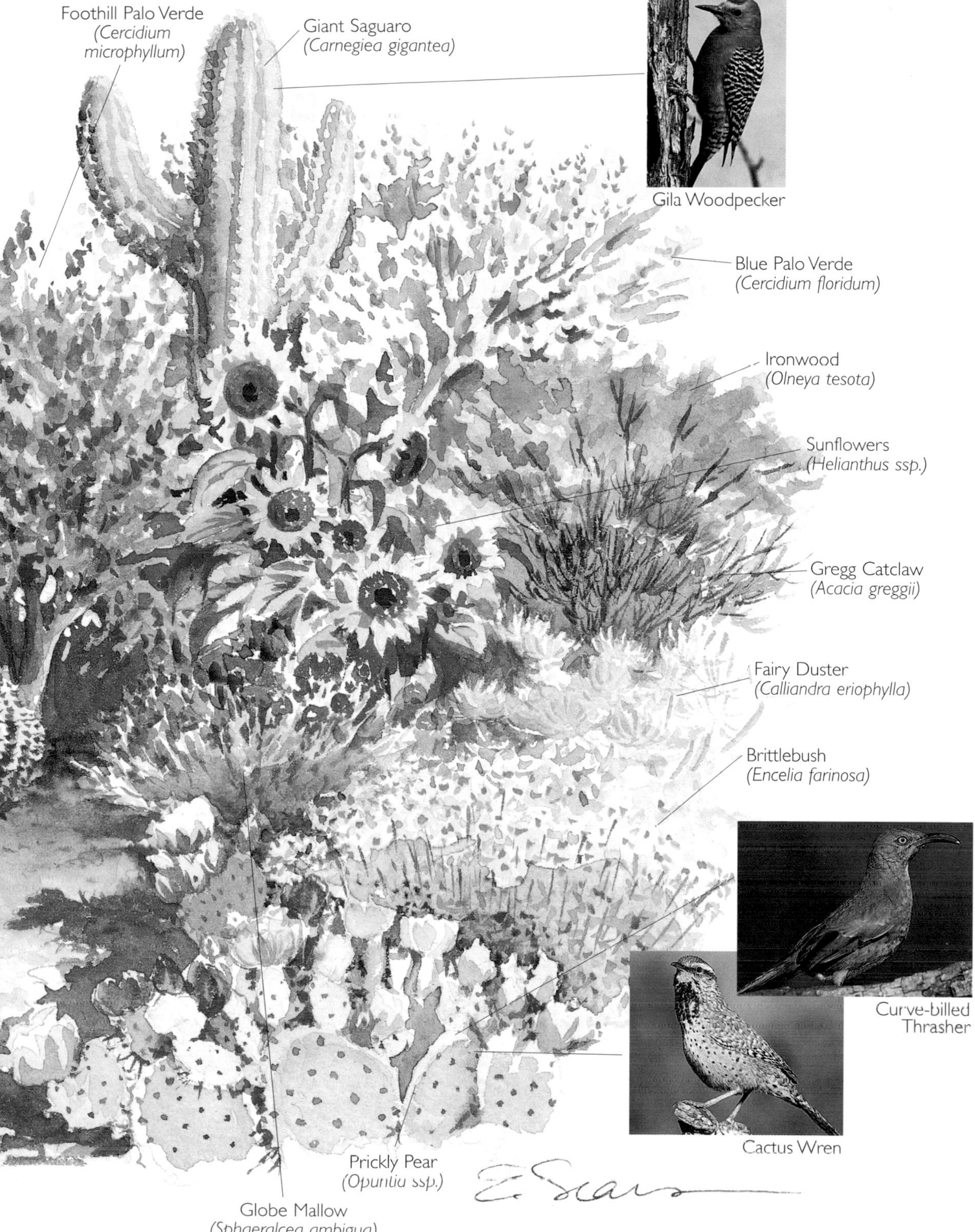

Foothill Palo Verde
(Cercidium microphyllum)
Giant Saguaro
(Carnegiea gigantea)
Gila Woodpecker
Blue Palo Verde
(Cercidium floridum)
Ironwood
(Olneya tesota)
Sunflowers
(Helianthus ssp.)
Gregg Catclaw
(Acacia greggii)
Fairy Duster
(Calliandra eriophylla)
Brittlebush
(Encelia farinosa)
Curve-billed Thrasher
Cactus Wren
Prickly Pear
(Opuntia ssp.)
Globe Mallow
(Sphaeralcea ambigua)

Northeastern States Backyard Bird Habitat

Common
Winterberry
(Ilex verticillata)
Mountain Ash
(Sorbus americana)
American Robin
Brown Thrasher
Flowering Dogwood
(Cornus florida)
House Finch
Sunflowers
(Helianthus ssp.)
Tufted Titmouse
Corn
(Zea mays)
Black eyed Susan (Rudbeckia hirta)
Bee-Balm (Monarda didyma)
Cardinal Flower (Lobelia cardinalis)
New England Asters (Aster novae-angliae)

MIDWESTERN STATES BACKYARD BIRD HABITAT

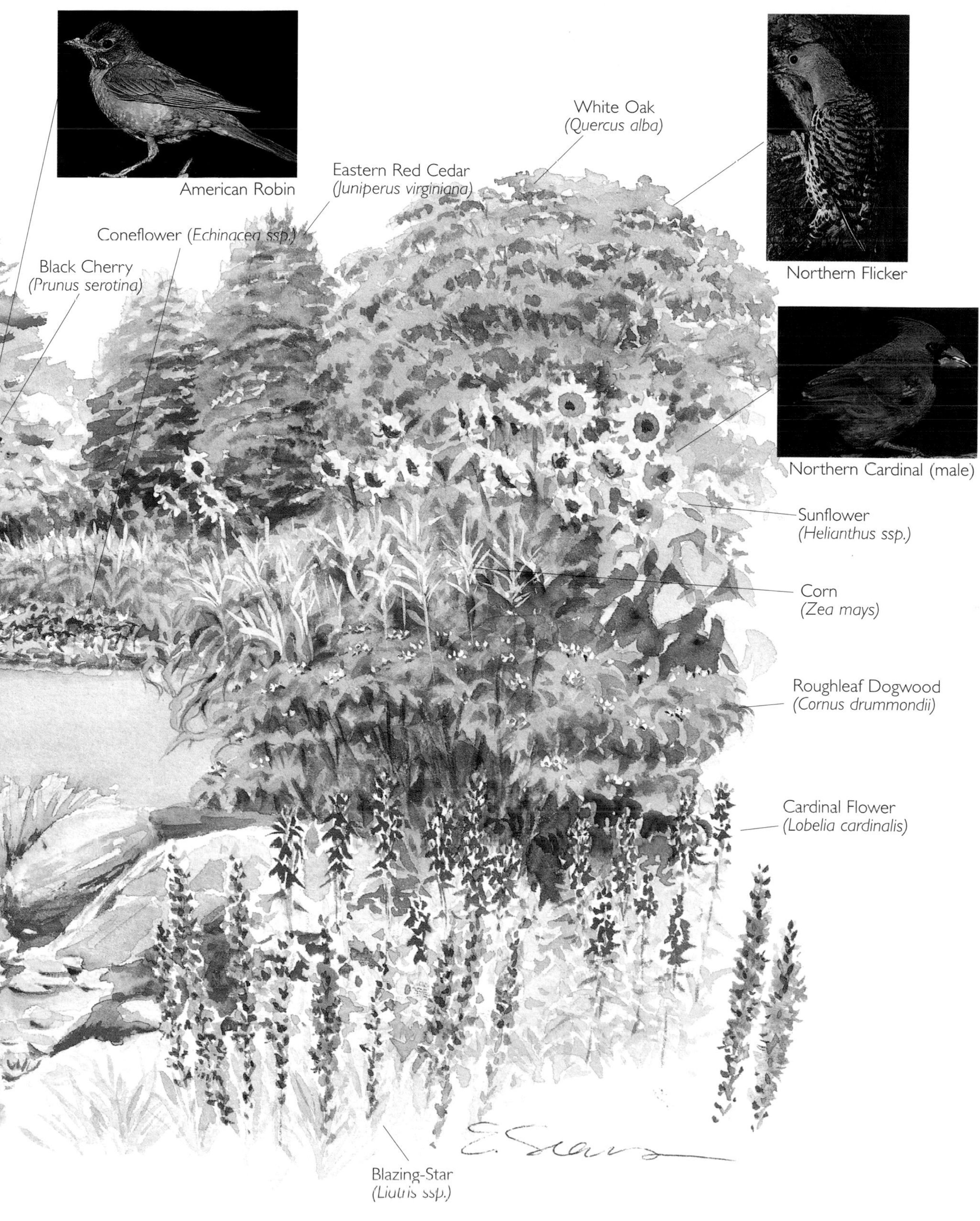
American Robin
White Oak
(Quercus alba)
Eastern Red Cedar
(Juniperus virginiana)
Coneflower (Echinacea ssp.)
Black Cherry
(Prunus serotina)
Northern Flicker
Northern Cardinal (male)
Sunflower
(Helianthus ssp.)
Corn
(Zea mays)
Roughleaf Dogwood
(Cornus drummondii)
Cardinal Flower
(Lobelia cardinalis)
Blazing-Star
(Liatris ssp.)

A. Golden-fronted Woodpecker.

B. Purple Martin.

C. Northern Mockingbird at feeder.

D. Northern Mockingbirds also eat American Holly *(Ilex opaca)* fruits.

E. Northern Cardinal (female).

F. Sunflower *(Helianthus ssp.)* seeds placed in feeders are favorites of Northern Cardinals.

G. Baltimore Orioles sometimes feed on sliced oranges *(Citrus ssp.)*.

SASKATCHEWAN

Backyard birders in Saskatchewan do not currently enjoy an official habitat-enhancement program, but they can turn to Wildlife Gardening in Saskatchewan: Building Backyard Biodiversity, *an excellent forty-four-page guide by Karyn Scalise. The booklet provides all the basic information necessary to create bird-friendly habitats in Saskatchewan using native trees, shrubs, and wildflowers. The following suggestions are based on her guide.*

For conifer trees, use junipers (Juniperus ssp.) *throughout the province and white spruce* (Picea glauca) *in the northern three quarters of Saskatchewan. Both provide fruit or seeds for finches, grosbeaks, crossbills, and sparrows.*

Among deciduous trees yielding fruits or seeds for birds, plant Manitoba maple (Acer negundo) *in the southern half of the province, alders* (Alnus ssp.) *in the northern two thirds, paper birch* (Betula papyrifera) *everywhere, and showy mountain ash* (Sorbus decora) *in a belt across the middle of Saskatchewan.*

Some native deciduous shrubs providing fruits or seeds eaten by birds include Saskatoon (Amelanchier alnifolia) *and silverberry* (Elaeagnus commutata), *suitable for use everywhere, and red elder* (Sambucus racemosa/pubens) *for use in a belt across central Saskatchewan.*

Selected native perennial wildflowers that produce seeds eaten by birds include Asters (Aster ssp.), *suitable for use everywhere; meadow blazing star* (Liatris ligulistylis)*; dotted blazing star* (Liatris punctata)*; penstemons* (Penstemon ssp.) *in the lower half of the province; and dock* (Rumex ssp.) *and goldenrod* (Solidago ssp.), *suitable for use everywhere.*

Several native perennial wildflowers feed hummingbirds. Try using columbine (Aquilegia ssp.) *in a belt across the middle of the province, fireweed* (Epilobium angustifolium) *everywhere, and one of the bergamots* (Monarda ssp.) *in southern Saskatchewan.*

Sunflowers (Helianthus ssp.), *native annual wildflowers, also produce seeds eaten by birds. They are suitable for use throughout southern Saskatchewan.*

To buy a copy of this booklet, contact the Blue Jay Bookshop, Nature Saskatchewan, listed in appendix 4.

Rocky Mountains

The high elevations and harsh climates found in the Rocky Mountain states naturally affect the trees, shrubs, wildflowers, and cultivated crops used for backyard habitat enhancement.

Pine trees—lodgepole *(Pinus contorta)*, Colorado pinyon *(Pinus edulis)*, western white *(Pinus monticola)*, and ponderosa *(Pinus ponderosa)*—produce seeds eaten by Blue Grouse, Black-capped and Mountain Chickadees, Red and White-winged Crossbills, and Pine Grosbeaks. They also provide protective cover and nesting sites for birds and are lovely to look at.

Colorado blue spruce *(Picea pungens)* seeds are consumed by several mountain birds, including Steller's Jays and chickadees. This spruce also provides

(continued on page 140)

ROCKY MTS.	**Trees**														**Shrubs**		
Birds	Western Red Cedar (*Thuja plicata*)	Sub-alpine Fir (*Abies lasiocarpa*)	Engelmann Spruce (*Picea engelmannii*)	Colorado Blue Spruce (*Picea pungens*)	Lodgepole Pine (*Pinus contorta*)	Colorado Pinyon (*Pinus edulis*)	Western White Pine (*Pinus monticola*)	Ponderosa Pine (*Pinus ponderosa*)	Western Hemlock (*Tsuga heterophylla*)	Gambel's Oak (*Quercus gambelii*)	Box Elder (Ashleaf Maple) (*Acer negundo var. interius*)	Paper Birch (*Betula papyrifera*)	Water Birch (*Betula occidentalis*)	Red-osier Dogwood (*Cornus stolonifera*)	Orange Honeysuckle (*Lonicera ciliosa*)	Twinberry (Bush Honeysuckle) (*Lonicera involucrata*)	Snowberry (*Symphoricarpos sp.*)
Mourning Dove																	
Black-chinned Hummingbird																	
Broad-tailed Hummingbird																	
Calliope Hummingbird																	
Rufous Hummingbird																	
Red-headed Woodpecker										●							
Downy Woodpecker										●				●			
Hairy Woodpecker														●			
Steller's Jay					●	●	●	●		●				●			
Clark's Nutcracker	●	●								●							
Black-billed Magpie					●	●	●	●									
Black-capped Chickadee					●	●	●	●	●			●	●				
Mountain Chickadee					●	●	●	●		●							
Plain Titmouse					●	●	●	●		●							
Red-breasted Nuthatch					●	●	●	●									
White-breasted Nuthatch					●	●	●	●		●							
Pygmy Nuthatch		●			●	●	●	●									
Eastern Bluebird	●													●			
White-crowned Sparrow																	
Black-headed Grosbeak		●															
Bullock's Oriole																	
Rosy-Finches (Gray-crowned, Black, Brown-capped)					●	●	●	●									
Pine Grosbeak					●	●	●	●						●	●	●	●
Cassin's Finch			●	●	●	●	●	●									
House Finch																	
American Goldfinch										●							
Evening Grosbeak	●							●			●			●			●

							Wildflowers & Weeds												Cultivated Crop Plants				
Sage (*Salvia sp.*)	Western Serviceberry (*Amelanchier alnifolia*)	Wild Red Raspberry (*Rubus idaeus*)	Rocky Mountain Raspberry (*Rubus deliciosus*)	Peach-leaf Willow (*Salix amygdaloides*)	Bebb Willow (*Salix bebbiana*)	Scouler Willow (*Salix scouleriana*)	Silvery Lupine (*Lupinus argenteus*)	Dwarf Lupine (*Lupinus caespitosus*)	Silky Lupine (*Lupinus sericeus*)	Longleaf Phlox (*Phlox longifolia*)	Desert Paintbrush (*Castilleja chromosa*)	Wyoming Paintbrush (*Castilleja linariifolia*)	Giant Red Paintbrush (*Castilleja miniata*)	Knotweed (*Polygonum sp.*)	Pigweed (*Amaranthus sp.*)	Miners Lettuce (*Montia perfoliata*)	Common Chickweed (*Stellaria media*)	Peppergrass (*Lepidium sp.*)	Sunflower (*Helianthus sp.*)	Wheat (*Triticum sp.*)	Oats (*Avena sp.*)	Corn (*Zea mays*)	Apple (*Malus pumila*)
															•				•	•			
•				•	•	•				•	•	•	•										
•										•	•	•	•										
•										•	•	•	•										
•										•	•	•	•										
																						•	
	•																					•	
		•	•																	•	•	•	
							•	•	•											•	•	•	
	•																			•		•	
	•																		•				
																					•		•
																				•	•		
	•																						
														•	•				•		•		
		•	•																		•		
		•	•																				
														•	•		•	•		•	•		
				•	•	•										•							
														•	•		•					•	
																			•				
		•																					

A COLORADO BACKYARD

Mention the word "Walden" and most people think of Henry David Thoreau's book and the pond where the great American philosopher and naturalist spent his most rewarding days. For Charlie and Sandy Fliniau, however, Walden is a little town of eight hundred people located 8,200 feet high in a bowl of the great Colorado Rocky Mountains. It's also the location of a lovely backyard habitat that Sandy created, frequented by birds common and rare.

The beginning was not auspicious when Sandy and her family moved into their then-yardless home—mounds of earth left over from construction ten years earlier filled a space only 66 feet wide and 125 feet long. There was one scrubby fir tree, 8 feet tall. A gardener by nature, she was nearly frantic at what she saw.

However, they soon terraced some of the property; excavated other parts; and hauled in topsoil, garden rocks, and even tree snags. First to be planted was a rock garden with perennials, strawberries, and other plants. Next came grass and small trees, followed by an acquaintance with birds that arrived in this suddenly transformed space.

Sandy recalls her progress toward wildlife gardening. "We began our yard with aesthetics in mind—not habitat—but it soon took on a different look. It seemed to me that each time I planted something, the birds had a reaction, usually positive. In a sense, they began to design their own habitat. I let nature take its course, and now, after more than thirty years, we have shade where there used to be sun and tall shrubs in front of short shrubs. Today, the shrubs and trees surrounding our property have joined hands from front to back."

Part of the lovely backyard habitat created by Sandy Fliniau at her Walden home high in the Colorado Rocky Mountains.

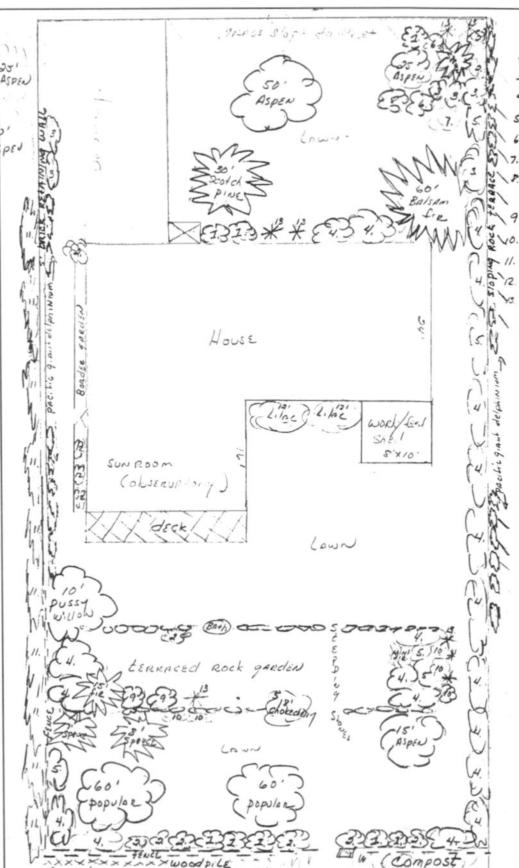

Wildlife habitat landscape plan for the Fliniau's property. This plan indicates heights of some of the plantings, but like the other plans it uses numbers to code most plant names. Sketch provided by Sandy Fliniau.

Trees and shrubs included blue spruce, subalpine fir, quaking aspen, western chokecherry, and common snowberry. Environmental con ditions at 8,200 feet in the Rocky Mountains are harsh: there is 9 to 12 inches of precipitation and typically twenty nonconsecutive frost-free days each year (sometimes it snows on summer picnics). Despite the difficulties, Sandy has been successful: her backyard habitat is alive with wild things and captivating in its beauty.

Notice is given that this backyard habitat is for the birds and other wildlife.

American Goldfinches and a Lazuli Bunting visiting one of the bird feeders.

Sandy operates thirteen bird feeders year-round, plus a few extras during winter. During peak winter months, she puts out a hundred pounds or more of sunflower and white millet seeds every week; chickadees are offered a suet-insect mix.

Meal worms are provided during the cold early days of spring. Later into spring and summer, the feeders are filled with expensive niger (i.e., thistle) seeds, which songbirds enjoy. During this feeding activity, Sandy faithfully keeps the habitat clean by removing seed waste. Water is provided year-round and heated in the birdbaths during winter, something the birds enjoy.

At least thirty bird species are on Sandy's backyard habitat list. These include Mountain Bluebirds, Townsend's Solitaires, Orange-crowned Townsend's, and Wilson's Warblers, along with Pine Siskins, Pine Grosbeaks, Evening Grosbeaks, and White-crowned Sparrows. In 1995, she hosted a large flock of Black-Rosy Finches, which created quite a stir among birders in the area. The Rosy-Finches continue to return each winter—both Black and Gray-crowned—and draw birders from far and wide to Sandy's extraordinary backyard.

An amazing concentration of rare Gray-crowned Rosy-Finches, and a Black Rosy-Finch, enjoying the winter menu on the Fliniau's back deck. Birders from across the nation, and even some birding tours, visit this wonderful backyard bird haven specifically to see and add the elusive rosy-finches to their life lists.

First sweep of the early morning, with rare Gray-crowned Rosy-Finches, and a Black Rosy-Finch, feeding on the back deck. Having these species so close is a birder's dream.

All photos by T. Charles Fliniau

Blue spruce (also called Colorado blue spruce) is an excellent tree providing shelter and nest sites for birds in backyard habitats. Although used widely in the eastern United States, I recommend its use mostly in its natural geographic range.

(continued from page 135)

excellent protective cover for birds, especially during winter, and nesting and/or roosting sites in spring, summer, and autumn.

Shrubs useful in Rocky Mountain habitats include common chokecherry *(Prunus virginiana)*, whose fruit (with poisonous pits) is eaten by Black-billed Magpies and Gray Catbirds. Blue elderberry *(Sambucus caerulea)* fruit is also eaten by Steller's Jays, Black-billed Magpies, Red-breasted Nuthatches, Eastern and Mountain Bluebirds, and Gray Catbirds. This elderberry sometimes attains small-tree size. Western mountain ash *(Sorbus scopulina)* fruit also is eaten by Gray Catbirds, and smooth sumac *(Rhus glabra)* fruit is eaten by American Robins.

Various currant species, including golden *(Ribes aureum)*, wax *(Ribes cereum)*, and prickly *(Ribes lacustre)*, also provide food for Black-billed Magpies, Lewis's Woodpeckers, Mountain Bluebirds, Gray Catbirds, and Sage Thrashers. However, currants host a disease of western white pines so they should not be planted in locations with large white-pine populations.

Wild strawberry *(Fragaria vesca californica)* can be used as a groundcover in moist, shaded locations at elevations below 7,000 feet. American Robins, Northern Mockingbirds, and Black-headed and Pine Grosbeaks eat its fruit. Grapes *(Vitis ssp.)* are eaten by Mountain Bluebirds.

Red wildflowers such as southwest penstemon *(Penstemon barbatus)* and firecracker penstemon *(Penstemon eatoni)* are attractive to Black-chinned, Broad-tailed, Calliope, and Rufous Hummingbirds. Red columbine *(Aquilegia formosa)*, red fireweed *(Epilobium angustifolium)*, and wild bergamot *(Monarda fistulosa)* also attract these lovely and fascinating birds.

Texas

Texas has many different types of habitats and ecosystems, and more than five thousand native plant species. The Native Plant Society of Texas divides the state into six distinctive plant regions: East, Coast, South, Central, West, and High Plains. Each region (see the map) has its own array of native plants, making it necessary to select ecologically suitable trees, shrubs, vines, wildflowers, or other plants for habitat enhancement in each region. That's why subregions are specified along with plant recommendations for Texas.

Ashe juniper *(Juniperus ashei)*, suitable for regions 1, 3, and 4, yields blue fruit in winter eaten by all three bluebirds, American Robins, Cedar Waxwings, and Northern Cardinals.

(continued on page 146)

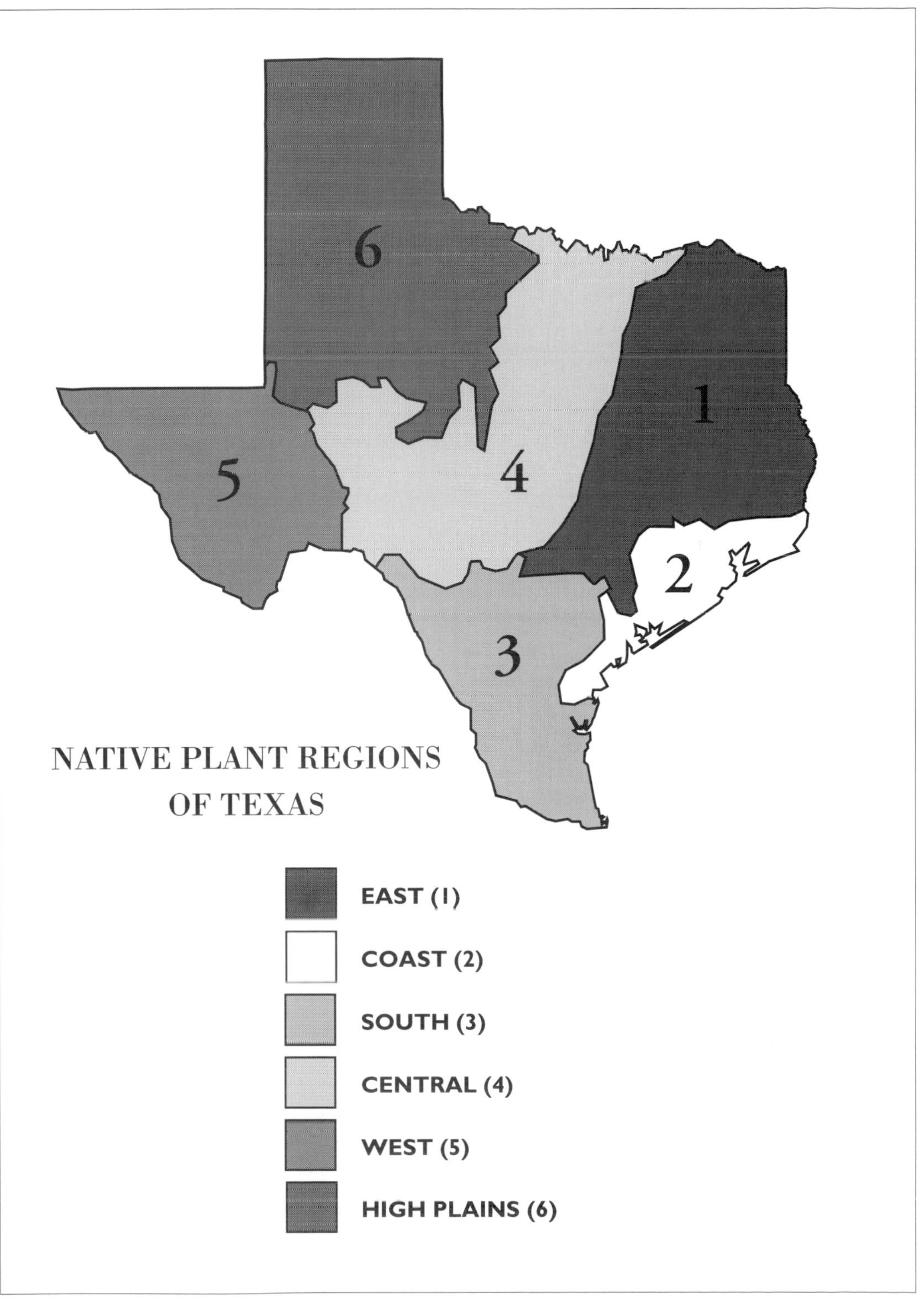

The native plant regions of Texas as shown in *Texas Natives: Ornamental Trees* by the Native Plant Society of Texas. Redrawn from a map published by the Native Plant Society of Texas.

TEXAS

Trees

Birds (*Texas regions, see map p. 141)	Eastern Red Cedar (*Juniperus virginiana*) 1, 4, 6*	American Beech (*Fagus grandifolia*) 1	Arizona White Oak (*Quercus arizonica*) 5	Bur Oak (*Quercus macrocarpa*) 2, 3, 4, 6	Plateau Live Oak (*Quercus fusiformis*) 2, 3, 4, 6	Southern Live Oak (*Quercus virginiana*) 1, 2, 3	Cedar Elm (*Ulmus crassifolia*) 1, 2, 3, 4, 6	Net-leaf Hackberry (*Celtis reticulata*) 1, 2, 4, 5, 6	Red Mulberry (*Morus rubra*) 1, 2, 3, 4, 5	American Holly (*Ilex opaca*) 1, 2	Yaupon (*Ilex vomitoria*) 1, 2, 3, 4	Elderberry (*Sambucus canadensis*) 1, 2, 4	Gregg Acacia (*Acacia greggii*) 2, 3, 4, 5, 6	Honey Mesquite (*Prosopis glandulosa*) 1-6	Fresno (Fraxinus *berlandieriana*) 2, 3, 4	White Ash (*Fraxinus americana*) 1, 2, 4	Black Cherry (*Prunus serotina v. serotina*) 1, 2	Cherry Laurel (*Prunus caroliniana*) 1, 2	Red Chokecherry (*Pyrus arbutifolia*) 1, 2	Chittam Wood (*Bumelia lanuginosa v. oblongifolia*) 1-6	Woolly-bucket Bumelia (*Bumelia lanuginosa*) 1-6	Western Soapberry (*Sapindus drummondii*) 1-6	Black Gum (*Nyssa sylvatica*) 1, 2	Pecan (*Carya illinoenensis*) 1, 2, 3, 4, 6
Northern Bobwhite			●	●	●	●					●		●	●		●	●	●	●					
White-winged Dove														●										
Inca Dove														●										
Common Ground Dove														●										
Ruby-throated Hummingbird																								
Black-chinned Hummingbird																								
Broad-tailed Hummingbird																								
Rufous Hummingbird																								
Red-headed Woodpecker		●	●	●	●	●	●		●			●					●	●						●
Golden-fronted Woodpecker			●	●	●	●	●																	●
Red-bellied Woodpecker		●		●	●	●	●		●			●					●	●						●
Downy Woodpecker		●	●	●	●	●	●																	●
Hairy Woodpecker		●	●			●	●										●	●						●
Northern Flicker		●	●	●	●	●	●			●							●	●						●
Blue Jay		●		●	●	●				●	●						●	●						●
Carolina Chickadee							●																	
Tufted Titmouse		●	●	●	●	●			●															
Eastern Bluebird	●							●		●	●	●										●	●	
Western Bluebird	●							●				●										●		
Mountain Bluebird	●							●			●	●										●		
Northern Mockingbird	●									●	●						●	●					●	
Curve-billed Thrasher	●																							
Northern Cardinal								●							●	●				●	●			
Pyrrhuloxia															●	●								
Painted Bunting																								
Harris's Sparrow																								
Orchard Oriole									●															
Bullock's Oriole												●												
Lesser Goldfinch																				●	●		●	
American Goldfinch																				●	●		●	

		Vines & Shrubs																Wildflowers & Weeds												Crop Plants		
Wax Myrtle (*Myrica cerifera*) 1, 2	Eastern Cottonwood (*Populus deltoides*) 1, 2, 3, 4, 6	Coral Berry (*Symphoricarpus orbiculata*) 1, 2, 4	Texas Honeysuckle (*Lonicera alba*) 1, 4, 5	Coral Bean (*Erythrina herbacea*) 1, 2, 4	Turk's Cap (*Malvaviscus drummondii*) 1, 2, 3, 4	Autumn Sage (*Salvia greggii*) 1, 3, 4, 5	Strawberry Bush (*Euonymus americanus*) 1, 2	Smooth Sumac (*Rhus glabra*) 1, 2	American Beautyberry (*Callicarpa americana*) 1, 2, 4	Trumpet Creeper (*Campsis radicans*) 1, 2, 3, 4	Pepper Vine (*Ampelopsis arborea*) 1, 2, 3, 4	Canyon Grape (*Vitis arizonica*) 5, 6	Heart-leaf Ampelopsis (*Ampelopsis cordata*) 1, 2, 3, 4, 6	Hiedra Creeper (*Parthenocissus vitacea*) 5, 6	Mustang Grape (*Vitis mustangensis*) 1, 2, 3, 4	Coral Honeysuckle (*Lonicera sempervirens*) 1, 2, 4	Carolina Moonseed (*Cocculus carolinus*) 1, 2, 4	Indian Paintbrush (*Castilleja indivisa*) 1, 2, 3, 4	Cedar Sage (*Salvia roemericna*) 4, 5	Mealy Sage (*Salvia farinacea*) 1, 3, 4, 5, 6	Scarlet Sage (*Salvia coccinea*) 1, 2, 3, 4	Standing Cypress (*Ipomopsis rubra*) 1, 3, 4, 6	Golden Wave (*Coreopsis tinctoria*) 1, 2, 3, 4	Greenthread (*Thelesperma filifolium*) 2, 3, 4, 6	Panicgrass (*Panicum ssp.*)	Bristlegrass (*Setaria ssp*)	Knotweed (*Polygonum ssp.*)	Pigweed (*Amaranthus ssp.*)	Doveweed (*Croton ssp.*)	Wheat (*Triticum aestivum*)	Oats (*Avena sativa*)	Corn (*Zea mays*)
●		●						●	●		●	●	●												●				●	●		●
																									●	●			●			●
																									●	●			●	●		
																									●	●			●	●		●
				●	●	●				●						●		●	●	●	●	●										
					●	●				●						●		●	●	●	●	●										
						●												●		●												
					●	●												●		●	●	●										
												●	●	●	●																	●
												●	●	●	●																	
												●	●		●																	
												●	●	●	●																	●
												●	●	●	●																	●
											●	●	●	●	●																	
												●			●																	●
		●	●				●		●					●			●															
			●											●			●															
		●	●											●			●															
●		●					●		●	●				●	●		●															
															●											●				●		●
●	●	●	●							●			●	●	●		●								●	●	●		●		●	●
												●													●	●		●	●			
																							●	●	●	●		●				
																									●	●	●			●	●	●
															●	●																
																●														●	●	
																												●				

A TEXAS BACKYARD

Mary Jackson's Treehouse Bed & Breakfast is in Henderson, Texas, 45 miles west of the Louisiana border. This is the Piney Woods Region of eastern Texas.

Attached to the bed-and-breakfast is an extraordinary backyard habitat certified by both the National Wildlife Federation's Backyard Wildlife Habitat Program and the Texas Wildscapes Backyard Habitat Program. The residential lot of some 45,000 square feet contains a section of hardwoods with a creek running through it. Since the 1970s, Mary has worked to develop this promising habitat, diversifying her plantings as her interest in wildlife gardening deepened. Roughly half the lot supports deciduous woodland and natural vegetation. She enhanced this area by adding brush piles and selectively clearing some portions; elsewhere, she let vegetation beneficial to wildlife grow unchecked. In the yard area, she added small trees, shrubs, and perennials beneficial to birds and butterflies, and established feeders, birdbaths, and nest boxes.

Among the trees on Mary's property are southern red oaks, white oaks, willow oaks, red maples, hickories, black walnuts, sweetgums, redbuds, dogwoods, and sassafras. Shrubs include holly of several species, privets, viburnums of several species, blueberries, and numerous others. A variety of flowers, some wild and others domestic, and ferns is also on the list.

All photos by Mary Jackson

A. The front of Mary Jackson's Treehouse Bed & Breakfast welcomes birders and other guests to her green oasis and wildlife wonderland in Henderson, Texas.

B. Wildlife-friendly landscaping along part of the building.

C. Major environmental damage inflicted on Hardy Branch, its floodplain, and adjacent woodland by a work crew from the City of Henderson, Texas. City workers trespassed on Mary Jackson's land—certified as a Backyard Wildlife Habitat by the National Wildlife Federation, and the Texas Wildscapes Backyard Habitat programs—without her knowledge or permission.

Additional backyard habitat enhancement using plants, bird feeders, and a low bird bath.

About half the property consists of woodland that's ideal wildlife habitat.

Mary is involved in several bird-related projects, including the annual Cornell Laboratory of Ornithology Project Feederwatch. More than forty bird species are on her backyard list, including Great Blue Herons, Ruby-throated Hummingbirds, four woodpecker species, Mourning and Inca Doves, Carolina Chickadees, White-breasted and Red-breasted Nuthatches, Brown Creepers, Carolina Wrens, Eastern Bluebirds, Gray Catbirds, Northern Mockingbirds, Summer Tanagers, Northern Cardinals, Rose-breasted Grosbeaks, Indigo Buntings, American Goldfinches, and Dark-eyed Juncos. Some wood warblers also have been sighted.

Habitat enhancement close to an area with high foot traffic.

A nest box installed near a wooded section of Mary Jackson's backyard habitat. Adding nest boxes helps replace loss of natural cavities needed by some birds.

(continued from page 140)

Many oak species grow in Texas. Blackjack oak *(Quercus marilandica)*, for example, is useful in regions 1, 4, and 6. Its acorns are eaten by various woodpeckers, Blue Jays, and Mourning Doves. This oak is also useful as a shade tree. Post oak *(Quercus stellata)*, suitable for use in all regions except 5, also provides food for Wild Turkeys, Mourning Doves, woodpeckers, and Blue Jays.

Carolina buckthorn *(Rhamnus caroliniana)* can be used in regions 1, 2, 3, and 4. It produces red fruit that turns to black, and is eaten by American Robins, Northern Mockingbirds, and Northern Cardinals.

Two dogwood species can be used in Texas. Flowering dogwood *(Cornus florida)* is best used in regions 1 and 2. Its red fruit is eaten by many birds, including Northern Flickers, Eastern Bluebirds, and Northern Cardinals. Rough-leaf dogwood *(Cornus drummondii)* can be used in regions 1 and 4. In autumn, clusters of its white fruit are eaten by Northern Bobwhites, Mourning and Inca Doves, and woodpeckers.

For a bird-food source useful throughout Texas, try sugarberry *(Celtis laevigata)*, which produces fruit eaten by bluebirds, American Robins, Northern Mockingbirds, Cedar Waxwings, and sparrows. On the other hand, if you want to feed Northern Bobwhites, try using bois d'arc *(Maclura pomifera)* in regions 1 and 2.

Deciduous holly *(Ilex decidua)* produces red fruit that's eaten by Northern Bobwhites, Blue Jays, Eastern and Mountain Bluebirds, American Robins, Northern Mockingbirds, and Cedar Waxwings. Use it in regions 1, 2, and 4.

Rusty blackhaw viburnum *(Viburnum rufidulum)* is a lovely tree with showy white flowers and dark purple fruit in autumn. It can be grown throughout Texas, except region 3, and produces fruits eaten by Eastern and Mountain Bluebirds, American Robins, Northern Mockingbirds, Cedar Waxwings, and Northern Cardinals.

Red buckeye *(Aeculus pavia)* has vivid red tubular flowers in early spring, which provide nectar for Ruby-throated, Black-chinned, and Rufous Hummingbirds. It prefers areas with mostly shade to full sun; plant it in regions 1, 2, and 4.

Huisache, or sweet acacia *(Acacia farnesiana)*, likes full sun and produces yellow-orange flowers in spring; its seed-filled beans ripen in autumn. It provides ideal nesting trees in backyard habitats for White-winged Doves in regions 1, 2, 3, 4, and 5.

Seeds of fragrant ash *(Fraxinus cuspidata)* are eaten by Northern Cardinals and Pyrrhuloxia; use it in backyard habitats in region 5. Green ash *(Fraxinus pensylvanica)*, however, is useful throughout the state except in region 5. Its fruit is eaten by Northern Cardinals and finches.

Various shrubs are also used in backyard habitat enhancement. The fruit of granjeno *(Celtis pallida)*, for example, useful in regions 2, 3, 4, and 5, is eaten by various wrens, Northern Mockingbirds, Pyrrhuloxia, and Northern Cardinals. Fragrant sumac *(Rhus aromatica)*, growing throughout Texas, produces fruit eaten by Northern Flickers and Northern Mockingbirds. The flowers of lantana *(Lantana horrida)*, suitable for regions 1, 2, 3, and 4, attract Ruby-throated, Black-chinned, and Rufous Hummingbirds. In addition, its fruit is eaten by Northern Cardinals, among other birds.

Some succulents also provide food for birds. Red yucca *(Hesperaloe parviflora)*, for example, can be used in regions 1, 3, 4, 5, and 6, where its nectar attracts Ruby-throated and Black-chinned Hummingbirds. The seeds and fruits of prickly-pear cactus *(Opuntia lindheimeri)*, found throughout Texas except region 1, provide food for many birds such as Wild Turkeys, Scaled and Gambel's Quail, Golden-fronted Woodpeckers, and Curve-billed Thrashers. Teddy-bear cholla *(Opuntia imbricata)* in regions 5 and 6 also provides especially safe nesting sites for birds such as Cactus Wrens and Greater Roadrunners.

There are at least a dozen species of vines that provide food for Texas birds. Cross vine *(Bignonia capreolata)*, for example, can be used in regions 1 and 2, where its flowers attract Ruby-throated Hummingbirds and an occasional migratory Rufous Hummingbird. In regions 5 or 6, try using thicket creeper *(Parthenocissus inserta)*, whose fruit attracts woodpeckers, Eastern and Western Kingbirds, bluebirds, Northern Mockingbirds, and Northern Cardinals. The fruit of Virginia creeper *(Parthenocissus quinquefolia)* is also useful in regions 1, 2, and 4 for attracting Northern Flickers, Great Crested Flycatchers, Tufted Titmice, Eastern Bluebirds, Northern Mockingbirds, Northern Cardinals, and numerous other species.

Finally, there are many other native wildflowers that also can be used to enhance Texas backyard habitats for birds. In regions 1, 2, and 4, for example, columbine *(Aquilegia canadensis)* flowers provide nectar for Ruby-throated, Black-chinned, Broad-tailed, and Rufous Hummingbirds. Similarly, cardinal flower *(Lobelia cardinalis)* can be used throughout Texas to attract hummingbirds. In region 5, Havard penstemon *(Penstemon havardii)* attracts hummingbirds, including Ruby-throated, Black-chinned, Broad-tailed, and Rufous. In comparison, Indian blanket *(Gaillardia pulchella)* and red gaillardia *(Gaillardia amblyodon)* can be used throughout Texas to produce nectar eaten by Ruby-throated, Black-chinned, Broad-tailed, and Rufous Hummingbirds, and seeds eaten by Painted Buntings.

American Southwest

The remarkable landscape of the American Southwest—Arizona, Nevada, New Mexico, and Utah—includes high mountain "islands" (many over 10,000 feet) covered with pine forests, canyons, deserts (i.e., Chihuahua, Great Basin, Mojave, and Sonora), foothills, grasslands, and wetlands. The Southwest's lowlands typically have elevations from 4,500 to 6,200 feet.

Most native trees, shrubs, cacti and other succulents, wildflowers, and other plants in the American Southwest are specialized and adapted to desert climates or high mountain elevations. Desert habitat species discussed here are suitable for attracting birds either by providing food (fruit and seeds) or favorable nesting sites.

Desert willow *(Chilopsis linearis)*, for example, provides limited shade, and has whitish-lavender flowers attractive to Black-chinned, Costa's, and Broad-tailed Hummingbirds, which feed on its nectar during late spring and summer. White-winged Doves also eat the seeds.

Blue paloverde *(Cercidium floridum)*, which grows on desert grasslands and lower desert slopes, has thorny twigs and lovely yellow flowers that bloom in late

(continued on page 150)

SOUTHWEST	Trees						Vines & Shrubs					Wildflowers & Weeds						
Birds	Engelmann Spruce (*Picea engelmannii*)	Blue Spruce (*Picea pungens*)	Ponderosa Pine (*Pinus ponderosa*)	Douglas Fir (*Pseudotsuga menziesii*)	Arizona White Oak (*Quercus arizonica*)	Gambel's Oak (*Quercus gambelii*)	Mountain Snowberry (*Symphoriocarpos oreophilus*)	Desert Lavender (*Hyptis emoryi*)	Tree Tobacco (*Nicotiana glauca*)	Foothill Paloverde (*Cercidium microphyllum*)	Desert Mistletoe (*Phoradendron californicum*)	Scarlet Larkspur (*Delphinium cardinale*)	Sunflower (*Helianthus ssp.*)	Ocotillo (*Fouquieria splendens*)	Condalias (*Condalia ssp.*)	Lycium (*Lycium ssp.*)	Panicgrass (*Panicum ssp.*)	Bristlegrass (*Setaria ssp.*)
Gambel's Quail																		●
Band-tailed Pigeon	●	●	●	●	●	●												
White-winged Dove					●	●							●		●	●		
Inca Dove																		
Black-chinned Hummingbird								●	●	●		●						
Anna's Hummingbird								●	●									
Costa's Hummingbird								●						●				
Broad-tailed Hummingbird												●						
Lewis's Woodpecker			●															
Acorn Woodpecker					●	●												
Gila Woodpecker											●							
Gilded Flicker																		
Steller's Jay			●		●	●												
Western Scrub-Jay					●	●												
Black-billed Magpie			●				●											
Mountain Chickadee			●			●												
Plain Titmouse					●	●												
Bushtit																		
Pygmy Nuthatch			●	●														
Curve-billed Thrasher															●			●
Pyrrhuloxia													●				●	●
Hooded Oriole																		
Bullock's Oriole															●			
Red Crossbill	●	●	●	●														
Lesser Goldfinch																		

											Cultivated Crop Plants & Misc.					
Russian Thistle (*Salsola kali*)	Pigweed (*Amaranthus ssp.*)	Spiderling (*Boerhaavia ssp.*)	Tansy Mustard (*Descurainia ssp.*)	Lupine (*Lupinus ssp*)	Deer Vetch (*Lotus ssp.*)	Filaree (*Erodium ssp.*)	Doveweed (*Croton ssp.*)	Spurge (*Euphorbia ssp.*)	Golden Crownbeard (*Verbesina encelioides*)	Miscellaneous Weed Seeds	Wheat (*Triticum aestivum*)	Oats (*Avena sativa*)	Corn (*Zea mays*)	Alfalfa (*Medicago sativa*)	Leaf Galls	Unidentified Flower Nectar
✿		✿	✿	✿	✿	✿		✿	✿					🌾		
											🌾					
							✿				🌾		🌾			
										✿	🌾					
												🌾	🌾			
													🌾			
													🌾			
											🌾		🌾			
											🌾		🌾			
												🌾				
															🌾	
											🌾		🌾			
	✿	✿					✿									
																🌾
										✿						

RARE HUMMINGBIRDS OF ARIZONA

Seventeen hummingbird species visit Arizona, including some rare species. The locations mentioned here are the best-known sites for finding some of the rarer hummingbirds.

Look for Berylline Hummingbirds in wooded canyons in the southeast. A Cinnamon Hummingbird was reported in 1992 at Patagonia, near Nogales. The few Lucifer Hummingbirds that visit Arizona are best seen either in Lower Cave Creek Canyon in the Chiricahua Mountains, or Joe's Canyon Trail (southern side) in the Coronado National Memorial in the Huachuca Mountains.

Look for Plain-capped Starthroats in scrub, foothills, and arid lowlands southward from Sonora and Nogales. White-eared Hummingbirds typically are seen in Ramsey Canyon in the Huachuca Mountains. Allen's Hummingbird, however, is more unusual in Arizona than many birders realize because of the difficulty of sorting out female Allen's and female Rufous Hummingbirds.

Violet-crowned Hummingbirds occur in southeastern Arizona's canyons and near Patagonia, along Sonoita Creek, on the southernside of the Santa Rita Mountains. Some are also reported in the Huachuca Mountains and in Cave Creek Canyon in the Chiricahua Mountains.

If you live near any of these locations, you may want to carefully check hummingbirds visiting your backyard habitat in the event that one of those mentioned is among them.

(continued from page 147)

March and April. Yellow paloverde *(Cercidium microphyllum)* has pale yellow flowers that blossom in April and May; it's associated with saguaro cactus. Both paloverdes provide nesting sites and insect food for Phainopeplas, hummingbirds, Verdins, Cactus Wrens, Northern Mockingbirds, and thrashers; quail and doves also eat their seeds.

Two species of mesquite are also useful for attracting birds: honey mesquite *(Prosopis glandulosa)* and velvet mesquite *(Prosopis velutina)*. White-winged, Common, and Inca Doves, along with Verdins, Ash-throated Flycatchers, Curve-billed Thrashers, Phainopeplas, and others, build nests in these trees or use them for shelter. Their seeds and pods are consumed by Gambel's Quail, doves, and Pyrrhuloxia.

Mexican elderberry *(Sambucus mexicana)*, a small evergreen tree, is also used as nesting sites by Northern Mockingbirds and vireos; its blue fruit is eaten by Pyrrhuloxia and a dozen other birds.

Arizona, or desert, ironwood *(Olneya tesota)* is an evergreen with spines. It produces purple flowers that bloom from May to June. Doves and quail, Verdins, and Cactus Wrens nest in these trees. A parasitic mistletoe, which produces reddish berries that Phainopepla eat, grows on ironwood tree branches. The bird helps spread the parasite to other trees, creating an interesting relationship between two or more plant species and birds.

Various shrubs are also included in the mix of vegetation used in backyard desert habitats. Gregg catclaw *(Acacia greggii)*, for example, provides nesting sites for Verdins, and its seeds are eaten by quail and doves. However, its sharp, hooked

POISON IVY

Nobody selects poison ivy (Rhus radicans), *a vine found across most of the United States and southern Canada, to enhance backyard habitats. Nevertheless, poison ivy produces fruit that is an important winter food for many birds and other wildlife. Birds that eat poison ivy include California Quail, Yellow-billed Magpies, Chestnut-backed Chickadees, Carolina Wrens, Eastern Bluebirds, and Purple Finches. If you find poison ivy on your property, you might consider leaving a small amount intact as part of the diversity of the habitat. In any case, people should avoid contact with the irritating ivy.*

Poison-ivy fruit. Most birders don't like this plant growing in their backyard habitats. Nevertheless, dozens of backyard birds—including Northern Flickers, Downy Woodpeckers, Gray Catbirds, and California Thrashers—relish eating poison-ivy fruit.

spines can rip clothing and inflict wounds on people's skin. Desert hackberry *(Celtis pallida)* is much favored by Band-tailed Pigeons and Bullock's Orioles for its orange fruit in summer and early autumn. Quail also find the dense shrub an excellent place in which to build their nests.

Quail, doves, sparrows, towhees, and finches also feed on seeds and use shelter provided by big saltbush *(Atriplex lentiformis)*, which sometimes can grow to a height of 12 feet. Gnatcatchers and Verdin use parts of the flowers of desert lavender *(Hyptis emoryi)* as a nest lining. Wolfberry *(Lycium ssp.)* flowers contain nectar and tiny insects on which hummingbirds feed, its fruit is eaten by other birds, and it provides protective shelter for various wildlife. Hummingbirds also feed on nectar and tiny insects in the flowers of ocotillo *(Fouquieria splendens)*. Quail and doves eat the seeds of hopbush *(Dodonaea viscosa)*.

Birders can also use lower-growing shrubs to enhance their backyard habitats. Sparrows and finches, for example, eat the seeds of brittlebush *(Encelia farinosa)*; quail and doves eat fairy duster *(Calliandra eriophylla)* seeds. Similarly, quail, doves, towhees, and finches eat four-wing saltbush *(Atriplex canescens)* seeds. The flowers of desert honeysuckle *(Justicia californica)* also attract hummingbirds.

Cacti and other succulents are strikingly beautiful—and a major part of the American Southwest landscape. They provide food and shelter for many birds and other wildlife.

The Joshua tree *(Yucca brevifolia)*, a Mojave Desert indicator species, is the largest of the yuccas. It's used by Northern Flickers and two dozen other bird species.

HELP PROTECT NATIVE CACTI AND SUCCULENTS

Cacti used for habitat enhancement projects—or any other purposes—must not be taken from the wild. If the source of a cactus is unclear, insist on documentation proving that the specimens are not part of illegal trafficking of these plants. Don't buy the plant without documentation.

To determine which cacti and succulents are federally endangered or threatened, check the list on the U.S. Fish and Wildlife Service's website (see appendix 2); numerous native cacti and succulents are on it.

Cholla *(Opuntia ssp.)* is a large, branching cactus in which Cactus Wrens, Verdins, and thrashers find safety and places to nest. Specimens of native species (not removed from the wild) are desirable for use in backyard desert habitats. Smaller *Opuntia* cacti are called prickly pears. Their flat pads support colorful flowers and produce fruits eaten by Gilded Flickers, Curve-billed Thrashers, Pyrrhuloxia, and Scott's Orioles; the last also takes nectar from cacti.

The giant saguaro *(Carnegiea gigantea)* produces the state flower of Arizona. It grows to 35 feet high—a wonderful part of any enhanced backyard habitat lucky enough to have one. Gila Woodpeckers and Gilded Flickers dig nesting holes in the trunk or tops of branches. When woodpeckers move out, Elf Owls (North America's smallest owl), flycatchers, and Cactus Wrens move in and occupy them. Gambel's Quail, White-winged Doves, Ladder-backed Woodpeckers, Hooded Orioles, and House Finches also relish eating giant saguaro fruits or seeds.

Wildflowers also can enhance backyard habitats for birds. Quail and doves, for example, eat the seeds of tufted evening primrose *(Oenothera caespitosa)* and poppies *(Eschscholzia ssp.)*. Quail, doves, finches, and sparrows also eat the seeds of globe mallow *(Sphaeralcea ambigua)* and blackfoot daisy *(Melampodium leucanthum)*. As elsewhere in the West, nectar and tiny insects in the flowers of various red and pink penstemons *(Penstemon ssp.)* also attract hummingbirds, which makes these wildflowers excellent additions to backyard habitats.

Pacific Northwest

Mention the Pacific Northwest—Washington, Oregon, and southern British Columbia—and naturalists think of old growth, temperate rain forests, the spectacular Cascades forming the spine of the region, towering volcanic peaks, great rivers like the Columbia, and the wildly rugged and beautiful Pacific Ocean coastline. It's an area rich in birds, other wildlife, complex geology, habitats, wildflowers, and wonderful trees with great personalities.

Western white pine *(Pinus monticola)* is a lovely tree for use in a backyard habitat. Its seeds are eaten by a variety of birds, including Mountain and Chestnut-backed Chickadees, Red Crossbills, and Pine Grosbeaks—all welcome species.

Two hemlock species, Western *(Tsuga heterophylla)* and Mountain *(Tsuga mertensiana)*, also provide food for Blue Grouse and Red Crossbills. Western red cedar *(Thuja plicata)*, found in moist lowland to mid-elevation areas, produces fruit eaten by Mountain Quail, Band-tailed Pigeons, Clark's Nutcrackers, and Evening Grosbeaks. In comparison, common juniper *(Juniperus communis)* and

AN OREGON BACKYARD

The Portland backyard of Denis and Eve Heidtmann has undergone a number of evolutions. At one time, the land was covered with a Douglas fir forest, and then later by a walnut orchard, which was subsequently converted to housing. Fortunately, many old Douglas fir trees survived in their neighborhood, adding beauty and charm to the area.

In 1985, Denis and Eve resolved to make part of their property wildlife-friendly. They replaced a considerable amount of lawn with native trees and shrubs, and added a pond and butterfly garden. The net effect was an open woodland habitat.

The Heidtmann's backyard habitat includes native Douglas fir, mountain hemlock, vine maple, shore pine (a variety of lodgepole pine), and some introduced species.

Eve Heidtmann

Jerry Pava

A. The Portland, Oregon, home of Denis and Eve Heidtmann, and some of its surrounding wildlife friendly habitat.

B. The pond is a key element in the Heidtmann's backyard habitat.

(continued on next page)

(continued from previous page)

Native shrubs in the habitat's floral diversity include Oregon grape, evergreen huckleberry, blue elderberry, Pacific red elderberry, common snowberry, mock orange, ocean spray, and Indian plum. Ferns, groundcovers, and wildflowers are also included in appropriate locations.

The Heidtmanns also installed feeders and constructed a pond in the yard, which Mallards use as a "courtship pond."

More than fifty bird species visit the Heidtmann backyard habitat. Among the larger and more colorful birds on their backyard list are Great Blue Heron and Wood Duck. A Great Horned Owl was present for a time. Smaller birds include Vaux's Swifts, Anna's and Rufous Hummingbirds, Red-breasted Sapsuckers, Western Flycatchers, Western Scrub Jays, Chestnut-backed Chickadees, Bewick's Wrens, Golden-crowned Kinglets, Swainson's Thrushes, Black-headed and Evening Grosbeaks, House Finches, Pine Siskins, and a number of warblers and sparrows.

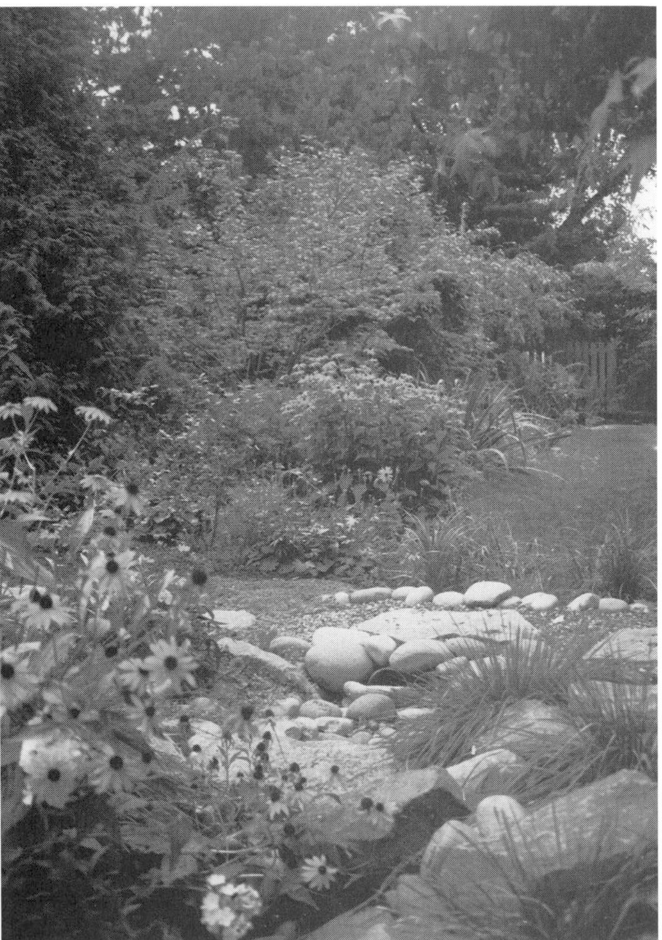

A lovely view from the rocky streambed to a grassy swale in the Heidtmanns' beautifully enhanced backyard habitat.

Eve Heidtmann

western juniper *(Juniperus occidentalis)* trees produce fruits eaten by Clark's Nutcrackers and Evening Grosbeaks.

Dwarf mistletoes *(Arceuthobium ssp.)* are western conifer parasites. If they appear on backyard conifers, keep them; their fruits are eaten by Blue Grouse, Mountain Bluebirds, Hermit Thrushes, American Robins, and Cedar Waxwings.

Three alder species—red *(Alnus rubra)* west of the Cascades, white *(Alnus rhombifolia)* east of the Cascades, and sitka *(Alnus viridis)* in mid-elevation to subalpine forests and valleys—also produce seeds eaten by Pine Siskins and Lesser and American Goldfinches.

Relatively few oak species live in the Pacific Northwest, but acorns from Oregon white oak *(Quercus garryana)* are eaten by Lewis's and Acorn Woodpeckers, Northern Flickers, Steller's and Western Scrub Jays, and Mountain Chickadees.

Several maple species—big leaf *(Acer macrophyllum)*, vine *(Acer circinatum)*, Douglas *(Acer glabrum var. douglasii)*, and Rocky Mountain *(Acer glabrum)*—are also residents of the Pacific Northwest. Purple Finches and Evening Grosbeaks eat their buds, flowers, and seeds.

Cascara buckthorn *(Rhamnus purshiana)*, a small tree or large shrub, likewise produces fruit (poisonous to people) eaten by Band-tailed Pigeons, Pileated Woodpeckers, American Robins, Varied Thrushes, and Brown Thrashers.

Oregon ash *(Fraxinus latifolia)*, which grows west of the Cascades, has winged seeds eaten by Pine Grosbeaks. Quaking aspen *(Populus tremuloides)*, found east of the Cascades, has buds and catkins eaten by Blue Grouse.

Among shrubs, use Pacific wax myrtle, or bayberry *(Myrica californica)*, in coastal areas and spruce forests. Chestnut-backed Chickadees, Northern Flickers, Western Bluebirds, Mountain Bluebirds, American Robins, and Varied Thrushes eat its fruit.

Western serviceberry *(Amelanchier alnifolia)*, found in forest clearings and rocky slopes, produces fruit eaten by Blue Grouse, Lewis's Woodpeckers, Black-billed Magpies, Townsend's Solitaires, Gray Catbirds, and Evening Grosbeaks.

Red-osier *(Cornus stolonifera)* and Pacific dogwood *(Cornus nuttallii)* also can be used to enhance backyard habitats. Their fruits are eaten by Band-tailed Pigeons, Lewis's Woodpeckers, and Pine and Evening Grosbeaks.

Pacific madrone *(Arbutus menziesii)*, appearing west of the Cascades on coastal ranges, produces fruits eaten by Mountain Quail, Varied Thrushes, Purple Finches, Cassin's Finches, and House Finches.

Common snowberry *(Symphoricarpos albus)*, a shrub growing about 5 feet high, produces white fruits eaten by Sharp-tailed Grouse, Black-billed Magpies, American Robins, Varied Thrushes, and Pine and Evening Grosbeaks. Spruce Grouse in British Columbia also eat these fruits.

(continued on page 158)

A BRIEF PACIFIC DOGWOOD HISTORY

This fine dogwood, Cornus nuttallii, *was named by American artist and ornithologist John James Audubon (1780–1851) in honor of Thomas Nuttall (1786–1859), a British-American ornithologist and botanist,who first discovered the species*

NORTHWEST	Trees									Shrubs						
Birds	Lodgepole Pine (*Pinus contorta*)	Ponderosa Pine (*Pinus ponderosa*)	Douglas Fir (*Pseudotsuga mezziesii*)	Grand Fir (*Abies grandis*)	Pacific Silver Fir (*Abies amabilis*)	Noble Fir (*Abies procera*)	Incense Cedar (*Calocedrus decurrens*)	Port Orford Cedar (*Chamaecyparis lawsoniana*)	Bitter Cherry (*Prunus emarginata*)	Sitka Mountain Ash (*Sorbus sitchensis*)	Cascades Blueberry (*Vaccinium deliciosum*)	Blue Elderberry (*Sambucus mexicana*)	Pacific Red Elderberry (*Sambucus racemosa*) [fruits poisonous to people]	Trailing Blackberry (*Rubus ursinus*)	Raspberry (*Rubus ssp.*)	Curl-leaf Mountain Mahogany (*Cerocarpus ledifolius*)
Blue Grouse			●	●	●	●					●					●
California Quail																
Band-tailed Pigeon									●		●	●	●			
Mourning Dove																
Black-chinned Hummingbird																
Calliope Hummingbird																
Rufous Hummingbird																
Lewis's Woodpecker	●	●							●			●	●			
Acorn Woodpecker												●	●			
Pileated Woodpecker									●			●	●			
Steller's Jay									●			●	●		●	
Western Scrub Jay									●			●	●			
Black-billed Magpie	●	●										●	●			
Mountain Chickadee	●	●														
Chestnut-backed Chickadee	●	●														
Bushtit																
Pygmy Nuthatch	●	●	●	●	●	●										
Western Bluebird													●	●		
Mountain Bluebird												●	●			
Cedar Waxwing									●	●		●				
Black-headed Grosbeak									●				●		●	
White-crowned Sparrow												●	●	●		
Gray-crowned Rosy-Finch	●	●										●				
Purple Finch									●							
Evening Grosbeak		●					●	●	●							

Wildflowers & Weeds															Cultivated Crop Plants & Misc.					
Penstemon (*Penstemon ssp.*)	Giant Red Paintbrush (*Castilleja miniata*)	Pink Monkey Flower (*Mimulus lewisii*)	Mayweed (*Anthemis cotula*)	Common Sunflower (*Helianthus annuus*)	Salal (*Gaultheria shallon*)	Eriogonus (*Eriogonum ssp.*)6	Knotweed (*Polygonum sp.*)	Pigweed (*Amaranthus sp.*)	Redmaids (*Calandrinia caulescens*)	Miners Lettuce (*Montia perfoliata*)	Common Chickweed (*Stellaria media*)	Peppergrass (*Lepidium ssp.*)	Clover (*Trifolium ssp.*)	Fiddleneck (*Amsinckia sp.*)	Sunflower (*Helianthus sp.*)	Wheat (*Triticum sp.*)	Oats (*Avena sp.*)	Corn (*Zea mays*)	Apple (*Malus pumila*)	Leaf Galls
					✿	✿							✿							
								✿	✿		✿		✿	✿			✿			
					✿											✿	✿			
				✿			✿	✿	✿	✿	✿			✿	✿	✿				
✿	✿	✿																		
✿	✿	✿																		
✿	✿	✿																		
																		✿	✿	
																✿		✿		
																✿	✿	✿		
																	✿	✿		
																✿		✿		
																			✿	
																				✿
													✿							
																✿	✿			
			✿	✿				✿		✿	✿						✿			
✿							✿					✿				✿	✿			

(continued from page 155)

Thimbleberry *(Rubus parviflorus)*, a blackberry species, yields fruit eaten by Blue Grouse, Band-tailed Pigeons, Mountain and Chestnut-backed Chickadees, and Sage Thrashers.

Wildflowers are also important parts of enhanced backyard habitats. To attract Black-chinned, Calliope, and Rufous Hummingbirds, among others, try planting species with red flowers, such as red columbine *(Aquilegia formosa)* in forest openings, red fireweed *(Epilobium angustifolium)* in cleared areas, and great hedge nettle *(Stachys cooleyae)* as high as midlevel mountain elevations.

Lovely skyrocket or scarlet gilia *(Ipomopsis aggregata)* also can be used to attract hummingbirds on dry rocky slopes up to sub-alpine elevations, and small-flowered paintbrush *(Castilleja parviflora)* is a good selection for the Olympic Mountains and from Three Sisters north in the Cascades.

BRITISH COLUMBIA

Backyard birdwatchers in British Columbia have available to them Naturescape British Columbia, a very helpful program that offers excellent publications on backyard enhancement. Following are some examples of native trees, shrubs, and wildflowers recommended in the Naturescape literature for enhancing a backyard in British Columbia.

Western white pine (Pinus monticola) *seeds are eaten by Mountain and Chestnut-backed Chickadees, Red Crossbills, and Pine Grosbeaks; Douglas-fir* (Pseudotsuga menziesii) *seeds are eaten by Winter Wrens and Red Crossbills. Common Redpolls, Pine Siskins, American Goldfinches, and Evening Grosbeaks eat western red cedar* (Thuja plicata) *seeds. Dwarf mistletoes* (Arceuthobium ssp.) *are conifer parasites whose fruits are eaten by Blue Grouse, Mountain Bluebirds, Hermit Thrushes, American Robins, and Cedar Waxwings.*

Alder (Alnus ssp.) *seeds are eaten by American Goldfinches, Pine Siskins, and Common Redpolls. Pacific dogwood* (Cornus nuttallii) *is another useful yard-enhancement tree whose fruit is eaten by Pileated Woodpeckers, Hermit Thrushes, and Cedar Waxwings.*

Among shrubs, red-osier dogwood (Cornus stolonifera) *fruit provides food for Cedar Waxwings and Evening Grosbeaks. Mountain ash* (Sorbus ssp.) *fruit also provides food for Cedar Waxwings. The fruits of blackberry* (Rubus ssp.), *red raspberry* (Rubus idaeus), *and elderberry* (Sambucus canadensis) *are also eaten by birds and other wildlife.*

The flowers of various shrubs, as well as wildflowers, attract Black-chinned, Anna's, Calliope, and Rufous Hummingbirds, which feed on their nectar and tiny insects. Examples include black twinberry (Lonicera involucrata), *wild azalea* (Rhododendron canescens), *red-flowering currant, or gooseberry* (Ribes sanguineum), *western columbine* (Aquilgia formosa), *cardinal penstemon* (Penstemon cardinalis), *and fireweed* (Epilobium angustifolium). *For more information about Naturescape British Columbia, see appendix 2.*

ALBERTA

In Alberta, a backyard habitat enhancement program called Naturescape Alberta encourages residents of the province to make their backyards more friendly to birds by adding native trees, shrubs, and wildflowers that produce seeds and fruit eaten by the birds. The program offers a guide that details ways in which residents can make their property more wildlife-friendly. Following are some examples of native vegetation that can be used.

The seeds of conifers such as black spruce (Picea mariana) *are eaten in winter by Blue Grouse, Boreal Chickadees, Red Crossbills, and Pine Siskins.*

Deciduous trees that provide food for birds include mountain alder (Alnus tenuifolia), *whose seeds are consumed by Common and Hoary Redpolls, Pine Siskins, and American Goldfinches. Seeds of birches* (Betula ssp.) *are eaten by Black-capped Chickadees and Common Redpolls.*

Several shrubs can be planted for the benefit of birds. Western serviceberry (Amelanchier alnifolia) *fruit is eaten by Townsend's Solitaires, American Robins, Western Tanagers, and Evening Grosbeaks. Chokecherry* (Prunus virginiana) *fruit is consumed by American Robins and Evening Grosbeaks. Cedar Waxwings and Evening Grosbeaks eat red-osier dogwood* (Cornus stolonifera) *fruit; mountain ash* (Sorbus ssp.) *fruit is food for American Robins and Cedar Waxwings.*

Various flowers are also helpful in providing food for birds. Ruby-throated, Calliope, and Rufous Hummingbirds, for example, obtain nectar and tiny insects from iris (Iris ssp.), *delphinium* (Delphinium ssp.), *phlox* (Phlox ssp.) *and wild geranium* (Geranium ssp.). *Common thistle* (Cirsium flodmanii) *seeds are eaten by American Goldfinches and various sparrows. For more information about Naturescape Alberta, see appendix 2.*

California

California, like Florida and Texas, is a large state with a complex ecology that warrants separate treatment.

Fremont cottonwood *(Populus fremontii)* is a widespread low-elevation species in California that is a good species for use in backyard habitats, especially when placed in groups. The spring catkins produce food for Cedar Waxwings and insects on the trees are eaten by wood warblers. Vireos, tanagers, and orioles also nest in these cottonwoods.

Common along California's foothills and coast, live oak *(Quercus virginiana)* can be used in full sun in backyard habitats with well-drained soils. Among birds that eat its acorns are Acorn Woodpeckers, Western Scrub Jays, Steller's Jays, and Northern Flickers.

White alder *(Alnus rhombifolia)* also can be used in backyard habitat enhancement efforts. It grows naturally in wet areas at elevations below 5,000 feet in

(continued on page 162)

CALIFORNIA / **Birds**	Western White Pine (*Pinus monticola*)	Sugar Pine (*Pinus lambertiana*)	Lodgepole Pine (*Pinus contorta*)	Ponderosa Pine (*Pinus ponderosa*)	Jeffrey Pine (*Pinus jeffreyi*)	Coulter Pine (*Pinus coulteri*)	Digger Pine (*Pinus sabiniana*)	Douglas Fir (*Pseudotsuga menziesii*)	California Walnut (*Juglans californica*)	Canyon Oak (*Quercus chrysolepis*)	Blue Oak (*Quercus douglasii*)	Oregon White Oak (*Quercus garryana*)	California Black Oak (*Quercus kelloggii*)	California Pepper Tree (*Schinus molle*)	Pacific Dogwood (*Cornus nuttallii*)	Red-osier Dogwood (*Cornus stolonifera*)	Pacific Red Elderberry (*Sambucus racemosa*)	Bitter Cherry (*Prunus emarginata*)	Trailing Blackberry (*Rubus ursinus*)	Pacific Wax Myrtle (*Myrica californica*)
California Quail										●	●	●	●							
Band-tailed Pigeon	●	●	●	●	●	●	●			●	●	●	●			●	●	●		
Costa's Hummingbird																				
Calliope Hummingbird																				
Anna's Hummingbird																				
Allen's Hummingbird																				
Lewis's Woodpecker	●	●	●	●	●	●	●								●	●	●	●		
Acorn Woodpecker									●	●	●	●	●				●			
Steller's Jay	●	●	●	●	●	●	●			●	●	●	●		●	●	●	●		
Western Scrub-Jay	●	●	●	●	●	●	●			●	●	●	●				●			
Yellow-billed Magpie										●	●	●	●							
Mountain Chickadee	●	●	●	●	●	●	●			●	●	●	●							
Chestnut-backed Chickadee	●	●	●	●	●	●	●													●
Plain Titmouse	●	●	●	●	●	●	●		●	●	●	●	●					●		
Bushtit																				
Pygmy Nuthatch	●	●	●	●	●	●	●	●												
Western Bluebird														●			●		●	
Mountain Bluebird																	●			
California Thrasher										●	●	●	●				●			
Black-headed Grosbeak																	●			
Lark Sparrow																				
White-crowned Sparrow																	●		●	
Hooded Oriole																	●			
House Finch	●	●	●	●	●	●	●										●			
Lesser Goldfinch																				

Trees

Wildflowers & Weeds																				Cultivated Crop Plants & Miscellaneous									
Yellow Bush Lupine (*Lupinus arboreus*)	California False Lupine (*Thermopsis macrophylla*)	Red Columbine (*Aquilegia formosa*)	California Fuchsia (*Epilobium canum*)	Scarlet Fritillary (*Fritillaria recurva*)	Scarlet Gilia (*Ipomopsis aggregata*)	Bromegrass (*Bromus ssp.*)	Ryegrass (*Lolium ssp.*)	Knotweed (*Polygonum ssp.*)	Pigweed (*Amaranthus ssp.*)	Common Chickweed (*Stellaria media*)	Mustard (*Brassica ssp.*)	Bur Clover (*Medicago ssp.*)	Clover (*Trifolium ssp.*)	Deer Vetch (*Lotus ssp.*)	Common Filaree (*Erodium cicutarium*)	Turkey Mullein (*Eremocarpus setigerus*)	Common Tarweed (*Madia elegans*)	Spikeweed (*Hemizonia pungens*)	Mayweed (*Anthemis cotula*)	Wheat (*Triticum sp.*)	Barley (*Hordeum vulgare*)	Oats (*Avena sp.*)	Fig (*Ficus carica*)	Apple (*Malus pumila*)	Cherry (*Prunus ssp.*)	Plum (*Prunus ssp.*)	Almond (*Prunus amygdalus*)	Grape (*Vitis ssp.*)	Leaf Galls
•	•					•	•		•			•	•	•	•	•					•	•							
																				•		•							
		•	•	•	•																								
		•	•	•	•																								
		•	•	•	•																								
		•	•	•	•																								
																								•					
																				•			•				•		
																				•	•	•							
																						•			•	•			
																				•	•	•	•					•	
																								•					
																						•		•					
																													•
											•		•																
																							•					•	
																												•	
														•					•		•	•		•				
								•	•	•					•	•	•	•		•		•							
								•	•	•					•		•	•	•										
																							•						
								•	•	•	•				•	•	•	•					•	•					
									•							•	•	•											

(continued from page 159)
ecological association with chaparral and ponderosa pine in foothills. When used in backyard habitats, it becomes a shade tree. Its seeds are eaten by Pine Siskins, Purple Finches, and related seed-eaters. Wood warblers use the tree for protective cover, nesting sites, and roosting.

Coyote willow *(Salix exigua)* prefers stream and river courses in desert conditions. It can be used in moist soils in backyard habitats. The catkins contain small seeds eaten by Nuttall's and Downy Woodpeckers, Western Kingbirds, Cassin's Kingbird, and Cassin's Finches.

A variety of shrubs can be used in California backyard habitats. Quailbush *(Atriplex lentiformis)* likes dry desert conditions and full sun. It produces protective cover for quails and nesting sites for other birds. Several dozen species of birds, including doves, Black Phoebes, Say's Phoebes, and gnatcatchers, eat its fruit.

The lovely purple and lavender flowers of desert willow *(Chilopsis linearis)* are very attractive to hummingbirds, which secure nectar and tiny insects in these flowers. Put desert willow in full sun and open areas. Hummingbirds are also attracted to the orange blossoms of Mexican honeysuckle *(Justicia spicigera)*, which blooms throughout the year. Several related species, available at local nurseries, are also visited by hummingbirds.

Toyon *(Heteromeles arbutifolia)*, a lovely native shrub that lives along coastal California, produces orange-red fruits during autumn that are eaten by woodpeckers, Northern Mockingbirds, Western Bluebirds, Hermit Thrushes, American Robins, Cedar Waxwings, and finches. When transplanting this shrub, which sometimes can be difficult, carefully follow recommendations of nursery staff who know local horticultural conditions.

Golden currant *(Ribes aureum)* produces fruits eaten by Band-tailed Pigeons, Lewis's Woodpeckers, Western Scrub Jays, Gray Catbirds, Sage Thrashers, Hermit Thrushes, Swainson's Thrushes, Townsend's Solitaires, Cedar Waxwings, and Black-headed Grosbeaks.

Mexican elderberry *(Sambucus mexicana)* produces white flowers that bloom from April to September. Its fruits—purple to blue-black to silvery—are eaten by Band-tailed Pigeons, Northern Flickers and other woodpeckers, Steller's Jays, Cactus Wrens, Mountain Bluebirds, American Robins, Northern Mockingbirds, Phainopeplas, Cedar Waxwings, Western Tanagers, Black-headed Grosbeaks, and House Finches.

When groundwater is available, mesquite *(Prosopis velutina)* provides protective cover, nesting sites, and food for many birds in desert habitats below 5,000 feet. These birds include Gambel's Quail, White-winged Doves, Mourning Doves, Inca Doves, Common Ground Doves, hummingbirds (Black-chinned, Costa's, Broad-tailed), Say's Phoebes, Black Phoebes, Song Sparrows, Black-throated Sparrows, and Cassin's Finches.

Wild strawberry *(Fragaria vesca californica)* can be used as ground cover in moist, shaded locations at elevations ranging from the foothills to mountain zones below 7,000 feet. California Quail, Mountain Quail, Western Scrub Jays, American Robins, Northern Mockingbirds, Song Sparrows, Black-headed Grosbeaks, and Pine Grosbeaks eat its fruit.

6 Bird Feeders

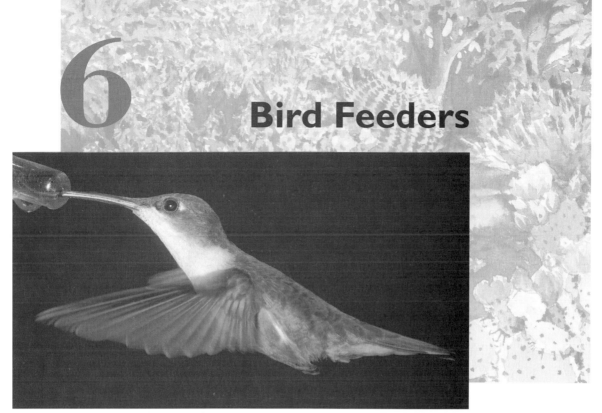

A female Ruby-throated Hummingbird feeding on sugar water at a hummingbird feeder.

One of the most enjoyable and popular backyard birdwatching activities is maintaining bird feeders. Why do people establish bird-feeding stations? It's delightful to watch a Northern Cardinal feeding on sunflower seeds against a cold January background of white snow. It's just as delightful to watch a beautifully dressed Red-bellied Woodpecker feeding on suet. And it's both delightful and nearly comical to watch a White-breasted Nuthatch walk headfirst down the trunk of a tree, fly to a tube or tray feeder, check the items on the menu—and then eat sunflower seeds.

Then there are hummingbirds. What extraordinary birds, displaying some of the most spectacular and colorful feathers in the bird world. They are avian helicopters that hover with ease in front of a hummingbird feeder or red cardinal flower, then zip forward or backward, sometimes within a foot of the people watching their remarkable performance. Hummingbirds are tiny birds but they have the boldness of giants!

When birders establish backyard feeders, they are approximating the foods and simulating a feeding experience that birds naturally seek in various habitats. However, feeders make it much easier for birds to find and consume food. Bird feeding is hugely popular—hundreds of millions of dollars are spent annually by backyard birdwatchers on feeders and sunflower seeds, niger seeds, cracked corn, suet, and other bird food.

In Arlene Koch's backyard habitat in rural Pennsylvania, hummingbirds have the right-of-way!

Given that winter bird feeding has been a popular recreational activity since the 1950s in the United States and Canada, does this abundant new food supply affect the geographic ranges—and even migration patterns—of some birds? The answer is yes. Roger Tory Peterson pointed out in *A Field Guide to the Birds* that bird feeding in the second half of the twentieth century resulted in range expansions of Tufted Titmice, Northern Cardinals, and some other species. These birds now have no need to withdraw southward to escape harsh winter conditions and can survive cold northern winters, thanks to plenty of sunflower seeds in bird feeders.

In addition, hundreds of Rufous Hummingbirds now visit hummingbird feeders during winter along the Gulf Coast. A few of these birds even appear at backyard feeding stations in the northeastern states. Previously, these hummingbirds were almost never reported during winter in the Northeast or along the Gulf Coast. Ornithologists now are watching with fascination for changes in geographic ranges and migration patterns of other birds.

TYPES OF BIRD FEEDERS

At one time, feeding birds consisted of little more than throwing a few scraps of bread onto the backyard lawn; those days are long gone. Now backyard birdwatchers use a wide range of both simple and sophisticated bird feeders, many of which are designed to accommodate the needs of specific types of birds, such as finches, woodpeckers, and hummingbirds.

Tube Feeders

Probably the most widely used feeders in the United States and Canada are tube feeders. They are made of clear plastic or occasionally other materials such as ceramics and filled with sunflower or niger seeds. Small seed-eating birds such as Black-capped Chickadees, Tufted Titmice, House Finches, and American Goldfinches perch at openings in the feeder and remove individual seeds with their bills. Sometimes a bird like a Tufted Titmouse pokes its whole head into the opening to extract seeds. Some birds eat the seed while remaining perched on the feeder, others quickly fly to a nearby tree or shrub to eat it.

It's difficult to say whether birds spot sunflower seeds in clear plastic tube feeders from a distance or are now so accustomed to finding food in hanging tube bird feeders that they automatically investigate anything that looks like one. I've seen birds visit a ceramic tube feeder hung in a backyard habitat where the food is not visible, yet they come regularly expecting to find food, and take sunflower seeds from its openings. In this example, birds in the area probably watch each other, and are quick to pick up clues that food is in the feeder when they see other birds getting seeds from it.

In addition to Droll Yankees, Inc. (see sidebar), Duncraft and Perky-Pet also manufacture tube bird feeders. Some of these are designed for use with mixed, niger, sunflower, and other seeds. Perky-Pet's Upside-Down Thistle Feeder allows birds to eat seeds while hanging upside down. This company also manufactures an all-metal Iron Silo tube feeder designed to discourage gray squirrels from raiding and damaging the feeder.

Many birdwatching equipment and supply stores sell some models from these companies, which gives backyard birdwatchers an opportunity to compare models before selecting those best suited to a particular backyard habitat. For contact information, see appendix 4.

Globe Feeders

Globe feeders are clear plastic spheres into which sunflower seeds are placed. Birds extract seeds from several holes in the globe, which is suspended from a tree limb or metal support by a small metal chain.

Domed Feeders

Droll Yankees, Inc., and other companies manufacture domed bird feeders—clear plastic dishes stocked with sunflower seeds or even mealworms for bluebirds. A metal rod extending up from the feeder dish supports a clear plastic dome, forming

INVENTION OF THE TUBE FEEDER

The best-known company that manufactures tube bird feeders is Droll Yankees, Inc. In 1969, Peter Kilham, founder of the company, invented these feeders. Today this company and other firms manufacture tube bird feeders in many different sizes and models. But that first Droll Yankees Model A-6F started a revolution in backyard bird feeding—and set a standard for the bird-feeder industry.

Because of their design and construction, tube bird feeders do not allow birds to quickly empty the entire contents, which saves time and effort in refilling the feeders and considerable money by not having to buy as much expensive sunflower, niger, and other seeds. Depending on the size of the feeder, weather conditions, and the number of birds visiting it, a tube feeder may not need to be refilled for several days during winter.

Droll Yankees, Inc., currently makes several dozen styles and models of tube feeders with various seed capacities, seed trays, and squirrel guards. They also make accessories such as feeder brushes, seed scoops, garden poles, and other hardware. By far, however, the tube feeders are the most popular and widely used Droll Yankees products. For contact information and a free catalog, see appendix 4.

Droll Yankees Inc.

Droll Yankees Inc.

A. A Droll Yankees tube feeder. In 1969, Peter Kilham invented the cylinder or tube style of bird feeders.

B. Two models of Droll Yankees bird feeders.

a protective umbrella covering the food dish below. Enough space is provided between the food dish and the bottom edge of the protective dome to allow birds to take the seeds or other food. There are various styles of domed feeders, all adapted from the basic design just described. Some allow adjustments for different size seeds or the dome to be raised or lowered to accommodate (or exclude) birds of different sizes, and some are squirrel-resistant. Domed feeders can be attached to a window with a special suction-cup device or hung from a tree limb or metal support.

Feeding Shelves

Another style of bird feeder widely used for sunflower seeds is a shelf feeder, which is a wooden platform on which sunflower seeds are placed. If you're handy in the woodworking shop, save some money and make your own; if not, commercially made models are available. Ask a local birding equipment supply store about feeding shelves and a suitable model for your needs.

Feeding shelves typically are placed directly outside a kitchen or dining-room window, perhaps on a nearby support. There are no specific dimensions for these shelves, but a common size is about 18 inches long and 8 inches wide. Some feeding shelves have roofs to protect the seeds and birds from rain or snow.

Among birds that use feeding shelves are Black-capped Chickadees, Tufted Titmice, White-breasted Nuthatches, Northern Mockingbirds, House Finches, Purple Finches, White-throated Sparrows, and other seed-eating species. In some locations, gray squirrels raid feeding shelves to feast on the abundant supply of sunflower seeds. (Squirrel guards are discussed on pages 183 and 228.)

Hopper Feeders

These feeders have a large central compartment, or hopper, covered with a roof, which is filled with sunflower or other seeds. Trays extend outward from both sides of the feeder. Birds such as Blue Jays, Black-capped Chickadees, White-breasted Nuthatches, Northern Cardinals, House Finches, Purple Finches, and Evening Grosbeaks perch or stand on the tray while eating seeds taken from a dispenser at the bottom of the hopper.

An advantage of hopper feeders is the large amount of sunflower or other seeds they hold, which makes it unnecessary to refill it frequently. Hopper feeders produced by Stonewood Manufacturing are made from 100 percent postconsumer plastic milk bottles, with a limited number of metal parts. This feeder may appeal to backyard birdwatchers with an avid interest in recycling and preserving natural resources and the environment. An alternative to plastic feeders is a wood Mega Hopper Feeder, manufactured by Coveside Conservation Products. It has an extra-large capacity and can be mounted on a pipe, wood post, or deck rail. (For contact information about these companies, see appendix 4.)

Table Feeders

Table feeders, designed to accommodate ground-feeding birds, are simply low tables or platforms several feet long and wide, supported by legs about 6 inches high, and set on the ground. An advantage of table feeders is that they help prevent some loss of seeds due to inclement weather, spoilage, and interference by other ground animals. A disadvantage is that feeding birds may be vulnerable to house cats and similar land-bound predators.

Sunflower seeds, cracked corn, and other seeds are spread on the table or platform. Some backyard birdwatchers also put other food on table feeders: stale bakery products, scratch feed, raisins, and ripe fruit such as bananas, apples, and orange and grapefruit sections. Birds that use table feeders include Black-capped Chickadees, Brown-headed Cowbirds, Northern Bobwhites, Northern Cardinals, Mourning Doves, White-throated Sparrows, and Dark-eyed Juncos.

A. American Goldfinches feeding on seeds at a hopper feeder, while a Downy Woodpecker uses a suet feeder on the end.

B. Brown-headed Cowbirds using a table feeder elevated a few inches above the ground.

Several companies manufacture table feeders for use on the ground. Stonewood Manufacturing's Ground Tray is the most ecologically sound design. Measuring 18 by 22 by 2 inches, it has optional 9-inch legs and a fine-mesh screen. It's also possible to make table feeders in the workshop.

Ground Feeding

Another way to feed seed-eating birds is simply to spread cracked corn and sunflower seeds directly on the ground. Northern Bobwhites, Mourning Doves, Northern Cardinals, White-throated Sparrows, and Dark-eyed Juncos visit these feeding areas to scratch around and eat the seeds. Although the ground-feeding method works, seeds are more susceptible to weathering, mold, spoilage, and other animals than when placed on slightly higher table feeders. Therefore, it's generally not recommended that seeds or other food be thrown on the ground to feed birds.

Hanging Coconuts

One of the do-it-yourself versions of bird feeders used by some backyard birdwatchers is half of a hollow coconut filled with a mixture of suet (i.e., animal fat, often from beef) and sunflower or other seeds. Three holes are drilled into the coconut at the widest part and wire is inserted through each hole and fastened together at the top. The feeder is suspended from a tree limb or metal pole by the wires. Some people use the other half of the coconut shell as a roof over the bottom half that contains the seeds. Another version has only part of one side of the coconut cut away, with sunflower seeds placed inside the hollow shell.

A variety of birds use these feeders, including Downy Woodpeckers, Black-capped Chickadees, Tufted Titmice, Red-breasted Nuthatches, White-breasted Nuthatches, and Evening Grosbeaks.

Thistle (Niger Seed) Stockings

Several types of thistle stockings are sold by various companies, including Duncraft. These devices are nylon-netting stockings about 10 inches long, into which thistle or niger seeds are placed. Birds such as American Goldfinches are able to poke their bills partway through the stocking's mesh and extract a thistle seed. The stockings are suspended from a tree or metal pole by using the stocking's drawstring. A disadvantage of using a thistle stocking is that its contents become wet when it rains or snows, causing mold to form.

Hanging Suet Logs

Another easy-to-make feeder is a piece of a tree branch, about 12 to 18 inches long and 3 or 4 inches in diameter, with six wide and reasonably deep holes bored into the log at various places. Suet is then placed firmly in the holes. It's desirable to use logs with the bark still firmly attached, which provides a suitable surface for birds to grip when they visit the log—and the bark adds to the attractiveness of the feeder. Suet feeders are a favorite among woodpeckers because they simulate the trees in which they naturally seek food and nesting cavities.

Suet-log feeders are manufactured by various companies and are available at birdwatching equipment and supply stores, nature centers, garden centers, and by mail order. Country Ecology, for example, produces three- and four-hole suet logs made of gray birch with wood dowel perches. A screw eye is inserted at the top end of the log, and the nylon cord included in the package allows the log to be suspended from a tree limb or metal pole. Country Ecology suet logs also can be ordered without perches. (See appendix 4 for contact information.)

Sometimes bird photographers use special hanging suet logs with holes bored into only one side of the log. Depending on where the camera is placed relative to the holes in the suet log, the resulting photograph may look like the woodpecker or other suet-eating bird is on an ordinary tree branch.

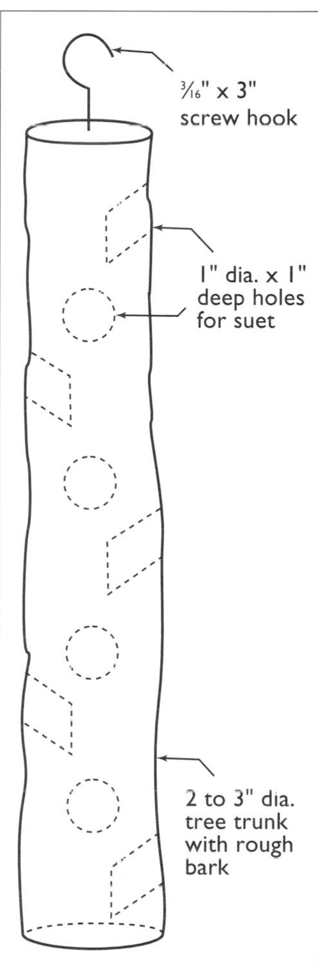

Plans for making a log suet feeder. Select a log with rough bark so birds can easily cling to the surface. Eastern red cedar is a good choice, and resists rotting. Redrawn from plans by Greg Oskay/Water Resources Design, Inc.

Suet, peanut butter, or some combination of these, plus sunflower or niger seeds, are packed into holes in the logs. Some suet logs have perches, others do not. A screw eye is put into one end of the log, which is then hung by a piece of wire from a tree limb or metal pole.

Among the many birds visiting hanging suet logs for food are woodpeckers, Black-capped Chickadees, Tufted Titmice, Red-breasted Nuthatches, and White-breasted Nuthatches. Other birds, including Blue Jays, Gray Catbirds, Yellow-rumped Warblers, Baltimore Orioles, Dark-eyed Juncos, and American Tree Sparrows, can be lured to hanging suet logs if a perch is added below each food hole.

Perhaps the most unusual bird that visited a backyard feeding station to eat suet was an American Kestrel, observed by ornithologist Gustav A. Swanson at his feeder. My own field studies of American Kestrel food habits demonstrate that a suet-eating kestrel is a rare bird.

Unfortunately, gray and other squirrels also enjoy obtaining a meal at a hanging suet log, but at the same time, they gnaw the sides of the food holes, making them larger. This does not endear squirrels to many backyard birdwatchers, and it may be necessary to try squirrel-proof suet logs. This can be accomplished by placing the wire suspending the log through a slippery plastic tube, which makes it difficult for squirrels to get enough footing to reach the log—at least that's the theory. Never underestimate the ability of squirrels to figure out how to get to bird feeders! These characters are not only master foresters, they're also master bird-feeder raiders.

Other Suet Feeders

The variety of containers that can dispense suet or a suet-seed mix is limited only by one's imagination. Try placing suet in tunafish cans secured in a wooden cradle nailed to a tree trunk. Hairy Woodpeckers and other woodpeckers perch on the wooden cradle with their tails propped against the tree trunk, which keeps the bird's feet and toes from contacting the metal. This is an important consideration in freezing temperatures when exposed (i.e., unfeathered) parts of birds, such as feet and toes, eyelids, eyes, and tongues, can stick to metal objects. One way to avoid this problem is to rub suet onto the metal surfaces. Most commercially manufactured metal suet feeders use plastic- or vinyl-coated wire. Of course, suet holders and feeders made of wood do not present this danger.

Duncraft has a pine shed-style feeder with roof to protect suet or seed blocks from inclement weather. Coveside Conservation Products offers several suet feeders made of wood and metal: a Mini Suet Feeder holding one suet cake in an upside-down position for woodpeckers, chickadees, nuthatches, and titmice; a Suet Chalet designed to hold one 4-inch suet cake vertically against a tree trunk for woodpeckers and nuthatches; and a Woodpecker Feeder designed to hold a suet cake and accommodate woodpecker perching behavior and postures.

Perky-Pet is another brand of western red cedar suet chalets, which hold a suet cake at each end of the feeder and have a sunflower or mixed birdseed compartment in the middle. Duncraft also has a Big Basket suet cake holder made of vinyl-coated wire, suspended by a 10-inch chain and hook; it likewise sells other metal or metal and wood suet holders. Heath Manufacturing Company makes several types of metal-cage suet feeders designed to hold one or two suet cakes, a redwood suet and seed feeder that holds two suet cakes and 3 pounds of mixed seeds, and a Suet 'N Seed Depot that holds 7 pounds of mixed seeds and two suet cakes. Hyde's Birdfeeder, Inc., makes several styles of galvanized hanging metal suet holders designed to hold one or two suet cakes, as well as a Barrel Suet Holder. Perky-Pet offers vinyl-coated metal suet baskets and has eight different types of suet cakes. (See appendix 4 for contact information about these companies.)

Stonewood Manufacturing offers backyard birdwatchers three different styles of suet feeders or holders made of 100 percent recycled plastic milk bottles, with wire mesh covering the area through which woodpeckers, nuthatches, titmice, and other birds can take bits of suet. One model, the Songbird, is designed mainly for songbirds and excludes European Starlings and grackles. A second model, the Post Box, is designed for mounting on fenceposts or trees, and holds one suet cake. A third model, the Banquet Feeder, allows birds access to both sides of a suet cake, includes in its design a tail prop for woodpeckers, and is equipped with a hanging chain. Birdwatchers who are avid environmentalists may want to examine these to determine if they're suitable for use in their backyard habitats.

Hummingbird Feeders

Hummingbirds require special feeders to deliver sugar water, a substitute for nectar in their natural diet. A wide array of hummingbird feeders is available in birdwatching equipment and supply stores, garden supply stores, some nature centers, and by mail order. Many are designed to resemble red flowers of various shapes and types.

Droll Yankees, Inc.'s hummingbird feeders resemble flying saucers, with up to eight openings at which hummingbirds can hover to obtain sugar-water solution. Red plastic disks surround the openings, making them more attractive to these birds.

Duncraft offers several different designs of hummingbird feeders, including a disk-like feeder, a tube with a plastic dome on top and a circular bottom with metal perches, and feeders with a red center and white or yellow rays to resemble a composite flower.

Hyde's Birdfeeder manufactures at least five models of hummingbird feeders, all of which have yellow or red ports, or openings, designed to resemble flowers. Some models also have bee guards. The reservoir capacity of these feeders ranges from 6 to 46 ounces, and all are suspended from a metal pole, tree limb, or other support.

Perky-Pet offers several dozen models and designs of hummingbird feeders. Their Gemstone feeder, for example, has a "Gem-Cut" glass feeder bottle, whereas the Wildflower Garden Feeder and Stem Set looks like a large composite flower with thirteen ports, through which hummingbirds can take sugar water or nectar solutions. Their most popular hummingbird feeders are in the Four Meadows series, but they also have drip-free models and many others. This company also sells several variations of Instant Nectar formulated for use in hummingbird feeders. It's a dry mixture that requires the addition of ordinary tap water before use.

There's been a debate within the backyard birdwatching community about whether red food dye is safe for use in sugar-water solutions. I know of no solid scientific evidence supporting a ban on red food dye. Indeed, Mitch Ericson, of Perky-Pet Products Co., reported in *Bird Watcher's Digest* that no research has been done on this issue. In my own experience, Maurice Broun (the first curator

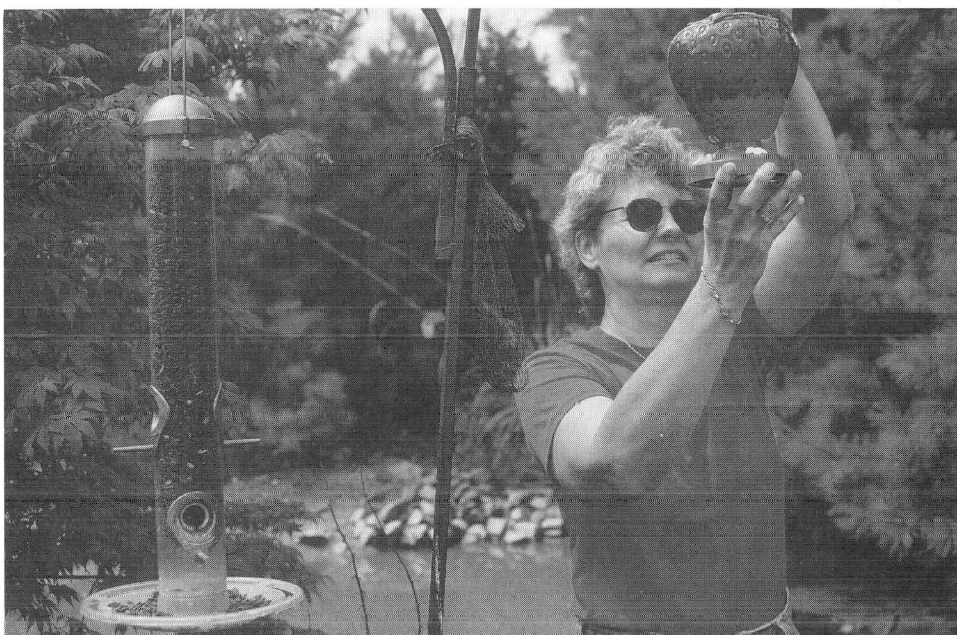

Judy Byrne hanging a hummingbird feeder filled with sugar water in her Pennsylvania backyard habitat.

of the Hawk Mountain Sanctuary) provided red sugar water in hummingbird feeders for decades without any evidence that it harmed the birds. Nevertheless, most hummingbird feeders now sold on the market have red or yellow plastic flowers or ports designed for use with uncolored sugar water.

Many backyard birdwatchers make their own sugar-water solution by dissolving one part of granulated sugar into four parts of water (by volume), boiling the solution for two minutes, and cooling it before filling the feeders. Extra solution is stored in the refrigerator. Do not use honey or artificial sweeteners.

At least seventy bird species other than hummingbirds sometimes visit hummingbird feeders, including Acorn Woodpeckers, Curve-billed Thrashers, Wilson's Warblers, Golden-crowned Sparrows, and Evening Grosbeaks.

Oriole Feeders

As for hummingbirds, several companies make feeders specifically designed to attract Baltimore Orioles and other orioles. Bird Company makes a 48-to-52-ounce-capacity device that looks like an oversized hummingbird feeder. Duncraft manufactures several oriole feeders. The Oriole Buffet holds half an orange on the top, 12 ounces of nectar in four feeding ports, and has four smaller spaces for grape jelly. Duncraft's Fruit Kabob is a clear plastic and metal feeder designed to hold orange slices. The feeder is suspended by a chain from a limb or pole. Completely different in design and materials is the Oriole feeder manufactured by Coveside Conservation Products. It's made of wood and has a skewer onto which half an orange is fastened; a perch provides easy access to the food. The feeder hangs with an attached cord.

Perky-Pet's oriole feeders, on the other hand, resemble larger versions of hummingbird feeders. The company also makes an orange-flavored Instant Nectar for orioles, a powder packed in a box to which tap water is added.

Of course, if these specialized devices are not at hand, Baltimore Orioles and other species usually consume popcorn and sliced fruit from tray feeders.

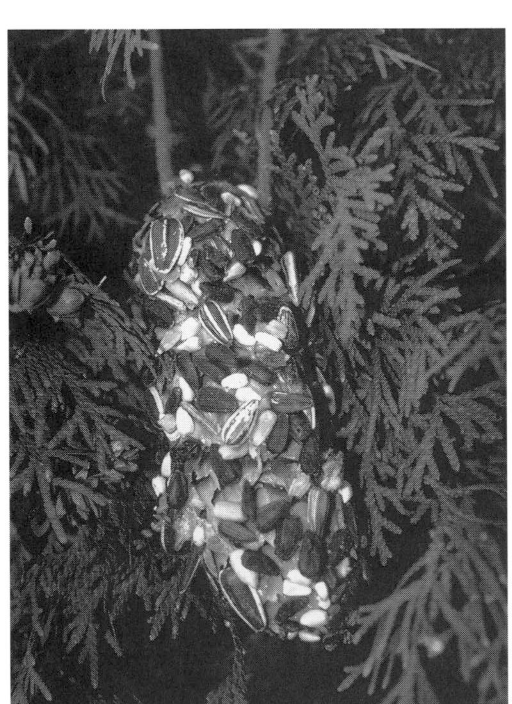

A pine cone feeder made with peanut butter and sunflower seeds is hung on a tree.

Peanut Strings

Stringing unshelled roasted peanuts onto a string and placing them on a pine tree or other evergreen at Christmas time is a simple project that can be done with small children to expose them to the enjoyment of backyard bird feeding. Blue Jays, woodpeckers, Tufted Titmice, and White-breasted Nuthatches are attracted to peanut strings.

Pine Cone Feeders

Another way of providing food for some birds, such as Black-capped Chickadees, Tufted Titmice, White-breasted Nuthatches, and other small birds, is to smear peanut butter into the open spaces of a pine cone, then press sunflower seeds into the peanut butter, which holds the seeds in place. Attach a colorful string to the top of the pine cone and suspend it from a tree limb, post, or other object. Making these bird feeders is a good Christmas-season project for young children, who can hang the cone feeders on a pine tree or other evergreen in a backyard habitat.

Popcorn Strings

During the Christmas season, it's also fun to thread popcorn and perhaps other fruits from shrubs onto a long string. Place the string on a pine tree or other evergreen for the benefit of birds. This is a nice project in which small children can participate and learn something about birds and their food habits.

Popcorn can be provided on feeding trays and elsewhere. Some backyard birders even feed popcorn to Baltimore Orioles in the spring, when they return to North America for the nesting season. Birds that eat popcorn include Blue Jays, Black-capped Chickadees, Tufted Titmice, Downy Woodpeckers, Hairy Woodpeckers, Red-bellied Woodpeckers, Brown Thrashers, Northern Cardinals, Baltimore Orioles, Eastern Towhees, and many sparrows.

Game-Bird Feeders

To feed game birds such as Northern Bobwhites and Ring-necked Pheasants, create a sheltered area by arranging poles like a teepee and then covering them with evergreen branches. The exact shape of the structure is unimportant as long as it creates a dry, sheltered ground area where corn kernels can be spread and cobs can be placed on the ground or positioned upright by being stuck onto a nail or other support.

Whispering Pines Enterprises makes an attractive Quail Hopper Feeder from mostly wood, with a 1½-gallon seed capacity, which is designed to be placed under a hedge or small bush (see appendix 4).

Bird Feeders with Built-In Microphones

One of the innovative variations on bird-feeder designs is the placement of a small microphone inside the feeder, tuned to the range of frequencies of birdsongs. The sounds of birds using the feeder are transmitted to a portable receiver/speaker inside the backyard birdwatcher's house. WingSong Bird Feeder, manufactured by Country Line Limited, is this type of feeder.

FEEDER FOODS

Sunflower seeds, niger seeds, corn, and suet are common items used in bird feeders, but innumerable others are also placed on the menu to attract birds to backyard feeders.

Seeds

Seeds of wild and cultivated plants are naturally important foods for many backyard birds; hence, their effectiveness in feeders. Sunflower seeds, the prime example, are sold in bulk quantities or packaged at birdwatching stores, nature centers, and garden supply stores, as well as at some feed mills in 25- or 50-pound bags. Following are typical seeds that birds eat at backyard bird feeders.

Birdseed mixtures are sold widely in supermarkets, garden supply stores, discount department stores, and elsewhere. Unfortunately, most prepared mixtures contain relatively large amounts of canary seeds, sorghum, and millet, which have less nutritional value than sunflower and niger seeds. Avoid the more inexpensive birdseed mixes. If you do buy mixtures, add sunflower, niger, and other seeds that birds prefer. You can purchase custom-blended seed mixtures at birdwatching stores.

Buckwheat seeds are eaten by Mourning Doves, Northern Cardinals, and Purple Finches; many other birds ignore them.

Canary seeds have low nutritional value, so you can blend sunflower and niger seeds with them. Northern Bobwhites, Mourning Doves, Red-bellied Woodpeckers, Tufted Titmice, Purple Finches, House Finches, and White-throated Sparrows all eat canary seeds; Mourning Doves and White-throated Sparrows particularly like them.

Corn on-the-cob or as whole kernels is an excellent food at feeding stations—especially from the prairies eastward to the Atlantic Ocean. Birds that eat corn include Ring-necked Pheasants, Wild Turkeys, Northern Bobwhites, White-winged Doves, Mourning Doves, Red-headed Woodpeckers, Northern Flickers, Blue Jays, White-breasted Nuthatches, Eastern Towhees, White-throated Sparrows, Harris's Sparrows, and Northern Cardinals.

If you are lucky enough to have the land available, consider planting about a half-acre with corn and sunflowers. Allow the crops to remain unharvested; many birds will find this half-acre and feed on the corn and sunflower seeds.

Cracked corn is also used in backyard feeding stations, but it spoils after becoming wet. Mourning Doves, Common Grackles, and White-throated Sparrows eat cracked corn. However, because it attracts squirrels, some birders dislike using it. If you make your own suet cakes, you can add yellow corn meal to the mixture.

Seeds from alfalfa, clover, and timothy are contained in hay chaff, which can be put on the ground or snow. Horned Larks, Savannah Sparrows, Vesper Sparrows, and Snow Buntings eat hay chaff.

Millet of various types—browntop, foxtail, German, Japanese, red proso, and white—is widely used in bird-food mixes. It's eaten by Mourning Doves, House Finches, various sparrows, and blackbirds.

German or golden millet is consumed by Mourning Doves, Brown-headed Cowbirds, House Sparrows, and White-throated Sparrows. Red proso millet is eaten by Mourning Doves, Brown-headed Cowbirds, House Sparrows, and White-throated Sparrows. White proso millet is eaten by Mourning Doves, Brown-headed Cowbirds, and House Sparrows, and occasionally by Northern Cardinals and House Finches.

A. Some birders with large backyard habitats plant rows of corn as food for birds and allow it to remain unharvested. This corn was grown in David and Arlene Koch's acres of habitat in eastern Pennsylvania.

B. Seeds from pumpkins can be harvested and used in bird feeders. Many birds eat them eagerly.

C. Sunflower seeds are the most eagerly consumed of all items offered at bird feeders. Most people buy them already processed, but some birders grow their own sunflowers and remove the seeds themselves, or allow the plants to remain unharvested in gardens or fields, where birds and other wildlife find them.

D. A sunflower left unharvested in a field.

Cantaloupe, pumpkin, squash, and watermelon seeds are as eagerly eaten as sunflower seeds. Look for Mourning Doves, Blue Jays, Black-capped Chickadees, Tufted Titmice, White-breasted Nuthatches, Rose-breasted Grosbeaks, Purple Finches, and Eastern Towhees to consume them. However, first put the seeds through a grinder to expose the edible kernels.

Apple seeds are eaten by Ruffed Grouse, Ring-necked Pheasants, Lewis's Woodpeckers, Tufted Titmice, American Robins, Varied Thrushes, Cedar Waxwings, and Purple Finches.

Niger (thistle) seeds are important but costly to offer in hanging feeders. American Goldfinches and House Finches especially relish them, but other birds that eat niger seeds are Mourning Doves, chickadees, Tufted Titmice, Purple Finches, Pine Siskins, Common Redpolls, Dark-eyed Juncos, and White-throated Sparrows.

Hulled oats (i.e., groats) are occasionally eaten in fields by Mourning Doves, Northern Flickers, Northern Cardinals, Purple Finches, Dark-eyed Juncos, and Snow Buntings.

Garden peas (seeds) sometimes are eaten by Band-tailed Pigeons, Baltimore Orioles, and Rose-breasted Grosbeaks. Similarly, in the southern United States, cowpea seeds are eaten by Mourning Doves and Northern Bobwhites.

Safflower seeds are offered on the menu at some bird-feeding stations, but only Northern Cardinals eat them, to a limited extent. Mourning Doves and White-throated Sparrows do so less frequently.

Sorghum, or milo, is another common seed in mixed birdseed products, but few birds prefer it. Mourning Doves eat it more than other birds, but occasionally Blue Jays, Common Grackles, Brown-headed Cowbirds, Northern Cardinals, and White-throated Sparrows will sample it.

Sunflower seeds are the number-one offering at backyard bird feeders, and all seed-eating birds eagerly consume them. However, some types are consumed more eagerly than others.

Black-oil sunflower seeds are at the top of the preferred list and are eagerly eaten by Black-capped Chickadees, Northern Cardinals, Evening Grosbeaks, Purple Finches, Mourning Doves, and House Finches.

Hulled sunflower seeds are preferred by American Goldfinches and House Finches. Common Grackles, White-throated Sparrows, Mourning Doves, and Northern Cardinals also eat them.

Black-striped sunflower seeds are eaten by Blue Jays, Common Grackles, Northern Cardinals, Evening Grosbeaks, and White-throated Sparrows. Mourning Doves, Blue Jays, chickadees, Tufted Titmice, House Finches, Purple Finches, American Goldfinches, and Dark-eyed Juncos also eat them.

Wheat kernels are eaten by a long list of birds in various parts of the United States. Examples include Mourning Doves, White-winged Doves, Ring-necked Pheasants, Northern Bobwhites, Curve-billed Thrashers, Red-winged Blackbirds, Brewer's Blackbirds, Snow Buntings, Rosy Finches, Blue Grosbeaks, Yellow-billed Magpies, Black-billed Magpies, Eastern and Western Meadowlarks, and Lark Sparrows. However, wheat kernels are of minor importance in the diet of seed-eating birds that visit backyard feeding stations.

Suet Cakes and Bricks

Beef suet is one of the standard foods offered to birds visiting backyard feeding stations, and most birdwatchers establish at least one suet feeder. Pileated Woodpeckers, Red-bellied Woodpeckers, Downy Woodpeckers, Hairy Woodpeckers,

Northern Flickers, other woodpeckers, Blue Jays, Black-capped Chickadees, Carolina Chickadees, Boreal Chickadees, Tufted Titmice, White-breasted Nuthatches, Red-breasted Nuthatches, and Brown Creepers all eat suet because it is a high-energy food.

Other steady suet-eaters include Gray Catbirds, Northern Mockingbirds, Brown Thrashers, Swainson's Thrushes, Gray-cheeked Thrushes, Hermit Thrushes, Wood Thrushes, American Robins, Eastern Bluebirds, Golden-crowned Kinglets, and Ruby-crowned Kinglets. Some wood warblers also eat suet: Orange-crowned Warblers, Cape May Warblers, Pine Warblers, Yellow-rumped Warblers, and Yellow-breasted Chats.

Even Orchard Orioles, Baltimore Orioles, Common Grackles, Scarlet Tanagers, and Summer Tanagers are reported eating suet occasionally, and Red-shouldered Hawks (in very cold weather) and Red-tailed Hawks are known to eat suet on rare occasions.

Suet can either be purchased commercially or made at home. A number of companies manufacture suet cakes and bricks for use in bird feeders. For example, C and S Products Co., Inc., makes suet cakes and bricks in dozens of blends and flavors. Likewise, Duncraft Bird Feeders sells a variety of suet cakes.

Commercially prepared suet cakes and bricks are convenient, easy to use, and designed to be placed in widely used suet baskets or holders. They can be purchased at birdwatching stores, garden shops, and some nature centers.

You also can make your own suet cakes or bricks from the recipe at right, which has served me well.

SUET CAKE RECIPE

Assemble the following ingredients.

*1 cup lard or beef suet**

1 cup chunky peanut butter

¼ cup granulated sugar

1 cup bread crumbs

2 cups oatmeal

1 cup cornmeal

1 cup whole-wheat flour

Melt the lard or beef suet and peanut butter, mix the dry ingredients, and pour into a cake pan. Harden the mixture in the refrigerator, cut into squares or cakes, and fill the suet feeders. Wrap extra cakes in waxed paper or plastic wrap and store in the freezer.

** Available in the refrigerated meat department of most supermarkets.*

Nuts

There is a considerable variety of wild and cultivated nuts eaten by birds such as Blue Jays, White-breasted Nuthatches, and Red-bellied Woodpeckers. Almonds can be chopped into smaller pieces and offered to White-breasted Nuthatches, Red-breasted Nuthatches, and occasionally Red Crossbills.

Eastern black walnuts (as opposed to other black-walnut species) are important wild nuts eaten by some birds and other wildlife. Red-bellied Woodpeckers in Kentucky, for example, eat black walnuts, and Black-capped Chickadees, Tufted Titmice, and White-breasted Nuthatches also accept black walnuts on a feeder menu. In the Midwest and northeastern United States, many birds that eat eastern black walnuts also eat butternuts or white walnuts.

English walnuts chopped into smaller pieces are eaten by Blue Jays, Black-capped Chickadees, Tufted Titmice, American Goldfinches, White-crowned Sparrows, and House Sparrows.

Peanuts were discussed in the section on peanut strings. Peanut kernels (i.e., whole peanuts removed from their shells) are sometimes offered at feeding stations where Blue Jays, Tufted Titmice, and White-throated Sparrows eat them. Peanut hearts, however, generally are not liked by most birds, although Common Grackles and White-throated Sparrows sometimes eat them.

Peanut butter is widely used by itself, mixed with suet, or mixed with suet and seeds, then placed in suet logs or other suet feeders. There is a controversy, however, about using pure peanut butter because some people claim birds can choke on this sticky substance. Therefore, to be safe, backyard birdwatchers sometimes mix cornmeal with the peanut butter before putting it in a suet log.

Pecans are grown and processed for human use in the southern states. Culls and scraps remaining after processing can be mixed with suet and used in suet logs for Red-bellied Woodpeckers, Tufted Titmice, White-breasted Nuthatches, and Rose-breasted Grosbeaks.

Fruit

Depending on where in the United States a feeding station is located, a wide range of both wild and cultivated fruit is popular bird food. For example, during summer, a fruit bowl containing fresh slices or small pieces of apples, bananas, pears, grapes, and oranges is attractive to Gray Catbirds, Northern Mockingbirds, thrushes, tanagers, Rose-breasted Grosbeaks, and orioles.

Apple slices or halves can be pushed into nails, twigs, or sharp objects on separate fruit feeders or in available spaces on other feeders. Northern Mockingbirds often are quick to spot apple slices. Hermit Thrushes, American Robins, Cedar Waxwings, Yellow-breasted Chats, and Purple Finches are other birds that eat apples.

Bananas are also easy to use in bird feeders. Split open a banana part way and lay it on a feeder tray, or remove the banana from its skin and lay slices on the tray.

A fruit bar with pieces of apple may attract some birds such as Northern Mockingbirds and selected other species.

Carolina Wrens, Gray Catbirds, Northern Mockingbirds, Yellow-breasted Chats, and Baltimore Orioles are some of the species that eat bananas.

Bayberry or wax myrtle fruits are consumed by some birds. Most bayberry species are found along the Atlantic coast, although one occurs along the Pacific coast. To offer these fruits, plant bayberry shrubs in a backyard habitat. In the East, bayberry fruits are eaten by Black-capped Chickadees, Carolina Chickadees, Tufted Titmice, Tree Swallows, Red-bellied Woodpeckers, Northern Flickers, Eastern Phoebes, Eastern Bluebirds, Hermit Thrushes, Gray Catbirds, Northern Mockingbirds, Brown Thrashers, Yellow-rumped Warblers, Scarlet Tanagers, Savannah (Ipswich form) Sparrows, and others. On the Pacific coast, bayberry fruit is eaten by Chestnut-backed Chickadees and Yellow-rumped Warblers, and occasionally other birds.

Backyard birders can use ripe blackberries to attract American Robins, Varied Thrushes, Gray Catbirds, Brown Thrashers, Yellow-breasted Chats, Orchard Orioles, Summer Tanagers, Northern Cardinals, Pine Grosbeaks, Eastern Towhees, Fox Sparrows, and many other species.

Blueberries, cultivated or wild, are eaten by Tufted Titmice, Gray Catbirds, Brown Thrashers, Eastern Bluebirds, Veeries, American Robins, Yellow-breasted Chats, Scarlet Tanagers, Bachman's Sparrows, Eastern Towhees, orioles, and numerous other birds.

Cherries, wild and cultivated, are fruits that some birds delight in eating, including Red-headed Woodpeckers, Red-bellied Woodpeckers, Northern Flickers, Gray Catbirds, Brown Thrashers, various thrushes, American Robins, Phainopeplas, Cedar Waxwings, Rose-breasted Grosbeaks, Evening Grosbeaks, and numerous other species to a lesser extent.

Some birds also eat cultivated cherries—at times taking three fourths of an orchard's crop. Species especially prone to eating cultivated cherries in various parts of the United States include Lewis's Woodpeckers, Red-bellied Woodpeckers, Steller's Jays, Gray Catbirds, American Robins, European Starlings, Cedar Waxwings, Western Tanagers, Brewer's Blackbirds, Bullock's Orioles, House Finches, Purple Finches, and Black-headed Grosbeaks.

Grapes, wild and cultivated, including white seedless grapes, are eaten by Ring-necked Pheasants, Ruffed Grouse, Wild Turkeys, Northern Bobwhites, many woodpeckers, Cassin's Kingbirds, Yellow-billed Magpies, thrushes, American Robins, Gray Catbirds, Northern Mockingbirds, thrashers (Sage, Brown, and California), Mountain Bluebirds, Western Bluebirds, Cedar Waxwings, Northern Cardinals, Baltimore Orioles, House Finches, Eastern Towhees, and Fox Sparrows. Grape jelly is also eaten by Yellow-rumped Warblers and Baltimore Orioles.

Oranges can be used at bird-feeding stations as part of a fruit bowl, with halves or slices placed on feeding trays or put onto feeders designed for fruit. Red-bellied Woodpeckers, Gray Catbirds, Summer Tanagers, Scarlet Tanagers, Rose-breasted Grosbeaks, and Baltimore Orioles eat slices of orange.

Halves or smaller pieces of pears are eaten by Northern Mockingbirds and American Robins. Baltimore Orioles, Purple Finches, House Sparrows, and Fox Sparrows sometimes also attempt to eat pears growing on trees.

In California and Oregon, Northern Flickers, American Robins, Varied Thrushes, House Finches, and Black-headed Grosbeaks eat prunes—particularly those on the ground.

Raisins have mixed success at backyard feeding stations. Blue Jays, Eastern Bluebirds, American Robins, Gray Catbirds, Northern Mockingbirds, Brown Thrashers, Cedar Waxwings, Summer Tanagers, Scarlet Tanagers, Northern Cardinals, Rose-breasted Grosbeaks, and Baltimore Orioles are known to eat them.

Strawberries are much loved by people and birds, including Gray Catbirds and American Robins.

Hummingbird Foods

Hummingbird feeders are filled with sugar water. The Hummer/Bird Study Group, Inc., recommends using a solution consisting of one part sugar dissolved into four parts water; it does not recommend using honey or artificial sweeteners. (The restriction on honey is important because it ferments quickly.)

The organization also recommends keeping hummingbird feeders filled with fresh sugar water throughout autumn, winter, and early spring in the East because a few western, cold-hardy species like Rufous Hummingbirds occasionally appear in the East during late autumn and winter. Some birds even visit feeders during very cold weather, with snow on the ground. They need to take fresh sugar-water solution from feeders if they are to survive harsh conditions. However, it's also necessary to frequently bring hummingbird feeders into a warm room to prevent the sugar water from freezing. I know of one case in which a Rufous Hummingbird

BIRD-FEEDING ORGANIZATIONS

Several national, nonprofit organizations focus on helping birdwatchers feed birds more effectively in backyard habitats. For contact information and websites, see appendix 1.

Cornell Laboratory of Ornithology. *This world-famous research center operates several bird-feeding projects. The best known is Project FeederWatch, which gathers and analyzes data from backyard birdwatchers.*

Hummer/Bird Study Group, Inc. *This organization is involved in hummingbird bird-banding studies and public education. Its quarterly newsletter,* Netlines, *contains articles, tips, and helpful recommendations about attracting and feeding hummingbirds.*

The Hummingbird Society. *The Hummingbird Society, another national, nonprofit organization, is dedicated to hummingbird conservation and habitat protection, public education, and research. Its quarterly magazine,* The Hummingbird Connection, *offers a wide range of articles about these birds.*

National Bird-Feeding Society. *Backyard birdwatchers who avidly feed birds at backyard feeding stations have much in common. They can share ideas and information by joining the National Bird-Feeding Society. Its newsletter,* The Bird's-Eye reView, *contains much useful information about bird-feeding methods, types of feeders, and types of food.*

survived a cold eastern winter thanks to a caring backyard birdwatcher who made an extraordinary commitment to assure the little bird would be fed.

Miscellaneous Foods

Baked goods can be offered at bird feeders; however, their nutritional value is less than that of many other foods. Nevertheless, bread (toasted or untoasted), cake, doughnuts, muffins, and rolls can be offered to birds. Baked piecrusts are also eaten by chickadees, bluebirds, Baltimore Orioles, and Scarlet Tanagers.

American cheese is eaten by Downy Woodpeckers, Carolina Wrens, and American Robins. Cottage cheese can be fed to rescued nestlings or young birds visiting feeders; however, cheese is not generally a preferred bird food.

As we've seen, sugar is a primary ingredient of sugar-water solutions used in hummingbird feeders. In the West Indies, some tropical birds eat granulated sugar directly from sugar bowls on tables, including woodpeckers, honeycreepers, and tanagers. In Key West, Florida, where some West Indian birds appear, this bird-feeding technique works occasionally.

MANAGING FEEDERS

Once you have selected the correct types of bird feeders and filled them, the next step is to place them properly to accommodate the feeding behavior of different bird species. This may include vertical height from the ground, means of mounting, and distribution within the backyard habitat.

Height

Birds that normally visit feeders elevated 4 feet or higher prefer black-oil sunflower seeds, whereas ground-feeding birds prefer white proso millet.

Feeders can be supported by wood posts or metal poles, or suspended by wires or special hooks from tree limbs. Birding stores sell various suspension devices and can make recommendations to accommodate a birdwatcher's particular backyard.

Wood posts, metal pipes, steel support poles, and even tree limbs can be used to support bird feeders.

When possible, it's desirable to place feeders in locations that face away from the generally prevailing wind direction.

Don't forget to include at least one table feeder to accommodate ground-feeding birds. As discussed earlier, certain birds will feed on sunflower seeds, cracked corn, and other seeds spread on a table or platform placed 6 inches off the ground.

Distribution

The placement of feeders around a backyard habitat and relative to one another can have a pronounced effect on the behavior of birds.

As we've seen, different birds prefer different feeders and foods. The most effective way of controlling where birds gather is to plan the placement of feeders designed for specific birds. For example, suet logs used by Downy and Hairy Woodpeckers can be hung from tree limbs some distance from a kitchen window. Place feeders with black-oil sunflower seeds close to windows to enjoy up-close views of Black-capped Chickadees, House Finches, Purple Finches, Northern Cardinals, and Evening Grosbeaks.

A less precise way to share the menu with as many different birds as possible is to place feeders at varying distances from the house. While a few feeders can be put very close to a window, also place several feeders 15 to 30 feet away and at different heights. This way, different birds can simultaneously visit feeders at which they are most comfortable, while avoiding conflicts with a few birds dominating other feeders.

Sometimes birds can be so aggressive as to disrupt the feeding of others. Individual hummingbirds can be very aggressive at feeders, trying to dominate a feeder to the exclusion of others. To solve this problem, add more feeders—but position them out of sight of each other; this helps distribute hummingbirds more evenly in the backyard.

Backyard birdwatchers should experiment for maximum effectiveness as they develop bird-feeding stations. Moreover, moving feeders around is inexpensive, provides insight into the food preferences of birds, and may even help prevent disease among bird populations.

Seasonal Considerations

In the temperate parts of North America, backyard bird feeding is normally done during the cooler autumn, winter, and early spring months. During very cold winter periods, feeding birds greatly helps them survive because they do not have to waste energy looking for food in natural places. Rather, birds quickly learn that it's easy to get food regularly at feeders, which is why it is important to not stop operating established stations during winter.

Certain species use feeding stations during summer, even when natural foods are readily available. Some species, such as American Goldfinches, wear their brightest breeding plumage during the summer, which is an added incentive to fill the feeders. However, some ornithologists and experienced birders are concerned that operating bird feeders during summer may harm newly fledged birds that have not yet learned necessary foraging skills vital to their survival. In other words, the "education" of newly fledged birds may be incomplete if they are only brought to backyard bird feeders by their parents during summer, so carefully consider if you really want to maintain bird feeders during summer.

A bird feeder that's been squirrel-proofed using a section of stove pipe as a baffle or guard.

Squirrel-Proof Bird Feeders

Many backyard birdwatchers object to having squirrels, in particular, eastern and western gray squirrels, raid their bird feeders. They dislike these mammals because they decimate seed supplies intended for birds and sometimes damage the feeders. To solve this problem, several companies make squirrel-proof bird feeders.

There are two basic approaches to squirrel-proofing. In the cage design, a tube feeder is placed inside a heavy-duty wire cage that admits smaller birds but prevents squirrels (and larger birds) from getting at the feeder. Droll Yankees, Inc.'s The New Generation Evergreen and TH A-6 Black Forest cages are classic designs. Duncraft, Hyde Bird Feeder, and Five Islands Products, Inc., also make variations on the caged-feeder design.

The second technique is to block the squirrel's approach by creating a barrier in the line or pole supporting the feeder. For instance, the Mandarin Squirrel-Away Baffle is an upside-down plexiglass funnel, which Arundale Products claims is absolutely squirrel-proof in combination with the Mandarin Sky Cafe and other feeders.

It's also possible to make your own squirrel-proof bird feeder using a long section of stovepipe. The one shown above worked well at one Pennsylvania backyard feeding station—until a black bear raided and demolished the feeder. Nothing makes a bird feeder bear-proof!

MAINTAINING FEEDERS

After you have selected, filled, and placed bird feeders properly, it's still necessary to keep feeders clean. Here are some recommendations for cleaning bird feeders:

- Clean feeders regularly. Once a month is satisfactory for thistle- (niger) and sunflower-seed feeders and suet feeders.
- Move feeders a foot or two each season to avoid a buildup of wet seeds and bird droppings on the ground below.
- Put plastic, ceramic, and glass feeders in a bucket of hot water with two capfuls of chlorine bleach. Remove as much grime as possible by hand and then wash as you would dishes. The same

can be done with wooden feeders, but use a nonchlorine disinfectant to avoid fading the wood. Some feeders, such as tube feeders, are almost impossible to clean without disassembling; bear this in mind when shopping for feeders.

- Wash feeders thoroughly with water after cleaning with bleach.

It's also necessary to prevent seeds from becoming moldy and spoiling. Here are some recommendations to solve this problem:

- Put only enough seeds in a feeder to last a single day.
- Store seeds in a dry container and keep them dry on feeders.
- Check that seeds don't become moldy or contaminated from droppings on platform feeders where birds stand among the seeds being eaten.
- Check the portals in tube feeders to prevent a buildup of contaminated and moldy seeds.
- Clean portals in tube feeders daily if moldy seed buildup is forming.

Hummingbird feeders require special procedures. The following tips are adapted from The Hummer/Bird Study Group, Inc.:

- Flush hummingbird feeders with hot tap water every few days, or at least once a week.
- Scour the inside of the feeder with a bottle brush. Alternatively, add a small amount of sand or a small quantity of nickel-plated BBs to the inside of the feeder bottle, fill with water, and then gently shake the bottle.
- Rinse the outside and inside thoroughly with hot water so that nothing remains. Do not use soap to clean the inside of hummingbird feeders.
- At least once a month, thoroughly clean feeders with a solution of ¼ cup of bleach to 1 gallon of water.
- Place the feeder in this solution for about one hour, then use a bottle brush if necessary.
- After removing the feeder from the bleach solution, rinse repeatedly and thoroughly with warm water.
- Air dry overnight before refilling the feeder with sugar-water solution.

If you don't want to clean feeders yourself, inquire at your local birdwatching equipment and supply stores; some offer these services, at least for tube feeders.

7 Nest Boxes

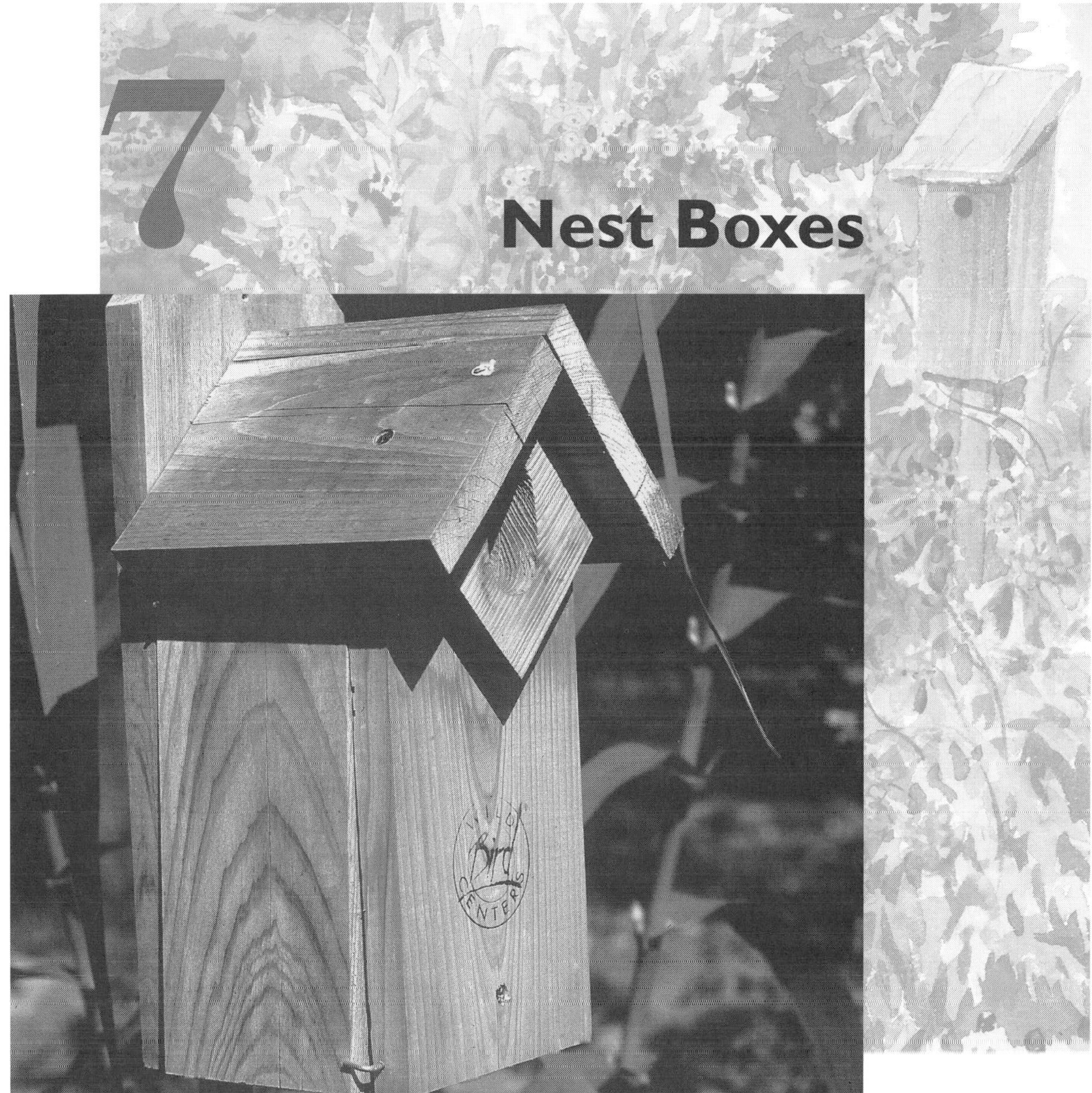

An Eastern Bluebird nest box in the frontyard habitat of Bob and Doris Jones in eastern Pennsylvania.

By now, our backyard habitat offers a rich variety of native trees, shrubs, flowers, and grasses, as well as well-stocked feeders. Such an enhanced habitat is an ideal place for birds to nest and raise their young. Nest boxes, or birdhouses, encourage species that nest in cavities to settle down in your backyard.

Some birds, such as Baltimore Orioles and Chipping Sparrows, may be attracted to backyards with protective trees and shrubs, but will never nest in nest boxes. On the other hand, birds like Tree Swallows, Black-capped Chickadees, House Wrens, and bluebirds nest in natural tree cavities or small openings in other structures. When natural nesting sites are unavailable, these birds seek alternatives. In this chapter, we discuss nest boxes and the birds that accept them.

THE ROLE OF NEST BOXES

It's delightful to hear chattering House Wrens rearing their nestlings in a box provided for them. Equally delightful are views of Eastern Bluebirds coming and going to a nest box along the edge of a large backyard field habitat, or a colony of Purple Martins using martin houses to raise their nestlings near a pond. Nest boxes are a critical component of a fully enhanced backyard habitat. No longer are birds only finding food or shelter, now they also are raising their young in structures provided for that purpose.

Nest boxes have considerable conservation value. As more woodland is cut for housing and land development, cavity-nesting birds are having difficulty finding suitable nesting sites. Adding to the problem are introduced European Starlings and House Sparrows, which compete aggressively for nesting sites with native cavity-nesting birds. Eastern Bluebird populations, for example, dropped to seriously low levels during the past forty years. That's when concerned birders and wildlife conservationists came to the rescue. By constructing thousands of bluebird nest boxes, establishing hundreds of miles of bluebird nest-box trails, and putting nest boxes in other areas such as enhanced larger backyard habitats, they helped the Eastern Bluebird populations rebound. The role that nest boxes played in the rescue was significant. A similar effort is underway to help the Purple Martin: thousands of Purple Martin colonies now thrive where none existed previously.

Many other cavity-nesting birds also accept nest boxes. Among game birds, Wood Ducks are the outstanding example. Wood Duck nest-box projects operate in many states and on many federal lands, including national wildlife refuges. The result is thousands of Wood Ducks raised each year.

Other birds that accept nest boxes include owls (Barn, Barred, Screech, Boreal, and Saw-whet), chickadees, titmice, nuthatches, Brown Creepers, Northern Flickers, wrens, swallows, woodpeckers, and Prothonotary Warblers. As would be expected, different species require different sizes and other characteristics in nest boxes. How to make nest boxes attractive to specific species is discussed later in this chapter. First, I offer general advice on establishing nest boxes.

A European Starling returning with food for its nestlings in a natural tree cavity. These birds, and House Sparrows, are introduced species. They are responsible for using many natural nest cavities needed by native cavity-nesting birds.

SELECTING AND MAINTAINING NEST BOXES

Materials

Whether you build or buy nest boxes, look for some basic materials and features. Do not use pressure-treated woods; they may contain dangerous chemicals. Three-quarter-inch-thick red cedar or bald cypress is the best wood for bird boxes. No paint or preservative is needed for nest boxes made of these woods; simply allow the boxes to weather naturally. Pine and exterior plywood will serve, but they won't weather as well. A preservative is needed on the outside surface of the nest box; I recommend a water-based exterior latex paint. Use white for Purple Martins and dull green for all other nest boxes. Do not paint the entrance hole or the inside of the box. Make sure that wood surfaces facing inside the box are not treated with preservatives or stains, which can create fumes and harm birds.

Some excellent plastic Purple Martin gourds are in widespread and successful use. The Purple Martin Conservation Association also offers its own plastic Super-Gourd martin house that's carefully designed for Purple Martins and highly recommended. (See appendix 4 for contact information.)

Drainage

Nest boxes are exposed to all weather conditions, including heavy rain. Unfortunately, rain sometimes gets inside a box and settles on the bottom, where a nest with eggs or young is located. To prevent rain from getting into a box or, failing that, to prevent it from remaining inside, the U.S. Fish and Wildlife Service has several recommendations:

- Make sure the roof is sloped to drain water off the top. The roof should overhang the outside of the box by approximately 1 inch on each side and the front.
- To prevent rain from entering the box, drill the entrance hole on a slight upward slant.
- To remove any water that may get inside a box, cut away each corner of the floor, and drill a few ¼-inch holes through the floor.
- The floor of the box should fit snugly in a slot in the walls (¼-inch deep).

Entrance Holes

The entrance on a bird box is placed on the front, below the roof. Different sizes are needed for different birds; in some cases, the size requirements are critical and specific. I discuss them later in this chapter.

Provide a rough surface on the inside and outside of the front panel. This makes it easier for adult birds to enter and leave, and for nestlings to leave when they're old enough. A few grooves also can be cut into the inside of the front panel below the entrance hole, where you can put a little wire mesh, cleats, or a little strip of wood, below the nest hole. This allows nestlings to look out and leave the box more easily. However, any wire mesh, cleats, or similar features should be free of sharp edges or points on which birds might injure themselves.

Do not put perches on nest boxes! Most natural cavities don't come equipped with them, and they will allow invasive European Starlings and House Sparrows to perch there and perhaps appropriate the box. A perch also helps a predator get inside a box to eat eggs or young.

Finally, bird nest boxes should have only one hole for entering and exiting; do not purchase boxes with more than one hole. Purple Martin houses are the exception: they have many entrance openings and compartments to accommodate entire breeding colonies.

Ventilation

When nest boxes are exposed to long periods of sunlight, their interior can become so hot that eggs or nestlings can be destroyed. That's why it's necessary to provide ventilation in boxes, which can be accomplished in two ways. You can drill some ¼-inch holes at a slight upward slant below the roof of the box, or you can leave a small gap between the two side walls and the roof (so that the roof is supported only by the front and back). Either approach is fine.

Placement

Part of the fun of putting nest boxes in a backyard habitat is watching birds use them to raise their young, so place them where they can be easily observed. Here are some additional suggestions:

- Mount boxes on metal poles, rather than tree trunks or limbs, to make them less vulnerable to predators.
- Limit small nest boxes for the same species (e.g., for wrens or bluebirds) to four per acre.
- Use only one large nest box per acre (e.g., for American Kestrels or Barn Owls).
- Keep nest boxes away from feeders to prevent territorial disputes.
- If you must mount a nest box in a tree, put only one in each tree.

Checking Boxes

Part of the process of maintaining nest boxes is checking the progress of the birds using them. These visits should be very brief. First, watch a box from a distance for a while to see if there is any activity. If you see nothing, gently tap the outside of the box and listen for sounds inside. Finally, open the box slightly, quickly peek inside, then securely close it.

Other creatures also adopt nest boxes, so be careful when opening them. Protect your eyes in case a European Starling, House Sparrow, mouse, squirrel, flying squirrel, snake, or insect makes a fast departure. I recommend allowing flying squirrels to continue using a box if they're inside—these charming little mammals are a delight to have around.

If insects or parasites such as mites, flies, or fleas are present, treat the inside of the box with a naturally occurring pesticide such as 1 percent rotenone powder or pyrethrum spray. Wasps can be discouraged by coating the inside top of the box with bar soap. Never use artificial pesticides on the inside of nest boxes.

Flying squirrels sometimes use nest boxes intended for cavity-nesting birds. If that happens, I recommend allowing these charming little mammals to keep using the box. They add lots of additional interest to backyard habitats.

Preparing Boxes for Winter

During autumn, at the end of the nesting season, backyard birdwatchers need to attend to some maintenance chores. After nest boxes are cleaned out, take them down and put them in storage or leave them in place; I recommend the latter. In warmer parts of North America, clean out nest boxes after the nestlings have fledged (i.e., left the boxes permanently). This is also a good time to make necessary repairs on boxes. Other animals may use nest boxes for shelter during winter. In spring, therefore, each box must be opened, cleaned, and made ready for use again by birds. Replace those in poor condition.

Pottery nest structures and Purple Martin gourds should definitely be stored inside for winter. If Purple Martin houses are kept outside, plug each entrance hole to prevent House Sparrows or European Starlings from entering and appropriating the compartments.

NEST BOXES FOR SPECIFIC BIRDS

Now let's consider some examples of nest boxes and other structures used to house specific backyard species.

Wood Ducks

Wood Ducks are especially receptive to using nest boxes, which is why federal and state wildlife agencies install them in suitable wetland habitats. However, it's pointless to put up Wood Duck nest boxes if marshes, lakes, ponds, and streams do not contain food and protective cover so ducklings can survive unharmed until they're able to fly.

Wood Duck nest boxes also can be placed on trees 10 to 15 feet inside a deciduous woodland that happens to be adjacent to a wetlands. Some ornithologists believe a woodland habitat is actually a more natural and appropriate place for them.

The nest-box plans provided here were developed by the U.S. Fish and Wildlife Service and are widely used throughout the United States. Hooded Mergansers and Tree Swallows occasionally nest in Wood Duck boxes, which are also attractive to squirrels, owls, European Starlings, and woodpeckers. Predators that raid these boxes include snakes, minks, raccoons, opossums, rats, and house cats.

Therefore, the ideal place to put Wood Duck nest boxes is over water or at the edge of a marsh, pond, lake, or stream. Wood Ducks tolerate other Wood Ducks

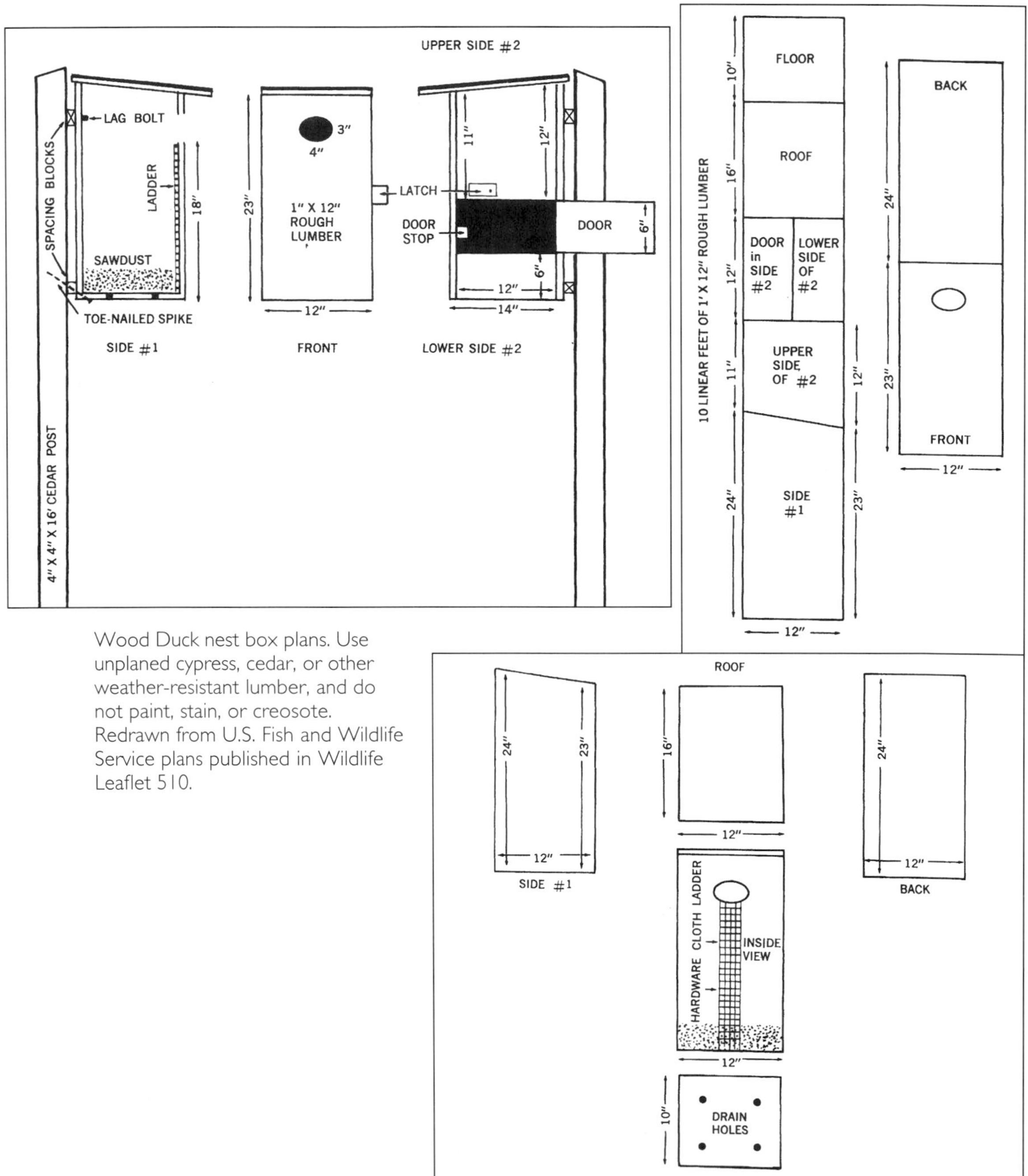

Wood Duck nest box plans. Use unplaned cypress, cedar, or other weather-resistant lumber, and do not paint, stain, or creosote. Redrawn from U.S. Fish and Wildlife Service plans published in Wildlife Leaflet 510.

nesting in boxes very close to each other—sometimes even clustered with two or more mounted on the same pole. However, when installing Wood Duck nest boxes, remember these requirements:

- Put 3 inches of hardwood sawdust or wood shavings on the bottom of the box.
- Mount the box on wood or metal posts, or on a tree.
- Be sure conical or flat metal predator guards are in place below the box, and extend 18 inches or more from the post or tree on which the nest box is attached. The guard should be at least 3 feet above high-water level for boxes over water.
- Place the box approximately 10 feet above the water or ground surface.

Maintenance of these boxes is essential. They should be cleaned each January and repaired as necessary. Stinging insects sometimes adopt boxes for home, so open them carefully to avoid injury. Prior to each nesting season, the inside of boxes can be sprayed with Lysol disinfectant, which may help discourage bees and wasps from using them.

Various types of wood can be used to construct Wood Duck nest boxes; the most commonly used are cypress, unplaned cedar, and weather-resistant lumber. Wood Duck boxes should not be treated with paint, stain, or creosote inside or outside. Simply allow the boxes to weather naturally.

Materials needed to construct the nest box discussed here include twenty-five 8- or 10-penny zinc-coated nails; one spike 4+ inches long; one ¼-inch lag bolt 6 inches long; one hinge (3-inch cabinet type with screws); an 18-inch strip of hardware cloth cut at least 3 inches wide (with sharp ends bent under); a cedar, cypress, or preservative-treated wood post 16 feet long and 4 by 4 inches in size; and enough hardwood sawdust or wood chips to form a 3-inch layer on the bottom of the box.

Wood Ducks lay ten to fifteen creamy or dull white eggs in nest boxes. Occasionally, two females lay their eggs in the same box, called a "dump nest," resulting in eighteen to forty eggs in one box. Incubation lasts about thirty days, after which the eggs hatch. The female does the incubating while the male remains nearby. In the case of dump nests, the two females sometimes take turns incubating or do so simultaneously.

You can also buy Wood Duck nest boxes from birding stores or Coveside Conservation Products (see appendix 4).

American Kestrels

American Kestrels readily use nest boxes for nesting. Place kestrel nest boxes on trees or poles near or in farm fields or old field ecosystems. Do not allow vines to grow up around the boxes, because snakes and other predators can use them to raid the boxes for eggs and nestlings. The height above ground can vary from about 10 to 30 feet, with the entrance hole facing south.

There are several design variations of American Kestrel nest boxes, but most work well. The design shown here is used by the Iowa Department of Natural Resources. Dimensions suggested for American Kestrel nest boxes are as follows: a box bottom 8 by 8 inches, a depth of 12 to 15 inches, an entrance height of 9 to 12 inches, and an entrance-hole diameter of 3 inches. Do not place perches on American Kestrel nest boxes—the kestrels do not require them and they allow European Starlings to enter and perhaps appropriate the box.

You can also purchase commercially manufactured American Kestrel nest boxes from birding stores or Coveside Conservation Products.

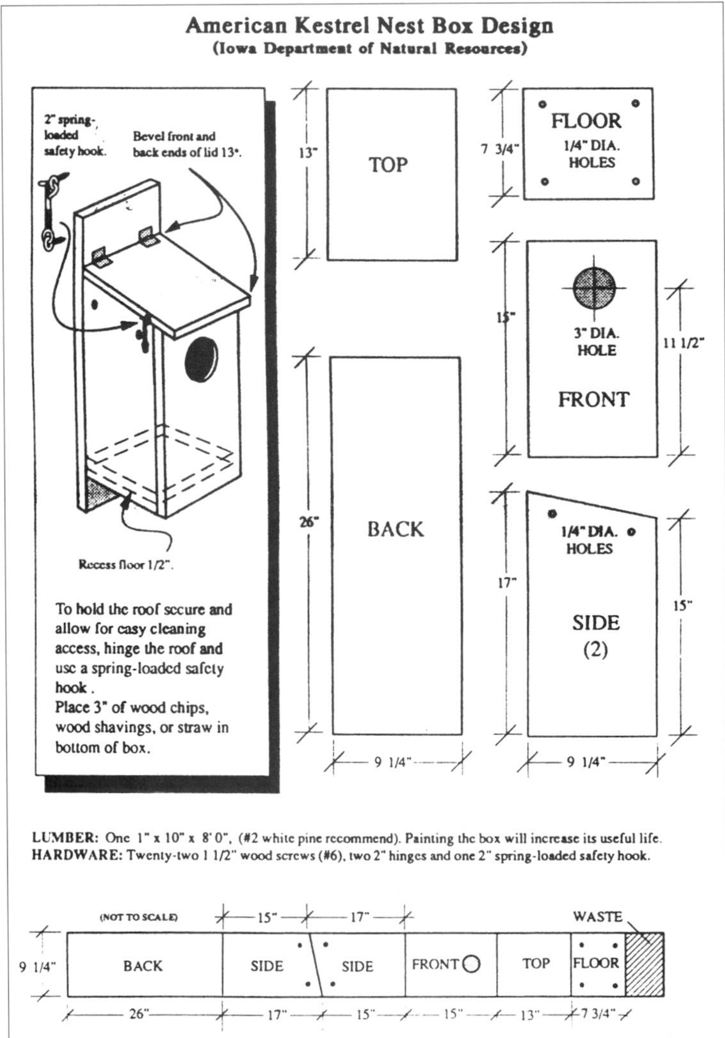

American Kestrel nest box plans. Courtesy the Iowa Department of Natural Resources.

American Kestrels lay three to six eggs, typically four, and usually on alternate days. The eggs are colored white, pinkish-white, or pale cinnamon with numerous brown spots. Incubation by the female lasts about thirty days. Usually only one brood is reared per year, although on rare occasions, a second nesting is attempted.

Owls

Barn Owls

Barn Owls accept boxes or similar structures in which to nest. Sometimes boxes are placed on the outside of a barn or silo, just inside with an opening leading from the outside into the nest box, or inside the building a short distance from the nest opening. Barn Owl nest boxes, placed appropriately throughout a rural area, can help reverse locally declining owl populations.

That's important, because Barn Owls are major predators of meadow voles and rats, and are among the best wildlife friends that farmers have.

Nest-box dimensions are as follows: a box bottom 10 by 18 inches, a depth of 15 to 18 inches, an entrance height of 4 inches, and an entrance-hole diameter of 6 inches. The box should be placed 12 to 18 feet above the ground. Commercially manufactured Barn Owl nest boxes are also available from Coveside Conservation Products.

Barn Owls lay five to seven white eggs, which are incubated by the female, with the male regularly feeding her rats, voles, and other delicacies. There is some confusion in ornithological literature regarding the incubation period of Barn Owl eggs. Depending on how it is counted, the incubation period lasts twenty-one to twenty-four days or thirty-two to thirty-four days.

Barn Owls are unusual in that they have been reported to nest at various times throughout the year, not only during spring when most other birds nest. Availability of prey may be one factor; they may delay nesting until enough food (mostly rats and meadow voles) is available to feed their young.

AMERICAN KESTREL NEST BOX TRAILS

In some areas, organizations install American Kestrel nest boxes across the landscape in what results as kestrel nest-box trails. Birders living in rural areas are ideally located to establish these trails. Indeed, long-term maintenance of nest-box trails can go a long way toward maintaining or increasing American Kestrel populations—and also provide excellent bird-conservation programs in which birders, Scouts, 4-H members, and other organizations can participate.

However, maintaining a kestrel nest-box trail over miles of rural countryside is time-consuming and labor-intensive. Each box must be cleaned in early autumn after the nesting season and kept in good repair. A correctly placed box can be reached only with a ladder. The cost of maintaining and replacing boxes adds up, so don't attempt to establish a kestrel nest-box trail unless you are able to devote adequate time and money to the effort. If you can, the knowledge you'll gain, coupled with the conservation value of the boxes, makes the effort very worthwhile.

Screech Owls

Screech owls readily accept nest boxes in which to raise their young. They prefer orchards or other semi-open areas, with nearby running water, lakes, or ponds.

The dimensions for screech owl nest boxes are as follows: a box bottom 8 by 8 inches, a depth of 12 to 15 inches, an entrance height of 9 to 12 inches, and an entrance-hole diameter of 3 inches. Put the box 10 to 30 feet above the ground.

Screech owls lay four or five white eggs, which are incubated by the female for about twenty-six days until they hatch. At night, the male brings food to the female on the nest. However, during the day, the male also may join the female in the nest box, using it for roosting.

For a relatively small bird, a screech owl can be extremely aggressive in defending its nesting territory. More than one backyard birder has been attacked when venturing too close to a screech owl nest. However, the delight in having these birds nesting in a backyard habitat or nearby is worthwhile to most birders.

These birds, of course, are fully protected by federal wildlife laws and treaties, so they must not be harassed or killed.

Woodpeckers

A number of woodpeckers accept nest boxes as substitutes for tree cavities.

Lewis's Woodpeckers

Lewis's Woodpeckers accept nest boxes of the following dimensions: a box bottom 7 by 7 inches, a depth of 16 to 18 inches, an entrance height of 14 to 16 inches, and an entrance-hole diameter of 2½ inches. Put the box 12 to 20 feet above the ground.

Lewis's Woodpeckers lay five to nine white eggs, which are incubated for fourteen days until they hatch.

Red-Headed Woodpeckers

One of the most lovely of North American birds, Red-headed Woodpeckers use natural tree cavities and nest boxes to raise their young. Here are the dimensions for building a nest box: a box bottom 6 by 6 inches, a depth of 12 to 15 inches, an entrance height of 9 to 12 inches, and an entrance-hole diameter of 2 inches. The box should be placed 10 to 20 feet above the ground.

Red-headed Woodpeckers lay four to seven white eggs (often five), which are incubated by both parents for fourteen days before they hatch. One brood is reared per year in the northern part of their range, but sometimes two broods are produced in the South.

Yellow-Bellied Sapsuckers

Yellow-bellied Sapsuckers have a unique way of securing food—they drill holes into live trees to allow sap to seep out and then lap up the sap and the insects it attracts. Sapsuckers accept nest boxes with the following dimensions: a box bottom 5 by 5 inches, a depth of 12 to 15 inches, an entrance height of 9 to 12 inches, and an entrance-hole diameter of 1½ inches. The box should be placed 10 to 20 feet above the ground.

Yellow-bellied Sapsuckers lay four to seven white eggs, which both parents incubate for about twelve days prior to hatching.

Downy Woodpeckers

Downy Woodpeckers are common birds at many backyard feeding stations throughout the United States, and may become nesting birds in some wildlife-friendly habitats if nest boxes are provided.

Here are the dimensions for Downy Woodpecker nest boxes: a box bottom 4 by 4 inches, a depth of 8 to 10 inches, an entrance height of 6 to 8 inches, and an entrance-hole diameter of 1¼ inches. The box should be placed 5 to 15 feet above the ground.

Downy Woodpeckers lay four or five white eggs, which both parents take shifts in incubating during the day; however, the male incubates the eggs at night. The incubation period is twelve days.

Hairy Woodpeckers

A larger version of the Downy Woodpeckers, Hairy Woodpeckers also visit backyard feeding stations and may be enticed to nest in backyard habitats if housing is provided.

The nest box for these woodpeckers should have a box bottom 6 by 6 inches, a depth of 12 to 15 inches, an entrance height of 9 to 12 inches, and an entrance-hole diameter of 1½ inches. The box should be placed 8 to 20 feet above the ground.

Hairy Woodpeckers lay four white eggs, which both parents incubate in shifts during the day; as with the Downy Woodpeckers, the male incubates them at night. The incubation period lasts about twelve days. One brood is reared per year.

Northern Flickers

Northern Flickers accept nest boxes as substitutes for natural cavities in which to nest. Flicker nest boxes should have a box bottom 7 by 7 inches, a depth of 16 to 18 inches, an entrance height of 14 to 16 inches, and an entrance-hole diameter of 2½ inches. The box should be placed 6 to 20 feet above the ground. Various companies manufacture Northern Flicker nest boxes; Coveside Conservation Products, for example, offers one in its catalog (see appendix 4).

There are usually six to eight white eggs in a Northern Flicker nest, which are incubated for about twelve days prior to hatching. During the day, the parents take shifts in performing the incubation duty, but at night the male does the incubation.

Pileated Woodpeckers

Pileated Woodpeckers are the largest woodpeckers found in the United States (assuming that the Ivory-billed Woodpecker is extinct). Its oval holes in trees provide distinctive, clear evidence that the big woodchoppers are present. While these birds normally use cavities that they excavate in trees, they also accept nest boxes as places to raise their young.

Pileated Woodpecker nest boxes should have the following measurements: a box bottom 8 by 8 inches, a depth of 16 to 24 inches, an entrance height of 12 to 20 inches, and a 3-by-4-inch entrance hole cut vertically. The box should be placed 15 to 25 feet above the ground.

Pileated Woodpeckers lay three or four white eggs, which are incubated by both parents for eighteen days until they hatch. There is one brood reared per year.

Flycatchers

Eastern Phoebes

Eastern Phoebes accept nesting platforms (not boxes) on which to build their nests. The platforms can be installed under eaves of barns (with open doors) and other outdoor structures, such as roofed firewood shelters. These birds also frequently build their nests under small bridges crossing creeks and streams.

The platform should measure 6 by 6 inches, the back 6 inches high, and the whole platform should be placed 8 to 12 feet above the ground under a roofed or other sheltered structure. If short pieces of knitting yarn are placed outside during spring, Eastern Phoebes may incorporate them into their nest construction—which adds all sorts of colors to the nest.

There are three to six white eggs—often five—in an Eastern Phoebe nest. The female incubates the eggs alone for about fifteen days. Sometimes two broods are reared per year.

Ash-Throated Flycatchers

Ash-throated Flycatchers are found in dry woodlands, forests along streams, brushy open country, and deserts in the western United States. A few occasionally wander into the eastern United States. They accept nest boxes in which to raise their young, so conservationists can provide additional potential housing for these birds.

Box dimensions are as follows: a box bottom 6 by 6 inches, a depth of 8 to 12 inches, an entrance height of 6 to 10 inches, and an entrance-hole diameter of 1½ inches. The box should be placed 5 to 15 feet above the ground.

A female Ash-throated Flycatcher lays four or five white eggs with some dark marks, which are incubated for fifteen days until they hatch. Prior to depositing the eggs, she lines the bottom of the nest box with soft materials, such as fur, hair, weeds, or even an old snakeskin.

Great Crested Flycatchers

The Great Crested Flycatcher is a bird of groves and woodlands, where they nest in natural cavities. These flycatchers also accept nest boxes.

Box dimensions are as follows: a box bottom 6 by 6 inches, a depth of 8 to 12 inches, an entrance height of 6 to 10 inches, and an entrance-hole diameter of 1¾ inches. Place the box 5 to 15 feet above the ground. Sometimes an old snake skin is added to the nest.

Great Crested Flycatchers lay four to eight—often five—pinkish-white or yellowish eggs, which the female incubates for thirteen to fifteen days.

Purple Martins

In eastern North America, Purple Martins are unique in that they are completely dependent on humans in their nesting habits. It is believed that this extraordinary interaction between the human and avian worlds began when Native Americans noticed that Purple Martins would accept dried, hollowed-out gourds as a cavity in which to nest and raise their young. Early European settlers continued the tradition. As a result, in a process known as "tradition shift," eastern martins will only nest in gourds or apartment-style structures provided by people. Purple Martins west of the Rockies continue to nest in natural cavities in trees, old woodpecker holes, or piling cavities.

Fortunately, there is great public interest in attracting Purple Martins to backyard habitats. Both nonprofit organizations and private individuals are devoted to their long-term welfare by providing housing for these colonial nesting birds. Among the organizations leading martin conservation efforts are the American Bird Conservation Association; Conservancy Purple Martin Society; National

WildBird Refuge, Inc.–Project Swallow; The Nature Society; Purple Martin Conservation Association; and The Purple Martin Society, N.A. The Purple Martin Conservation Association, for example, operates a Purple Martin Colony Registry, on which landlords register their martin colonies and provide data on nesting success. Contact information for these organizations is in appendix 1.

First, we look at martin gourds and apartment houses; then we consider how to establish and manage a martin colony in your backyard.

Housing Purple Martins

Over generations, Purple Martins have learned to accept both dried, hollowed-out gourds and apartment-style houses as spaces in which to nest and raise their young. A typical gourd has two hanging holes drilled at the top and four to six small drain holes drilled into the bottom. Gourds are hung individually or in groups from a support pole or other structure. If you opt for a natural gourd, the entrance hole should have a diameter of 2¼ inches. Backyard birdwatchers can purchase gourd seeds and a gourd-growing booklet from the Purple Martin Conservation Association. Cleaned gourds, ready to be painted and used, can also be purchased from this organization (see appendix 1).

Several companies produce plastic Purple Martin nesting gourds. NATURE-line by Plasticraft makes its gourds with reprocessed plastic and a UV inhibitor to withstand the sun's effects. Carroll Industries manufactures 8-inch plastic martin gourds, which are shipped in two halves that snap together. James R. Hill III, founder of the Purple Martin Conservation Association, privately manufactures the SuperGourd by Bird Abodes, which is a one-piece, plastic structure designed to

James R. Hill III/Purple Martin Conservation Association

Chris J. Slabaugh Sr/American Bird Conservation Association

A. A Purple Martin at an advanced design SuperGourd, which is now the industry standard.

B. Purple Martin gourds, single-unit houses, and apartment houses on farmland surrounding the American Bird Conservation Association headquarters in Nappanee, Indiana.

resemble a gourd. A special threaded access port allows a hand to be inserted into the gourd. (See appendix 5 for contact information.)

However, the most widely used Purple Martin nesting structures are referred to as apartment houses: large wooden or metal birdhouses, often with multiple levels, containing several separate compartments. Common features include porch-like shelves, porch dividers, owl guards (i.e., outward-curving rods that prevent owls from reaching into compartments), perching arms, and access doors for inspection and cleaning. Popular models are manufactured by Nature House, Inc., and Coates Manufacturing, Inc. Lone Star Purple Martin Houses manufactures excellent aluminum apartment houses, particularly because they provide deep compartments (12 inches), which give martins more room to nest and make it more difficult for owls to reach in and take nestlings.

Thomas Borkholder of Trendsetter also makes quality aluminum apartment houses for Purple Martins. Other companies manufacture and sell wooden Purple Martin houses, which vary in design and quality; an excellent source is the Birds' Paradise (see appendix 5).

In eastern North America, you should paint gourds or houses white—Purple Martins are accustomed to that color and it keeps the interior cooler. As with other nesting structures, adequate ventilation and drainage are also needed for each compartment, and insulation may be needed in the attic of some houses. Floor dimensions for martin houses should be no less than 6 by 6 inches, and preferably 7 by 12 inches. The height can be 7 inches, with entrance holes placed 1 inch above the floor. The size of the entrance hole should measure 2⅛ inches. If housing plans do not conform to these sizes, modify them accordingly. Moreover, if porch dividers are not shown on the plans, add them.

Predators of various types are attracted to Purple Martin colonies: raccoons, squirrels, hawks, owls, crows, rats, snakes, and—in some areas—fire ants. Equip support poles with external predator guards. You can use tape or Teflon spray on poles to stop fire ants, or put a grease ring around a low section of the pole. A more conventional pole guard is needed to prevent raccoons and snakes from climbing to the housing.

Do not allow vines and shrubs to grow up around martin housing; martins will avoid it, apparently recognizing that it is vulnerable to predators such as cats, raccoons, and squirrels. Likewise, martins dislike houses connected to wires or cables; because some predators can climb wires, they should not be used to support martin housing.

Managing Purple Martin Colonies

The Purple Martin Conservation Association has developed a number of management recommendations for Purple Martin landlords. The association maintains an excellent website that I encourage anyone interested in martins to study. The following tips on purple martins are culled from the association's website.

Colonies must be established in the correct location. Martins will not accept housing enclosed or obstructed by trees. Martin houses should be at least 40 to 60 feet away from trees of equal height. Ideally, gourds or apartment houses should be situated 10 to 15 feet above the ground in open airspace, between 30 and 120 feet from a birder's house. (Human dwellers actually attract martins, probably because they repel natural predators.) The Purple Martin Conservation Association also recommends using a telescoping pole or a comparable device so that the house can be raised and lowered vertically, affording the landlord easy access to compartments. Avoid apartment houses that only provide access through the roof, entrance holes, or layers of the house.

Purple Martins in eastern North America lay three to eight white eggs—frequently four or five—which are incubated by the female for about fifteen days until they hatch. Prior to depositing her eggs, the female lines the gourd or apartment with soft materials such as grasses, leaves, string, and bark.

It is critical to open martin housing at the correct time and not to close it too quickly. In a behavior referred to as *site tenacity*, an adult martin almost always returns to the same site where it nested successfully the previous year. It is the subadults—last year's fledglings—that inhabit new breeding sites. They appear about four weeks after the first adult martins are seen. Because they have not yet developed site tenacity, the subadults are easily repelled from new housing, particularly if it is colonized by aggressive birds such as House Sparrows and European Starlings. Thus, the way to lure subadult birds into new housing is to open it only at the proper time when these birds arrive. The migration map produced by the Purple Martin Conservation Association (see page 200) is helpful in adjusting timing for opening and closing.

At established nesting sites, adult martins generally arrive within one or two weeks of the previous year's arrival date. Established martin houses should always be kept closed until some adult birds appear—in some places, as late as the end of June. Depending on where a colony is located, the arrival timing differs. In the North, adult martins arrive during an eight- to twelve-week period; in the South, the arrival period can extend for sixteen to twenty weeks. During these periods, landlords should keep careful watch on the housing to prevent House Sparrows and European Starlings from using it for their nesting activities. If either of these birds do, evict them promptly (neither species is protected by state or federal law). Sometimes birds such as flycatchers, wrens, Tree Swallows, and bluebirds—all protected by state and federal laws—attempt to nest in martin housing. If this happens, plug the compartment entrances and put

PURPLE MARTINS AND MOSQUITO CONTROL

In the 1960s, reports appeared in the press claiming that Purple Martins eat two thousand mosquitoes per day and urging people to erect Purple Martin houses to establish nesting colonies. The implication was that Purple Martins represent a natural and effective means of controlling mosquitoes.

Ornithologist Herbert Kale of the Florida Audubon Society was fascinated by these claims. After reviewing scientific papers about martin food habits and related data, he found the claims were not supported by scientific data. In fact, mosquitoes are a negligible part of a Purple Martin's diet, although martins eat many other insects. Therefore, don't expect Purple Martins to control mosquitoes.

nest boxes for these birds elsewhere in the backyard habitat. Hopefully, they'll discover and use their own nest boxes, after which the martin housing can be opened.

Martins recognize their own nesting compartments based on height, relative orientation, and even compass direction. This means that landlords must take great care to mark the precise height and orientation of martin houses so they can be restored to their original positions after nest checks. Likewise, landlords with only one house in their colony should be leery of replacing the house entirely; if the new structure is significantly different, the returning adults may reject it. It is better to phase in a second house alongside an established one over the course of a season.

As with all birdhouses, martin apartments or gourds should be kept in good repair. If nests become wet after severe rainstorms, remove the nest material and replace it with clean, dry, hardwood shavings. To control parasites, put DE (diatomaceous earth) in each compartment. Do not use pesticides in any nest boxes. Clean the houses in autumn with a 10 percent solution of bleach, then rinse

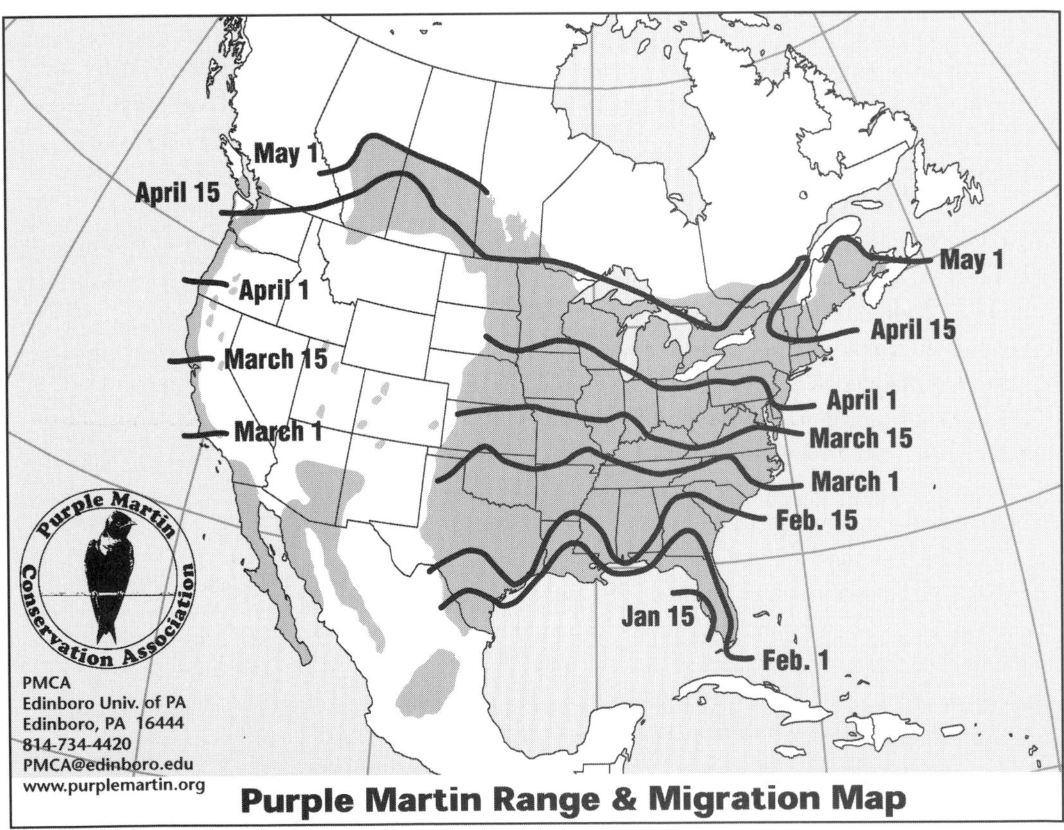

Purple Martin breeding range, migration map, and spring arrival timetable. Black lines represent average first arrival dates of older adult martins at sites of established colonies. Smaller or younger colonies may have slighter later return dates. The northward spring migration of Purple Martins coincides with warming temperatures that support emergence of flying insects martins eat. Martins have at least three northward migration routes from South America: around the Gulf of Mexico through Mexico; across 600 miles of open Gulf waters from Yucatan to the Gulf coast; and across the West Indies to Florida. The spring and autumn migrations from North to South America are about 5,000 miles each. Map provided by the Purple Martin Conservation Association.

thoroughly with water, and air-dry them. If possible, store houses indoors during the winter; if not, plug the entrance holes so interlopers can't get in.

Landlords can provide crushed, dried eggshells or oystershells in a container near the housing so that calcium and grit are added to the martins' diet. If eggshells are used, rinse them thoroughly, dry them in the oven, and then crush them. Some landlords provide nesting materials such as dry pine needles, twigs, or straw scattered over the ground near the colony. Using a garden hose, soak an area of soil near the colony to produce mud; this also can be done for Cliff Swallows, Barn Swallows, and American Robins.

DAWNSONGS

Adult Purple Martins use dawnsongs to lure subadult martins to colonies. If you haven't succeeded in attracting Purple Martins to housing, try playing a tape recording of martin "dawnsinging" for an hour or two before dawn or at other times of the day. Martin landlords can also use recordings to attract subadult martins to new or unused housing. A dawnsong recording is played during the two- to four-month period when Purple Martins are migrating northward during spring (see migration map). Recordings are available from the Purple Martin Conservation Association.

Swallows

Tree Swallows and Violet-Green Swallows

When bluebird nest boxes are placed near lakes or ponds, Tree Swallows and Violet-green Swallows also accept them to raise their young. Box dimensions are as follows: a box bottom 5 by 5 inches, a depth of 6 to 8 inches, an entrance height of 4 to 6 inches, and an entrance-hole diameter of 1½ inches. Place the box 5 to 15 feet above the ground. You can purchase Tree Swallow or Violet-green Swallow nest boxes from Country Ecology or birdwatching stores.

To attract these swallows, build and install nest boxes of the size indicated in open fields or near ponds or lakes. Place the boxes about 100 feet from trees or shrubs, and separate individual boxes by about 300 feet.

Tree Swallows and Eastern Bluebirds often occupy the same habitat and sometimes the two species will accept a pair of neighboring boxes, either facing opposite directions on the same pole or a short distance apart (25 feet). If you establish a number of such pairings, for the best results they should be separated by 300 feet.

Tree Swallows lay four to six white eggs, which the female incubates for thirteen to sixteen days. One brood is reared per year. Violet-green Swallows also lay four to six white eggs, which are incubated for thirteen to fourteen days.

Barn Swallows

Unlike some swallows that nest in cavities, burrows, or nest boxes, Barn Swallows do not accept boxes. However, they do accept nesting platforms placed under the eaves of a barn or garage (provided the doors are kept open at all times). The platform should measure 6 by 6 inches, have a back 6 inches high, and be placed 8 to 12 feet above the ground under the eaves of buildings. Barn Swallows build their mud nests on the platform. To provide a nearby supply of mud for their use, use a garden hose to soak some bare soil with water.

Barn Swallows lay four or five white eggs with brown spots. The eggs are incubated for fifteen days by both parents in shifts of approximately fifteen minutes during the day. At night, however, the female remains on the eggs as the male perches nearby. Sometimes two broods are raised in a year.

Wrens

Three species of wrens in North America accept nest boxes or similar structures in which to nest.

Carolina Wrens need nest boxes with one dimension slightly different than is used for other wrens. When constructing their nest box, use the following dimensions: a box bottom 4 by 4 inches, a depth of 6 to 8 inches, an entrance height of 4 to 6 inches, and an entrance-hole diameter of 1½ inches. The box should be placed 5 to 10 feet above the ground. For Bewick's Wrens and House Wrens, use the same dimensions for nest boxes except for the entrance-hole diameter, which should be 1¼ inches. As with Carolina Wrens, the box should be 5 to 10 feet above the ground. Alternative dimensions and design for House Wrens are shown in the drawing below.

Backyard birdwatchers should be aware that House Wrens sometimes interfere with nesting attempts of other birds by puncturing the eggs in nearby nests. This is natural behavior and birders should not attempt to intervene or remove the wrens;

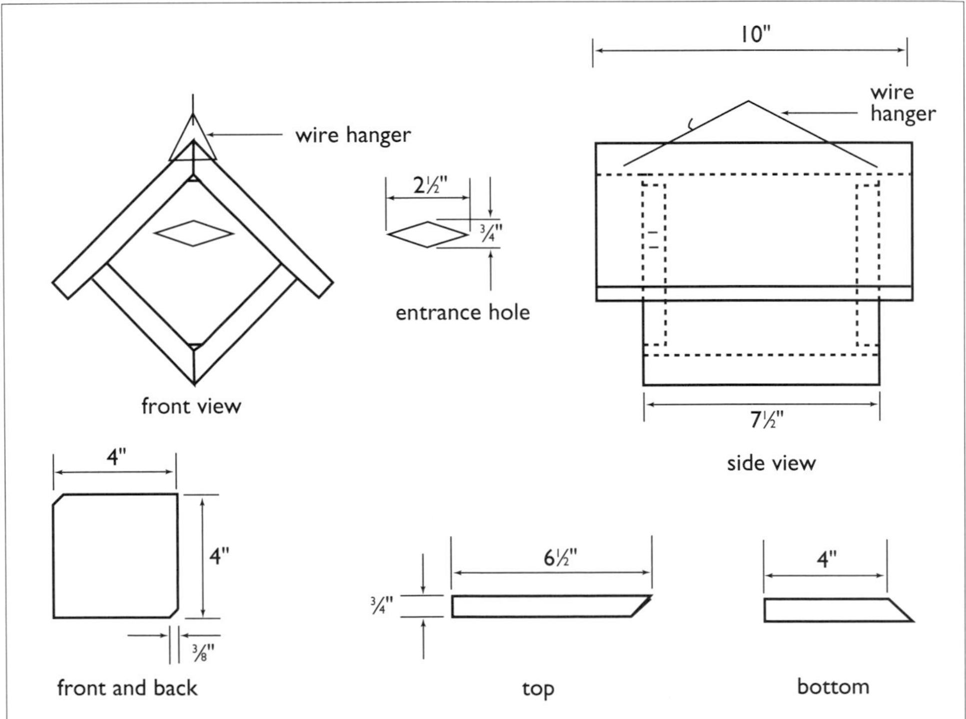

Plans for making a House Wren nest box. Using an oblong entrance allows House Wrens to put small twigs, fine grass, and hair into the box as nesting material. One section of the bottom should be attached with screws to allow removal for cleaning. Hang the box from eaves of a house, trellis, or tree limbs. Redrawn from plans by Greg Oskay/Water Resources Design, Inc.

they are protected by federal and state laws. If House Wrens are not wanted, don't put wren houses in a backyard habitat. In another interesting behavior, House Wrens are known to fill nearby unused boxes with dummy nests fashioned from twigs.

Carolina Wrens lay four to eight (often five or six) white to pale pink eggs marked with vivid brown spots. The female incubates the eggs for fourteen days before they hatch, as the male feeds her on the nest. As many as three broods can be raised in the South in a year, but elsewhere two broods are typical. Bewick's Wrens deposit four to eleven white eggs with dark spots, which the female incubates for fourteen days. House Wrens typically lay six or seven white eggs speckled with brownish and reddish spots. The female incubates the eggs for approximately thirteen days. Two broods can be reared in a year.

Chickadees

Black-capped Chickadees and their relatives are also cavity-nesting birds that accept nest boxes. Dimensions for constructing chickadee nest boxes are as follows: a box bottom 4 by 4 inches, a depth of 8 to 10 inches, an entrance height of 6 to 8 inches, and an entrance-hole diameter of 1⅛ inches. The box should be placed 4 to 15 feet above the ground.

Not all backyard birdwatchers make their own chickadee nest boxes. However, Country Ecology sells chickadee nest boxes or you can buy them at birdwatching stores.

Black-capped Chickadees typically lay six to eight white eggs with pale reddish spots, which are identical to those of the Carolina Chickadee. The female Black-capped Chickadee incubates her eggs for about twelve days, as the male feeds her on the nest.

Titmice

Tufted Titmice and their relatives naturally nest in tree cavities, but they also accept nest boxes as a substitute. The dimensions are as follows: a box bottom 4 by 4 inches, a depth of 10 to 12 inches, an entrance height of 6 to 10 inches, and an entrance-hole diameter of 1¼ inches. The box should be placed 5 to 15 feet above the ground.

Tufted Titmice generally lay five or six white or creamy-colored eggs speckled with small dots. The female incubates the eggs for thirteen or fourteen days until they hatch, covering the eggs with soft nesting materials when she leaves the nest box. The male often feeds the female while she is engaged in her motherly duties inside the nest box.

Nuthatches

Four species of nuthatches naturally nest in tree cavities, but they also use nest boxes. Three of these birds require one size nest box, the other a different size.

Red-breasted, Pygmy, and Brown-headed Nuthatches each can use the same size box with dimensions as follows: a box bottom 4 by 4 inches, a depth of 8 to 10 inches, an entrance height of 6 to 8 inches, and an entrance-hole diameter of 1¼ inches. The box should be placed 5 to 15 feet above the ground.

Red-breasted Nuthatches usually lay five or six white eggs marked with reddish-brown spots. They are incubated by the female for twelve days prior to hatching. One brood of young is reared per year. Pygmy Nuthatches, residents of ponderosa and other pine forests in the west, lay four to nine white eggs with dark markings. The incubation period is fifteen or sixteen days before hatching, and one brood is raised each year. Brown-headed Nuthatches generally lay five to six white eggs that are extensively marked with small reddish-brown spots and blotches. After the eggs are incubated for about fourteen days, they hatch. One brood is reared each year.

White-breasted Nuthatches require a slightly different size nest box, with dimensions as follows: a box bottom 4 by 4 inches, a depth of 8 to 10 inches, an entrance height of 6 to 8 inches, and an entrance-hole diameter of 1⅜ inches. The box should be placed 5 to 15 feet above the ground.

White-breasted Nuthatches lay five to ten eggs (typically eight), white with pale brown and lavender spots. The female incubates the eggs for twelve days until they hatch. One brood is raised each year.

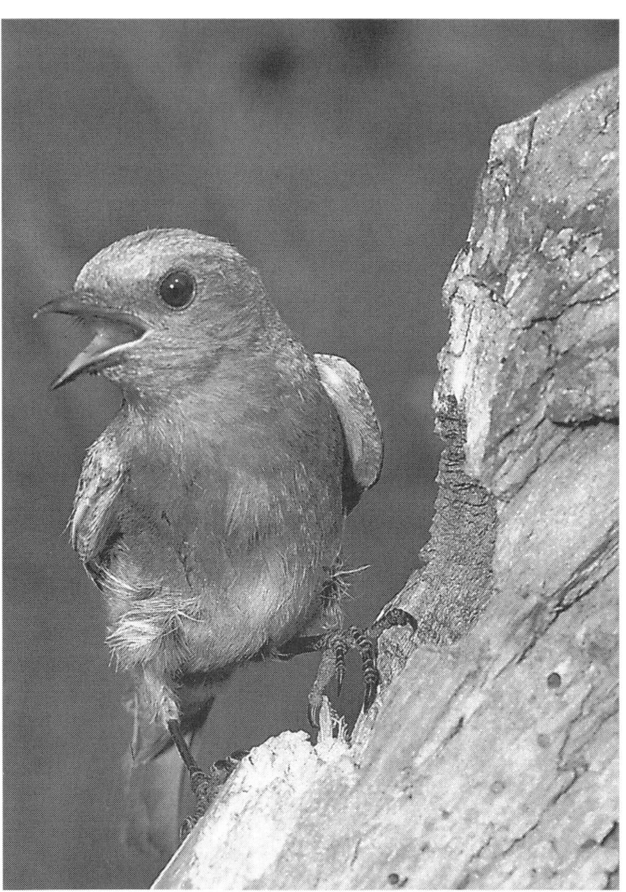

A male Eastern Bluebird at the entrance to its nest in a cavity in a wood fence post beside a rural road. Bluebird nest boxes now serve as substitutes for rapidly disappearing natural cavities in posts and trees.

Bluebirds

There are three species of bluebirds in North America: Eastern, Mountain, and Western. All are members of the thrush family, lovely and popular birds. Moreover, many people are taking action to help bluebird populations survive and to remain an important part of the wildlife community, which is especially true in rural areas.

This activism began with the discovery in the middle of the twentieth century that the populations of Eastern Bluebirds and some Mountain and Western Bluebirds were seriously declining. The discovery sounded alarms among birdwatchers, ornithologists, and conservation biologists. The reasons for the drop in Eastern Bluebird populations are varied.

- substantial loss of many trees and shrubs, such as flowering dogwood and American holly, whose fruits were important winter food supplies

- adverse weather conditions during which vital trees, shrubs, and fruits were coated with ice and unavailable as food
- widespread use of pesticides such as DDT (now banned) that killed some bluebirds on direct contact and many more because their insect food supply was severely reduced or eliminated
- widespread loss of essential habitat and natural nesting cavities
- serious competition for food and cavity nesting sites from European Starlings and House Sparrows.

That's when birdwatchers began building bluebird nest boxes and establishing trails in an effort to offset the loss of natural cavity-nesting sites. Both are now well-established conservation traditions in the United States and Canada.

Let's look more closely at bluebird conservation and how backyard birders can participate. I've already discussed gardening, but it bears repeating here that rural birders can play an important role in bluebird conservation by planting fruit-producing trees, shrubs, and vines in their backyard. During winter, particularly when severe weather conditions prevail and natural food is scarce, the food they provide is critical. The best food plant species for the different regions of the United States are shown in the charts in chapter 5.

North American Bluebird Society

The North American Bluebird Society, Inc., is the leading conservation, public-education, and research organization dedicated to bluebirds, although its interests also include other cavity-nesting birds. Through its magazine, *Bluebird* (formerly *Sialia*), members are informed of the latest happenings in the world of bluebirds.

The Society also established industry standards for the design, dimensions, and construction of bluebird nest boxes; evaluates nest-box samples provided by manufacturers; and gives a seal of approval on boxes meeting the Society's standards. By purchasing nest boxes meeting North American Bluebird Society standards, backyard birdwatchers can be sure they're offering bluebirds the best and safest in housing.

The Society has a speaker's bureau that schedules presentations of bluebird programs to bird clubs, Audubon groups, and other public gatherings.

Nest Boxes

Backyard birdwatchers can help Eastern, Mountain, and Western Bluebirds maintain adequate breeding populations by putting up bluebird nest boxes in large backyard habitats or by establishing bluebird nest-box trails in rural areas.

Although various bluebird nest-box plans are available, I recommend using the design and dimensions provided by the North American Bluebird Society, Inc. Plans and dimensions for Mountain and Western Bluebird boxes are the same, whereas Eastern Bluebirds require somewhat different dimensions. (Note: The entrance hole for the Mountain Bluebird nest box should be 1 9/16 inches rather than 1 1/2 inches.)

Bluebird nest boxes can be purchased at birdwatching stores, garden supply shops, and other places. However, buy nest boxes whose design, dimensions, and construction meet standards developed by the North American Bluebird Society, Inc., and are approved by that organization; look for a small sticker of approval.

Place bluebird nest boxes in areas with low vegetation, away from trees and shrubs, and not close to fields or other areas that receive frequent and heavy applications of pesticides. Also avoid places with large populations of House Sparrows. A good rule-of-thumb is to place a bluebird nest box at least 100 feet from any

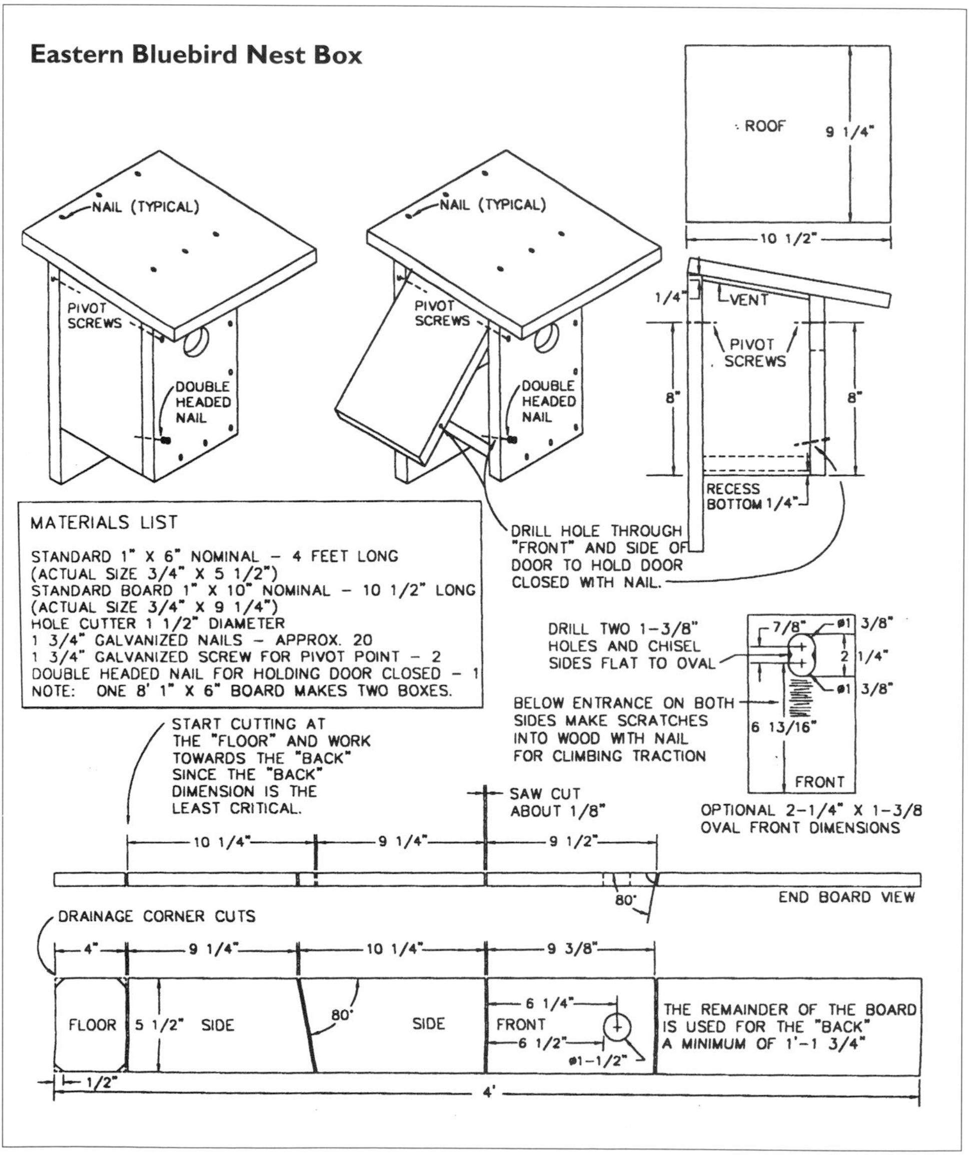

North American Bluebird Society nest-box plans for the Eastern Bluebird. Redrawn from plans developed by the North American Bluebird Society.

protective vegetation. However, provide an extra perch or two near the box; bluebirds make good use of them.

To support a bluebird box, use a piece of galvanized ¾-inch (inside diameter) pipe that's 8 feet long. Two feet of the pipe is put into the ground, leaving 6 feet above ground for mounting the nest-box bottom at eye level, approximately 5 feet above the ground. There's also room to put a predator guard below the box.

Eastern Bluebirds generally lay four or five pale blue eggs (rarely white), which are incubated for about fourteen days by the female before hatching. Sometimes

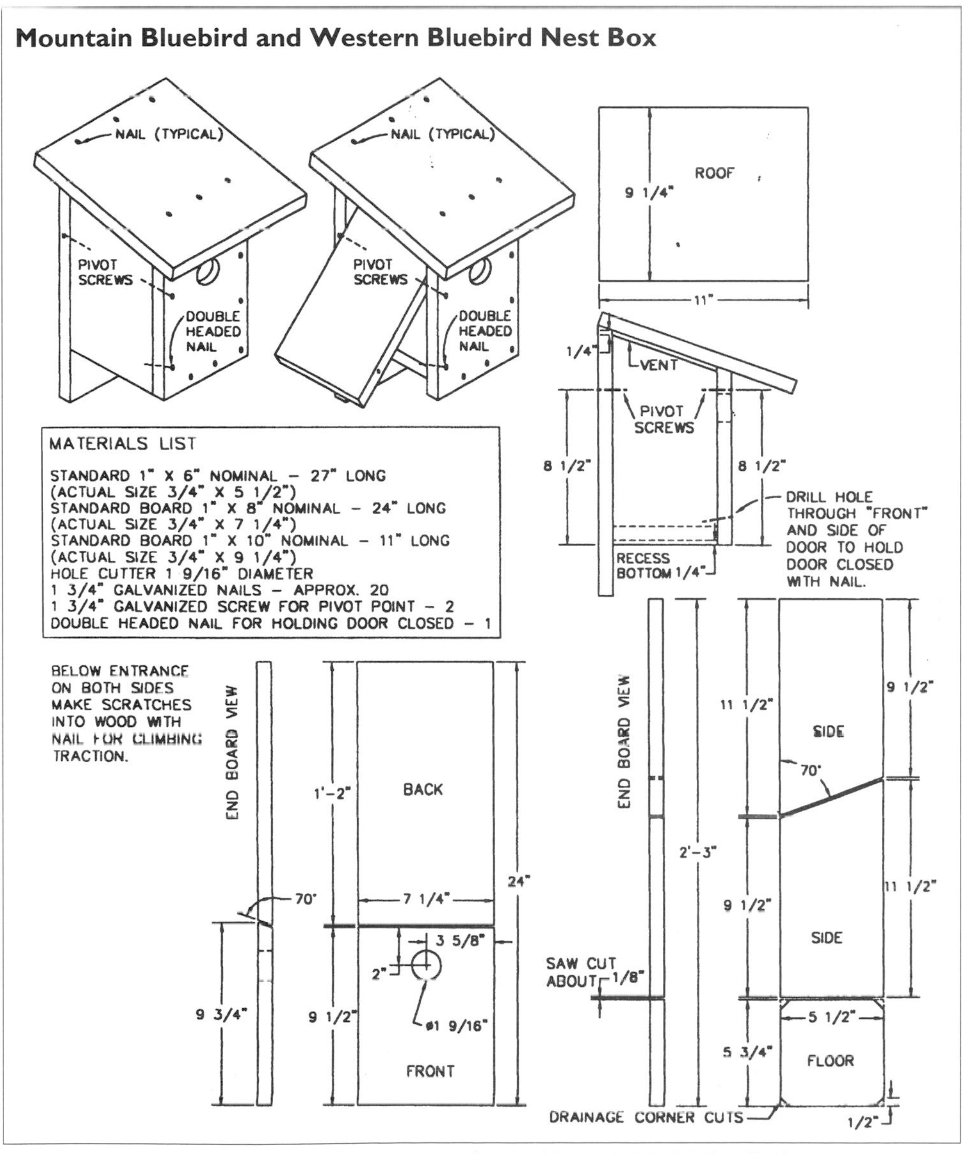

North American Bluebird Society nest box plans for the Mountain Bluebird and Western Bluebird. Redrawn from plans developed by the North American Bluebird Society. (Note: The entrance hole for the Mountain and Western Bluebird nest box is 1 9/16 inches rather than the 1 ½ inches for the Eastern Bluebird.)

three broods are reared each year, with subsequent nesting efforts containing one less egg per clutch. Western Bluebirds lay five to eight pale blue eggs. The eggs are incubated for thirteen to seventeen days before hatching. Two or three broods can be reared each year. Mountain Bluebirds lay four to eight pale blue eggs, which are incubated for twelve to sixteen days. Two broods sometimes are raised each year.

As we discussed previously, Tree Swallows and Eastern Bluebirds sometimes occupy neighboring boxes of the same dimensions. Two bluebird nest boxes mounted on the same support, facing opposite directions, can be occupied by Eastern Bluebirds and Tree Swallows without difficulty. Alternatively, two bluebird nest boxes can be mounted on separate posts about 25 feet apart.

Wrens, swallows, chickadees, titmice, and nuthatches may also adopt the bluebird boxes for their nesting activities—especially when boxes are placed too near trees or other protective vegetation. Enjoy those birds, too, and welcome them into the backyard wildlife community. Each is protected by state and federal laws, so it's illegal to disturb them, evict them from a box, or remove or otherwise harm their eggs or nestlings.

A bluebird nest-box trail is a series of boxes placed in a habitat suitable for Eastern, Mountain, or Western Bluebirds. Many trails cover miles of rural roadside, but you can also establish bluebird trails in cemeteries, pastures, and other places where there's open space with low ground cover. Again, avoid areas where pesticides are used.

After a bluebird trail is established, monitor the birds and boxes regularly. Keep written records of what's happening and take corrective action if problems are discovered. Written records also provide comparative information from year to year, and enjoyable reading on winter evenings when inclement weather keeps you indoors.

Information preserved in notebooks may have scientific importance. Ornithologists, conservation biologists, and ecologists may be able to use long-term bluebird data if they're available for research purposes. Similarly, the North American Bluebird Society, Inc., may welcome copies of long-term bluebird data for research and educational projects. Examples of useful data include number of eggs in a clutch, laying dates, number of eggs that hatch, number of young surviving per box, and predation rates.

Parasites and Predators

A variety of parasites occurs in bluebird nests, including fleas, mites, lice, and ants. With the exception of ants, their presence in moderate numbers is natural. The best way to prevent ants from climbing support poles and entering nest boxes is to put Teflon tape or spray around a portion of the support pole. If other parasites become too numerous, discard the nest after the young bluebirds fledge.

The larvae of bluebird blowflies *(Protocalliphora sialia)* drink blood from nestlings at night. It is not uncommon or unnatural for a nest to contain some larvae—say, fewer than fifty. In larger numbers—as many as 240 have been reported in a single nest—the larvae pose a lethal threat to the nestling. When exceptionally large numbers of blowfly larvae appear, remove the nestlings, discard the nest in a paper bag that's burned or placed in the garbage, and fashion a new, dry-grass nest inside the nest box. The nestlings can then be placed back in the nest—hopefully to enjoy a healthy nestling period prior to fledging. There is no danger that adult bluebirds will abandon nestlings touched by humans because they, like most birds, can't smell any scent left on the nestlings. A replacement nest should only be put in an occupied nest box when the nestlings are between nine and eleven days old.

Predators may be attracted to bluebird nest boxes and the eggs or nestlings they contain. While predation from raccoons, opossums, domestic house cats, and snakes is expected along bluebird trails, most birdwatchers with a box in their backyard habitat prefer that bluebird nesting efforts are successful.

One way to deter raccoons and snakes is to use a predator guard or baffle. Many different types are available. One that's fairly simple to make and use is a 2-foot length of 6- or 7-inch-diameter galvanized stovepipe. A piece of ½-inch wire mesh hardware cloth is then cut into a circle and fastened inside the end of the stovepipe to prevent snakes from getting past the mesh. The whole assembly is then attached with metal brackets to the galvanized support pipe a little below the bottom of the nest box. This should prevent raccoons, snakes, and other climbing predators from getting inside the box entrance hole.

American Robins

American Robins are always welcome in backyard habitats. However, they commonly build their nests in the crotch of a tree or shrub. Nevertheless, it's possible to assist American Robins in finding a place to nest by providing a sheltered nesting platform.

Place these structures about 6 feet or higher on the trunk of a tree in a shaded location or under a shaded overhang of a porch or outbuilding. Whether American Robins accept nesting platforms depends to some extent on the availability of natural nesting supports in a particular backyard.

If you want to make a nesting platform, the back should measure 8 inches high, 7 by 8 inches in floor size, and be made of ¾-inch red cedar or bald cypress. Install it between 6 and 15 feet above ground. Allow the wood to weather naturally.

American Robins lay three to five pale blue eggs in mud nests lined with grasses, weeds, cloth strips, string, and other materials. Eggs are incubated by the female for twelve to fourteen days before hatching. As many as three broods can be raised per year.

Some birdwatching stores sell American Robin nesting platforms, and Coveside Conservation Products also sells them; its platform can be used by American Robins, Eastern Phoebes, and Barn Swallows. When Barn Swallows use the platform, it's placed under the eaves of a barn, shed, or garage (remember to keep the doors open).

To further help American Robins nest in your backyard habitat, you can create a "mud puddle" by soaking some soil with a garden hose; this gives the birds an accessible mud supply for lining their nests.

Tom Adams

A view of the backyard of Pat and Tom Adams in the suburbs of Boston. Trees and shrubs were selected to provide food, shelter, and nest sites for birds. Flowers attractive to birds (and butterflies) have also been added, including butterfly bush, butterfly weed, bee balm, asters, black-eyed Susan, and coneflowers. Over 30 bird species appear on their backyard list.

Prothonotary Warblers

Prothonotary Warblers are colorful and beautiful wood warblers. As a cavity-nesting species, they accept nest boxes as substitutes for natural tree cavities. Their nest-box dimensions are as follows: a box bottom 5 by 5 inches, a depth of 6 inches, an entrance height of 4 to 5 inches, and an entrance-hole diameter of 1⅛ inches. The box should be placed 4 to 8 feet above the ground.

Backyard birders living near wooded swamps and forests within the breeding range of this species have wonderful opportunities to help these lovely birds. Place nest boxes on trees or other supports rising from water or on the edge of water.

Prothonotary Warblers usually lay four to six creamy-colored eggs marked with blotches of brown. The female incubates the eggs for about thirteen days before they hatch. Each year, two broods can be raised in the South, one brood in the North.

8 Water and Shelter

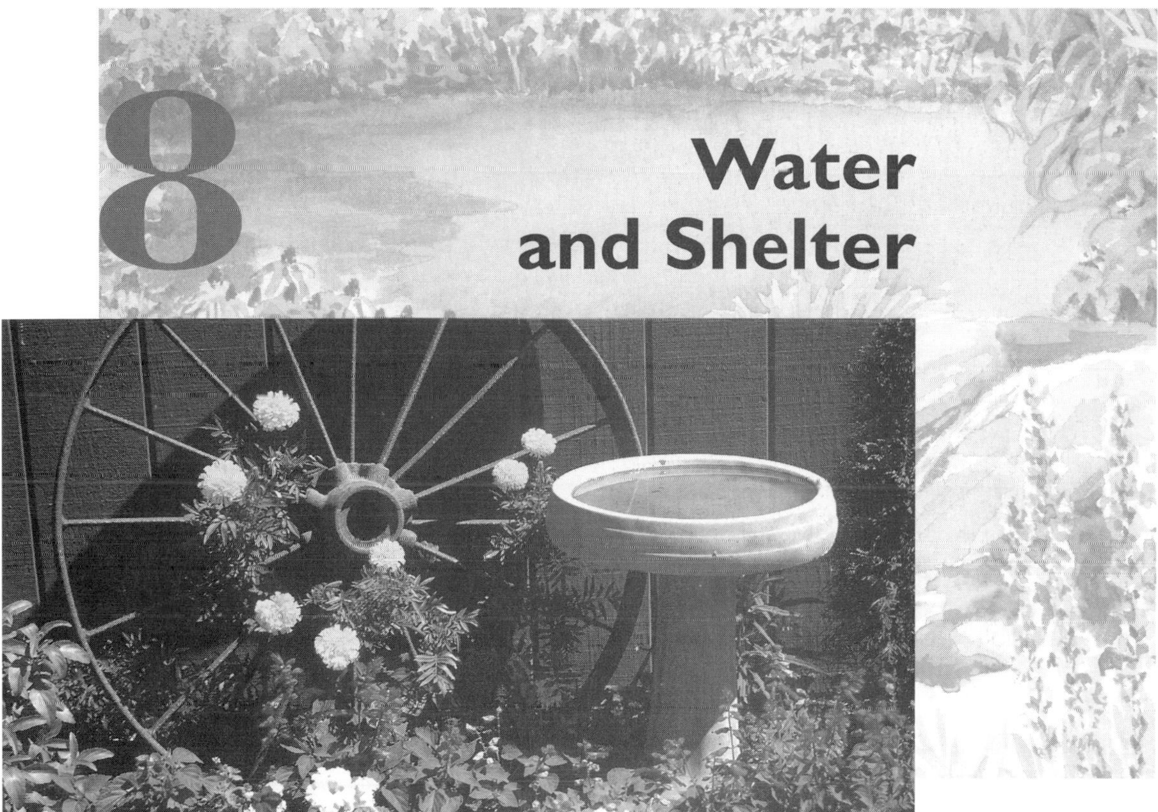

An incorrectly placed pedestal birdbath in a summer garden. With the bath too close to protective vegetation, house cats or other predators could capture wet birds when they are vulnerable and have difficulty flying.

The last essential components of the enhanced backyard habitat are water for drinking and bathing and protective cover. The easiest way to fill the need for water is by adding birdbaths. At the other end of the spectrum, a pond with circulating water benefits a whole range of birds and can become the centerpiece of a stunning backyard habitat. As discussed in chapter 5, gardening is important because it provides natural shelter and cover for birds. Brush piles, stone walls, and similar structures also play a role, and they are also considered in this chapter.

BIRDBATHS

When songbirds bathe, their feathers become soaked with water and it is very difficult for them to fly properly. It can take several minutes to shake water from the feathers and then preen them. Bathing and preening birds are especially vulnerable to capture by house cats, hawks, and other predators. Therefore, you should give some thought to the placement of a birdbath in a backyard habitat. A good place is about 10 feet from shrubs or other protective cover that birds can reach quickly so a cat hiding nearby won't completely surprise them. (And, of course, be sure that the birdbath is clearly visible from a kitchen or dining-room window for your own enjoyment.)

Pedestal Birdbaths and Simple Dishes

The simplest birdbath is a shallow dish, such as the lid of a garbage can, laid on the ground and filled with water. However, birds bathing this way are quite vulnerable to predators.

More common are pedestal birdbaths, which offer birds more protection. A pedestal birdbath should be no deeper than 3 inches in the deepest section, with shallow sections (i.e., ½ inch deep) and gradually sloping sides. You can also add less water or place flat stones in the center of the birdbath on which the birds can stand. If possible, the inside of the birdbath should be a dark color because water is more visible to birds against a dark than a light color.

If the bottom of the birdbath is slippery, put nonskid stickers used in bathtubs on the bottom to give birds a rougher surface and more traction when bathing. Cement birdbaths are sufficiently rough to provide adequate footing for birds. Some birders prefer to find or make their own birdbaths. Possibilities include a flat stone or a tree stump with a shallow bowl to hold water.

In any noncirculating birdbath, it's necessary to replace the water frequently so birds come into contact with fresh water. An occasional thorough cleaning of the birdbath bowl is also necessary. Be certain that no chemicals or soap used in cleaning remains on the bowl's surface.

Avian Aquatics, Inc., makes a small "waterfall rock" for use in pedestal birdbaths. (For the address of this company and others mentioned in this chapter, see appendix 4.) A small pump is included inside the waterfall, which allows bath water to recirculate and cascade over the rock, producing a gurgling sound that's very attractive to songbirds.

Molded Birdbaths

There are molded birdbaths made from ABS polymer and designed specifically for backyard habitats. These are convenient to use and for blending into the appearance of a backyard habitat. Avian Aquatics, Inc., for example, makes various shapes and sizes of molded birdbaths, all coated with a sandy surface for sure footing. Those colored tan are recommended for warmer climates; those colored charcoal are for colder climates. This company also manufactures hanging birdbaths and molded birdbaths that recirculate water.

An American Robin bathing in summer in a natural spring.

When molded birdbaths are used in a backyard habitat with low wildflowers planted near them, a natural setting enhances the overall appearance of the birdbath and the surrounding area.

Drippers and Misters

The sound of dripping water is irresistible to songbirds. Allow water to drip into a birdbath or some other container at a rate of about one drip per second. You can use a hanging bucket or a garden hose equipped with a device to regulate very slow water flow into the bowl of a pedestal birdbath. Thrushes, wood warblers, sparrows, and many other birds are likely to use birdbaths with water dripping into them. They can significantly increase the attractiveness of a backyard habitat for many birds. Commercially manufactured birdbath drippers, some models with a water timer, are sold at birding stores. Avian Aquatics, Inc., sells several models and styles. Similarly, songbirds of many species, especially hummingbirds, enjoy bathing in a fine water mist. To accommodate this behavior, birding stores and Avian Aquatics sell several models of misters for use in backyard habitats, some of which can be adjusted for use as a dripper.

Heaters

Many backyard birders in colder climates use small electric heaters in birdbaths to prevent the water from freezing and to keep the water warm for the enjoyment of birds. Birds will flock to heated birdbaths in winter.

However, in extremely cold temperatures, problems can occur. I know of one case in Minnesota where a number of European Starlings died while using a heated birdbath in extremely cold weather (–20°F). They splashed water onto their feet and feathers, which then froze. A plastic-coated wire fencing over the birdbath allowed birds to drink without getting wet, solving the problem. The situation in Minnesota is very unusual, but it is wise to be careful using heated birdbaths when air temperatures drop below freezing.

Several companies manufacture birdbath heaters, including Avian Aquatics, Inc., and Nelson Manufacturing Company.

Artificial Creeks

Categorized somewhere between birdbaths and full-fledged ponds are small premolded ponds that can be installed in backyard habitats. For example, Avian Aquatics sells a product called the Bird-Creek Recirculating Bird Pond in 3-by-5-, 5-by-6-, and 3-by-11-foot lengths. The assembled creek consists of a gravel creek bed, over which water flows at a depth of

Sandy Fliniau

A snow-surrounded, electrically heated birdbath in the Colorado Rocky Mountain backyard habitat of Sandy Fliniau. Birds love taking a warm bath during winter, and many backyard birdwatchers now provide heated birdbaths for birds.

1 to 2 inches. A small pump circulates the water. Edging rocks and creek gravel are not included. Some birding stores sell these and similar products.

BUILDING PONDS AND POOLS IN BACKYARD HABITATS

One of the most important water components of many backyard wildlife habitats is a small pond or pool, usually with an accompanying cascading waterfall. This is pleasant to see and satisfies the essential water needs of birds that use the habitat.

Greg Oskay of Water Resources Design, Inc., in Indianapolis, Indiana, designed an excellent backyard wildlife pond and waterfall, and has made his design available for do-it-yourself landscapers.

A liner is necessary to keep water in the pond from soaking into the ground. Try to find a used swimming-pool liner to save money; some swimming-pool companies give away used liners or sell them for a few dollars. The liner's color is unimportant because it will be covered with soil. Alternatively, you can buy a liner made for small backyard ponds; however, these are expensive.

Build the pond in a spot that blends into the backyard habitat landscape and is also visible from your house or deck. Avoid putting the pond under a tree to prevent leaves from falling into it. Remember that aquatic plants need four or more hours of sun every day.

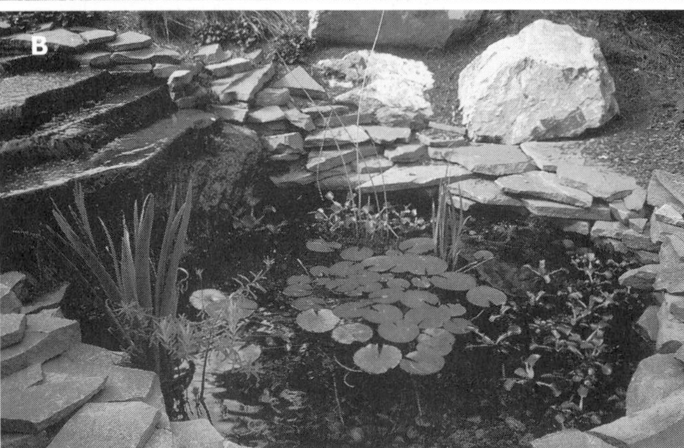

A. A small backyard garden pond in Bucks County, Pennsylvania.

B. Another small backyard garden pond with a waterfall in rural Pennsylvania. The sound of running or dripping water is appealing to backyard birds.

The size and shape of the pond are unimportant, but should look natural; that means avoiding circles and straight lines. To plan the pond's shape, place a length of rope or garden hose on the ground, adjusting it until you like the shape.

Be sure the pond's sides are not angled at more than a 3:1 slope; otherwise, the soil that eventually covers the bottom will slide off the liner. As a rule-of-thumb, the width of the pond should be six times the greatest desired water depth; for example, a pond 2 feet at the center should be at least 12 feet wide. To serve the widest range of backyard birds, it's important that there be very

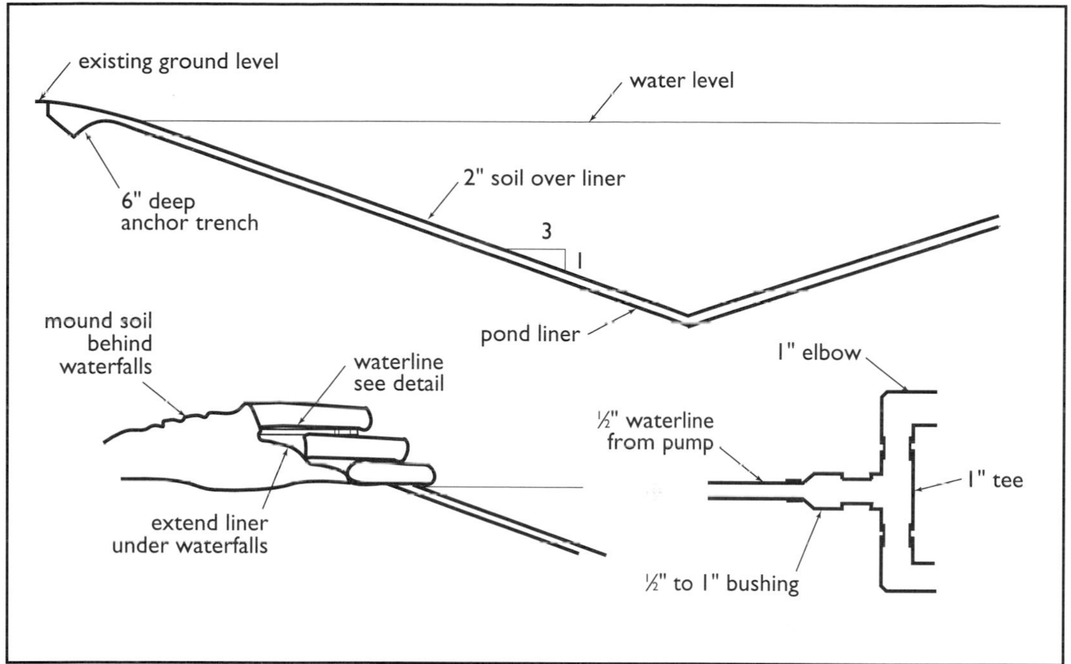

Selected details from a plan to make a backyard wildlife pond. Shown are pond cross-section, waterfall detail, and diffuser detail. Redrawn from plans by Greg Oskay/Water Resources Design, Inc.

shallow sections in the pond—no more than ½ inch deep. Shallows are required by migrants including Wilson's Warblers and American Redstarts, as well as by regular visitors including Gray Catbirds, Brown Thrashers, Northern Cardinals, and sparrows. Create the shallows as you first dig the pond or build up shallow sections with flat stones, gravel, and sand after the liner is in place.

Once you have determined the shape and depth of the pond, excavate 4 inches deeper than the desired depth to compensate for the liner and soil covering it. The excavated soil will be used to cover the pond liner and to create a mound behind the waterfall (discussed later).

The next step is to dig an anchor trench around the outside of the pond to keep the liner from sliding. The trench should be about 6 inches deep and 12 inches wide. Make an overflow for the pond by maintaining an area 12 inches wide and slightly lower than the pond. Remove all sharp objects (e.g., roots and stones) that can puncture the liner, then smooth out the soil that's placed on top of the liner.

Be sure to retain slack in the liner, then fold the top edge into the anchor trench. Place soil in the trench and compact it; then put rocks over the compacted soil. Any excess liner can be trimmed off. Plant grass and flowers on the remaining disturbed areas.

A circulation system is necessary to prevent the water in the pond from becoming stagnant. I always suggest a small waterfall, which greatly improves the natural appearance of the pond. In Greg Oskay's design, a ¼-horsepower sump pump is placed on rocks in a deeper part of the pond (not the absolute bottom); the pumped water comes out above the waterline of the pond and gently cascades down a waterfall. Use stones of various sizes and shapes to build the waterfall; try garden supply stores or local quarries if you can't find any on your property. If you build up a mound of earth behind the waterfall, it appears that a natural spring is providing the water. The plumbing and electrical cords can be concealed under rocks and soil.

To fill the pond, use a garden hose or wait until rain fills it naturally. (If the pond is situated near your house, you can even use runoff from the roof.) Avoid washing soil off the liner, and allow the water to age for a few days before adding plants or fish. Try using emergent aquatic plants to reduce algae problems: push their roots into the soil and hold them down with a few rocks, or set pots containing the plants on the bottom of the pond; conceal the pots with stones and rocks. The following aquatic plants can be used in your backyard habitat pond: arrowhead, arrow arum, blue flag iris, bull rush, lizard tail, swamp buttercup, spike rush, and water lily. Local nurseries and garden supply stores may have additional native species available.

To prevent plants spreading and taking over the pond, avoid cattails, lotus, and pickerel weed. By all means, do not use purple loosestrife *(Lythrum salicaria)*—it's beautiful but extremely invasive. You can use a dip net to remove algae if it becomes a problem. To control mosquitoes, try using flathead minnows, available in fishing bait shops.

Several important precautions regarding water should be taken when establishing a pond in a backyard wildlife habitat. First is water quality. If you use city tap water treated with chlorine or other chemicals, aim the hose into the air, which puts oxygen in the water before it falls into the pond. Alternatively, allow rainwater to fill the pond or pool (even that water supply sometimes contains contaminants).

Finally, if young children play in a backyard habitat with a pond or pool, make absolutely sure they can't fall in. It may be necessary to put a fence around the pond or pool until the children are old enough to recognize the danger.

CONVERTED SWIMMING POOLS

Most people with in-ground swimming pools naturally use them for swimming. However, if a pool has fallen into disuse, it can be converted to a wildlife pond for ducks, herons, kingfishers, frogs, and other aquatic creatures, such as dragonflies and damselflies.

I know of one in-ground swimming pool that was converted into a pool for wildlife with excellent results. Patric and Amy Ginsbach are well along in restoring native habitat on their acres of vital stopover habitat near McAllen, Texas. Because they didn't use their pool much, Pat decided to convert it into a wildlife pond. He drained the water from the pool and used a silicone sealant around the top of the tile and pool edge. He also sealed the drain and other valves around the pool, but in such a way that use of the swimming pool can be restored in the future.

Pat then added 50 cubic yards of cheap, clean, non-topsoil fill to the swimming pool, filling it to roughly the halfway point. This resulted in the new wildlife pond being about 1 foot deep at the shallow end and 4 feet deep at the other end. He then watered the soil lightly, sowed about 25 pounds of winter rye on the moist soil, and let it sprout. For the next three months, he grew the best rye crop possible in the soil.

Amy Ginsbach

In-ground swimming pools in backyard habitats occasionally are converted into wildlife ponds. This one is in the backyard habitat of Patric and Amy Ginsbach near McAllen, Texas.

Then Pat added water to the pond using a small feeder line from the regional irrigation district, which allows water to flow into the pool every few days when someone downline needs irrigation water. Occasionally, the pool overflows, but this waters other trees and shrubs in the backyard habitat.

Water lilies were added, as was arrowhead and other aquatic plants. He also planted aquatic plants along the edges of the new wildlife pond to give it a natural appearance. Some fish already were in the pool, carried in with irrigation water, and goldfish were added. There has never been an algae problem.

Among wildlife that use the wildlife pond and adjacent backyard habitat are raccoons, an occasional Black-bellied Whistling-Duck, Great Blue Herons, Little Blue Herons, Green Herons, Green Kingfishers, Elf Owls, Great Kiskadees, snakes (including a big indigo), frogs, dragonflies, and damselflies.

SHELTER

It's desirable to create brush piles, rock piles, and other natural forms of cover in a backyard habitat so that birds can hide when danger threatens. Some people also build rock piles for small birds to hide in and for other creatures such as chipmunks, harmless snakes, and spiders to establish homes.

Brush Piles

Building a brush pile is straightforward, but there is a right way to do it. Use limbs, branches, and twigs pruned from trees and shrubs in your backyard habitat, as well as limbs blown down during storms. Vegetation used in the brush pile decomposes slowly, recycling nutrients into the soil, so you should continue to add material to the top of the pile. Discarded Christmas trees can also be used in brush piles.

Brush piles of various sizes, shapes, and constructions can be placed in odd corners of backyard habitats to provide increased protecting cover for small birds and other wildlife.

If you prefer not to have the brush pile

WETLAND RESTORATION

Wetland restoration is an increasingly important wildlife conservation project undertaken by people owning relatively large tracts of land. Typically, farmers are involved in this activity because they own large acreages, some of which may have been wetlands such as freshwater marshes. The cost of restoring a wetland that covers an area as small as 4 acres is substantial: tens of thousands of dollars. Many farmers simply do not have money available for wetland restoration.

Fortunately, a federal governmental program is available to restore some wetlands. Partners for Fish and Wildlife may pay for most (and sometimes all) of the costs associated with approved wetland-restoration projects. The U.S. Fish and Wildlife Service, working in cooperation with the Natural Resources Conservation Service (formerly the Soil Conservation Service), state wildlife agencies, and some county conservation districts, identifies suitable sites for restoration. The service then enters into a legal agreement with a farmer or other landowner to restore an approved site to wetland status.

After they are accepted into the program, the partners plan, design, restore, and monitor the new wetland for a period of at least ten years. The landowner does not lose ownership of the land; after the ten-year period (or another agreed-upon term), total control of the wetland reverts back to the farmer or landowner. Meanwhile, the farmer received tens of thousands of dollars of conservation services—plus a lovely wetland—all without cost (or nominal cost, in some projects).

An outstanding example of wetland restoration occurred near me in Lehigh County, Pennsylvania. A 4.5-acre degraded wet area owned by a farmer concerned with conservation issues has been restored to a beautiful and biologically productive wetland.

The U.S. Fish and Wildlife Service provided funding, heavy equipment, and labor. All but about $500 was paid by the Service—a tremendous bargain that works for the best interest of birds and other wildlife now living in or visiting the wetland. After the restoration was completed, the Pennsylvania Game Commission installed Wood Duck nest boxes and Mallard rings (tubes), in which these birds nest successfully. These structures are maintained by the Game Commission once a year, usually during a cold winter period when it's possible to walk over the ice on the marsh to get to the boxes and rings. Today, one sees a lovely 4.5-acre freshwater marsh that's spring-fed, circled with cattails and other aquatic-loving shrubs and wildflowers, and rich in birds and other wildlife.

A restored wetland on the farm of Forrest Wessner Jr. near Germansville, Pennsylvania. The restoration was done in cooperation with the Partners for Fish and Wildlife program available throughout the United States.

as an obvious part of your backyard habitat, it can be partly hidden with a screen of shrubs, which provide more protective cover and food for birds.

One way to begin construction of a brush pile is with a bottom layer of crossed limbs; then add to the pile in pyramid form so it has a hollow core. The higher you build the pile, the finer the branches, with leaves and pine boughs eventually on top. If you leave small entrance and exit holes on the sides of the brush pile, small birds can get inside for protective cover. However, make the entrance and exit holes small enough so that house cats can't enter. If you're a gardener, you can plant beans, squash, and trumpet vines beside the pile and train them to grow up and over it.

A. Rock piles offer backyard birdwatchers another way of providing protective shelter for small birds and other wildlife. Sometimes they also serve as perches for birds. This rock pile, with a dead tree trunk included, is in the backyard habitat of David and Arlene Koch in eastern Pennsylvania.

B. A gray fox resting in the shelter of a stone wall.

Although the National Wildlife Federation advocates building brush piles, some local health departments may object, claiming they harbor rats. This is generally not true, but remove the brush pile if anyone objects.

Rock Piles and Stone Walls

In addition to brush piles, many backyard birders construct rock piles and stone walls to provide cover for small birds and other wildlife. Construction of rock piles and rough stone walls is simple; however, as with brush piles, it is important to leave interior space to shelter small birds. Depending on where you live, small- and medium-sized rocks may or may not be readily available. Rocks of appropriate

Firewood shelters can also give birds shelter from rain, snow, and wind. If a small creek or brook is nearby, they sometimes provide nesting sites for Eastern Phoebes and perhaps Barn Swallows.

sizes and shapes can be purchased from gardening and landscaping companies, quarries, and other sources. Sometimes people want to remove rocks from their property, so it may be only a matter of asking and hauling them away. Some backyard birdwatchers plant native ferns and wildflowers along the base of a rock pile, which adds a touch of color to the scene.

Wood Piles

In rural temperate areas of North America, many people stack firewood in their yards. When firewood is loosely stacked, it offers protection similar to a brush pile or stone wall. If firewood is stacked neatly in an open-sided but roofed shelter, birds such as sparrows and finches can find shelter under the roof during inclement weather. In addition, birds such as Eastern Phoebes and Barn Swallows sometimes find the underside support timbers of the shelter's roof a suitable place for building their nests and raising their young. (When birds select these structures for nesting purposes, water is usually nearby; this is why Eastern Phoebes often build nests on the underside support beams of bridges.) Some backyard birdwatchers install platforms and shelves under the roofs of firewood shelters and similar structures to encourage birds to nest.

Perches

Many people overlook the importance of perches in enhancing a backyard habitat. Birds need ready perches close to feeders, birdbaths or ponds, and other parts of the habitat. Certain birds do not actually eat at feeding stations, but only secure food and then retire to a nearby perch to eat it. Dead trees and branches secured in an upright position make aesthetically pleasing perches. They should be 3 or 4 feet high near a pool or birdbath, but they can be as high as 20 feet in other locations.

A Mourning Dove perched on a dead tree in the backyard habitat of David and Arlene Koch in eastern Pennsylvania. Perches are often overlooked when backyard habitats are enhanced. One way of bringing a perch into a habitat is to mount upright a dead tree with several branches near bird feeders, a pond, or elsewhere. Small perches can also be put beside birdbaths, natural springs, or other places birds visit frequently.

9 Problems in Backyard Habitats

In the early 1950s, when the Red-tailed Hawk was shot illegally in Pennsylvania, some raptors and certain other birds were not protected by state or federal wildlife laws. Now all birds of prey, and nearly all other birds, are fully protected by state and federal laws. Exceptions are European Starlings and House Sparrows.

Backyard birdwatchers can expect many hours of trouble-free pleasure watching birds feeding, nesting, bathing, and going about their daily lives. This chapter looks at some of the problems that can occasionally develop in backyard habitats, however, and attempts to provide solutions.

LEGAL CONSIDERATIONS

With the exception of a few nonnative birds such as European Starlings and House Sparrows, birds in the United States are protected by state and federal wildlife laws, as well as certain international treaties. Legally, birds are the property of the state, which acts on behalf of its citizens in managing and protecting them. It is illegal to kill, injure, or otherwise capture or handle wild birds, nests, eggs, feathers, or body parts. That's as true for Northern Cardinals and White-throated Sparrows as it is for Sharp-shinned Hawks and Great Horned Owls.

However, in the case of game birds, hunting seasons are established under federal and state regulatory frameworks, for specific periods, and for specific numbers of each species.

In the case of injured or orphaned birds, licensed wildlife rehabilitators are legally permitted to capture, handle, and treat them, and then, if possible, to release them. Backyard birdwatchers are not permitted to take any of these actions. This subject is discussed in more detail later in the chapter.

All fifty states, Indian nations, and territories comprising the United States have agencies designated to deal with wild birds, with their own laws and regulations that vary considerably. Overlaid upon state laws are federal laws and international treaties that sometimes override state laws and regulations.

For practical purposes, however, backyard birdwatchers who have a question or bird-related problem should first contact a wildlife agency at the state level. Most problems related to backyard birds fall into the state's jurisdiction.

The U.S. Fish and Wildlife Service is the federal agency responsible for legal protection of wild birds in the United States. It also deals with federally endangered or threatened birds, other wildlife, and plants.

Examples of federally endangered birds are California Condors, Snail Kites, Red-cockaded Woodpeckers, Cape Sable Seaside Sparrows, and Golden-cheeked Warblers. It's unlikely you will encounter these species in backyard habitats. Nevertheless, if you have problems with a federally endangered or threatened species, contact the Service for further instructions. More information about endangered species, as well as lists of endangered or threatened species, is posted on its website (see appendix 2).

Pet house cats and feral cats that roam outside collectively are major predators of North American songbirds, responsible for millions of bird deaths each year.

BACKYARD PREDATORS

Many types of predators discover backyard habitats and attempt to capture birds visiting bird feeders, nest boxes, or birdbaths. Sharp-shinned Hawks and Cooper's Hawks are the most commonly encountered raptors at feeders. Both are bird hawks, whose normal diet is small- to medium-size birds. Free-roaming house cats are also serious backyard predators; raccoons, opossums, skunks, snakes, and various other animals may prey on birds as well. Let's look more closely at predation in backyard habitats.

House Cats

It's estimated that there are more than 66 million pet house cats in the United States. Approximately 35 percent are kept indoors; the remaining 65 percent roam outdoors. The 40 million house cats left to roam outside become breeding feral cats if they're not spayed/neutered. They represent a major bird-conservation problem because they are very efficient killers of wild birds. One Wisconsin study estimated that between 7.8 million and 219 million wild birds were killed annually by house cats roaming rural areas of that state! As many as 114 free-roaming cats per mile were estimated in some parts of Wisconsin.

Here are the basic facts regarding house cats roaming outdoors:

- Putting bells on a cat's collar won't hinder it from killing wild birds; because birds don't associate the sound with danger, they won't be warned off.
- Well-fed cats will still kill birds because of their natural predatory instincts.
- Most small animals brought to licensed wildlife rehabilitation centers after being victims of house-cat attacks die from internal injuries or infections sustained from contact with bacteria and viruses in the cat's mouth. Only about 20 percent of cat-attack victims survive even after treatment by rehabilitators or veterinarians.
- In some areas, songbird populations and heron and egret rookeries suffered catastrophic population declines as a result of house-cat and raccoon predation.

An important study of house-cat (and raptor) predation at backyard feeding stations in the United States was conducted during the winter of 1989–90 by the Cornell Laboratory of Ornithology using data secured by 5,500 backyard birders participating in Project FeederWatch. Only 10 percent of birders reported predation of any kind at their winter bird feeders. When house cats preyed on backyard feeder birds, they did so more readily when bird food was put on the ground and when suet and seed mixes were used, than when seeds such as niger and peanuts were used. Curiously, house-cat predation was not associated with any particular backyard characteristics; cats captured whatever prey was available. In addition, a small number of cats was responsible for most feeder-bird deaths. The Cornell researchers doubt whether maintaining bird feeders produces a higher rate of songbird mortality than what occurs in natural settings.

Finally, the Cornell researchers suggested that bird feeders might be fairly safe havens from predators because the many birds visiting them would soon detect raptors, house cats, or other predators and quickly sound the alarm. In addition, when songbirds visit feeders for food, they spend less time searching elsewhere, which means less time that they are exposed to predators.

To address the problem of house-cat predation, the American Bird Conservancy operates a special program called Cats Indoors! The Campaign for Safer Birds and Cats, which educates Americans about cat predation and

CATS INDOORS!

Courtesy of the American Bird Conservancy

The logo for the American Bird Conservancy's Cats Indoors! The Campaign for Safer Birds and Cats.

encourages pet owners to keep pet cats indoors at all times. By taking that simple step, millions of wild birds will be saved each year, and pet house cats will enjoy longer, healthier, and happier lives. The conservancy is eager to partner with other organizations on this important wild bird conservation effort.

Although I'm aware of how sensitive this issue is to some cat owners, I strongly encourage backyard birdwatchers who own house cats to adopt this bird-conservation strategy: simply don't allow pet house cats to go outside. For more information and campaign information kits, write to the American Bird Conservancy (see appendix 1).

Dogs

Dogs occasionally become a problem at backyard bird-feeding stations, especially when allowed to roam unrestrained. Dogs are capable of capturing and killing songbirds, including Northern Mockingbirds and Northern Cardinals. Problems with dogs at backyard bird feeders must be dealt with promptly.

The best solution is to put a long leash on the dog so that it has plenty of room to move around, but can't get to birds visiting feeders. Alternatively, a dog can be given a fenced-in area in which to roam without impacting bird-feeding activities elsewhere in a backyard habitat.

If a neighbor's dog is running near your backyard bird feeders, ask your neighbors to remove their pet before it causes injury to birds. Alternatively, call your

A. Virginia opossums sometimes venture into backyard habitats, and eat seeds at bird feeders. Backyard birders can either ignore (or even appreciate) them, or use humane live traps to capture and release them elsewhere. However, please consult with your state wildlife agency before using any live traps. Wildlife laws pertaining to mammals vary in different states.

B. A predator guard installed below a Wood Duck nest box in a wetland.

local animal-control officer, humane society, or Society for the Prevention of Cruelty to Animals (SPCA) and ask for assistance in removing the dog.

In the case of stray dogs whose owners are not known, ask your local humane society or SPCA to capture the dog and place it in a shelter. In some municipalities, animal-control officers do this or work with a humane society or the SPCA. Be aware, however, that this can be a death sentence for a stray dog. If possible, try to find a local nonkill animal shelter that will keep the stray for as long as necessary to find a new owner.

Raccoons, Opossums, and Skunks

Raccoons can be serious predators on bird eggs or nestlings in nest boxes. Use a predator guard or baffle on the poles or posts that support nest boxes. Predator guards can be purchased in birding stores or fashioned at home.

In theory, raccoons, opossums, and skunks can all be live-trapped and transported to another location for release. However, some states may prohibit releasing raccoons because they are major carriers of rabies. Likewise, skunks are major carriers of rabies, not to mention their odorous spray. Check with your state wildlife agency before attempting any live-trapping.

Some backyard birdwatchers prefer to turn the problem over to a commercial animal-control company. Ask what the company intends to do with an animal that's live-trapped and removed from your property. If you don't like their reply, hire another company.

An alternative solution is to provide separate feeders for raccoons, opossums, or skunks somewhere in the backyard habitat away from and preferably out of sight of bird feeders.

Birds of Prey

Occasionally, hawks are attracted to songbirds that gather at backyard feeding stations; unfortunately, it's not uncommon for backyard birders to become upset when a hawk appears. I've heard birders complain about hawks hanging around their feeders and occasionally killing a bird, and read similar complaints in various publications. I'm always disappointed by this response. On the other hand, I'm delighted that the National Bird-Feeding Society urges its members to watch and appreciate hawks and owls in wildlife communities, including backyard habitats.

Hostility toward hawks reflects an incomplete understanding of raptors and

LIVE TRAPS

One of the major advances in dealing with backyard wildlife problems is the use of live traps. No longer is shooting an animal the only solution. These nonlethal devices are baited, an animal enters to get the bait, and both ends of the box-like trap quickly close, humanely capturing the animal inside. It is then taken to another location, opened, and the animal is released unharmed.

Live traps of various sizes can be purchased at hardware and garden stores. Some humane societies also loan live traps to people to capture and remove squirrels or other animals from a house or backyard. However, state wildlife agencies may require permits to deal with protected animals—squirrels included—or license commercial animal-control companies to deal with these problems.

the ecological role they play, which is to help remove weak, sick, and old birds and other wild animals from habitats and ecosystems. Negative attitudes also conflict with state and federal wildlife laws that protect birds of prey—a major conservation advance that took hawk watchers and raptor biologists decades to achieve. Conservation biologists do not want a backward shift toward hostility and persecution of hawks and owls. Therefore, it's vital that backyard birdwatchers learn about the natural history and ecology of birds of prey, their roles as predators in wildlife communities, and why raptors sometimes appear at backyard feeding stations. The answer to the last question is simple: there's lots of potential prey concentrated in a restricted environment—exactly the situation hawks and owls naturally seek.

Because all hawks and owls are protected by laws and international treaties, my recommendation is to observe and appreciate hawks that suddenly appear near a bird feeder. It is rare for a birder—or even professional raptor biologists—to see a hawk capture a bird.

Two species in the genus *Accipiter*—Sharp-shinned Hawks and Cooper's Hawks—most commonly appear during winter at backyard feeding stations. Occasionally, the largest of the three accipiters, the powerful and spectacular Northern Goshawk, is attracted to a feeding station. When that happens, birders really have a hawk in their backyard habitats! Sometimes Red-tailed Hawks, Merlins, and American Kestrels appear, and an occasional Red-shouldered Hawk or Broad-winged Hawk visits a backyard bird feeder.

The same comments and recommendations apply to owls. Who are we to say that nature is wrong in creating these fascinating birds? However, when Great Horned Owls appear at Purple Martin nesting colonies, the landlord should immediately install owl guards (they should already be in place).

The major Cornell Laboratory of Ornithology study mentioned previously also shed some light on raptor predation at backyard feeding stations. Of the 5,500 backyard habitats studied, only 10 percent (567) reported predation of *any* kind at their bird feeders during the study period (the winter of 1989–90). In most cases where predation did occur, only a single act was reported. Overall, the study suggests that raptor predation has a minor impact on feeder-bird populations. House cats easily outstripped raptors as killers of feeder birds.

Del McNew

House Sparrows are among the ten most common bird species preyed upon by birds of prey visiting bird-feeding stations.

From a seasonal perspective, predation by Sharp-shinned Hawks and Cooper's Hawks peaked in early winter. There was more raptor predation at feeders in the Southwest and West Coast regions than elsewhere, and less than expected in the Northeast. Hawks and falcons visited bird feeders especially when there was a lot of activity in progress. Interestingly, only ten bird species accounted for 92 percent of the birds captured by raptors: Mourning Doves, Dark-eyed Juncos, Blue

Jays, House Sparrows, European Starlings, Pine Siskins, House Finches, American Goldfinches, Northern Cardinals, and Rock Doves (pigeons).

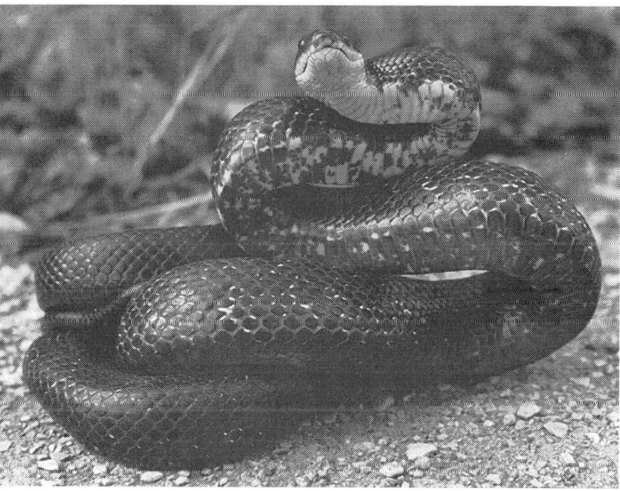
Black snakes are among several species that sometimes prey on bird eggs and young.

Snakes

Snakes occasionally enter nest boxes to take eggs or nestlings. If you discover that this is occurring, you may choose to remove the offending reptile to prevent bird predation. However, do not automatically assume the snake must go—snakes perform valuable roles by controlling rats and mice in a nontoxic fashion. Small, nonvenomous snakes are unlikely to molest birds and should not be disturbed. In addition, some states legally protect snakes, so you should first contact your state wildlife agency for recommendations.

Most snakes that appear in backyard habitats are nonvenomous species. How folks deal with a snake depends entirely on the person. Some people, avid naturalists or amateur herpetologists, capture the snake, transport it a considerable distance from the backyard, and then release it. Many people, however, call a local herpetologist, nature center, animal-control officer, humane society, SPCA, or state wildlife agency, asking them to relocate the snake.

The situation changes when a venomous snake ventures into a backyard habitat. Depending on where in the United States you live, the reptile might be a copperhead, rattlesnake, cottonmouth moccasin, or coral snake. Always take venomous snakes seriously; they are capable of killing adults, children, and pets. Don't try to deal with the reptile yourself, unless you know exactly what you're doing. You need experienced help to safely remove these dangerous creatures from a backyard habitat—that means a telephone call to your state wildlife agency. It's helpful if the location of the reptile is known when assistance arrives, so keep track of its movements—but keep people and pets away from the reptile.

Note, however, that I don't mention killing the snake. Venomous snakes are increasingly persecuted; some are also considered endangered and legally protected in some states.

BACKYARD PESTS

Squirrels

Squirrels are the number-one backyard wildlife problem in the opinion of many backyard birdwatchers. Indeed, birdwatchers encounter few problems more frustrating than having squirrels raiding bird feeders to eat sunflower seeds and other foods. There are three basic approaches to the squirrel problem: confound them, get rid of them, or divert them.

A variety of squirrel guards or baffles can be purchased or home-made to prevent squirrels from gaining access to bird feeders. The one shown at right (B) worked at one Pennsylvania backyard feeding station until a black bear wrecked the feeder and the squirrel guard while raiding the feeder.

Arundale Products, Inc., manufactures several types of squirrel guards. Model AR154 Mandarin Squirrel-Away Baffle is a 17-inch, transparent, recycled Plexiglas dome designed for use with hanging feeders regardless of manufacturer. It hangs above a bird feeder, like an umbrella, and prevents squirrels from climbing or jumping down onto the feeder. The Mandarin Wrap-Around Skirt is a pole baffle that wraps and snaps onto the bottom of its Sky Cafe bird feeders. It, too, prevents squirrels from climbing or jumping onto the bird feeder located directly above the skirt.

Alternatively, try to live-trap a squirrel using a Havahart Trap (manufactured by the Woodstream Corporation) without injuring the animal. Then transport it miles away and release it in an appropriate habitat. However, other local squirrels probably will discover the feeding station, taking the place of the animal that was removed. It also may be illegal in some states to live-trap without a permit, so contact your state wildlife agency before capturing a squirrel. In some states, licensed animal-control companies can do the job for you. Some humane societies loan live traps to people with this problem.

A third alternative to keeping squirrels away from bird feeders is to establish special squirrel feeders in an isolated corner of your backyard habitat. Ears of corn are used in these feeders; peanuts are also suitable.

Deer and Elk

In some parts of the United States, such as the Rocky Mountains, mule deer sometimes raid backyard bird feeders to share the menu. Even bigger problems occur when an elk invades a backyard habitat. George Harrison's *The Backyard Bird Watcher* includes a photograph of five elk browsing in a yard in Estes Park, Colorado. Now *that's* a big problem!

Deer and elk can wreck bird feeders, feed on backyard vegetation, become frightened and accidentally crash through windows, and generally create situations that are difficult to control. Deer and elk are large animals and not easily discouraged from eating sunflower seeds, apples, and other bird foods. Dealing with them in backyards is one of the most complex tasks faced by wildlife professionals. However, it all depends on a person's point of view. Many backyard birders love to watch deer and don't care if shrubs or other vegetation are eaten; the beauty of seeing these lovely mammals up close is worth the expense. You can establish a deer or elk feeding area in a remote corner of a larger backyard habitat, and try to attract the mammals there with apples or stale bread. Apple trees can be planted to provide food for deer. However, some state wildlife agencies oppose this approach because deer or elk may gather at the feeding location, become tame, and then get killed crossing roads.

Richard Holmes

Invisible Fence Co.

Del McNew

A. A squirrel raiding a suet feeder.

B. A squirrel baffle made from a stovepipe was effective at a Pennsylvania bird feeder in preventing gray squirrels from reaching seeds in the feeder.

C. A high-technology method of preventing squirrels, raccoons, and other mammals from raiding bird feeders for seeds is to use a WildBills Squirrel-Free Bird Feeder WB12. It's an electronic feeder that gives mammals a mild electric shock that quickly trains them not to come to this type of feeder.

D. A mule deer eating from a bird feeder in the backyard habitat of Connie Redak in Boulder, Colorado.

If you do not want deer or elk visiting your backyard and its feeders, your options are limited. One solution is to put up a very high (and costly) fence around your property. Or you can contact your state wildlife agency and ask for assistance. Most state wildlife agencies take the quick-and-easy approach—shoot the animals—although that approach is increasingly being questioned. Nonlethal solutions to deer and elk problems are being developed, including sophisticated fertility-control methods to regulate local deer or elk populations. Of course, these techniques do not remove individual animals that already trespass on backyard habitats. The best solution, perhaps, is to coexist with the creatures and learn to appreciate them.

Black Bears

In some states, black bears wander out of wilderness areas into rural, suburban, and even urban areas where folks maintain bird feeders. A hungry bear may raid the feeders for a meal of sunflower seeds, damaging or wrecking the feeder in the process. Although it is rare, be aware that black bears do attack people. Therefore, be careful if one is in your backyard. Do not attempt to feed it or otherwise throw food to it, and do not approach the animal. If a black bear makes an isolated appearance, marvel at the animal, replace the feeder when the coast is clear, and add another species to your backyard mammal list. However, if a black bear decides your backyard is a great place to enjoy regular meals, promptly contact your state wildlife agency and ask them to live-trap the animal so they can transport and release it in an appropriate wilderness area. Do not attempt to do this yourself: it's dangerous *and* illegal for private individuals to do so.

PROBLEMS WITH BACKYARD BIRDS

Disease

Because so many birds concentrate at feeding stations in backyard habitats, the risk of disease appearing and spreading among them is increased. There are a number of diseases that birds can suffer. Let's look at some that infect wild birds—and ways to lessen or eliminate diseases at bird feeders. Much of this information is derived from the National Wildlife Health Center, a federal agency.

Common Bird Diseases at Feeding Stations

There are five important diseases that can affect birds visiting backyard feeding stations.

- Salmonellosis is caused by *Salmonella* bacteria, which birds ingest by eating food that's been contaminated by droppings.
- Trichomoniasis is caused by a protozoan parasite found in contaminated food and water. Birds contract the disease when they eat or drink contaminated items.
- Aspergillosis is caused by a fungus growing on damp bird feed, such as sunflower seeds. It also can be present in waste seed on

the ground below bird feeders. Birds contract the disease by inhaling spores from the fungus, which grow inside the bird and spread to air sacs and lungs, causing bronchitis, pneumonia, or both.

- Avian pox is identified in afflicted birds when wart-like growths appear on a bird's unfeathered face, legs, or feet. It's spread by contact with virus-contaminated objects and by infected mosquitoes.
- Mycoplasmosis recently was discovered in songbirds. The conjunctivitis epidemic (i.e., an eye-membrane infection) in House Finches in the eastern United States and Canada from 1994 through 1996 is a vivid example of how the disease can spread throughout bird populations. Mycoplasmosis is spread by direct contact with other birds, airborne droplets, or dust. House Finches contracted the disease by visiting feeders with seed openings that were contaminated when infected birds put their heads in to take seeds in their bills, or came into close contact with infected birds using tray feeders.

When disease afflicts individual birds or entire populations, birds are weakened; become more susceptible to environmental stress; are poorly nourished; and generally are not alert, active, and well preened. They also are more vulnerable to predators such as Sharp-shinned Hawks, Cooper's Hawks, and free-roaming house cats. Generally, sick birds perish fairly quickly, by whatever means.

While some disease is a normal part of wild bird populations, it's not normal to have it develop and spread because of backyard bird-feeding activities. That means backyard birdwatchers must keep bird feeders, birdbaths, and nest boxes clean. However, even the best efforts sometimes are not entirely successful. Therefore, at the first sign that a single bird visiting a feeder is suffering from disease, take prompt action to combat the problem before other birds are infected.

The National Wildlife Health Center recommends eight ways to prevent disease from appearing and/or spreading at bird feeding stations.

- Make sure there is ample space at feeders for the number of birds coming to enjoy the food. If necessary, add more feeders to your backyard habitat.
- Frequently clean up waste seeds and droppings below and on feeders. Put the waste in disposal bags or use a workshop vacuum to clean up waste materials and droppings. Obviously, do not use the vacuum in wet areas or on anything wet! In addition, put fresh, pure water in birdbaths and pools.
- Eliminate sharp corners or edges on feeders to prevent birds from getting injuries, through which bacteria can cause infections.
- Clean and disinfect bird feeders frequently using one part (by volume) of household chlorine bleach to nine parts of water. The

entire empty feeder should be cleaned and then immersed in the solution for about three minutes, followed by air-drying. If sick birds visit the feeder, disinfect it once a week; otherwise, do the process twice a month.

- Put clean food in bird feeders; never use old, moldy, musty, or wet food. If a food-storage container contains spoiled food, it's necessary to disinfect it, as well as scoops and other items associated with the container.
- Rodents such as mice can contaminate stored bird food, so keep them out of storage containers.
- Neighbors who feed birds also must use disease-prevention methods because birds visit feeders in adjacent or nearby backyard habitats.
- By keeping bird-feeding equipment clean and well maintained, disease prevention is achieved, assuring healthy birds at backyard feeders.

For more information about bird diseases and disease prevention, contact the National Wildlife Health Center (see appendix 1).

Collisions with Windows

The tendency of birds to fly into glass windows can be a problem at houses and other buildings with large picture windows. One ornithologist estimated that at least 100 million birds are killed annually by flying into reflective windows. Nobody knows how accurate those estimates are, but it's clear that lots of birds are killed this way.

There are two aspects to the problem. During spring, when male Northern Cardinals and other birds are establishing and defending their nesting territories, they may see their reflection in a window or another shiny object and think they are confronting a rival male. The result is that birds attempt to fight and chase away their own reflections. Obviously, this does not work, and the attacking bird can become so battered or intimidated by its own reflection that it dies or leaves the area. Neither situation is acceptable.

The second problem with glass picture windows happens when a bird sees a reflection of surrounding habitat, such as a wooded area or garden, and attempts to fly to that habitat—only to crash directly into the glass, injuring or killing itself. Again, this situation is not acceptable.

What to do? A range of solutions is used, some more effective and successful than others. Netting, obtained at garden stores, can be placed in front of a glass window to prevent birds from hitting the glass. This works and is used on picture windows in houses, nature centers, and other buildings.

Another solution is to break up reflections on a large window to scare birds away from the glass; put up cut-out designs of snowflakes or bird silhouettes, for example. Stickers that serve the same purpose can be purchased in birding stores; sometimes they work, sometimes they don't.

Another solution is to put a curtain or hanging cloth strips behind a window to break up reflections. A cloth or curtain also can be hung in front of reflective glass to prevent reflections from forming. A much more costly—but perhaps permanent—solution is to slightly tilt windows inward at the bottom when they are installed, perhaps preventing reflections from developing. If new windows or replacements are being installed, it's helpful to use tinted, low-reflective glass. Frosted glass can be used in some situations, although one can't see through it.

In some situations, relocating bird feeders or other items that attract birds farther from a reflective window solves the problem.

Drilling Woodpeckers

Many people are dismayed to find woodpeckers drilling holes into their wood siding, particularly redwood or western red cedar and exterior plywood. Other woodpeckers drum on wood or metal objects, such as rain gutters, making wonderful sounds (from the woodpecker's viewpoint). These problems often occur during autumn, winter, and spring. Species known to engage in this behavior include Northern Flickers, Acorn Woodpeckers, Red-bellied Woodpeckers, Downy Woodpeckers, Hairy Woodpeckers, and Pileated Woodpeckers.

Dealing with these birds is a challenge. You can try spraying the offending bird with a garden hose or putting fake hawks, owls, and snakes near places where woodpeckers drill to discourage them from drilling on buildings. Alternatively, try putting wind chimes or other threatening objects where woodpeckers are at work. Still another creative solution is to install a Wood Duck house close to the place used by the woodpeckers. The birds may accept the alternative, drilling holes in the duck house rather than the human house. Or, try painting any wood exposed to woodpeckers.

Although there are no completely successful solutions to this problem, using an alternative siding may be the best available option. What is not acceptable or legal is shooting or harming woodpeckers that are protected by state and federal laws.

Dealing with an injured or orphaned bird, such as a nestling American Robin, can be a challenging task. Most so-called orphaned nestlings are not orphaned; their parents are away briefly, getting food or watching from a nearby tree or shrub. However, the best way to help birds that are orphaned is to ask a licensed wildlife rehabilitator to fetch the bird, and work with it. It's illegal for anyone without state and federal licenses to handle, hold in captivity, or try to rehabilitate all protected birds.

Injured or Orphaned Birds

Dealing with injured or orphaned birds is a complex process for which few backyard birdwatchers are prepared. The best action is to contact a state and federally licensed wildlife rehabilitator who's experienced and equipped to handle and treat birds.

If a rehabilitator is not located nearby, contact the International Wildlife Rehabilitation Council for the name and telephone number of one in your area (see appendix 1). Your state wildlife agency may also provide the name of a licensed wildlife rehabilitator. Check governmental listings in your telephone directory.

COHABITAT

Enhancement of backyard habitats for birds sometimes creates a space allocation problem. Ray Congdon of Auburn, Washington, solved such a problem by setting aside part of his backyard as a cohabitat play area for his children.

Ray Congdon

ADDITIONAL RESOURCES

Several agencies and organizations can provide additional information and advice about problems in backyard habitats.

- *Contact the county agricultural agent or extension service for free literature and recommendations, many of which will be helpful. However, remember that agricultural agents may recommend the use of pesticides, herbicides, and other chemicals that backyard birders should avoid.*
- *Contact your local or state chapter of the National Audubon Society (or independent Audubon Societies in some states). If there is no local chapter where you live, use the National Audubon Society website to find the nearest one (see appendix 3).*
- *Contact The Humane Society of the United States for information about nonlethal methods of solving some backyard wildlife problems (see appendix 1).*

10 The Active Birder

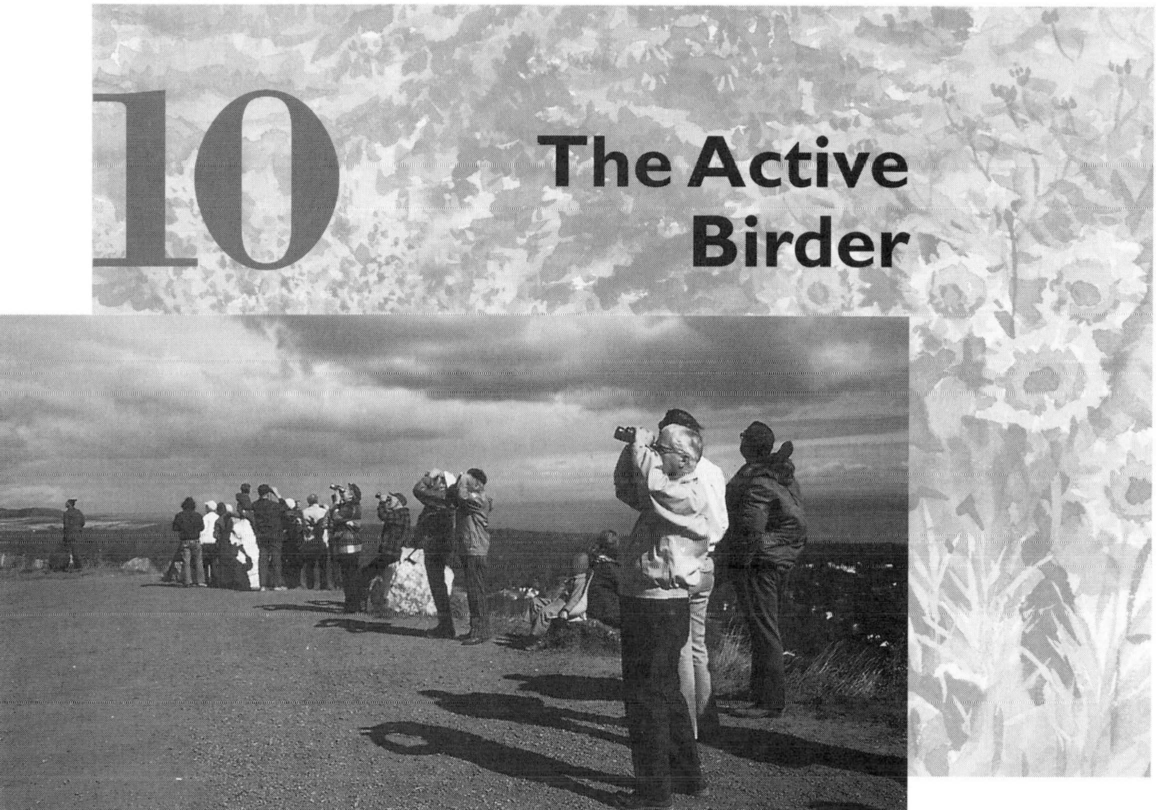

Hawk watchers enjoying hawk migrations at the Hawk Ridge Nature Reserve in Duluth, Minnesota.

You have developed a habitat to attract birds and a growing understanding of its clientele. What now? In this chapter, we consider ways to make the most of the birdwatching experience, both at home and in your community.

THE PRACTICE OF WATCHING

Because the objective of recreational birdwatching is to enjoy looking at birds, one should give some thought to getting close to birds and techniques of watching. For many, the hobby centers around watching birds as they visit feeders. If a feeder is placed a few feet from a kitchen window, feeder birds can be watched at extremely close range.

When you venture out into the yard or farther afield, different tactics come into play. The most basic approach is simply to sit down in an interesting spot and wait quietly for birds to appear. Not infrequently, they'll appear as they go about their normal activities, sometimes rewarding birders with good views of many species. Sitting and waiting is especially useful when birding in woodlands or woodlots. The key is to be quiet, patient, and still. But beware that deer ticks in some parts of the United States, such as the Northeast, can carry the bacteria that causes Lyme disease in people and pet dogs and cats. So, after sitting in wooded areas, check your body thoroughly for any ticks.

Hawk watchers routinely use this technique at lookouts on hawk-migration routes and at migration bottlenecks. Find a good place to sit and join other birders in scanning the horizon and sky for migrating raptors. On the best days, hundreds or even thousands of hawks may pass—sometimes so close that binoculars are unnecessary.

Bird photographers sometimes use blinds, that is, small structures, portable or permanent, in which the photographer hides to get closer views of birds. Blinds are sometimes found at nature centers and national wildlife refuges. In a sense, recreational birders use their houses and automobiles as blinds. If a permanent feature of your backyard is a magnet for birds—a spring or a wetland area—you might consider constructing an observation blind to create close viewing opportunities.

It is possible to actively attract birds with sound. Some years ago, a beginning birder came along on a Christmas Bird Count in which I was participating. We were walking in a park, and as we approached some evergreen shrubs and trees, I made "pishing" and squeaking sounds with my lips and by kissing the back of my hand. The novice looked startled. Fortunately, a Black-capped Chickadee flew from one of the shrubs and was added to the count. Pishing and squeaking sounds sometimes entice birds into view. I explained this to the beginning birder, who picked up a valuable birding technique.

You can also purchase products such as the Audubon Bird Call at birding stores. Used correctly, they make all sorts of chirps and squeaks that entice hiding birds into view. I've had good success using one on my field trips.

Some birdwatchers also use commercial birdsong recordings (discussed in chapter 3) to lure birds closer for observation or photographing. A portable, battery-operated tape recorder plays the appropriate songs at high volume. However, be forewarned: If this luring is done repeatedly during spring—when birds are nesting and respond dramatically—it's possible to so intimidate a male defending his territory that he can be driven away, ruining the nesting effort. This is unethical birding behavior, a violation of the ABA Code of Ethics, and probably illegal.

Don't restrict backyard birdwatching to feeders, birdbaths, and birdhouses. Carefully check for birds in all parts of your backyard habitat and in all levels of vegetation. Many backyard habitats have at least one large tree. During spring and autumn, when birds are engaged in seasonal migrations, they may land in the tops of large trees to rest and feed. Take full advantage of these opportunities for some of the best spring and autumn birding; wood warblers, vireos, and tanagers can all be seen among the upper branches.

Time of day is an important factor in birdwatching. For many of us, the time of day that we engage in birdwatching is determined by work schedules. Many people are restricted to early mornings and evenings, before they leave for work and after they return home.

All else being equal, the best times to engage in backyard birdwatching are during the early morning hours when birds are seeking food, and in the evening before sunset when birds again are searching for food before night arrives. This is also when diurnal birds seek protective habitat in which to rest and sleep for the night. Of course, backyard birds also visit feeders and birdbaths throughout the day,

Evelyn Helm

A view of the Junipers, Evelyn Helm's Japanese-style garden in Sun City, Arizona. The garden takes its name from a group of Pfitzer junipers trained in the bonsai manner. The understory is planted with trailing Vinca major, which lowers the temperature in summer by ten degrees or more. Elsewhere are Xylasma trees, a towering Chinese lace-bark elm, and a huge loquat, which produces a tasty fruit relished by birds. A red torii adds an oriental accent. There are 30 species on her backyard habitat list, including Gambel's Quail, Cactus Wrens and three species of hummingbird—Anna's, Costa's, and Black-chinned.

so on weekends have binoculars ready for use at the best viewing window in your house. You never know when an unusual bird might appear or when some fascinating or dramatic interaction of several birds will happen unexpectedly.

Although backyard birdwatching happens in all seasons of the year in the United States and Canada, spring and autumn are particularly favorable and productive. Large numbers of migrating songbirds move northward to spring and summer breeding grounds, or southward during autumn to wintering grounds in the southern United States, Latin America, and the West Indies. However, there are important differences between spring and autumn bird migrations.

Backyard birdwatchers new to the hobby soon discover that spring songbird migrations offer exceptionally enjoyable birding opportunities because birds are in fresh, bright breeding plumage. Many species, including male thrushes, tanagers, and wood warblers, are in their most colorful and brightest dress—making them very enjoyable to see. Many migrating songbirds stop in backyard habitats to rest, feed, and drink. Enjoy them!

Who can forget their first sighting of a male Eastern Bluebird, Mountain Bluebird, or Scarlet Tanager? Or the sight of a Cape May Warbler, Blackburnian Warbler, Hooded Warbler, or American Redstart feeding among fresh green leaves on a backyard tree? In addition to the aesthetic pleasure of seeing birds in fresh spring plumage, it's when the birds are usually the easiest to identify. Spring is an excellent season for you to venture into the hobby.

In contrast, it is in autumn that birds are molting; they're wearing drab dress, often different from their appearance in spring. Thus, identifying birds during autumn migrations is more of a field challenge, particularly in the case of vireos, wood warblers, some finches, and sparrows—even experienced birders have difficulty identifying autumn wood warblers. Many migrating songbirds also stop in backyard habitats during autumn to rest, feed, and drink before continuing southward to their wintering grounds. Enjoy them, too, and try to identify as many as possible despite their drab autumn plumage.

MAINTAINING LISTS

When birdwatchers keep a list of the woodpeckers, finches, sparrows, and other species that visit their backyard feeders, a simple form of the life list is produced. There are many reasons why amateur birders make lists; perhaps the most basic and powerful reason is to recall past seasons and delightful sights of birds at feeders, birdbaths, and birdhouses—great moments of wildlife viewing pleasure.

At the other end of the spectrum are bird checklists published by birding and ornithological organizations in North America. These publications list the species a birdwatcher can reasonably expect to see within a given area, as well as "accidental" birds—those whose appearance would be extraordinary but not unprecedented. Not all backyard birdwatchers are interested in these lists, but all should be aware of them.

Common Birding Lists

Backyard Lists

The most common type of bird list maintained by birdwatchers is the backyard or home life list. It's a dated list of all the bird species observed in a backyard habitat. Birding stores sell printed field checklists that can be used to maintain a backyard life list. Alternatively, mark backyard life list birds in your field guide or enter them into a computer database. The number of birds likely to be included on a backyard list ranges from two or three dozen to close to two hundred species.

A feeder life list contains birds seen using feeders in a backyard habitat. It lists all birds that visit feeders, including feeders specially designed for hummingbirds or woodpeckers (i.e., suet feeders).

Another life list that can be maintained is the breeding bird list. It lists species, such as Northern Mockingbirds, Gray Catbirds, Brown Thrashers, Eastern Bluebirds, American Robins, and House Finches, that successfully nested in birdhouses; nest boxes; or trees, shrubs, and other vegetation in your backyard habitat.

The number of breeding birds likely to nest successfully in your backyard habitat depends on the size and quality of habitat enhancement, as well as the number and suitability of birdhouses and nest boxes that you provide.

Local Life List

A local life list includes birds observed in backyard habitats and local areas close to a particular backyard. Expanding the geographic area allows inclusion of many more birds not normally expected in backyards; for example, Northern Pintails, Hooded Mergansers, Bald Eagles, and Golden Eagles. You'll probably also want to maintain a local life list.

State and National Life Lists

Many birders keep state and national life lists, and you'll probably want to do so. Again, you can use field checklists, your field guide, or computer programs to keep track of species new to your state and national life lists.

World Life List

A world life list contains birds seen anywhere in the world, with dates and locations. Few birders have seen more than half of the approximately 9,700 species in the world, and that achievement is extremely time-consuming and expensive, sometimes to see just one particular species. If you assiduously include birds seen on vacations and business trips, you might reasonably expect to have between five hundred and a thousand birds on your world life list. The number is determined by where you travel, the amount of time and in which seasons you were birding, your bird identification skills, and luck.

Professional Checklists

American Ornithologists' Union Check-List

The seventh edition of the American Ornithologists' Union *Check-List of North American Birds* is the accepted source for North American bird names (for certain exceptions, see the ABA section below). Its list contains the known geographic distribution for each species listed, technical information related to taxonomy, and details regarding species not accepted for inclusion on the main list. Most backyard

John Boyer

A. A Cooper's Hawk standing with prey remains in the backyard of John and Nancy Boyer. All wildlife is welcome in this small sanctuary.

B. Part of the main bird feeding area on David and Arlene Kochs' property in Pennsylvania. Birds continually use the feeders, regardless of season.

A large colony of nesting King Penguins on South Georgia Island.

birdwatchers will never use this checklist, but their activities are directly influenced by the information it contains.

For example, common English names used in field guides are based on information in the AOU checklist. State and federal laws that protect birds also include common and scientific names from the AOU checklist. Its influence, therefore, reaches into the activities of every birdwatcher.

American Birding Association Checklist

The ABA Checklist: Birds of the Continental United States and Canada is another slim checklist. Some serious birders use this checklist to determine whether they can include a rare sighting on their own North American life list. However, the ABA and AOU checklists do not necessarily contain the same species or number of species. When pressed to select, however, professional ornithologists always choose the AOU list.

The ABA checklist is much less complex than the AOU list, with far fewer pages. It's a simple list on which birders can check off names of birds they've seen. It includes a summary of "accidental" species that have reached North America from elsewhere in the world, including the Fork-tailed Swift, Bahama Swallow, and Eurasian Bullfinch.

Since the 1998 publication of the seventh-edition AOU checklist, the fifth-edition ABA checklist has some obsolete information. However, a new ABA checklist is in preparation.

Field Checklists

Many backyard birdwatchers use small card-like pocket lists on which daily, weekly, monthly, or even yearly bird sightings are checked off. These lists are available free at many wildlife refuges, parks, and nature centers. Birding stores also sell them. You can use these lists as a convenient way of keeping permanent records of the birds you've seen. It's the information recorded on daily field lists that birdwatchers use to compile life lists.

Birdwatchers can organize lists in any number of ways, the most common of which are by world, North American, state, county, local, backyard, and yearly. From 1933 to 1962, Catherine L. Barlieb was avidly engaged in birding in Bethlehem, Pennsylvania. She was meticulous only to record birds within the city limits—no matter how tempting it was to add an additional species seen just over the city line. No bird was added to her list unless she was absolutely certain that it had been correctly identified. The result of her Bethlehem life list was 210 species.

The lure of the list is strong for adventurous birders—which means going far beyond one's backyard. Many birders also maintain North American life lists, and hard-core ABA members venture worldwide to see new birds.

There are also a few species, such as the Ivory-billed Woodpecker and Bachman's Warbler, that were alive earlier in the twentieth century but are now most likely extinct. Hence, a few older birders have them on their life lists, but it's impossible for birders today to see them.

Listing Software

A number of companies have developed computer programs to help birders create and maintain lists. To keep up with new software releases, check the About.com Birding Page website. For more information about this program and other websites, see appendix 3, Birding on the Internet.

Bird Brain A program called Bird Brain (produced by Ideaform, Inc.) allows birders using Macintosh computers to prepare numerous types of lists, including backyard lists, life lists, and year lists. Bird Brain incorporates changes in accepted species, bird names, and sequence of presentation published in the AOU's seventh edition of the *Check-List of North American Birds.* A printed reference manual accompanies the software. For more information about Bird Brain and other birding products, see appendix 4, Company Addresses.

Ramphastos Birding Software Ramphastos Birding Software produces a PC-based listing and identification program called YardBirds for birdwatchers, with eastern and western North America versions. The program combines detailed information on more than a hundred bird species with listing functions.

Santa Barbara Software Products Many North American bird watchers use lifelist software developed by Santa Barbara Software Products. The choice of species is based on *Birds of the World: A Checklist* by James Clements rather than the seventh edition of the AOU's *Check-List of North American Birds* (i.e., the international standard for

A Blue Jay at a bird feeder.

determining which species occur in North America). The company's website includes sections for birding software demonstrations.

Thayer Birding Software Thayer Birding Software offers a range of computer software for birders using either PC or Macintosh computers. Its website has detailed information about its CD-ROMs (Birds of North America v2.5) and applications (Birder's Diary v2.5) for preparing life lists.

Rare Bird Sightings

Rare birds do appear unexpectedly. In autumn 1994, an adult male Rufous Hummingbird appeared at a feeder in Cambridge, Washington County, New York. It's one of two accepted records of that species for New York. In Berks County, Pennsylvania, in December 1995, a Varied Thrush appeared at bird feeders; it was the first record for the county. In Des Moines, Iowa, from January to April 1977, the only record of a Pygmy Nuthatch for that state was documented with photographs. My own favorite example is the Kermadec Petrel I filmed in October 1959, at Hawk Mountain Sanctuary in eastern Pennsylvania. The petrel—normally found in the South Pacific Ocean—had been carried thousands of miles by a hurricane. My record of this bird sighting is the only one in continental North America.

On October 3, 1959, this Kermadec Petrel unexpectedly appeared at Hawk Mountain Sanctuary in Pennsylvania. The record is the only one for North America. Photo from a 16 mm motion picture by the author.

As soon as you recognize a rare bird, the first step is to document the bird carefully and completely. The easiest way to do this is to take lots of videotape footage of the bird, showing as many different views as possible. Use the camera's highest magnification, preferably with the camera mounted on a tripod. Alternatively, take 35 mm color slides or color prints of the bird. If only black-and-white film is available, use that. As a last resort, sketch the bird, showing conspicuous features, and note the date, location, time of day, and name of observer on the sketch.

Once you have documented the bird, you should seek independent confirmation of the identification. This is particularly important if your sighting is the first recorded in a state, or even in North America. The best way to confirm the bird's correct identification is to telephone a local chapter of the National Audubon Society, a wildlife conservation organization, or a nature center. Explain the significance of the bird and the need to have an experienced birder confirm the bird's identification. Speed is vital because birds can fly away from a feeding station and an important record can be lost. Unfortunately, this sometimes happens.

After documentation and confirmation, report details of the sighting to your state's rare bird records committee. Most states have these committees, sometimes in association with a state ornithological society or Audubon society. The committee will indicate the manner in which details of the record should be submitted. If photographs or videotape are included, keep copies for yourself. Keep in mind that state rare bird records committees are not infallible, and there may be different opinions regarding the validity of rare bird records.

The final step in dealing with a rare bird sighting is publication of details of the record. This may include photographs made from a documentary videotape, 35 mm color transparencies, or black-and-white negatives showing the bird in the best possible position to show essential field marks.

A national record would rate publication in *The Auk*, *Condor*, *Journal of Field Ornithology*, or the *Wilson Bulletin*. State records are published in state ornithological journals. New species for a county list can be published in local bird newsletters or a state ornithology journal.

It may be appropriate to seek permanent preservation of the original videotape or photographs in a professionally curated collection of these types of images. Check with your state museum or archives, a major natural history museum, or a local historical society—provided these institutions are equipped to store and curate these materials using professional standards.

BIRDING ORGANIZATIONS AND PROJECTS

National Audubon Society

One of the best ways to become more involved in birding and conservation is by joining a National Audubon Society (NAS) chapter and participating in its activities. There are more than 510 local chapters of the Society. Each has its own programs and projects, field trips, publications, activities, and flavor. To look for a local chapter, check the Society website and look for state listings. The NAS state offices listed on the website can provide information about local chapters (see appendix 3).

It's the local chapters that organize and schedule many of the Society's bird projects. The oldest and best-known birding project is the annual Christmas Bird

Count (CBC), which has been sponsored by the Society since 1900. The original 1900 CBC was a protest by twenty-seven conservationists against the annual "side hunt," a gruesome contest to determine who could shoot and kill the most birds on Christmas Day!

CBCs have grown to include 45,000 participants from fifty states, all Canadian provinces, Central and South America, and several Pacific Islands that are wintering grounds for some North American birds. Approximately 1,700 CBCs are held annually.

Each CBC lasts for one day sometime between December 18 and January 3. Each group selects its own date and covers a designated circle 15 miles in diameter during a twenty-four-hour period. Birding is done on foot, in vehicles, and indoors by watching birds at backyard feeders. Data are then submitted to the NAS for compilation, analysis, and publication. In 1998, the NAS teamed with the Cornell Laboratory of Ornithology to use computers to work on the CBC. Using Cornell's BirdSource website, each CBC can expedite data receipt and analysis on-line. After nearly a hundred years, the CBC has entered cyberspace!

Christmas Bird Counts are among the few databases representing the birdlife of the entire North American continent. Although considered crude by some scientists, analysis of CBC data provides approximate annual snapshots of the health and status of North America's birds—and the environment on which they depend for their survival. Data from CBCs is used with other information in developing the NAS's WatchList of 115 species of declining birds. The WatchList is the centerpiece of the Society's bird conservation programs.

Participating in Christmas Bird Counts can be educational and informative. Do not hesitate to participate in a CBC because you don't know enough about birds or their identification; there's no better way to improve birding skills than to learn useful tips during a day-long CBC. Most skilled birders are very willing to help beginners by sharing their knowledge.

Contact information for the National Audubon Society and the Cornell Laboratory of Ornithology is in appendix 1.

Project FeederWatch

Project FeederWatch, an annual project that began in 1987 and was developed and coordinated by the Cornell Laboratory of Ornithology, is conducted each winter by approximately twelve thousand volunteer backyard birdwatchers across the United States and Canada. They monitor and count the numbers of each bird species visiting their backyard feeders throughout the winter. Periodically, participants use forms to enter their data into the Project FeederWatch database.

Project FeederWatch has numerous goals. In particular, it collects long-term data on North American winter bird populations, attempts to detect serious population declines or explosions, and tracks nomadic or wandering movements of certain species. The project also identifies which habitats, feeders, and foods are attractive to birds and determines which bird populations need more ornithological research.

When bird-feeder data are received at the Laboratory, ornithologists organize and analyze it, then publish their results in *Birdscope*. Additional findings are

A female House Finch on a crabapple tree.

published in scientific journals and books, and Laboratory ornithologists also present their findings at conferences and meetings. This cooperation of backyard birdwatchers results in important scientific contributions and new knowledge about backyard birds—plus an annual continental snapshot of birds and their numbers visiting feeders across North America.

The Cornell Laboratory of Ornithology also conducts other feeder-related projects in which you can participate. For example, one year Project FeederWatch participants in the Midwest and Northeast noticed sick and dying Pine Siskins, American Goldfinches, and Common Redpolls at their feeders. In New York, Common Redpolls were particularly hard hit. Alarmed at the situation, backyard birders contacted the Laboratory, which then contacted the National Wildlife Health Center. Already aware of the problem, the Center confirmed the diagnosis of bacteria in the sick and dead birds as Salmonella.

Similarly, the House Finch Disease Survey monitors monthly the presence and distribution of severe conjunctivitis in eastern populations of the House Finch. Birds infected with the disease, which is caused by the parasitic bacterium *Mycoplasma gallisepticum*, have eyes that are red, swollen, runny, and sometimes crusty; some infected birds are blinded. Mortality among infected birds is very high, not due to the disease itself but rather to indirect causes, such as starvation and predation.

The disease was first noticed in eastern House Finch populations during the winter of 1993–94 in Maryland and Virginia; it then concentrated in states and provinces north to Quebec and south to Georgia. It now has spread to the Rocky Mountains. Between November 1994 and March 1997, ornithologists at the Cornell Laboratory received and analyzed almost twenty-five thousand data forms reporting birds suffering from conjunctivitis.

Contact information for the Cornell Laboratory of Ornithology is in appendix 1.

Big Day Counts

Big Day Counts are birding events in which participants try to see and hear as many species as possible in a specific geographic area within a twenty-four-hour period. The emphasis is on compiling a very long list of birds, as opposed to quality birding in which good, long views are enjoyed.

There are variations on Big Day Counts, such as the annual World Series of Birding organized by the New Jersey Audubon Society. In this affair, teams of birders try to compile the largest number of birds seen. Teams have sponsors pledging to pay specified amounts for each species reported by the sponsor's team. This aspect of the event raises thousands of dollars for bird and wildlife conservation.

Birding Hotlines or Rare Bird Alerts

Many birding organizations in the United States and Canada collect and disseminate information about rare or unusual birds through birding hotlines or Rare Bird Alerts. You call a hotline number and listen to a recorded announcement; this is how most birders learn about rare birds present in a particular location. In addition to seeing a potential new life-list bird, there are opportunities to meet other birders and network with them.

A useful list of birding hotlines and Rare Bird Alerts was published in the July–August 1998 issue of *Bird Watcher's Digest*, or check the ABA's website (see appendix 3).

CHIRP

In addition to the thousands of certified backyard habitats in North America (see chapter 5), a number of neighborhood and community habitat-enhancement projects have been successful. A remarkable story of community activism took place in Alpine, California.

Maureen Austin had the idea. Fascinated by what she had achieved in her own backyard, she began giving talks at local organizations about her organic herb gardens. Interest grew, and eventually Maureen established a nonprofit organization called CHIRP for Garden Wildlife (Center to Help Instill Respect and Preservation). CHIRP encourages property owners to create and certify enhanced habitats, and lends technical assistance.

A schoolyard habitat project followed; then, a community-wide habitat-enhancement project was launched. By the summer of 1998, more than eighty homes, two schoolyards, a number of businesses, the chamber of commerce, and the local fire department all planted trees, shrubs, and wildflowers in a coordinated effort to create a community garden. In 1998, the National Wildlife Federation certified Alpine, California, as the nation's first Community Wildlife Habitat. The public continues to express its interest, and Alpine is now a model for similar programs throughout the United States. All that's needed are local leaders like Maureen Austin to show the way.

Enhancing Local Parks

There are many birding and bird-related public-service projects in which you can become involved. You can work with local parks departments, install and maintain bird feeders, or recommend where birdhouses or nest boxes should be placed. Establishing a bluebird nest-box trail is another possible park project. Or make and install Wood Duck, American Kestrel, wren, and woodpecker nest boxes, or American Robin nesting platforms.

In eastern Pennsylvania, the Wildlife Information Center is beginning the Lehigh Valley Park Lands Biodiversity Project, in which volunteers conduct biodiversity inventories of parks. The program is starting with birds, but eventually will include other major wildlife and plant groups. When adequate data are available for a particular park, the information will be published and made available to park managers and municipal officials for enhanced park management.

Schoolyard Habitats and Birding Projects

There are increasing opportunities to serve as a mentor to students because the National Wildlife Federation has a

Lehigh Parkway South is another good birding park in Allentown, Pennsylvania.

growing roster of some one thousand schoolyard habitat projects throughout the United States. For example, New Hampshire and Pennsylvania now have schoolyard habitat programs.

Some schools are also involved with the Cornell Laboratory of Ornithology's Project Feederwatch. This allows students and teachers to participate in scientific research and report data secured from bird-feeding stations located outside classroom windows. The Laboratory's newsletter, *Classroom Birdscope*, contains articles (including scientific analysis of data from observations at schoolyard feeders) and illustrations by participating students. Some students and teachers are also involved in the Cornell Nest Box Network.

Joint Projects with Youth Organizations

There are many ways in which you can become involved with youth organizations such as the Boy Scouts, Girl Scouts, 4-H Clubs, Boys and Girls Clubs, and similar nonprofit organizations. Offer to lead local birding field trips for children. For the Boy Scouts and Girl Scouts, you can be a resource person for scouts seeking bird-study merit badges.

Maintaining Feeders at Retirement or Nursing Homes

One way in which backyard birdwatchers can share their enjoyment of birds is to maintain bird feeders outside the windows of retirement or nursing homes. Elderly or ill people can enjoy watching the birds eating sunflower seeds at the feeders.

Who can say that such sights do not stimulate an ill person toward recovery, or give pleasure and hope to a lonely retired person? You might propose that the facility provides the feeders and seeds, and that the birdwatchers maintain them. A local Audubon chapter might adopt this as a special project.

Garden Scarecrows

Putting scarecrows in gardens is fun. However, do scarecrows actually scare birds away from fruit or vegetable crops? That's a project that backyard birders with gardens can study carefully—and perhaps answer adequately.

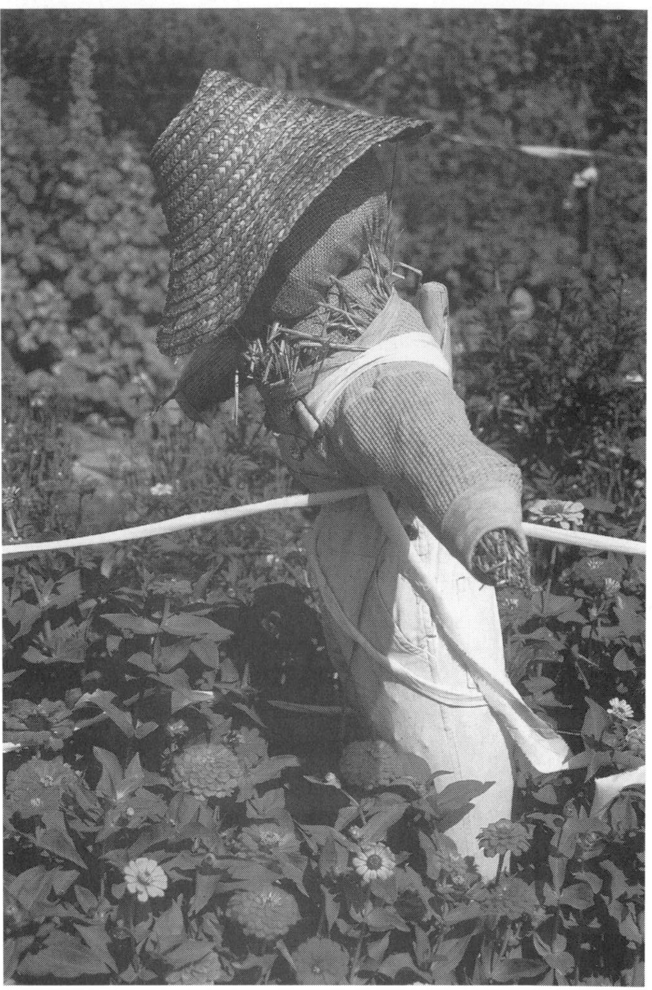

Many home gardeners and backyard birdwatchers put scarecrows in their gardens as a nonlethal way of deterring birds from eating too many fruits or vegetables. Whether they actually are effective is questionable, but they nevertheless add an interesting "extra" to a garden.

11 Expanding Your Horizons

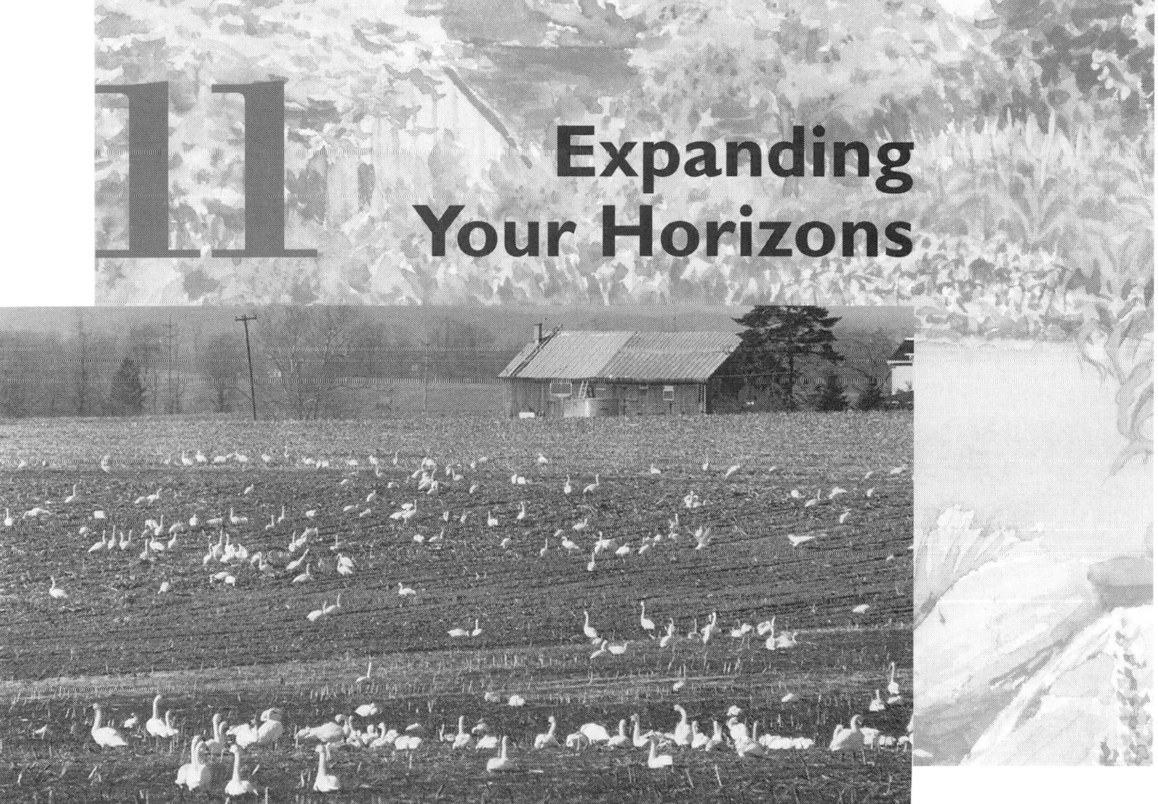

Roadside Tundra Swan watching in March in the vicinity of Washington Boro, Lancaster County, Pennsylvania, is a delightful activity.

Watching birds in a backyard habitat is how many of us entered the world of birdwatching, and it is here that we develop our basic birding skills. By creating, studying, and enjoying a backyard habitat, we move beyond birding as a hobby and begin to see the important connections between birding and conservation. We realize that habitat preservation is fundamentally linked with birding.

Many backyard birders eventually move farther afield and begin to explore local, regional, state, and national birding locations. Without suggesting that birders leave the backyard, in this final chapter I look at how backyard birders can take advantage of a wider scope of birding opportunities.

LOCAL AND REGIONAL BIRDING

Depending on where you live, local birding may mean birdwatching in a city, town, suburban area, or rural area. Each offers different habitats, environmental conditions, and birding opportunities. Birdwatchers in towns, suburbs, and rural areas are to be expected, but there also are excellent birding sites in virtually every major city in the United States and Canada, even in very large and dense cities such as New York City or Chicago.

To find out about good local birding spots, first check with your public library or the academic library at a nearby college or university. Many libraries maintain databases of local organizations, and they may also have local or regional bird-finding guides. Other information sources include the Audubon chapter in your community, other wildlife organizations such as nature centers, and birding equipment and supply stores.

The ABA is a major source for purchasing bird-finding guides; it offers a large selection for the United States, Canada, and elsewhere in the world. For a price list and contact information, see appendix 1. The Internet is another source for local birding information. Try searching the BirdLinks or the National Audubon Society's website, which contains links to hundreds of local Audubon chapters (see appendix 3, Birding on the Internet).

Large Cities

Beyond one's backyard or apartment balcony, the key to enjoying successful birdwatching in a large city is to do some backyard habitat enhancement and visit nearby natural areas.

Most large cities in the United States and Canada have parks, nature centers, cemeteries, woodlands, old fields, marshes and wetlands, river or lake shores, reservoirs, sewage and waste treatment plants, even landfills, that are attractive to birds during different seasons of the year. They all offer birding opportunities.

At first, the idea of enjoying exciting birdwatching in a city, especially a large, intensely developed one such as New York City, must seem ludicrous. In fact, nothing could be farther from the truth. Experienced birdwatchers in New York City agree that it's an excellent place for birding, with several bird-rich areas: Central Park in Manhattan, Van Cortlandt and Pelham Bay parks in the Bronx, and Wolfe's Pond and other sites on Staten Island, as well as Jamaica Bay adjacent to JFK International Airport.

At least 270 species of birds have been reported in Central Park, which covers 840 acres in the middle of Manhattan. The Ramble is a particularly productive area of the park for spring and autumn birding. With 33 acres of canopied woodland, shrubs, and rock outcroppings, there are elevated vantage points to observe migrating wood warblers foraging in treetops. Indeed, warbler-watching is especially productive in Central Park (the city lies on a bird migration flyway).

Unusual birding events happen in New York City. In 1993, a pair of Red-tailed Hawks unsuccessfully attempted to nest on a ledge of a tall building at 74th Street and Fifth Avenue—across the street from Central Park. A nesting attempt the next year failed as well, but in 1995, the male Red-tail found a new mate—a bird that was injured and rehabilitated at a licensed facility in New Jersey, released, and found her way to New York City. Three young Red-tails were fledged, and the hawks remained near their building nesting site for about a month before wandering away. The next year, the male Red-tail found another mate—this time a female he had bonded with in 1992 (this was revealed by band numbers read through a telescope). Again, three nestlings were fledged in the middle of Manhattan! Introduced Peregrine Falcons have also nested successfully in certain locations in New York City.

Seattle, Washington, is another example of several good birding areas within the city. The campus of the University of Washington, especially the Arboretum, has many native and introduced trees, shrubs, and other plants that birds find to their liking; both breeding birds and migrants have been found there.

Fields on the campus bordering Union Bay also are productive birding sites. Among birds seen in the marshland are Marsh Wrens, Green Herons, American Bitterns, and Virginia Rails. On upland fields, look for Western Meadowlarks, White-crowned Sparrows, and Savannah Sparrows; during October, Horned Larks, Water Pipits, Lapland Longspurs, and Snow Buntings also are seen in these fields, as well as American Tree Sparrows, Golden-crowned Sparrows, Lincoln's Sparrows, and Fox Sparrows. In the adjacent bay, you can see European Wigeons, Blue-winged Teals, Cinnamon Teals, Gadwalls, Redheads, Barrow's Goldeneyes, and Hooded Mergansers.

During certain winters, Snowy Owls can be seen at various locations in Seattle; Cooper's Hawks, Sharp-shinned Hawks, Short-eared Owls, and Northern Shrikes also have been sighted in winter.

Smaller Cities and Towns

There are hundreds of smaller cities and thousands of towns in the United States and Canada. Birders living in them typically go birding in local parks, lakes and ponds, greenways (see sidebar), nature centers, cemeteries, sewage treatment plants, and other open-space areas. Despite their size, certain towns throughout the United States are extremely important stopover habitats, and their preservation efforts can have a huge impact on the survival of migrating songbirds.

Santa Barbara, for example, is a beautiful city set against the Santa Ynez Mountains on the Pacific Ocean in Southern California, where more than four hundred bird species have been reported. Among birding sites of interest are the Santa Barbara Botanic Gardens, which has displays of native plants and offers worthwhile birding for species found in oak woodlands and chaparral. Nearby, in Rocky Nook Park, a preserved stand of coastal live oaks, look for Oak Titmice, Bushtits, Hutton's Vireos, and California Towhees. Ducks and other waterbirds are seen during migration seasons at the Andree Clark Bird Refuge. Western and Ring-billed Gulls live there year-round and are quite tame.

GREENWAYS

In suburban areas, you can sometimes find greenways—corridors of land sometimes formerly used by railroads—that have been converted to trails connecting isolated woodlands, wetlands, fields, and other habitats. They make for fine hiking or biking trails, but they also offer excellent birdwatching because they often parallel rivers or creeks and generally cut across a variety of habitats. That means you have a good chance of sighting representative birds from each habitat. Your local parks department or planning commission can tell you how to reach any greenways in your area.

A world away is Grinnell, Iowa, a cornbelt town of about nine thousand people surrounded by large expanses of agricultural lands. The area offers limited habitat diversity, and few wooded areas in which migratory birds can find stopover shelter. Towns like Grinnell play a crucial and unexpected role in providing stopover habitat for migratory songbirds during spring and (to a lesser extent) autumn. Migrating birds stop in Grinnell for hours or days to rest and feed in wooded areas in the town's cemetery, along the shores of Lake Arbor, in a city park, on the campus of Grinnell College, and even in tree-lined streets. Birders visiting these locations typically see Red-eyed, Blue-headed, and Yellow-throated Vireos; wood warblers; Great Crested Flycatchers; Eastern Wood Pewees; Scarlet Tanagers; Indigo Buntings; and Rose-breasted Grosbeaks. Occasionally, a Great Blue Heron, Green Heron, or Black-crowned Night-Heron appears on Lake Arbor.

Suburban Areas

Backyard birdwatchers living in suburban areas have many local birding sites to explore if they decide to venture beyond their own yards. Suburbs have less development than cities, far fewer people, and more pastures and woodlands, parks, wetlands, cemeteries, and other potential wildlife habitats. As discussed previously, the greater the diversity of habitats, the greater the number of birds likely to appear. Creeks, rivers, ponds, and other wetlands are strong magnets for waterfowl and shorebirds.

Suburban areas are home to many county, state, and national parks in the United States. Many are maintained in a natural state, which preserves bird habitats and creates birdwatching opportunities. A typical example is Jordan Creek Parkway, a county park five minutes from my door in Whitehall, Pennsylvania. The park offers winding hiking trails, woodlands, a small old field, and a creek. The park is accessible to many urban and suburban birdwatchers and it gets regular use from birders, especially during spring and autumn when migrating songbirds visit it as stopover habitat.

MUNICIPAL RESERVOIRS

Large reservoirs in suburban or rural areas that serve cities located miles away are prized locations for birders. Reservoirs are magnets for waterfowl, especially during spring and autumn migration periods. In eastern Pennsylvania, for example, hundreds of Tundra Swans sometimes stop to rest and feed at reservoirs during spring and autumn, along with even larger numbers of Snow Geese. These are spectacular birding attractions. Herons and egrets also are seen along shallow edges of reservoirs. Great Blue Herons are fairly common, but Great Egrets, Snowy Egrets, Black-crowned Night-Herons, and their relatives are seen only occasionally. When a reservoir's water level is drawn down, often in late summer and early autumn, the exposed mudflats attract migrating shorebirds.

In Jordan Creek Parkway alone, I've spotted dozens of birds, including Turkey Vultures, Ospreys, Red-tailed Hawks, Belted Kingfishers, Northern Flickers, Downy Woodpeckers, Blue Jays, Scarlet Tanagers, and Dark-eyed Juncos. There are thousands of similar suburban parks throughout the United States and Canada that offer good birding opportunities. In some parks, trained naturalists assist birders by directing them to particularly good spots, mentioning unusual birds recently seen in the park, and providing checklists of the park's birds.

Rural Areas

Offering open space and much less development, rural areas are a natural destination for backyard birdwatchers seeking a change of pace. Distinct habitats include agricultural fields, old fields, woodlots, woodlands, wetlands, running waterways (i.e., creeks, streams, and rivers), and ponds and lakes.

Roadside Birding

In rural areas, a great deal of quality birding can be done in the car and along roadsides. That's especially true in areas with panoramic views of the landscape, where binoculars and spotting scopes enable you to see and identify birds at great distances. From my car I've seen, at acceptable viewing distances, Bobolinks, Red-winged Blackbirds, and Eastern Meadowlarks flying to and from fields in which they were nesting. Another rural birding technique is to watch for birds perched on utility wires and poles or on dead branches and trees. Red-tailed Hawks, American Kestrels, and other raptors, as well as swallows, kingbirds, bluebirds, and sparrows, commonly use exposed perches. Roadside birding is quite popular among raptor enthusiasts during autumn, winter, and spring; however, the technique is less effective during summer, when leaves on deciduous trees and shrubs hide the birds from view.

A spectacular example of rural roadside birding is in Lancaster County, Pennsylvania, in February and March when Tundra Swans feed on waste corn and other plants in farm fields near Washington Boro. As many as ten thousand of these beautiful birds gather for a few weeks on the nearby Susquehanna River before continuing their northward migration to their Arctic breeding grounds. Each morning, after sunrise, the big white birds begin moving around on the river. Soon flock after flock flies overhead and eastward to fields a few miles inland. Because swans are white and large, hundreds of them can be seen on fields from great distances. Drive along the road to get as close as possible to the swans; from there, inside your vehicle or standing on the shoulder of the road, use binoculars or spotting scopes to scan the fields.

Wetland Restoration Projects

In some rural areas in the United States, cooperative wetland restoration projects are developed via a partnership among private landowners (usually farmers), the U.S. Fish and Wildlife Service, and conservation and soil agencies. Restored wetlands are havens for Wood Ducks, other ducks and geese, herons and egrets, and rails. Be sure to check these spots if you're near one. (For more on wetland restoration, see page 218.) Because public funding helped pay for the restoration, the public is allowed to visit restored wetlands for birdwatching purposes. Nevertheless, good birding etiquette requires birders to ask permission from the owner, who usually lives nearby; it doesn't take much time to extend this courtesy. In general, birders should never trespass on privately owned rural land (which may or may not be posted) without obtaining the owner's permission.

Rural Wildlife Management Areas

Throughout the United States, state wildlife agencies own and maintain many wildlife management areas, primarily in rural areas. Although their names vary from state to state, they are, in essence, public hunting lands; you should avoid them during hunting seasons. However, most are good birding locations at other times of the year because they preserve many habitats rich in birdlife. You can obtain detailed information about these areas from your state wildlife agency.

BIRDING ACROSS THE UNITED STATES

U.S. Parks

Some of the finest birdwatching locations in the United States are the state and national parks. Many national parks preserve spectacular natural features such as wetlands, woodlands, rivers, and deserts. These areas support a rich diversity of wildlife, including birds, which is why birdwatching in national parks can be very rewarding and is highly recommended. The parks are generally safe and suitable for family birding adventures. The larger parks have a range of visitor facilities, and some provide useful checklists of birds known to occur there, which are great birding aids and very useful when compiling a national or world life list.

WATCHABLE WILDLIFE VIEWING AREAS

In many states there are watchable wildlife viewing areas identified by and marked with signs. The public is encouraged to use these locations because they offer excellent opportunities to view and photograph birds and other wildlife. Watchable wildlife viewing guides are also published for several dozen states; eventually, every state will have its own guide.

The Oregon Wildlife Viewing Guide *by Julie Goodnight and Sara Vickerman was the first to be published (by Defenders of Wildlife). James A. Yuskavitch wrote a similar book, entitled* Oregon Wildlife Viewing Guide, *as part of a series published by Falcon Publishing Company, of Helena, Montana. Each guide has maps of the selected sites, color photographs, and basic wildlife information. They are inexpensive books that you'll find useful when searching for good birding locations.*

State Parks

Every state operates a network of parks that provide outdoor recreational activities. There are thousands of state parks in the United States. Many state parks make special efforts to preserve a diversity of wildlife habitats ranging from sand dunes, and even deserts, to mountains, old fields, old-growth forests, rivers, and wetlands. Many provide excellent birding opportunities.

The majority of state parks are located in rural areas. For practical purposes, you will need a car to reach them because public transportation does not serve most of these places. Urban birders without cars should not despair; join a birding carpool, perhaps organized by a local National Audubon Society chapter, or a private group of birders that plans visits to state parks known as outstanding birding hotspots.

Cape May Point State Park, with 190 acres at the extreme southern tip of New Jersey, is an outstanding birding hotspot. It's internationally known as a major autumn migratory bird-concentration bottleneck along the Atlantic Coast of the United States. Tens of thousands of migrating raptors, shorebirds, waterbirds, and songbirds are observed there every autumn (September through November) by thousands of avid birders from across the United States and around the world, who also pump millions of ecotourist dollars into the local economy. On days when northwesterly winds prevail, huge numbers of migrating hawks fill the sky, some perching on trees and shrubs in the vicinity of the lighthouse. Occasionally, hundreds of Peregrine Falcons are seen in a single day. Those are truly never-to-be-forgotten red-letter birding days!

If Wild Turkeys are of more interest to you than hawks, Myakka River State Park near Sarasota is the place to go in Florida. Not only is this park Florida's largest, encompassing 28,875 acres, it's also an impressive place. Consisting of dense forest and part of the Myakka River, birders drive along a winding road looking for Wild Turkeys that appear early in the morning and late in the afternoon. In addition to gobblers, a boardwalk extending into Upper Myakka Lake allows birders to see various ducks during winter and year-round resident waders. Among the wonderful birds sometimes observed are White Ibises, Red-shouldered Hawks, Pileated Woodpeckers, Northern Mockingbirds, and Northern Cardinals.

Heading west to other states, Tishomingo State Park covers 1,541 acres of highland forest about 20 miles from Iuka, Mississippi. Tishomingo offers fine birding opportunities in a pine, oak, and hickory forest. An especially good birding area is in the vicinity of a bridge over Bear Creek.

Among Tishomingo's breeding birds are Broad-winged Hawks, Pileated Woodpeckers, Great Crested Flycatchers, Blue-gray Gnatcatchers, White-eyed Vireos, Yellow-throated Vireos, and a fair number of wood warblers including Pine, Prairie, Yellow-throated, Kentucky, and Hooded Warblers. Summer Tanagers and Bachman's Sparrows are also nesting species found at Tishomingo.

Texas is another outstanding birdwatching state, with countless excellent locations rich in birdlife. In fact, in *Birding Texas* by Roland Wauer and Mark Elwonger, 67 of the 210 sites featured in the book are state parks. Bentsen-Rio Grande Valley State Park, located in the Rio Grande Valley region, is one of the most famous and important. Encompassing 588 acres, with habitats including chaparral, Oxbow Lake, a thorn forest, and Tamaulipan scrub, a wealth of birdlife awaits birders and photographers.

Hawk watchers using an elevated platform at Cape May Point State Park, New Jersey. Autumn hawk and other bird migrations are impressive at this major Atlantic Coast migration bottleneck.

Among regularly seen species are Green Jays, Plain Chachalacas, Golden-fronted Woodpeckers, Long-billed Thrashers, Altamira and Audubon's Orioles, and Olive Sparrows. At night you can hear nocturnal species including the Pauraque. Waterbirds include both Ringed and Green Kingfishers; flycatchers include Couch's Kingbirds and Great Kiskadees. Hawkwatchers are particularly eager to see rare Hook-billed Kites that occur along the Rio Grande; other rare species that inhabit the park include Red-billed Pigeons, Clay-colored Robins, and Tropical Parulas.

National Parks

The national park system in the United States is the finest in the world. It was also the first in the world, begun in 1872 with the establishment of Yellowstone National Park. Not only do our splendid national parks protect the nation's finest scenery, they also preserve the widest possible array of habitat types all across this great land. As a result, many national parks offer outstanding birdwatching opportunities. Let's discuss a few representative examples.

Acadia National Park along the Maine coastline is one of the most beautiful parks in the United States. One of its major units is located on Mount Desert Island, where most birders enter the park. Driving along the road paralleling the park's coastline is a very pleasant summer experience, with gulls and other birds often in view. Sewall Bog is another famous birding spot, where Lincoln's Sparrows, Common Yellowthroats, and Palm Warblers nest. In addition, both Acadia National Park and non-park lands on Mount Desert Island are hotspots for nesting wood warblers. During autumn, hawk migrations can be seen from the summit of Cadillac Mountain. It's a spectacular location, with sweeping panoramic views over the ocean, bay, and surrounding landscape; on very clear days, you can see a hundred miles inland. A paved road winds its way to the summit, which makes that vantage point very accessible to see whatever birds may be present.

A section of the spectacular Maine coastline in Acadia National Park.

Farther south, on the border between North Carolina and Tennessee, you'll want to explore one of America's greatest natural areas—Great Smoky Mountains National Park. Its 800 square miles contain some of the finest southern Appalachian Mountains scenery in the nation. Parts of the park are at elevations of no less than 5,000 feet, with sixteen mountain peaks rising higher than 6,000 feet.

Although acid rain has damaged some high spruce and fir forests above 6,000 feet, much of major interest remains undamaged. That includes mixed hardwood–hemlock–black cherry–sugar maple forests between 6,000 and 4,500 feet. At lower elevations, famous cove hardwoods contain some of the largest species diversity in the United States. Thus, from beautiful valleys to splendid mountain peaks, you are offered an amazing range of habitats in which birds thrive.

A few of the many birds living in Great Smoky Mountains National Park are Ruffed Grouse, Northern Ravens, Red-breasted Nuthatches, Brown Creepers, Winter Wrens, Black-throated Green Warblers, and Scarlet Tanagers; much less common are Saw-whet Owls, Olive-sided Flycatchers, Pine Siskins, and Red Crossbills. Dark-eyed Juncos are common above 3,000 feet. The ideal time for a birder to visit the park is during spring and early summer—roughly late April through early July.

From a birdwatcher's viewpoint, Everglades National Park is one of the finest destinations in the nation, particularly from late autumn to early spring. Although many types of birds are found in this park, waterbirds are especially well known. Here, most North American species of herons and egrets are encountered: Great Blue Herons, Great Egrets, Snowy Egrets, Little Blue Herons, Tricolored Herons, Reddish Egrets, Cattle Egrets, Green Herons, Black-crowned Night-Herons, and Yellow-crowned Night-Herons. Some birds of special note are Anhingas, Roseate Spoonbills, Snail Kites, Bald Eagles, Short-tailed Hawks, White-crowned Pigeons, Mangrove Cuckoos, and Black-whiskered Vireos. If you're compiling national and world life lists, you'll want to make a special effort to see them.

Big Bend National Park, along the Rio Grande in Texas, is another outstanding national park rich in birdlife. With more than 800,000 acres and elevations rising from 1,850 to 7,835 feet, it's famous among birdwatchers. More than 450 species of birds have been reported there, making its bird list the largest for any national park in the United States.

Among the many species of birds of particular interest are the Golden-fronted Woodpecker, Lucifer Hummingbird, Black-capped Vireo, and Colima Warbler. Birders also seek the so-called "Mexican Duck" variation of the Mallard, Golden Eagles, Peregrine Falcons, and Prairie Falcons, as well as Common Black-Hawks, Zone-tailed Hawks, and Gray Hawks. You can also add the Scaled Quail and Greater Roadrunner to your life lists. Don't forget to look and listen for both Eastern and Western Screech-Owls.

Everglades National Park in Florida is one of the major birdwatching hotspots in the United States.

There are numerous other superb national parks that together provide wonderful birding opportunities. Compared with the most famous, such as Yellowstone National Park, some seem little used and even overlooked. Explore them and enjoy their birding delights; you'll be amazed how many new life-list birds you'll see and how rich is the full scope of birding.

Wildlife Refuges

Various kinds and sizes of wildlife refuges are scattered throughout the United States, some with specific wildlife conservation purposes. Many are national wildlife refuges owned and operated by the U.S. Fish and Wildlife Service. Most are located at strategic spots in waterfowl wintering, migration, and breeding areas. Although waterfowl is their primary focus, hundreds of other birds also visit or live there.

There are also private wildlife refuges. The National Audubon Society, state Audubon Societies, some local Audubon chapters, and other private conservation organizations own and operate some of the best private bird refuges. Let's look at a representative sample.

National Wildlife Refuges

The largest refuges, and often the most important, are hundreds of national wildlife refuges operated by the U.S. Fish and Wildlife Service. They range in size from a few to tens of thousands of acres. Collectively, they provide essential habitat for nearly all species of birds and other wildlife known to occur within the United States and its territories.

For birdwatchers, one of the most famous and important is the Bear River Migratory Bird Refuge in Utah. During spring and autumn migrations, millions of waterfowl and other birds visit it, creating amazing birdwatching opportunities. Birders visit Bear River especially to see large numbers of waterfowl and shorebirds. The refuge provides helpful visitor educational materials, including free checklists of birds, and the staff is pleased to answer questions.

The Brigantine division of the Edwin B. Forsythe National Wildlife Refuge near Oceanville, New Jersey, is one of the most important along the Atlantic Coast.

The Brigantine division of the Edwin B. Forsythe National Wildlife Refuge, New Jersey, is one of the best, and most popular, birding locations along the Atlantic coastline.

Because the refuge is located on some of the Atlantic Flyway's busy waterfowl corridors, large numbers of geese and ducks use this refuge—as do many other wading birds and shorebirds. However, there's great variation in birdlife during different months of the year. In August, birders look for migrating shorebirds and gatherings of wading birds. Duck-watching is productive during September, and large numbers of Snow Geese start arriving in October, with peak numbers from the middle of November to the middle of December. From late April through May, wading birds and shorebirds appear in good numbers, and newly hatched Canada Geese goslings are easily viewed.

Bombay Hook National Wildlife Refuge in Delaware is another outstanding refuge along the Atlantic Coast. Encompassing more than 15,000 acres of wetland habitat, it is home to Canada Geese, Snow Geese, numerous ducks, and many shorebirds. Birds of prey, including Ospreys and Bald Eagles, also live on Bombay Hook, which adds to the refuge's attractiveness for birdwatchers and bird photographers.

On the Pacific Coast, a number of wildlife refuges provide excellent birdwatching opportunities. Two of the most famous are Tule Lake National Wildlife Refuge and Lower Klamath National Wildlife Refuge—both components of the Klamath Basin National Wildlife Refuges—located on the border between California and Oregon. Roger Tory Peterson considered these amazing places among the nation's best birding spots.

These freshwater refuges are located on the Pacific Flyway, and in late October are used heavily as resting sites by ducks and geese migrating to wintering grounds from central California southward to Mexico and from as far away as South America. In April and May, vast numbers of waterfowl again stop at Tule and Lower Klamath.

The refuges host such notables as White-crowned Sparrows, Golden-crowned Sparrows, and Brewster's Blackbirds, but they are most famous for ducks, of which there are literally millions. Words cannot do justice to the spectacle. Among the most abundant are Gadwalls, American Wigeons, Mallards, Northern Shovelers, Northern Pintails, Canvasbacks, Ruddy Ducks, and vast numbers of White-fronted, Snow, and Ross's Geese. An auto road around Tule Lake, other refuge roads, and California Route 161, at Lower Klamath, give birders and photographers excellent vantages.

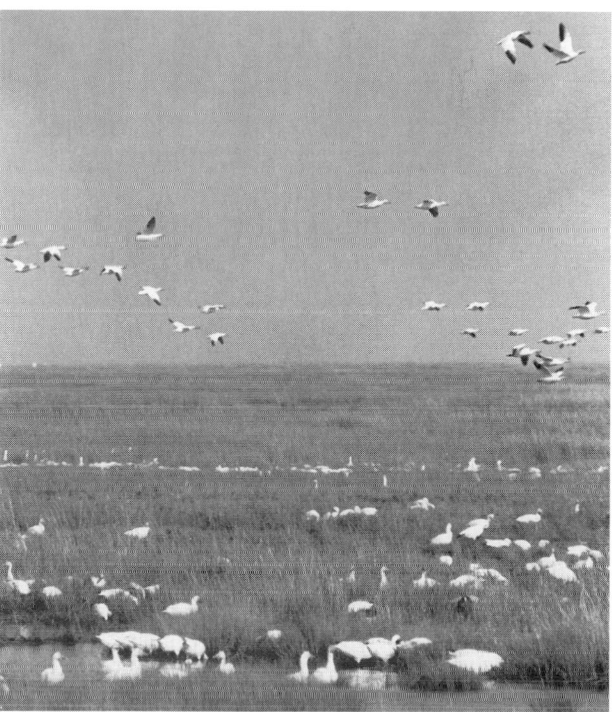
Snow Geese at Brigantine refuge.

Local Wildlife Refuges

In addition there are wildlife refuges owned by counties or cities, some of which are mentioned in the last chapter. You should always explore these places for local birding field trips because many are excellent, and only a short distance from home.

Mill Grove, John James Audubon's first home in America, is an excellent example of a 175-acre wildlife refuge and museum owned by a county—in this case, Montgomery County, near the town of Audubon, Pennsylvania. This beautiful historic house, built in 1762, was young Audubon's home for two years while he managed the family estate and operated a lead mine, explored nearby forests and meadows, conducted the first bird-banding experiment by putting a thin silver thread around the leg of a young Eastern Phoebe that was in a nest on the property, and met his future wife Lucy, who lived on a nearby estate. At Mill Grove John James Audubon also began painting birds and other wildlife, which would eventually make him world famous.

Today, visitors to Mill Grove enjoy free visits to the historic house, its priceless collection of Audubon art (including a complete set of his famous *The Birds of America*), an original Audubon painting, and a restored studio and working area. Birders can also wander over the property's 175 acres of lawns, meadows, woodland, a slope above the Perkiomen Creek, and miles of trails from which to bird. More than 175 species of birds have been cataloged at Mill Grove, including Mourning Doves, Northern Flickers, Eastern Phoebes, House Wrens, Wood Thrushes, American Robins, Gray Catbirds, Baltimore Orioles, Northern Cardinals, and Song Sparrows. May is a particularly good time to visit this wonderful wildlife sanctuary because flowering shrubs are in bloom and spring bird migrations are in full swing.

Castalia Pond, covering 10 acres in the middle of the little Ohio town of Castalia, is an example of a local wildlife refuge that provides excellent birding opportunities—particularly for seeing waterfowl and other waterbirds. Between December and March, birders often see species such as Pied-billed Grebes, American Black Ducks, American Wigeons, Redheads, and Common Goldeneyes on visits to the pond. What's especially enjoyable is how extremely close birders and photographers can come to birds on Castalia Pond. That's an extra bonus to the birding experience.

Private Wildlife Refuges

Privately owned refuges also have a significant ecological impact and are of interest to birders. A few of the most famous and productive are described here.

Hawk Mountain Sanctuary, near Kempton, Pennsylvania, was the world's first refuge for birds of prey. It's part of the famous Kittatinny raptor corridor—a hawk migration route in parts of New York, New Jersey, and eastern Pennsylvania—and an outstanding example of a privately owned refuge with an international reputation. Every autumn, from September through November, thousands of migrating hawks are observed at Hawk Mountain and nearby hawk lookouts, sometimes at close range and always to the delight of birdwatchers, wildlife photographers, and students. It's an ornithological spectacle that frequently draws birders back for decades.

Farther south, Corkscrew Swamp Sanctuary, near Immokalee, Florida, is a large property of more than 10,000 acres owned by the National Audubon Society. Corkscrew is a wonderful natural area, rich in birds, other wildlife, and native flora. Visitors traverse an elevated, mile-long boardwalk extending into the sanctuary's major areas. Among birds sometimes seen are Little Blue Herons, American Anhingas, White Ibises, Limpkins, Barred Owls, Red-cockaded Woodpeckers, and Brown-headed Nuthatches. Many consider Corkscrew Swamp Sanctuary the crown jewel of the National Audubon Society's wildlife refuge system.

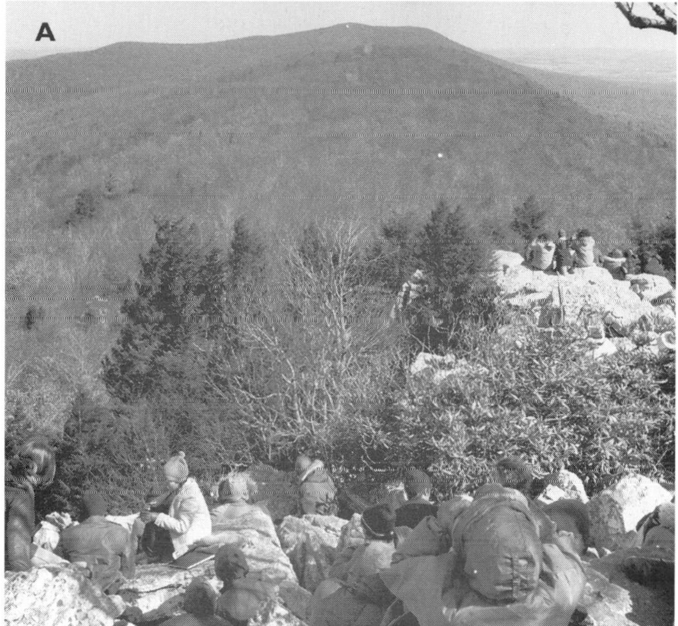

A. November hawk watchers on the North Lookout at Hawk Mountain Sanctuary, Pennsylvania.

B. Corkscrew Swamp Sanctuary is one of Florida's finest natural areas and a popular birding destination. The sanctuary is owned by the National Audubon Society.

Birding Festivals

Each year, there are dozens of birding festivals throughout the United States that focus on various types of birds and aspects of birding. These events offer wonderful opportunities for birdwatchers to meet, exchange ideas and information, attend programs and workshops, and purchase merchandise.

The economic aspect of birding festivals is important because it demonstrates to local businesses and government officials that birding is a powerful economic force in local areas. In other words, protecting birds and their habitats brings hard cash into communities in the form of birding tourism. Make no mistake about it, birders spend lots of money at festivals—sometimes millions of dollars over several days—to the benefit of local motels, restaurants, service stations, and other vendors.

WildBird magazine's annual North American directory of these events is a good source of information about birding festivals. The January issue, for example, typically provides a comprehensive roundup organized by state. Let's look at a few examples.

In Alaska, the Garnet Festival is held in April at Wrangle. The emphasis is on seeing large numbers of Bald Eagles (the world's second largest concentration), shorebirds, harbor seals, and Stellar's sea lions. It's quite a birding opportunity.

California hosts ten festivals between January and November. In January, there is the Morro Bay Winter Bird Festival and the Imperial Beach BirdFest in San Diego. In late September, the Annual Kern Valley Turkey Vulture Festival is held, timed and designed to give birders an opportunity to see several thousand Turkey Vultures migrating across the area, along with other migratory landbirds. Toward the end of the year, the Lodi Crane Festival is held in early November, which boasts of up to 10,000 Sandhill Cranes as well as Cinnamon Teals, Nuttall's Woodpecker, Spotted Towhees, and many other birds.

Florida holds three birding festivals between early April and mid-November. In mid-October, the Buteos on the Beach festival is held in Hollywood. The emphasis is on migrating hawks and Snail Kites, but other species such as Limpkins and White-crowned Pigeons also are seen. Organizers of the event offer guided field trips to the Everglades and Corkscrew Swamp.

In Illinois, three birding festivals are scheduled between January and mid-May. In early March, the Prairie Chicken and Waterfowl Weekend at Springfield gives birders the opportunity to see Greater Prairie Chickens, Short-eared Owls, grassland birds, and thousands of waterfowl at a limited-access reserve.

During the latter part of September, birders can attend the Effigy Mounds Hawkwatch in Harper's Ferry, Iowa. Birders watch migrating hawks, receive tips on raptor identification from a professional staff, and experience an educational program with live raptors.

Loons are lovely, fascinating birds and the subject of several festivals, including the Walker Lake Loon Festival at Walker Lake, Nevada. It's there that a major inland concentration of Common Loons takes place in mid-April. As many as 1,400 loons are seen in a single day. Other festivals that focus on loons include the Loon Festival in late summer at Moultonborough, New Hampshire.

New Jersey has five bird festivals of one type or another. Four are organized at Cape May, including the popular World Series of Birding, which pits teams of birders against each other to see and hear the largest number of species within a specific period. In addition, a Wings 'n Water Festival and art show is held in mid-September at Stone Harbor.

Some festivals have whimsical themes, such as Buzzard Sunday, held in mid-March in Cleveland. Birders from that event visit Hinkley, Ohio, to watch the return of the season's first Turkey Vultures.

Texas, of course, does everything in a big way, so why not birding festivals? In late February and early March, for example, A Celebration of Whooping Cranes and Other Birds is held in Port Aransas. Emphasis is on taking birders on guided boat trips to see and photograph endangered Whooping Cranes. In September, the Hummer/Bird Celebration is held in Rockport.

In Utah, Sandhill Crane Days is held in September at Hyrum. It enables birders to enjoy large numbers of waterfowl and shorebirds, as well as a thousand Sandhill Cranes at Bear River Migratory Bird Refuge.

BIRDING IN CANADA

Canada offers the birder some wonderful birding opportunities, particularly in its provincial and national park system and birding festivals of international stature.

Provincial Parks

Algonquin Provincial Park in Ontario is a superb wilderness area rich in birds and other wildlife, including gray wolves. Adventurous birders will certainly enjoy a foray into this 7,725-square-kilometer area.

There are three ways in which birders can explore Algonquin Provincial Park's lakes, rivers, beaches, bogs, cliffs, and forests. A 56-kilometer-long Parkway Corridor along Highway 60 cuts through the southwestern part of the park making motoring access easy. It's also possible to hike in the park, and venture into remote sections by 1,500 kilometers of canoe routes (for which maps are available). More than 3,000 camping spaces are available. Unfortunately, blackflies are a problem from mid-May to late June and mosquitoes a nuisance from late May into July, making August through mid-October especially good times to visit this wilderness.

With 250 bird species on its list, Algonquin offers birders wonderful observation possibilities, such as Common Loons, Spruce Grouse, Gray Jays, Mourning Warblers, White-winged Crossbills, Lincoln Sparrows, and Evening Grosbeaks.

The Public Wolf Howls held in late August under the direction of the park's staff are famous. If you're there at that time of year, don't miss this unique opportunity to hear these splendid animals—arguably the voice of the wild.

In Québec, few birding sights are more astonishing than the spectacle of up to fifty thousand Northern Gannets that make Bonaventure Island, part of Île-Bonaventure-et-du-Rocher-Percé Provincial Park, off the little town of Percé on Québec's Gaspé Peninsula, their breeding grounds and summer home. It's North America's largest nesting concentration of these birds, and the second largest in the world. Smaller numbers of Common Murres, Razorbills, Atlantic Puffins, and Black-legged Kittiwakes also nest on the island. Birders can board a tour boat in Percé and circle the island's high cliffs, which are covered with thousands of nesting Northern Gannets.

National Parks

Canada also has some excellent national parks that are known around the world for their rich birdlife. Point Pelee National Park is one of Canada's most famous birding locations, particularly for migrations of wood warblers (as well as Monarch Butterflies). Strategically

(continued on next page)

(continued from previous page)
located on the north shore of Lake Erie and acting as a funnel or migration trap, Point Pelee is a magnet for migrating birds. Northward migrations in spring are especially spectacular—indeed, so many northward-bound wood warblers stop there in spring that it's known as the "Warbler Capital of North America." That reputation is justified: nearly all the species of wood warblers found in North America have been sighted in this park. Prothonotary, Golden-winged, Blue-winged, Orange-crowned, Magnolia, Cape May, Blackburnian, Wilson's, and Canada Warblers, plus many others, all are on the list. Autumn migrations are also outstanding. In September, hundreds—sometimes even thousands—of migrating Broad-winged Hawks, Sharp-shinned Hawks, American Kestrels, and other raptors concentrate at the southern tip of Pelee, providing excellent observation opportunities. More than 360 bird species appear on the park's list.

Northern Gannets nesting on Bonaventure Island, Québec.

Bird Festivals

Numerous bird festivals in Alberta, British Columbia, Ontario, and Sas-katchewan are held between late January and November—some depending on the migratory status of specific birds.

In British Columbia, for example, the Salmon Arm Grebe Festival is held in mid-May at Salmon Arm. As many as three hundred Western Grebes are seen in their spectac-ular courtship displays—a wonderful birding experience. Another British Columbia event, the Snow Goose Festival, is held on November weekends at Delta. It offers birders opportunities to see twenty-five thousand Lesser Snow Geese returning from Russia.

In Ontario, the Festival of Hawks is held at the Holiday Beach Conservation Area near Amherstburg on weekends between mid-September and early October. Particular emphasis is on helping birders observe autumn hawk migrations that concentrate by the thousands at Holiday Beach. A large, three-level tower is available to gain elevation and a better vantage. In addition to seeing migrating hawks and other raptors, other migrating birds also concentrate at this site, including as many as two hundred hummingbirds and fifty thousand Blue Jays. Large numbers of migrating Monarch Butterflies, dragonflies, and bats are also seen.

Birding and Habitat Enhancement Organizations

Numerous nonprofit organizations are involved in of backyard birdwatching, habitat improvement, and bird feeding. Those listed here are either the best known or are involved with specific species, such as Purple Martins and bluebirds.

Alliance for the Chesapeake Bay
Headquarters
6600 York Rd.
Baltimore MD 21212
410-377-6270
Fax 410-377-7144
www.acb-online.org

Satellite offices
225 Pine St.
Harrisburg PA 17101
717-236-9019
Fax 717-236-9019

P.O. Box 1981
Richmond VA 23218
804-775-0951
Fax 804-775-0954

American Bird Conservancy
1250 24th St. NW, Suite 400
Washington DC 20037
202-778-9666
Fax 202-778-9778
abc@abcbirds.org
www.abcbirds.org

American Bird Conservation Association
Route 3, 111-2nd B. Rd.
Nappanee IN 46550-9517
www.tyrell.net/~deadbird/abca.htm

American Birding Association
P.O. Box 6599
Colorado Springs CO 80934-6599
800-850-2473, 719-578-1480
member@aba.org
www.americanbirding.org

Audubon International
46 Rarick Rd.
Selkirk NY 12158
518-767-9051
Fax 518-767-9076
www.audubonintl.org

Backyard Wildlife Habitat Program
See National Wildlife Federation

Canadian Wildlife Federation
2740 Queensview Dr.
Ottawa ON K2B 1A2
Canada
800-563-WILD (800-563-9453)
613-721-2286 (Ottawa Area)
www.cwf-fcf.org

Cats Indoors! Campaign
See American Bird Conservancy

Conservancy Purple Martin Society
3090 55th Terrace, SW
Naples FL 34116-8034
billd@naples.net
www.tyrell.net/~deadbird/cpms.htm

Cornell Laboratory of Ornithology
159 Sapsucker Woods Rd.
P.O. Box 11
Ithaca NY 14850-1999
800-843-2473, 607-254-2425
www.birds.cornell.edu

Humane Society of the United States
2100 L St. NW
Washington DC 20037
202-452-1100
www.hsus.org

Hummer/Bird Study Group, Inc.
P.O. Box 250
Clay AL 35048-0250
205-681-2888
Fax 205-681-1339
HummerBSG@aol.com
www.hbsg.org

Hummingbird Society
249 E. Main St., Suite 4
P.O. Box 394
Newark DE 19715
800-529-3699
Fax 302-369-1816
info@hummingbird.org
www.hummingbird.org

International Wildlife Rehabilitation Council
4437 Central Place, Suite B-4
Suisun City CA 94585-1633
707-864-1761
Fax 707-864-3106
iwrc@inreach.com
www.iwrc-online.org

National Audubon Society
700 Broadway
New York NY 10003
212-979-3000
Fax 212-979-3188
www.audubon.org

National Bird-Feeding Society
P.O. Box 23
Northbrook IL 60065-0023
847-272-0135
feedbird@aol.com
www.birdfeeding.org

National WildBird Refuge, Inc.
4913 Dreyfous Ave.
P.O. Box 7066
Metairie LA 70010-7066
504-888-3711
Fax 504-888-5510
www.gnofn.org/~swallow

National Wildlife Federation
Backyard Wildlife Habitat Program
8925 Leesburg Pike
Vienna VA 22184-0001
703-790-4434
Fax 703-790-4468
www.nwf.org

National Wildlife Health Center
USGS, Biological Resources
6006 Schroeder Rd.
Madison WI 53711-6223
608-264-5411
www.emtc.usgs.gov/nwhchome.html

Native Plant Society of Texas
P.O. Box 891
Georgetown TX 78627
512-238-0695
Fax 512-238-0703
www.npsot.org

Nature Society
Purple Martin Junction
Griggsville IL 62340
217-833-2323
Fax 217-833-2123
www.natsoc@adams.net
www.naturesociety.org

North American Bluebird Society, Inc.
P.O. Box 74
Darlington WI 53530-0074
608-329-6403
Fax 608-329-7057
nabluebird@aol.com
www.cobleskill.edu/nabs/

North American Nature Photography Association
10200 W. 44th Ave., #304
Wheat Ridge CO 80033-2840
303-422-8527
Fax 303-422-8894
nanpa@resourcenter.com
www.nanpa.org

Ottawa Field-Naturalists' Club
P.O. Box 35069 Westgate
Ottawa ON K1Z 1A2
Canada
613-722-3050
www.achilles.net/ofnc/fletcher.htm

Purple Martin Conservation Association
Edinboro University of Pennsylvania
Edinboro PA 16444
814-734-4420
Fax 814-734-5803
pmca@edinboro.edu
www.purplemartin.org

Purple Martin Society, N.A.
8921 Royal Dr.
Burr Ridge IL 60521-8332
630-655-2028
Fax 630-655-2028
HOBB99E@prodigy.com
Tsuchma@aol.com
www.purplemartins.com

Roger Tory Peterson Institute of Natural History
311 Curtis St.
Jamestown NY 14701
716-665-2473, 800-758-6841
Fax 716-665-3794
bill@rtpi.org
www.rtpi.org

Wildlife Information Center, Inc.
P.O. Box 198
Slatington PA 18080-0198
610-760-8889
www.wildlifeinfo.org

Wild Ones–Natural Landscapers, Ltd.
P.O. Box 23576
Milwaukee WI 53223-0576
www.for-wild.org

WindStar Wildlife Institute
3603 Fry Rd.
Jefferson MD 21755
301-834-9238
wildlife@windstar.org
www.windstar.org/wildlife

Government Programs

Many state wildlife agencies operate programs dedicated to birding and habitat improvement. Many states certify backyard habitats; others offer literature on habitat enhancement. A few federal programs are of interest to backyard birders as well.

STATES AND PROVINCES

Alberta's Naturescape Program

The Naturescape Alberta program is organized and administered by the Red Deer River Naturalists, with support of the Federation of Alberta Naturalists. It encourages backyard habitat gardening and enhancement for the benefit of birds and other wildlife. A publication, *Naturescape Alberta: Creating and Caring for Wildlife Habitat at Home*, is available.

Naturescape Alberta
c/o Red Deer River Naturalists
Box 785
Red Deer AB T4N 5H2
Canada
403-347-8200

Federation of Alberta Naturalists
Box 1472
Edmonton AB T5J 2N5
Canada
780-427-8124
www.naturescape.ab.ca

Arizona Game & Fish Department

The Arizona Game & Fish Department publishes *Landscaping for Desert Wildlife*, containing helpful desert landscaping suggestions.

Arizona Game & Fish Department
Attn: Carolyn Engel-Wilson
2221 W. Greenway Rd.
Phoenix AZ 85023
602-789-3622
www.gf.state.az.us/welcome.html

British Columbia's Naturescape Program

British Columbia's Naturescape Program seeks to restore, preserve, and enhance the province's urban and rural wildlife habitat, and allow citizens to become more associated with nature on a daily basis. The program is sponsored by numerous governmental partners including Environment Canada (Canadian Wildlife Service) and the Province of British Columbia, plus nine private partners.

The Naturescape Kit contains literature (*Naturescape British Columbia: Caring for Wildlife Habitat at Home—Provincial Guide*, *Naturescape British Columbia: Caring for Wildlife Habitat at Home—Native Plant and Animal Booklet, Georgia Basin*, *Naturescape British Columbia: Caring for Wildlife Habitat at Home—Resource Booklet, Southern Interior*, and *Naturescape British Columbia: Caring for Wildlife Habitat at Home—Native Plant and Animal Booklet, Southern Interior*), instructions on how to upgrade habitats, and a membership card.

Naturescape British Columbia
P.O. Box 9354 Stn. Prov. Gov.
Victoria BC V8W 9M1
Canada
www.elp.gov.bc.ca/hctf/nature.htm

Florida Wildlife Habitat Program

The Florida Wildlife Habitat Program is administered by the Department of Wildlife Ecology and Conservation, Institute of Food and Agricultural Sciences, at the University of Florida. State residents may request a free registration kit that includes a guide entitled *Planting a Refuge for Wildlife: How to Create a Backyard Habitat for Florida's Birds and Beasts.* Qualified applicants receive feedback and recommendations, additional resource materials, and a personalized certificate recognizing their efforts.

Department of Wildlife Ecology & Conservation
Attn: Joe Schaefer
P.O. Box 110430
University of Florida
Gainesville FL 32611-0430
www.wec.ufl.edu/Extension

Idaho Backyards for Wildlife Program

The Backyards for Wildlife Program developed by the Idaho Department of Fish & Game encourages urban residents to enhance their backyard habitats to attract birds and other wildlife. Interested residents may obtain *Backyards for the Birds: A Guide for Attracting Wild Birds to Your Yard in Idaho* and other literature about backyard wildlife habitat enhancement, bird feeding, and nesting requirements. Applicants with approved habitats receive a sign for display in their backyard.

Idaho Nongame Wildlife Program
Idaho Department of Fish & Game
600 S. Walnut
P.O. Box 25
Boise ID 83707-0025
208-334-2920
www2.state.id.us/fishgame/ngurban.htm#land

Illinois Department of Natural Resources

The Illinois Department of Natural Resources offers several publications that backyard birdwatchers should read before enhancing a backyard wildlife habitat: *Landscaping for Wildlife*, *Prairie Establishment and Landscaping*, and *Wood Projects for Illinois Wildlife*.

Illinois Department of Natural Resources, Division of Natural Heritage
Lincoln Tower Plaza
524 S. 2nd St.
Springfield IL 62701-1787
217-785-8774
dnr.state.il.us/conservation/naturalheritage/florafauna/

Iowa Department of Natural Resources

Iowa does not have an official backyard wildlife habitat program, but does have available for a nominal fee *Attracting Backyard Wildlife* and other brochures.

Wildlife Diversity Program
Iowa Department of Natural Resources, Wildlife Research Station
1436 255th St.
Boone IA 50036-7557
515-432-2823
www.state.ia.us/government/dnr/organiza/fwb/wildlife/pages/pubs.htm

Kansas Backyard Wildlife Habitat Improvement Program

The objective of the Kansas Backyard Wildlife Habitat Improvement Program is to assist homeowners in enhancing their backyards for birds and other wildlife. The program provides technical assistance, distributes brochures and other printed information, and invites state residents with enhanced backyard wildlife habitats to enroll in the program. There is a small registration fee. Upon approval, the applicant receives a certificate and sign to display in the yard. Mailings of special new backyard wildlife materials occasionally are sent to each person on the certified list.

Kansas Department of Wildlife & Parks, Fisheries & Wildlife Division
512 SE 25th Ave.
Pratt KS 67124-8174
www.kdwp.state.ks.us/brochures/brochures.html

Kentucky Backyard Wildlife Program

The Kentucky Department of Fish & Wildlife Resources operates a backyard habitat enhancement program in association with the Salato Wildlife Education Center in Frankfort. The program aims to establish demonstration gardens and habitat exhibits; organize workshops dealing with birding and gardening; and provide information about landscaping with native plants. You can obtain a Backyard Wildlife Habitat Kit for a modest fee.

Kentucky Department of Fish & Wildlife Resources
#1 Game Farm Rd.
Frankfort KY 40601
800-858-1549, 502-564-7863
www.state.ky.us/agencies/fw/backyard.htm

Maine Backyard Wildlife Demonstration Garden

The Maine Department of Inland Fisheries & Wildlife maintains a backyard wildlife demonstration garden.

Maine Wildlife Park
Route 26
Gray ME 04039
207-657-4977
http://janus.state.me.us/ifw/education/wildlifepark.htm

Manitoba's Naturescape Program

Naturescape Manitoba provides information about the benefits of small areas of habitat, and remaining natural habitats in and around Winnipeg, wildlife's needs, and ways in which citizens can enhance backyards for the benefit of wildlife. Summaries of native species are also provided.

Naturescape Manitoba
Rodney Penner
Project Coordinator
204-986-3166

City of Winnipeg's Urban Habitat Stewardship Resource Network
c/o Cheryl Heming, City Naturalist
204-986-2036
www.cwhp.mb.ca

Maryland Wild Acres Program

The Maryland Department of Natural Resources operates the Wild Acres Program, discussed on pages 106–107.

Fish, Heritage, & Wildlife Administration
Maryland Department of Natural Resources
Attn: Wild Acres Coordinator
Tawes State Office Bldg.
Annapolis MD 21401
410-260-8570, 410-260-8555
www.dnr.state.md.us/wildlife/wildacres.html

Michigan Backyard Wildlife Demonstration Area

The Wildlife Division of the Michigan Department of Natural Resources maintains a wildlife demonstration area at its Private Lands Office to show the public how a small area (e.g., a backyard) can be enhanced to attract birds and other wildlife. The agency is also preparing a Habitat Manual to provide landowners with detailed information on enhancement of backyard wildlife habitats. Its website also has information regarding backyard habitat enhancement.

Private Lands Office
Michigan Department of Natural Resources
8903 E. Stoll Rd.
East Lansing MI 48823
517-641-4638
www.dnr.state.mi.us/Wildlife/Heritage/Pubs/backyard.htm

Minnesota Garden Landscape Design Program

The Minnesota Department of Natural Resources has posted on its website detailed information regarding the design of five different types of gardens using native plant species: evergreen shaded garden, native shade garden, prairie garden, suburban garden, and wet meadow garden. Each may be attractive to some birds and butterflies. The Department also sells several books about various aspects of backyard habitat enhancement: *Woodworking for Wildlife*, *Landscaping for Wildlife*, and *Wild about Birds: The DNR Bird Feeding Guide*.

Minnesota Department of Natural Resources Information Center
500 Lafayette Rd.
St. Paul MN 55155-4040
651-296-6157, 888-MINNDNR (888-646-6367)
www.dnr.state.mn.us/backyard/

Nebraska Game & Parks Commission, and Nebraska NebGuides

The Nebraska Game & Parks Commission offers useful literature on backyard enhancement, including bird and wildlife identification, birdhouses and nest boxes, planting vegetation to enhance yards, and feeding wildlife. The Commission does not have an official backyard habitat certification program.

Nebraska Game & Parks Commission
2200 N. 33rd St.
Lincoln NE 68503
402-471-0641

New Hampshire Project HOME

The New Hampshire Fish & Game Department operates Project HOME: Homes for Wildlife in the Schoolyard. It's an interdisciplinary curriculum for grades K–6, including a six-hour training workshop for teachers, plus an excellent curriculum guide, *Homes for Wildlife*.

Project HOME is not designed for backyard habitats, but some of its information applies to them. Backyard birdwatchers may want to obtain the guide to extract pertinent information for use in backyard habitats.

New Hampshire Fish & Game Department
2 Hazen Dr.
Concord NH 03301
603-271-3211
www.wildlife.state.nh.us/wildlife_profiles.htm

New Jersey Wildlife Sanctuary Program

New Jersey's rapid loss of critical stopover resting and feeding habitat in southern Cape May County—the most southerly in the state—is jeopardizing the role that the Cape May peninsula plays as a major autumn migration funnel and trap for millions of migrating songbirds, raptors, and other species. The Cape May Stopover Protection Project is a narrowly focused partnership to preserve and restore migratory bird and butterfly habitats.

The New Jersey Audubon Society operates a backyard habitat program for homeowners located within the lower 10 kilometers (6 miles) of the Cape May peninsula. It includes a demonstration backyard landscaping and education program at the Society's Center for Research and Education in Cape May Court House, New Jersey. As of 1998, approximately one hundred property owners had participated in free backyard landscaping workshops, receiving up to $300 worth of plants and advice from professional landscape designers. They also received a placard for display on their property.

The Endangered & Nongame Species Program is involved in another backyard habitat restoration program called "Landscaping for Birds on New Jersey's Barrier Islands." It asks landowners to landscape their barrier-beach island properties with native trees, shrubs, and other plants to provide food for songbirds migrating southward along the New Jersey coast during autumn and, to a lesser extent, spring.

The New Jersey Division of Fish, Game & Wildlife hopes to have backyard wildlife habitat-enhancement programs expand elsewhere in the state, and publishes several free information circulars.

Endangered & Nongame Species Program
Tuckahoe Field Office
2201 County Route 631
Woodbine NJ 08270
or
Center for Research and Education
New Jersey Audubon Society
600 Route 47 N.
Cape May Court House NJ 08210
609-861-0770
www.nj.com/audubon/

Oklahoma Wildscapes Certification Program

Oklahoma's certification program is discussed on pages 107–108.

Oklahoma Wildscapes Certification Program, Nongame Wildlife Program
Oklahoma Department of Wildlife Conservation
1801 N. Lincoln
Oklahoma City OK 73105
405-521-4616
www.state.ok.us/~odwc/

Oregon Department of Fish & Wildlife Naturescaping Program

The Oregon Department of Fish & Wildlife's Naturescaping Program does not have a certification process, but it does offer a book, informational handouts, and Naturescaping classes in autumn taught by volunteer instructors. In addition, the Department's website guides browsers through the process of conceiving, planning, and implementing a backyard habitat, and there's a Wild in the City demonstration area at the Department's headquarters.

Oregon Department of Fish & Wildlife
2501 SW 1st Ave.
P.O. Box 59
Portland OR 97207
503-872-5260
www.dfw.state.or.us/ODFWhtml/Education/Naturescaping.html

Pennsylvania Game Commission

The Pennsylvania Game Commission does not have a backyard certification program. However, it partnered with the Pennsylvania Audubon Society and the Alliance for the Chesapeake Bay to offer workshops for homeowners, teachers, nursery employees, and other people, which encourages them to make backyards wildlife-friendly.

The Working Together for Wildlife program has pamphlets about nest boxes, seeds, and plantings. In addition, it publishes *Wildlife Notes*, which provides biology and natural history information about numerous mammal and bird species. Other publications include *Wings Out Your Window* and *Resources on Creating Backyard & Schoolyard Habitat in Pennsylvania*. It also offers *Woodcrafting for Wildlife* and *Homes for Wildlife: A Planning Guide for Habitat Enhancement on School Grounds*, which were published by the New Hampshire Fish & Game Department, with portions adapted for Pennsylvania.

The Publications section of the Commission's website has information about birds and mammals, suggestions for helping wildlife, and *Wildlife Notes*.

Pennsylvania Game Commission
2001 Elmerton Ave.
Harrisburg PA 17110-9797
717-787-4250
www.state.pa.us/PA_Exec/PGC/pubs/w_notes/wl_notes.htm
www.state.pa.us/PA_Exec/PGC/pubs/50birds/50birds1.htm
www.state.pa.us/PA_Exec/PGC/pubs/ten.htm

South Carolina Department of Natural Resources

The Wildlife Diversity Section of the South Carolina Department of Natural Resources offers publications entitled *Backyard Wildlife Management* and *Boxes for Birds*.

Nongame & Heritage Trust Program
South Carolina Department of Natural Resources
P.O. Box 167
1000 Assembly St.
Columbia SC 29202
803-734-3888

South Dakota Department of Game, Fish, & Parks

The South Dakota Department of Game, Fish, & Parks publishes an excellent book, *Sharing Your Space: A Homeowner's Guide to Attracting Backyard Wildlife*, which covers topics such as landscape planning, South Dakota's natural landscapes, wildlife habitat needs, attracting wildlife, and insect and wildlife problems.

South Dakota Department of Game, Fish, & Parks
Wildlife Division
523 E. Capitol
Pierre SD 57501
605-773-3485

Texas Wildscapes Program

The Texas Wildscapes Program seeks to develop wildlife habitats where residents of the state live or work. It is discussed on page 108.

Texas Wildscapes Program, Nongame & Urban Program
Texas Parks & Wildlife
4200 Smith School Rd.
Austin TX 78744
512-389-4800 in Austin
972-293-3841 in Dallas/Ft. Worth
281-456-7029 in Houston
210-348-6350 in San Antonio
www.tpwd.state.tx.us/nature/plant/wldscapp.htm

Vermont Department of Fish & Wildlife

The Vermont Department of Fish & Wildlife offers various materials pertaining to the enhancement of backyard wildlife habitats.

Backyard Wildlife Habitat in Vermont contains information about protective cover, food, shelter, and water; developing and maintaining a backyard habitat; and related subjects. A free 35 mm slideshow with eighty slides (available to state residents for two weeks without cost) accompanies this book. The department also has brochures about several subjects, including birding, bluebirds, and invasive plants. The *Natural Heritage Harmonies* newsletter is published several times each year.

Vermont Department of Fish & Wildlife
103 S. Main St.
Waterbury VT 05671-0501
802-241-3700
www.anr.state.vt.us/fw/fwhome/index.htm

Washington Backyard Wildlife Sanctuary Program

With 35,000 acres of wildlife habitat lost annually in Washington state, wildlife officials are working to preserve and restore habitats. Washington's Backyard Wildlife Sanctuary Program recruits urban and suburban residents to create enhanced habitats. For a nominal fee, residents can order a Backyard Wildlife Sanctuary Packet containing a *Landscaping for Wildlife* pamphlet, lists of native plants suitable for specific parts of the state, and other backyard habitat enhancement recommendations. Participants receive a signed certificate and an outdoor sign indicating their yard is part of the Backyard Wildlife Sanctuary Program.

East of Cascades Ridge:
Washington Department of Fish & Wildlife
Backyard Wildlife Sanctuary Program
8702 Division St.
Spokane WA 99218
509-456-4082

West of Cascades Ridge:
Washington Department of Fish & Wildlife
Backyard Wildlife Sanctuary Program
16018 Mill Creek Blvd.
Mill Creek WA 98012
425-775-1311
www.wa.gov/wdfw/wlm/byw_prog.htm

West Virginia Division of Natural Resources/Wildlife Resources Section

West Virginia's Wildlife Resources Section operates a West Virginia Wild Yards Program that encourages and aids citizens in backyard habitat enhancement for birds and other animals. A Wild Yards packet contains an introduction to the West Virginia Wild Yards Program, habitat information, information about birds and other animals in a backyard landscape, recommendations about planning wildlife landscapes, and sources of other printed materials.

After enhanced backyards reach a mature state, owners are encouraged to complete an application for certification from the West Virginia Wild Yards Program. After review and approval by department biologists, certified Wild Yards are added to a registry maintained by the program. Owners of certified yards also receive a certificate and sign suitable for placement in the Wild Yard. The program also publishes a quarterly newsletter that is mailed to participating citizens.

West Virginia Wild Yards Coordinator
Wildlife Resources Section
West Virginia Division of Natural Resources
P.O. Box 67
Elkins WV 26241
304-637-0245
asterling@dnr.state.wv.us
www.dnr.state.wv.us/wvwildlife/landscaping.htm

FEDERAL

U.S. Environmental Protection Agency (Region 5)

The U.S. Environmental Protection Agency (Region 5) office operates a Natural Landscaping initiative with excellent materials available on habitat enhancement. The EPA's voluntary Natural Landscaping initiative encourages people to use native trees, shrubs, flowers, and other plants in backyard habitats.

A brochure entitled *Natural Landscapes for Midwest Landowners* is available, as well as *A Source Book on Natural Landscaping for Local Officials*, prepared by the Northeastern Illinois Planning Commission. The EPA's website also has sections for forest, prairie, and wetlands flowers, birds and bees and more, the Wild Ones Handbook, weed laws, and a tool kit. Printed and online copies are available from the EPA.

Natural Landscaping Initiative
U.S. Environmental Protection Agency (Region 5)
77 W. Jackson Blvd.
Chicago IL 60604-3590
312-886-7901
www.epa.gov/greenacres

U.S. Fish & Wildlife Service

The U.S. Fish & Wildlife Service offers several booklets with useful information pertaining to backyard birdwatching and habitat enhancement: *Homes for Birds*, *Attract Birds*, and *Backyard Bird Feeding*. These booklets, the list of federally endangered or threatened species, and much more are also posted on the Service's websites.

U.S. Fish & Wildlife Service, Consumer Information Center, 3C
P.O. Box 100
Pueblo CO 81002
www.fws.gov/r9mbmo/pamphlet/songbrd.html
www.fws.gov/r9endspp/lsppinfo.html

Northeast Forest Experiment Station

The Northeast Forest Experiment Station, part of the Forest Service (U.S. Department of Agriculture), has several publications designed for larger landowners seeking to manage woodlands for birds and other wildlife: *Managing Urban Woodlands for a Variety of Birds*, *Managing Cavity Trees for Wildlife in the Northeast*, and *Guide to Wildlife Tree Management in New England Northern Hardwoods*.

Northeastern Forest Experiment Station
Five Radnor Corporate Center
100 Matsonford Rd., Suite 200
P.O. Box 6775
Radnor PA 19087
610-975-4017

Birding on the Internet

Access to the Internet opens up a whole world of information on birding topics. In addition to sites of general interest to birders, I have included sites that (1) are associated with Audubon societies and birding clubs, (2) address conservation issues, (3) provide information on nest boxes and bird feeders, and (4) are dedicated to specific birds. Expert birder Paul Hess brought many examples to my attention. *Internet Guide to Birds and Birding: The Ultimate Directory to the Best Sites Online* by Jack Sanders, published by Ragged Mountain Press, is another excellent source of birding websites.

GENERAL

Cornell Laboratory of Ornithology

The Cornell Laboratory of Ornithology is one of the world's leading centers of bird research, education, and conservation. Its large website has nearly two dozen sections, including several projects of great importance in which backyard birdwatchers, who need no scientific training, can participate, such as Project Feeder Watch, the Great Backyard Bird Count, the Warbler Watch, and the Broad-winged Hawk Survey.
birds.cornell.edu

National Audubon Society

The National Audubon Society website is one of the largest dealing with birds and conservation. Sections of interest to all birdwatchers include activities and conservation, birds and science, chapters, news, local Audubon resources, and national campaigns that focus on wetlands, endangered species, forests, Everglades restoration, national wildlife refuges, and more. Some of the society's programs described include the WatchList, Christmas Bird Counts, Important Bird Areas, Project FeederWatch, and Cats and Birds.
www.audubon.org

National Wildlife Federation's Backyard Wildlife Habitat Program

This website explains how to become involved in the Backyard Wildlife Habitat Program. It also has links to the U.S. Environmental Protection Agency's website, which contains an excellent review of local weed laws.
www.nwf.org/habitats/index.html

About.com Birding Page

The About.Com birding website includes articles, a post office for sending and receiving free bird postcards, and links to many other birding sites. You can sign up for a free weekly electronic birding newsletter. I recommend this site for its wide array of birding information, including backyard habitat enhancement, bird food and feeding, birdbaths, birdhouses, and related topics.
birding.about.com/index

Birding on the Web

This is one of the most comprehensive websites for birders. It links daily birding mail for each state, some Canadian provinces, and other bird-related topics, as well as links for Rare Bird Alerts telephone numbers in the United States, Canada, and Trinidad and Tobago.

Hot Links has more birding information and Bird Chat Digest offers birding-related information derived from up-to-date sources. Birding on the Web also has links to exhibits (e.g., the bird art of Louis Agassiz Fuertes at Cornell University) and illustrations from rare bird books.

Particularly useful for birders planning international travel are world bird lists that use three different sources: American Birding Association, American Ornithologists' Union, and Sibley-Monroe.
wwwstat.wharton.upenn.edu/~siler/birding.html

Bird Links to the World

This website contains numerous links pertaining to birding worldwide. Beginning backyard birdwatchers seeking a global perspective about birding—including links to backyard activities such as bird feeding and birdhouses—will find this an excellent site.
www.ntic.qc.ca/~nellus/links.html

Birdnet: The Ornithological Information Source

This website is a combined effort of the Ornithological Council, which consists of the following nine major North American ornithological organizations: American Ornithologists' Union, Association of Field Ornithologists, CIPAMEX (a Mexican organization), Colonial Waterbirds Society, Cooper Ornithological Society, Pacific Seabird Group, Raptor

Research Foundation, Society of Caribbean Ornithology, and Wilson Ornithological Society. Birdnet provides information about the scientific study of birds. Links to each organization provide detailed information about membership costs, benefits, publications, and other activities. Also included are ornithological issues, legislative news about migratory birds, and *The Ornithological Newsletter*.
www.nmnh.si.edu/BIRDNET

Birder Home Page

This website has a great diversity of options and information, including links for Checklists, Rare Bird Alerts, Hot Spots for Birders, Geographic Birding Guide, Favorite Birds, Backyard Birders, Organizations, and Chat About Birds. There's also information about bird books, magazines, optics, other equipment used by birders, and scientific and fun areas.

Links for birding organizations contain dozens of websites in the United States, such as American Birding Association, Audubon Naturalist Society, and Tennessee Ornithological Society. Internationally, dozens more birding organizations have links to their websites. A backyard birder planning a foreign trip can find useful overseas birding ideas and information here.
www.birder.com

Fugleskue Birdwatch

This is perhaps the most extraordinary website for birders in the world. It's maintained by Tor Ivar Bjønness in Tonsberg, Norway. What's so extraordinary are the way it's organized and its large number of links connecting to all major birding sites in the world. It's regularly updated with additional links, making it even more useful.

Fugleskue Birdwatch begins with BirdLink Pages, then moves to search engines helpful in finding birding-related websites followed by links to birding magazine, newsletter, and journal websites, as well as more bird resources. It also provides links and places to find and purchase bird books, including book dealers who specialize in bird and natural history books. Icons with "COM" indicate commercial rather than nonprofit organizations.

Whether you're a beginning backyard birdwatcher or an advanced birder roaming the world, this site is essential.
home.sol.no/~tibjonn/index.htm

The Virtual Birder

This website is devoted to online "field trips" to important birding locations. Rare Bird Alerts information is also included, plus e-mail opinions and space to request new features.
www.virtualbirder.com/vbirder

Peterson Online

All birders should check this website, which contains information about Roger Tory Peterson, America's Master Birder, his books and other bird- and nature-related materials, favorite links (even one about dragonflies and damselflies), selected articles from *Bird Watcher's Digest*, and more.
www.petersononline.com/birds

CANADIAN

There's a thriving birding community in Canada, and the following two sites provide extensive links to Canadian birding sites.

Birding in Canada

This excellent site is maintained by Gord Gallant. Every Canadian birder, and those planning to visit Canada, should use the bird lists for the entire country, its provinces, and local areas. Especially innovative is a national directory of Canadian birders with their e-mail addresses (updated almost daily). American birders will look upon this extremely useful tool with envy.

Additional information and/or links deal with books and selected reviews, a chat line, updates for birding events, hotlines from the provinces, Canadian Christmas Bird Counts, Canadian bird observatories, hawkwatching sites, details about Canadian publications, and more.
www.interlog.com/~gallantg/canada

Canadian Wildlife Service/Canadian Bird Trends Database

This website is the "Canadian Bird Trends Database" of the Canadian Wildlife Service. Interested birders will welcome examining population trends based on Canadian Breeding Bird Surveys, updated annually and the best information available.

When data for certain species are available, users can retrieve information by common or scientific name, taxonomic group (order or family), habitat guilds (e.g., cavity-nesting species, wetlands, and woodlands), migratory pattern (neotropical migrant, short-distance migrant, year-round resident), or ecozone. There are also links to related topics or sites, including CITES (Convention on International Trade in Endangered Species).
www.cws-scf.ec.gc.ca/canbird/news/bt99/index-e.html

AUDUBON SOCIETIES

Local Audubon Societies

Only a small number of local Audubon Societies have major websites. Those included here are the best.

Anchorage Audubon Society

This chapter of the National Audubon Society seeks to enhance learning opportunities regarding wildlife and the environment, and to advance wildlife conservation and environmental protection via action, education, and research. The website has detailed position papers on statewide conservation matters and issues, and information about birding sites in Alaska.

www.audubon.org/chapter/AK/anchorage/start.htm

Chicago Audubon Society

The Chicago Audubon Society's website provides a summary of that organization's birding, conservation, education, and research activities. It includes an activity calendar, links to other birding and ornithology sites, articles from the Society's newsletter, and information on membership and educational opportunities.

www.audubon.org/chapter/il/chicago/

Audubon Society of Greater Denver

The Audubon Society of Greater Denver has an effective birding and conservation program. Among the Society's offerings are birding field trips and classes pertaining to a wide range of topics. It also operates a nature center. The website includes activities, special events, travel departures, archives for the armchair traveler, brainteasers, and an encyclopedia search function.

www.audubon.org/chapter/co/asgd/

Houston Audubon Society

The Houston Audubon Society seeks "thoughtful conservation" of natural resources; protects, preserves, and enhances wildlife habitat; and encourages environmental-protection legislation. The Society operates fourteen wildlife sanctuaries and controls more than 2,000 acres on the upper Texas coast and adjacent areas—all important conservation areas.

Its website includes a calendar of events; Rare Bird Alerts; information on membership, volunteer programs, and educational opportunities; and links to numerous other Audubon Societies and birding organizations.

www.io.com/~pdhulce/audubon.html

Los Angeles Audubon Society

The Los Angeles Audubon Society is one of the larger local chapters of the National Audubon Society. It operates a full program of birding, conservation, and educational activities. Its website section titles include general information, bookstore, programs and trips, especially for birders, get involved, calendar of events, and special announcements.

The Society's bookstore has a very large online catalog of books and other birding items. Backyard birdwatchers welcome lists of plants used to enhance backyard habitats for birds and other wildlife.

Birding activities include weekly field trips to local areas, pelagic trips, and several overseas destinations each year. Monthly meetings generally deal with birds and bird conservation. The Society publishes *Armchair Activist*.

The Society's conservation projects deal with California Condors, the reintroduction of Bald Eagles to Catalina Island and Peregrine Falcons to the Santa Monica Mountains, issues related to Mono Lake, and other concerns.

Educational activities include Audubon Adventures for children in grades four through six, students participating in science fairs, and scholarships for elementary schoolteachers for one-week periods at the National Audubon Society's Ecology Workshops for Educators in Greenwich, Connecticut.

The Society also has a two-thousand-volume library of books, field guides, periodicals, and other materials.

www.laaudubon.org

New Columbia Audubon Society (Washington, DC)

In our nation's capital, the New Columbia Audubon Society is the local chapter of the National Audubon Society. Its website has a calendar of events, articles from its newsletter, information about local birding sites and conservation within the City of Washington, and links to other birding sites. Backyard birdwatchers will find information pertaining to native plants of particular interest.

www.audubon.org/chapter/dc/newcolumbia

New York City Audubon Society

The New York City Audubon Society's website is organized in eleven parts, including conservation, education, field trips, harbor herons, photography, and programs.

This organization's conservation efforts pertain to wetlands development proposals, including threats to Jamaica Bay. The Society also publishes *Urban Audubon*. Volunteer opportunities are available. Beginning backyard birdwatchers in the New York City metropolitan area can learn much by attending this organization's meetings.
www.interboro.com/nycaudubon

Seattle Audubon Society

Founded in 1916, the Seattle Audubon Society is one of the oldest, largest, and most active in the Pacific Northwest. The Society has a keen interest in birds, birding, educational opportunities, and important conservation issues. It publishes *Earthcare Northwest* and *The Action Cormorant*.

Its website has sections for birding, field trips, conservation, education, public advocacy, and links to other websites. A catalog of books and other items sold in its sales shop is also on the website.
www.seattleaudubon.org

Tucson Audubon Society

The Tucson Audubon Society is involved with local, state, and national conservation issues, as well as many bird and other wildlife activities and efforts. It owns Mason Audubon Center, a 20-acre oasis of heavily vegetated ironwood desert on the northwestern side of Tucson. The Center is used for educational, research, and other purposes.

Public education is a major focus of the Society. Its Institute offerings, such as the 29th Annual Institute of Desert Ecology in 1999, are very popular. It also publishers the *Vermilion Flycatcher*.

Its website has sections dealing with membership, monthly programs, conservation, education, volunteers, Institutes, nature shop (with product catalog), newsletter, field trips, workshops, Mason Audubon Center, Arizona birding, and bird-of-the-month.
www.audubon.org/chapter/az/tucson/

State and Regional Audubon Societies

A number of state and regional Audubon Societies have significant websites. Some are affiliated with the National Audubon Society, others are independent.

Audubon-California

Audubon-California has fifty-three chapters of the National Audubon Society, making it one of the larger state segments of the national organization.

Its website has eight main sections dealing with news and forthcoming events, environmental educational programs, conservation policy, links to most of the fifty-three state chapters, who the organization is, brief details about its sanctuaries, legislative affairs, and information about frequently asked bird questions.
www.audubon-ca.org

Connecticut Audubon Society

Founded in 1898, the Connecticut Audubon Society is an important bird and wildlife conservation organization in Connecticut. It has numerous advocacy, conservation, and educational programs, and operates several centers and wildlife sanctuaries.

The Society's website has sections for advocacy, education, ecotravel, CAS news, seasonal guide, membership, questions and answers, nature notes, general information, and press releases. There is also a section for CAS centers and sanctuaries.
www.ctaudubon.org

Delaware Audubon Society, Inc.

The Delaware Audubon Society is a statewide chapter of the National Audubon Society. Its website has sections devoted to the organization, action alerts, birding, books, bulletin board, conservation, current issues, news, wildlife and habitat, and links to other websites.

The Society seeks to increase appreciation of the natural environment and encourages environmental protection and conservation. It holds field trips, has public and school educational programs, organizes Armchair Activists, and engages in other activities. Protection of Delaware Bay and the coastal zone area is a priority focus of the organization.
de.audubon.org

Florida Audubon Society

The Florida Audubon Society was founded in 1900 to stop the slaughter of wading birds. In 1905, it helped form the National Audubon Society.

The Society's website contains sections dealing with who they are, where they are, publications, news and upcoming events, legislative affairs, chapter services, Birds of Prey Center, environmental education, sanctuaries, conservation policy, nature centers, Audubon Council, frequently asked questions, and links to other websites.

The two organizations now work closely and cooperatively on many projects and programs. There are forty-five joint Florida and National Audubon Society

chapters within Florida. Membership in the Florida Audubon Society includes membership in the National Audubon Society. The *Florida Naturalist* is included with each membership.
www.audubon.usf.edu/

Maine Audubon Society

The Maine Audubon Society is the voice of bird, other wildlife, and natural resources conservation in Maine. It has a large and active program in the state. Members receive four issues of *Habitat: Journal of the Maine Audubon Society*, the primary publication issued by the Society.

Its website deals with conservation issues, environmental centers, field trips, educational resources, volunteer opportunities, *Habitat Magazine*, bookshop, membership, birding in Maine, checklist of Maine birds, feeding birds, weekly bird alert, natural history information, Maine endangered species list, news, and links to other websites. Backyard birders and wildlife habitat-enhancers will be pleased with the information about these topics.
www.maineaudubon.org/bird.htm

Massachusetts Audubon Society

Founded in 1896, the Massachusetts Audubon Society is one of the oldest and the largest independent state Audubon organization in the United States. It is the largest conservation organization in New England. The Society is involved with many facets of nature and the environment, but birds remain a very strong focus of many of its programs. The organization publishes *Sanctuary* magazine.

Its large website has sections entitled news and action, nature connection, membership, birds and beyond (including daily bird sightings in the state), a kids' section, the large bookshop (which also sells audio and videotapes, CD-ROMs, and much more), jobs, and links to other websites.
www.massaudubon.org

Michigan Audubon Society

Established in 1904, the Michigan Audubon Society is that state's oldest conservation organization. It has forty-four local chapters, and maintains fourteen bird and wildlife sanctuaries. *The Jack Pine Warbler* is the Society's ornithological journal, with *Michigan Birds and Natural History* also containing much bird information. The Society also operates a bookshop.

The Society's website has sections about the organization, how you can help, environmental fast-action project, fast-action alerts, Purple Martin project, Jack Pine Warbler, Michigan Bird and Natural History, announcements, Rare Bird Alerts, ecotourism, field trips, campouts, bookstore, calendar of events, chapters, sanctuaries, Sandhill Crane & Art Festival, and links to other bird and wildlife sites.
www.audubon.org/chapter/mi/mas

Minnesota Audubon

Working in cooperation with local National Audubon Society chapters in Minnesota, Minnesota Audubon seeks to preserve and improve the state's ecological diversity through public policy advocacy and environmental education, with strong emphasis on birds, other wildlife, and habitats.

The website has sections for staff, events, programs, what's new, Audubon links, and how folks can help.
www.audubon.org/chapter/mn/mn/new.html

Audubon Society of Missouri

The Audubon Society of Missouri, founded in 1901, is one of the oldest statewide organizations of its kind in the United States. It seeks to preserve and protect birds and other wildlife within Missouri and beyond. It's also affiliated with the National Audubon Society. Annual membership includes *The Bluebird*, issued quarterly. Two birding weekends are held annually, in spring and autumn, plus birding educational activities, and birding fellowship.

Its website has sections entitled calendar of events, Chip Mill News, environmental news, book reviews, and links to other environmental and outdoor websites.
www.audubon.org/chapter/mo/mo/

Montana Audubon

Montana Audubon is a collection of local chapters of the National Audubon Society coordinated under the state office. Collectively, they place emphasis on conservation (e.g., cottonwoods and wetlands), education, and recreational birding.

Its website has 15 sections, including birding and field trips, activism, environmental education, local chapters, issues, Audubon apparel, and bird hotline (a Rare Bird Alert).
mtaudubon.org/

Audubon Nebraska

Audubon Nebraska is the state office of the National Audubon Society. There are also several local Audubon chapters that work closely with Audubon Nebraska.

Its website has sections for calendar of events, legislative affairs, wild thoughts,

Nebraska's natural resources, just for kids, educational programs, sanctuaries and wildlife viewing, local chapters, and bird news.

www.audubon.org/chapter/ne

Audubon Society of New Hampshire

The Audubon Society of New Hampshire is involved in birding and other wildlife, and conservation, educational, and research programs.

Its website has sections for birding information, current research, environmental policy issues, ask the naturalist, programs and field trips, centers, sanctuaries, chapters, join us and volunteer, armchair shopping, and a site index. There are also additional parts to the various sections; for example, a Rare Bird Alert is part of the birding information section.

www.nhaudubon.org

New Jersey Audubon Society

The New Jersey Audubon Society, founded in 1897, is another of the nation's oldest Audubon organizations. It is independent from the National Audubon Society. The Society owns twenty-seven nature preserves; is involved in conservation, educational, and research activities; and publishes *New Jersey Audubon Society*, *Records of New Jersey Birds*, and *Green Gram*. Its Cape May Bird Observatory issues the *Peregrine Observer* and *Kestrel Express* for Observatory members.

Its large website contains major sections about conservation, education, research, information about the organization, a birder's forum, nature notes, a calendar of events, a guide to numerous birding sites in the state, and other topics.

www.njaudubon.org/

Audubon Society of New York State

This completely independent organization is not affiliated with any other local, state, regional, or national branches of the National Audubon Society.

Its website contains information about four wildlife sanctuaries in New York State, the New York Loon Conservation Project, birds of prey protection, and water-quality protection.

Its parent, Audubon International, has on its website backyard habitat enhancement programs of interest to backyard birdwatchers, and other useful bird and wildlife information.

www.audubonintl.org/home.html

National Audubon Society in New York State

Within New York State, the National Audubon Society has strong membership support via thirty-two local chapters. They engage in a wide range of bird- and wildlife-related activities and programs. Several nature centers and wildlife sanctuaries are part of Audubon's overall New York State program. A complicated administrative arrangement oversees National Audubon Society in New York State.

The National Audubon Society website for this state has sections dealing with advocacy, bird conservation, Audubon Centers (refuges and sanctuaries), environmental education, forests, wetlands, wildlife, smart growth, WatchList, Birdathons, and Christmas Bird Counts, as well as backyard birding.

www.audubon.org/chapter/ny

Pennsylvania Audubon Society

Although a Pennsylvania Audubon Society was established in 1896, the second in the United States, that original Society became defunct. In 1998, a new Pennsylvania Audubon Society was created. This Pennsylvania Audubon Society supports twenty-five local Audubon Society chapters. Public education is an important part of the activities. For example, it issued Native Plants in the Creation of Backyard, Schoolyard and Park Habitat Areas as part of its Audubon Protecting Animals through Habitat Program. The Society also seeks protection (where necessary) for designated Important Bird Areas (some major sites are omitted in their listing).

The Society website contains sections devoted to a newsletter, the state office and its staff, history of the Society, weekly Rare Bird Alerts, a Pennsylvania Songbirds teachers guide (K through 12), population and habitat campaign, birding festivals, PA Birds Listserve, towers and birds, as well as links to other state websites.

www.audubon.org/chapter/pa/pa/

Texas Audubon Society

The Texas Audubon Society is the state office of the National Audubon Society. It is a network of nineteen local chapters of the National Audubon Society. Bird and wildlife conservation is a major activity of the Society.

The Texas Audubon Society's website has sections for the organization, chapters, news and upcoming events, Great Texas Birding Classic, volunteers, publications, sanctuaries, a children's section, conservation, resources, and links to other sites. The Society also maintains a Texas WatchList containing names of bird species exhibiting declining populations.

www.audubon.org/chapter/tx/tx

Audubon-Washington

Audubon-Washington has an active conservation and education program designed to protect the state's birdlife, other wildlife, habitats, and other natural resources. Numerous local Audubon chapters work with the state office. Some programs deal with backyard birdwatching and habitat enhancement.

Its large website has sections for Audubon centers, birdwatching in Washington State, important bird areas, Audubon and birding events, and links to other sites.

www.audubon.org/chapter/wa/wa/index.html

Audubon Society of Western Pennsylvania

Founded in 1914, the Audubon Society of Western Pennsylvania is a vital force in bird study, education, and conservation in a nine-county section of western Pennsylvania. The Society operates two wildlife sanctuaries and has volunteer opportunities available.

Its website has sections for native plants useful in backyard gardening and landscaping, birding, conservation, education, a sales shop, and links to other websites.

www.aswp.org

Tennessee Valley Audubon Society

The Tennessee Valley Audubon Society serves three counties (i.e., Limestone, Madison, and Morgan) in northern Alabama. It has an extensive program of birding field trips, an annual Christmas Bird Count, Birdathon, May migration counts, festivals, and workshops.

Its website has sections, each with subsections, about people, calendar of events, birds, resources, and links to other sites.

fly.hiwaay.net/~pgibson/tvas/

Audubon Naturalist Society

Founded in 1897, the Audubon Naturalist Society is a major birding, conservation, and educational organization in the Washington, DC, area. It has a long record of public service in the city and states surrounding it. Notable past members included Rachel Carson, Roger Tory Peterson, and Justice William O. Douglas.

The Society's website has sections for what's new, special events, conservation alerts, watching nature, The Voice of Audubon (i.e., bird sightings updated weekly), events calendar, and its bookshop. *Audubon Naturalist News* is available online, and the ANS bookshop is well stocked with books and other birding products.

www.audubonnaturalist.org

BIRD CLUBS AND SOCIETIES WITH WEBSITES

State and Local Bird Groups

Baltimore Bird Club–Backyard Birding

The Baltimore Bird Club's website contains significant information useful to beginning backyard birdwatchers. Homes for Birds deals with eleven bird species or groups that use bird houses, their selection, construction materials, placement, protection from predators, protection of habitat, and references.

Backyard Bird Feeding has an introduction, explains how to get started, a feeder selection, how to use feeders, attracting birds with foods and feeders, dealing with uninvited feeder guests, questions regarding feeding birds, and references.

Landscaping to Attract Birds has an introduction, discusses basics of landscaping, land scaping benefits, plants that wild birds like, instructions for getting started, and a reading list. This website also has links to yard lists, backyard reports, and specific backyard birds.

204.255.212.10/~tross/by/backyard.html

Brookline Bird Club

The Brookline Bird Club in Massachusetts is a very active birding organization involved with all aspects of the hobby.

Its website has sections containing many links to other sites, dealing with the club, field trip schedules, local birds, rare birds, and other birding sites. Links are further organized into helping injured birds, supporting conservation, joining other bird clubs, building a library, counting birds, documenting birds, evaluating equipment, trip planning, trips, bird guides online (books and CD-ROMs), and nests. There are also links to Rare Bird Alerts in New England. The Club's Code of Ethics is also posted.

www.world.std.com/~jane/bbc.html

Alabama Ornithological Society

Founded in 1952, the Alabama Ornithological Society is the leading bird study and conservation organization in Alabama.

It encourages development of a greater knowledge of the state's birds and conservation of Alabama's natural resources.

Topics on its website include a site index, new information, membership information, Alabama Bird Records Committee information, permits and other details about Blakeley Island, conservation committee matters, Rare Bird Alerts hotline reports, submitting rare bird observations, a checklist of the state's birds, Christmas Bird Count dates and related information, North American Migration Count information, links to other Alabama birding sites, and selected regional and national birding connections.

www.bham.net/aos

Carolina Bird Club

Unlike most state ornithological organizations, two states (North Carolina and South Carolina) form the Carolina Bird Club, Inc. Founded in 1937, it has a distinguished history of birding and ornithological activities in the Carolinas.

Its website contains sections dealing with Rare Bird Alerts, newsletter excerpts, *The Chat* (the organization's scientific journal), meeting dates, state records committees, and links to other birding sites.

www.carolinabirdclub.org/

Colorado Field Ornithologists

This organization is the leading bird-study group in Colorado. It promotes field study, conservation, and enjoyment of birds; reviews rare bird sightings; maintains the Colorado Bird Records Committee; publishes the *Journal of the Colorado Field Ornithologists*; conducts field trips; organizes and hosts workshops; and has an annual convention.

Its website contains sections dealing with officers and directors, Colorado Records Committee, official state bird list, field trips, journal, Colorado Breeding Bird Atlas, bird photographs and video clips, and links to birding sites.

www.cfo-link.org/leadpage.html

Georgia Ornithological Society

The Georgia Ornithological Society, founded in 1936, is the primary scientific bird study and conservation organization in Georgia.

Its website has sections for the organization, membership, research and grant information, publications (including *The Oriole* and *GOShawk*), merchandise, Rare Bird Alerts, species accounts and sightings, trip reports, Georgia Audubon Societies and bird clubs (addresses and/or links to other sites), bird checklists, Records Committee, Breeding Bird Atlas, Christmas Bird Counts, North American Migration Count, bird photograph index, Society history, and links to other birding resources.

www.gos.org

Kansas Ornithological Society

The Kansas Ornithological Society, founded in 1949, has as its focus the study, conservation, and enjoyment of wild birds.

The Society's website has sections for the organization's officers, meetings and membership, history and mission, projects, Kansas Bird Records Committee, Rare Bird Alerts, publications, links to other sites dealing with conservation (regional, national, and international bird), and birding links.

www.ksbirds.org/kos/index.html

Louisiana Ornithological Society

Organized in 1947, the Louisiana Ornithological Society is the state's leading bird-study group. It collects and disseminates information about Louisiana's birdlife, promotes bird appreciation and value (economic considerations included), conservation, and the social aspects of birding. Some activities pertain to backyard birding.

Its website has sections dealing with the organization's history, officers, Louisiana birding organizations, state bird checklist, Bird Records Committee, *LOS News* (a newsletter), sales, meetings, pelagic trips, local contacts, Rare Bird Alerts, links to other birding organizations, and Featured HotSpot.

Weather is important to backyard birdwatchers in Louisiana and the whole Gulf Coast area, because it affects bird migrations that cross those areas. Backyard birdwatchers with a scientific background and interest may enjoy exploring links to sites that provide satellite and radar images of meteorological conditions in the Gulf of Mexico and selected areas along the Gulf Coast.

www.losbird.org

Maryland Ornithological Society

Founded in 1945, the Maryland Ornithological Society (MOS) is a leading statewide bird-study organization. Local chapters of the society sponsor field trips and programs. Collectively, they are a strong and effective organization working for preservation and protection of Maryland's birdlife and habitats. The Society owns nine bird sanctuaries, each preserving a unique ecological area.

The MOS website has sections about the Society, activities, bird lists, bird programs, birding in Maryland, chapters, members' corner, publications, records committee, what's new, bird links, press room (news releases), BirdReporter, MD/DC BirdFinder, Maryland Partners in Flight, private sanctuary program, Shorebirding, and more.

www.mdbirds.org

New Mexico Ornithological Society

The New Mexico Ornithological Society, founded in 1962, is the leading bird-study organization in New Mexico.

Its website has sections about the Society, publications and sales, a hotline (a Rare Birds Alert), checklist of New Mexico birds, Bird Records Committee, research grants, and numerous links to other birding and ornithology websites.

biology.unm.edu/~nmos/home.html

South Dakota Ornithologist's Union

The South Dakota Ornithologist's Union, founded in 1949, provides the incentive and direction necessary to stimulate study, research, and documentation of the state's birds. It has two meetings each year, and publishes *The South Dakota Breeding Bird Atlas*, *The Birds of South Dakota*, and *Bird Notes*.

The Union's website has sections dealing with the organization, announcements, publications, birding hotspots, rare bird hotlines, South Dakota birding records, and links to other sites.

www.homepages.dsu.edu/droged/SDOU/default.htm

Tennessee Ornithological Society

Founded in 1915, The Tennessee Ornithological Society is one of the nation's best state bird-study organizations. It's a federation of more than a dozen local chapters, each of which schedules meetings and field trips. Two annual statewide meetings allow birders to explore unfamiliar important birding locations.

Its website has sections dealing with the Society, birding in the state, upcoming events, local TOS chapters, *Tennessee Breeding Bird Atlas*, Tennessee Bird Records Committee, and literature on the state's birdlife. The TOS is well known for its flagship journal, *The Migrant*; it also publishes *Tennessee Warbler*.

www.funnelweb.utcc.utk.edu/~awjones/TOS.html

Texas Ornithological Society

The Texas Ornithological Society is a leading state bird-study organization. Its purpose is to secure and disseminate knowledge about birds; encourage their observation, study, and conservation; and establish local birding clubs. The Society publishes *The TOS Newsletter* and a biannual scientific periodical, *The Bulletin of the Texas Ornithological Society*. In 1995, it also published the third edition of the *Checklist of the Birds of Texas* containing 591 species.

Its website has sections for *Texas Birding* magazine, upcoming meetings, becoming a member, membership advantages, publications, two TOS sanctuaries, officers, Society regions, and a search engine allowing website visitors to search for articles published in its bulletin.

www.io.com/~pdhulce/tos/tos.html

Virginia Society of Ornithology

Since 1929, the Virginia Society of Ornithology has been the state's voice for birding and ornithology. The Society has twenty-four local chapters, documents the state's birdlife, seeks to stimulate interest in birds, and encourages bird conservation. The VOS journal, *The Raven*, contains scientific information about the state's birds. The Society also publishes a quarterly newsletter.

Its website has sections about the Society, current events, Birdline and Rare Bird Alerts, chapters, officers, a general store, and links to other birding sites.

www.ecoventures-travel.com/vso

Washington Ornithological Society

The Washington Ornithological Society plays an important role in bird study and conservation in the State of Washington. Annual meetings alternate between venues—once east, then west—of the Cascades, including workshops and birding field trips. The Society issues *Washington Birds* and a newsletter called *WOSNEWS*. The Society also prepares the state's official bird list.

Its website has sections pertaining to membership and contact information, WOS publications, WOS sales catalog, upcoming meetings, upcoming field trips, Checklist of Washington Birds, Rare Bird Alerts, sightings reports, website tour, and links to other birding organizations.

www.wos.org

Regional and National Bird Clubs and Societies

An easy way to access information about nine major North American ornithological organizations (but not the ABA) is to access their BIRDNET website with links to each organization's site.

www.nmnh.si.edu/BIRDNET/index.html

Delaware Valley Ornithological Club

The Delaware Valley Ornithological Club, founded in 1890, is one of the oldest regional ornithological societies in the United States. Many club members are involved in bird conservation, it maintains a collection of bird skins housed at the Academy of Natural Sciences in Philadelphia, and sometimes issues special awards for excellence in bird study and ornithology. Many prominent amateur and professional ornithologists and other naturalists are (or were) members of this organization, whose roster reads like a who's who in twentieth-century American ornithology.

The DVOC publishes *Cassinia*, a scientific bird journal, and *Philadelphia Larus*, a newsletter. In the twentieth century, it also published Witmer Stone's *Bird Studies at Old Cape May*, Earl L. Poole's *Pennsylvania Birds: An Annotated List*, and several smaller checklists.

Its website has sections for a brief club history, mission, membership information, images (photographs of rare birds), program calendar, field trip schedule, and hotlines (Rare Bird Alerts).

www.acnatsci.org/dvoc

DelMarVa Ornithological Society

The DelMarVa Ornithological Society is the leading bird-study organization in the State of Delaware. Monthly meetings are held at the Delaware Museum of Natural History. It annually sponsors several dozen field trips in Maryland, New Jersey, eastern Pennsylvania, and elsewhere. *Delmarva Ornithologist*, published annually, is the Society's ornithological publication. The Delaware Records Committee evaluates rare or unusual bird records for possible inclusion on the state's bird list.

Its website has sections regarding membership information, *DOS Flyer* (a newsletter), DOS contacts, field trips, Maurice Barnhill's Delaware Birding Locations, St. Jones Research Reserve Survey, Delaware RBA (Rare Bird Alert), hotlines, and links to other birding sites.

www.acnatsci.org/dos

American Birding Association

The American Birding Association is North America's leading birding and listing organization, although its activities extend beyond merely keeping life lists.

Its large website has eighteen areas of birding interest identified by icons, including About ABA, ABA news, publications, conventions and conferences, job opportunities, sales, membership, Partners in Flight, volunteer opportunities, education, conservation, young birders, birders' resources, International Migratory Bird Day, Rare Bird Alerts, what's new, bird art on the Web, and links to other birding sites.

www.americanbirding.org

American Ornithologists' Union

Founded in 1883, the American Ornithologists' Union is the largest professional ornithological organization in the New World. Its membership consists of professional and amateur ornithologists, and its activities are centered strongly on original research into all aspects of birds and their biology, behavior, ecology, evolution, and natural history. The AOU publishes *The Auk* (the leading scientific ornithological journal in the Americas), *Ornithological Newsletter*, *Ornithological Monographs*, a series of longer occasional special publications, *Check-List of North American Birds*, and a multipart species monographic series called *Birds of North America*.

Its website has sections about the organization, The Council, publications, membership, AOU Resolutions, proceedings, and research awards.

pica.wru.umt.edu/AOU/AOU.html

Association of Field Ornithologists

Founded in 1922 as the Northeastern Bird-banding Association, the Association of Field Ornithologists has amateur and professional ornithologists as members. It publishes *Journal of Field Ornithology*, the focus of which includes original life history studies, advances in conservation, and assessments of existing ideas and concepts.

The AFO website has sections about the organization, officers and councilors, membership, *Journal of Field Ornithology*, editorial assistance, Alexander F. Skutch Medal, Bergstrom Memorial

Awards, and links to other ornithological organizations.
www.afonet.org/index.html

Cooper Ornithological Society

The Cooper Ornithological Society, founded in 1893, is one of America's oldest ornithological organizations. Its name honors James G. Cooper, an early California naturalist. The objectives of the COS are bird study, advancement of interest in birds, conservation of birds and other wildlife, and publication of ornithological knowledge. *The Condor* is its primary ornithological research periodical. *Studies in Avian Biology* are monographs or symposia proceedings of general ornithological interest. Information published by the Society is technical, intended for professional and advanced amateur ornithologists.

Its website has sections about the President's message; COS and its bylaws, officers, board of directors, and committees; just for students; announcements; awards; resolutions; and publications.
www.cooper.org

Professional Birding Association, Inc.

This organization places its primary emphasis on hard-core bird listing, including invitational birding competitions. However, it also has serious interests in bird conservation, and educational programs that instill in students and other people a deep and caring appreciation of birds. Backyard birdwatchers unfamiliar with how intense competitive birding can be may want to check this website for a totally different perspective of birding and bird listing.

Its website has sections for about us, conservation efforts, upcoming events, products and services, membership discounts, bird art gallery, and hot birding spots.
www.probirding.com

Wilson Ornithological Society

Founded in 1888, The Wilson Ornithological Society honors Alexander Wilson, the father of American ornithology. The Society stresses the important role played by amateur ornithologists in ornithology. Many important ornithological contributions from amateurs are published in *The Wilson Bulletin*, the organization's periodical. The home of The Wilson Ornithological Society is the Bird Division of the University of Michigan's Museum of Zoology. The Society's library, one of the finest in North America, contains about 3,000 books and 4,800 bound serial volumes, plus tens of thousands of reprints and other materials.

Its website has sections devoted to the organization, Society officers, membership information, *The Wilson Bulletin*, annual meetings, The Josselyn Van Tyne Memorial Library, research awards, *Guide to Graduate Studies in Ornithology in North America*, surplus bird books and periodicals for sale, and more.
www.ummz.lsa.umich.edu/birds/wos.html

WEBSITES WITH EXTENSIVE LINKS

Several sites contain links to birding, ornithology, wildlife, and habitat websites. The most useful are described here.

Birding and Ecological Sites in CASCADIA

This website is a goldmine of birding and wildlife links. It's arranged in three parts: Cascadia, North America, and Worldwide. Birders should explore all parts for a grand tour of the world of birding and related topics.
www.scn.org/earth/tweeters/links.html

Northern Prairie Wildlife Research Center

Although this website is not strictly a birding site, it contains lots of information about birds and other animals of interest to birders, as well as links to numerous other websites.
www.npwrc.usgs.gov

Wildlife Websites

This website, maintained by Bill Standley of Central Coast Consulting, is for wildlife ecologists needing a wide range of wildlife and ecology information. However, birdwatchers will also find it useful.

The site has sections for government, professional, nonprofit, university, birds, mammals, herps, fisheries, endangered species, reference, jobs, products and services, other site indexes, and search Bill's Wildlife Sites.
www.wildlifer.com/wildlifesites/index.html

CONSERVATION

American Bird Conservancy

The American Bird Conservancy is a leading bird conservation organization involved with a wide range of important activities and programs.

Its website has sections about the ABC, membership, Cats Indoors, field guides, Important Bird Areas, what's new, staff, climate change and birds, international, pesticides and birds, Partners in Flight, policy council, small grants, search, and feedback.
www.abcbirds.org

Audubon International

This national bird conservation, education, and research organization (not related to any other local, state, or national Audubon organizations) is involved in several bird-conservation programs, including backyard habitat enhancement, and habitat planning and improvement on golf courses, schools, and business properties.
www.audubonintl.org

National Audubon Society

The National Audubon Society's Bird Conservation Initiatives programs include important efforts and activities, such as WatchList, Christmas Bird Counts, Important Bird Areas, Cats Indoors! Campaign, its Coffee and Birds initiative, and BirdSource.

The Society's large website has major sections devoted to conservation and action, birds and science, kids education, membership and support, chapters, search, news, local Audubon resources, about Audubon, Audubon and the Internet, books-gifts-travel, and joining Audubon.
www.audubon.org

Office of Migratory Bird Management

The U.S. Fish & Wildlife Service's Office of Migratory Bird Management's large website has these sections: introduction, what you can do, get involved, participate in international projects, and sources of information about migratory birds.
migratorybirds.fws.gov/

Smithsonian Migratory Bird Center

Conservation of migratory birds is the Smithsonian Migratory Bird Center's mission. It conducts field research, organizes and operates public educational campaigns, and prepares and issues popular and technical books and other publications.

Its website sections include cocoa corner, coffee corner, bird lists, education, bird of the month, fact sheets, and publications. In addition, the large Smithsonian Migratory Bird Center section has parts about the Center, staff, milestones, investigate the problem, training young scientists, innovations in conservation, getting the message out, outreach programs, publications, and the SMBC network.
web2.si.edu/smbc/start.htm

Vermont Institute of Natural Science

The Vermont Institute of Natural Science is one of the most active bird conservation organizations in New England. Its bird research programs focus on Common Loons, Peregrine Falcons, and migratory songbirds. It also collects and publishes bird sightings, and operates the Vermont Rare Bird hotline.

The VINS web site has sections about general information, membership and support, Montpelier and Manchester facilities (the headquarters is at Woodstock), programs and events, education, Vermont Raptor Center, research, news and publications, citizen science, Partner Projects, birding, nature shop, employment opportunities, New Wildlife Center, and links to other bird and wildlife websites.
www.vinsweb.org

Wildlife Information Center, Inc.

The Wildlife Information Center, Inc., is a wildlife conservation organization interested in birds of prey, raptor migration, biodiversity and habitat protection, conservation education, and ornithological and ecological research. The Center's newsletter, *Wildlife Activist*, has feature articles; news about the Kittatinny Raptor Corridor Project and other wildlife concerns; and numerous bird, wildlife, conservation, ecology, and natural history book reviews.

Its website has sections about membership, interns, endangered species, Bake Oven Knob Hawk Count, Kittatinny Raptor Corridor Project, library and archives, wildlife, publications, news releases, research projects, and educational program.
www.wildlifeinfo.org

FEEDING AND NEST BOXES

About.com Birding Page

This website has numerous links to other sites providing detailed information about building birdhouses, nest boxes, and bird feeders. Measurements for boxes and houses are provided on most of the sites.
birding.about.com/hobbies/birding/mbody.htm

Barn Owl Headquarters

This website has great information about Barn Owls, including plans for building Barn Owl nest boxes. A variety of unusual materials can be used to construct them.
www.members.tripod.com/Tommy51/index.html

U.S. Fish & Wildlife Service

The U.S. Fish & Wildlife Service posts useful information on nest boxes and bird feeding on its website. Internet versions of its print booklets are available.

www.fws.gov/r9mbmo/pamphlet/house.html

Baltimore Bird Club

The Baltimore Bird Club's website has links to other bird-feeding sites, including the U.S. Fish & Wildlife Service's site.

204.255.212.10/~tross/by/backyard.html

University of Nebraska

The University of Nebraska's website has excellent information about bird feeding, construction of bird feeders, and a list of references. There is also detailed information about feeding hummingbirds, flowers to which they are attracted, and references.

www.ianr.unl.edu/pubs/wildlife/g669.htm

www.ianr.unl.edu/pubs/wildlife/g1331.htm

SPECIFIC BIRDS

As we've seen, birding has a number of special branches devoted to specific bird groups. Several fine websites address specific birds or groups of birds. Backyard birdwatchers will also want to examine *Hinterland Who's Who*, produced by the Canadian Wildlife Service, for dozens of brief life history accounts of North American birds.

www.cws-scf.ec.gc.ca/hww-fap/eng_ind.html

Vultures

Throughout the twentieth century, New World vultures were classified as birds of prey. Now they are classified among storks. However, for convenience, hawk watchers still deal with them as raptors.

Turkey Vulture Society

The Turkey Vulture Society is a data center for scientific information pertaining to vultures. The Society's website has sections devoted to introduction, sketches and photographs, newsletter, vulture's purpose, biology, buzzard, Harpy, library, more vulture roosts (links to other sites), membership application form, and help.

www.accutek.com/vulture

Waterfowl

Northern Prairie Wildlife Research Center

The Northern Prairie Wildlife Research Center's large website has sections for what's new, NPWRC site map, biological resources, publications database, announcements, information, and help and feedback.

Beginning backyard birdwatchers can especially benefit by reviewing the paintings and text in the U.S. Fish & Wildlife Service's booklet *Ducks at a Distance: A Waterfowl Identification Guide* by Bob Hines. The site also has the Central Flyway Waterfowl Council's *Waterfowl Identification in the Central Flyway*, which contains excellent paintings.

www.npwrc.usgs.gov/index.htm

www.npwrc.usgs.gov/resource/tools/duckdist/duckdist.htm

www.npwrc.usgs.gov/resource/tools/waterfwl/waterfwl.htm

Hawks, Eagles, and Falcons

Bake Oven Knob Hawk Watch

The Bake Oven Knob Hawk Watch in eastern Pennsylvania is one of the nation's longest running autumn hawk migration studies. Begun in 1961, year 2000 marks the fortieth anniversary for this ongoing effort. The Center's website has sections about the Bake Oven Knob Hawk Watch and the Kittatinny Raptor Corridor Project.

www.wildlifeinfo.org

Cape May Hawk Watch

Cape May Point is located at the tip of the Cape May peninsula at the southern end of New Jersey. During autumn, it's a major hawk (and other bird) migration bottleneck, with thousands of raptors counted annually. The Hawk Watch count is organized by the New Jersey Audubon Society's Cape May Point Bird Observatory.

The Cape May Hawk Watch website has sections for a brief discussion of the geography and its relationship to hawk migration, past yearly hawk counts, and a link to the Cape May Bird Observatory website.

www.njaudubon.org/sites/hwcmbo.html

Carolina Raptor Center

The Carolina Raptor Center is involved in raptor rehabilitation, conservation, education, and research. Its website has sections about who we are, you can help, resources, education, raptor repair shop, gift shop, bird brains, job opportunities, contact us, and links to other raptor websites.

www.birdsofprey.org

Golden Gate Raptor Observatory

The Golden Gate Raptor Observatory is located on Hawk Hill, overlooking San Francisco Bay. It is California's most important hawk-migration observation site.

The Observatory's website has sections for timing, raptor quiz, conservation, education, research, volunteers, frequently asked questions, map to Hawk Hill, Hawk Hill weather, and mission.

www.ggro.org

Hawk Migration Association of North America

The Hawk Migration Association of North America's website has links to selected hawkwatching websites throughout North America. The site also has sections about the organization, membership, chapters, listserv, news, regions, data, forms, projects, awards, weather, references, and links to other websites.

www.hmana.org/index.htm

Hawk Mountain Sanctuary

Hawk Mountain Sanctuary, established in 1934, was the world's first refuge for birds of prey. It is located on 2,400 acres on the Kittatinny Ridge near Kempton, Pennsylvania. Its autumn hawk migration counts are the world's longest running data base.

Hawk Mountain's website has sections about the sanctuary, migration, events, news, bookstore, membership, and core programs. Hawk count numbers are posted daily in autumn.

www.hawkmountain.org

Hawk Ridge Nature Reserve

The hawkwatching lookout at Hawk Ridge Nature Reserve, in Duluth, Minnesota, is one of the oldest and most important locations in the western Great Lakes area. Visitors stand along the side of a lightly traveled road, overlooking part of Lake Superior, watching raptors approach. Tens of thousands are seen and counted each autumn.

The Reserve's website has sections for introduction, directions, migration, hawk count, statistics of common raptors, naturalist program, banding research station, banding station totals, Minnesota Ornithologists' Union weekend, Hawk Ridge support, and links to other raptor sites.

www.biosci.umn.edu/~mou/ridge.html

Hawks Aloft, Inc.

Hawks Aloft, Inc., a New Mexico organization, is involved in raptor conservation, education, and research programs.

Its website has sections about calendar, contact us, education, employment, field studies, kids, membership, newsletter, related sites (links to other raptor sites), species profiles, sponsors, wish list, and who are we.

www.rt66.com/~hawksnm

HawkWatch International, Inc.

HawkWatch International, Inc., focuses its activities in the American West, Florida Keys, and Mexico. Research, education, and conservation are its primary activities, which are clarifying the status of hawk migrations in the western United States.

The organization's website has sections for welcome, contribute to the message board, about us, where we work, calendar, adopt-a-hawk, species spotlight, membership, employment, board and staff, help us soar, and links to other raptor sites.

www.hawkwatch.org

Peregrine Fund & World Center for Birds of Prey

The Peregrine Fund and its headquarters, the World Center for Birds of Prey, is an international leader in captive breeding of birds of prey—in particular, Peregrine Falcons. Through its efforts, restoration of Peregrine Falcons in North America was achieved after DDT was banned in the United States and Canada. Other raptors from various parts of the world are also captive-bred at this facility.

The Peregrine Fund's website has sections for introduction, World Center for Birds of Prey, visitor's center, conservation projects, notes from the field, press room (news releases), membership, catalog, archive of American falconry, search, and links to other raptor sites.

www.peregrinefund.org/index.html

Raptor Center at the University of Minnesota

The Raptor Center at the University of Minnesota is known worldwide for its advanced veterinary medicine and raptor programs. It offers raptor-related residency and externship programs for veterinarians and upper-level student veterinarians.

Some of its website sections deal with welcome, how to find us, events, adoption, membership, gift store, education, publications, what to do with an injured raptor, raptor facts, and Highway to the Tropics (satellite-tracking of migrating Bald Eagles, Ospreys, and Swainson's Hawks). Of particular interest to birdwatchers, students, and teachers are superb Osprey, Bald Eagle, and Swainson's Hawk migration data

obtained via satellite-tracking. The migration routes for some birds are shown in step-by-step sequences on maps, giving viewers impressive insights into the migratory movements of these individuals. Teaching units, bibliographies, and other information supplement the migration information.
www.raptor.cvm.umn.edu

Shorebirds

Western Hemisphere Shorebird Reserve Network

The Western Hemisphere Shorebird Reserve Network websites contain a migration map, wetland news, quick information, shorebird facts, projects, shorebird sites, threatened shorebird sites, international shorebird surveys, resources, and other more technical information.
www.manomet.org/whsrn.htm

Internet Information on Shorebirds

The Internet Information on Shorebirds website contains a large number of links to other sites dealing with the entire range of shorebird interests—birding, conservation, education, research, photographs, and much more.
www.utm.edu/~phertzel/shbird.htm

Shorebird Sister Schools Program

Birders, teachers, students, parents, and youth leaders will want to examine the U.S. Fish & Wildlife Service's Shorebird Sister Schools Program containing significant information about shorebirds. The Atlantic Flyway version has English, Spanish, Portuguese, Japanese, and Russian language editions.

The Shorebird Sister Schools Program website has sections about update, shorebirds, conservation, exhibition, for kids, teachers, resources, hotline, Atlantic Flyway, sister cities, and links to other shorebird websites.
www.fws.gov/r7enved/sssp.html

Shorebird Watcher

Dick and Jean Hoffman's The Shorebird Watcher website has sections devoted to news and links, information, species, festivals, voice, gallery (of photographs), and bibliography. Backyard birders will find it fascinating and educational to explore its many parts and links.
pw1.netcom.com/~djhoff/shorebrd.html

Owls

Owl Pages

This website has plenty of excellent owl information packed into its many sections, which cover biological, ecological, conservation, and natural histroy aspects of owls worldwide. There are also sections on owl-related collectibles.
www.owlpages.com

Hummingbirds

There is considerable public interest in hummingbirds and numerous websites devoted to them. On the following selected websites, backyard birdwatchers can obtain excellent, basic, useful information about all aspects of hummingbirds, including attracting and feeding these birds in backyard habitats.

Hummingbird.net

Hummingbirds are avian jewels, and this outstanding website has much excellent, fascinating, and useful information about the North American hummingbird species. Major sections of the site deal with welcome, hummer notes, species, attracting hummingbirds, feeders, migration maps, natural history, research, anecdotes, The Gallery, reviews (e.g., books and feeders), organizations, bibliography, and online resources, as well as links to other hummingbird websites.
www.hummingbirds.net

Hummer/Bird Study Group, Inc.

The Hummer/Bird Study Group's website, with excellent hummingbird photographs, has sections for mission and history, winter banding, attracting and feeding hummingbirds, membership, calendar of events, banding stations, fundraisers, and links to other hummingbird sites.
www.hbsg.org/

Hummingbird Society

The Hummingbird Society's website has sections about the founder, advisors, The News, help wanted, frequently asked questions, photos, join, kids, sponsors, banding, wallpaper, catalog of sales items, found an injured hummingbird, and links to other hummingbird websites. There are English, Dutch, Portuguese, and Spanish versions of this site; users simply click the desired version.
www.hummingbird.org

Hummingbird Website

The Hummingbird Website is an outstanding place to obtain substantial information about these lovely birds. There are sections on the site for seventeen species, behavior, gardens, gallery, questions and answers, historical, legends, nests, stories, quiz, poetry, identify, migration, search, exotic, rarities, iridescence, links, store, and hummingbird tours and vacations.
www.portalproductions.com/h/

Purple Martins

American Bird Conservation Association

The American Bird Conservation Association is very involved in maintaining colonies of nesting Purple Martins at its headquarters in Nappanee, Indiana. The Association provides helpful information to backyard birdwatchers interested in these birds. An annual ABCA Year End Report is published and several books are distributed. Its website's Home link must be clicked to access Purple Martin information (i.e., numerous links to other martin websites). Association membership information is also provided on the home page.
www.tyrell.net/~deadbird/abca.htm

Chuck's Purple Martin Page

This is the private website of Purple Martin landlord Chuck Abare. It has sections for preface, attracting martins, the great housing debate, erecting a martin house, suggested reading, odds and ends, search engine, meet the author, e-mail and comments, and links to other Purple Martin sites.
www.ro.com/~yankee

Danny's Purple Martin Place

Danny Frazier maintains this website. It has sections about attracting Purple Martins, taking care of your colony, resources, fundamentals, bits and pieces, The Purple Martin Web ring, and links to twenty-one other martin websites.
www.brightok.net/~dfrazier

Hirondelles Noires

This website is maintained by Carol Arcand for French-speaking Canadians. It contains basic information for Purple Martin landlords, plus photographs.
pages.infinit.net/prosubis/index.htm

Nature Society

The Nature Society in Griggsville, Illinois, provides Purple Martin housing and conservation information to the public. This organization also publishes *Nature Society News*.

The Society's website has sections for migration map, scout reports, Purple Martins, The Griggsville Story, *Nature Society News*, martin housing, Nature Society Museum, and J. L. Wade.
www.naturesociety.org

Purple Martin Conservation Association

The Purple Martin Conservation Association is a leader in providing the public with Purple Martin biology, ecology, nesting, and conservation information. During the northward spring martin migration, the site is updated daily using data from a continental network of more than three thousand Scout-arrival Study cooperators. The Association also publishes *Purple Martin Update*.

The Association's large website has sections for letter from the Director, about Purple Martins, scout dates, information request, management tips, membership benefits, Project Martinwatch, research and conservation, update magazine articles, martin mentors, Landlord of the Year, martin terminology, volunteer opportunities, education and grants, The Purple Martin Forum, slide show, catalog, links, and web ring.

The Purple Martin Forum is an essential resource for people interested in these birds. The Forum is owned and maintained by the Purple Martin Conservation Association. It is an interactive site, allowing people to post messages and articles, ask questions, give opinions, and otherwise share their martin experiences.
www.purplemartin.org

Purple Martin Society

The Purple Martin Society's website has sections about the organization, migration, emergency, photographs, online manual, research and development, what's new, housing, cutting edge, gourds, other resources, advisories, roosts, dictionary, topic search page, and web author. The organization also publishes *The Scout Report*, a newsletter mailed to members.
www.purplemartins.com

Purple Martins in Texas

Purple Martins in Texas is part of the Texas Environmental Studies Institute's website. It has sections for migration map, ecology, sightings, and migratory data (previous decades). The site also has sections for Monarch Butterflies and Ruby-throated Hummingbirds in Texas.
riceinfo.rice.edu/armadillo/ftbend/TESI/tesi.htm

Bluebirds

Bluebird Association of Maine

The Bluebird Association of Maine is dedicated to saving and increasing the number of Eastern Bluebirds in that state. Its website has sections for officers, bluebird history, facts, nest boxes, predators, notes, join BAM, and links to other bluebird sites.

w3.ime.net/~cordman/bluebird/bam.html

Bluebird Fancying

There is much helpful information on this website, which has sections for general information and habitat, bluebirds in peril, bluebird species, more habitat, erection of bird boxes, birdhouse construction, dimensions of birdhouse pieces, supplemental feeding (mealworms), and links to nine other bluebird sites.

www.iocc.com/~twash/bluebirds.html

Bluebird Society of Pennsylvania

The Bluebird Society of Pennsylvania, an affiliate of the North American Bluebird Society, seeks to protect and encourage Eastern Bluebirds to nest, engages in public education, monitors bluebird research, establishes bluebird nest-box trails, conducts quarterly meetings, and holds annual conferences.

The organization's website has sections dealing with Eastern Bluebirds, nest boxes, photo of the month, other information sources, current and upcoming events, and a place to submit nest box reports.

www.voicenet.com/~clarens/BSP/1BSP.HTM

Iowa Department of Natural Resources

The Iowa Department of Natural Resources has bluebird information useful to backyard birdwatchers. Its website has sections about a bluebird's year, enemies, bluebird nest-box trails, general nest-box guidelines, references, and Iowa's bluebird nest-box plans.

www.state.ia.us/government/dnr/organiza/fwb/wildlife/pages/bbird.htm

Nest Box

This website contains information about bluebirds and other birds, backyard birding, and general birding. There are sections for backyard birding, field birding, bluebirds, photo galleries, and birding links. Beginning backyard birdwatchers will especially enjoy exploring the backyard birding section.

www.nestbox.com

New York State Bluebird Society

Monitoring and increasing Eastern Bluebird populations in New York State, educating the public about bluebirds, conducting bluebird research, and cooperating and coordinating bluebird projects are objectives of the New York State Bluebird Society.

Its website has sections for welcome, our mission, membership, bluebird information, nest-box plans, for sale, free nest boxes, adopt-a-box, help, meetings and exhibits, report nesting, and links to other bluebird sites.

www.geocities.com/RainForest/2414/nysbs.htm

North American Bluebird Society, Inc.

The first website backyard birdwatchers should check when seeking bluebird information is the North American Bluebird Society's site. It has sections about the organization, join NABS, affiliate organizations (state and local bluebird societies or organizations), nest-box plans, fact sheets, predator control, educational gift items, educational packages, bluebird poster/pocket field guide, frequently asked questions, research grants, range map, bluebird nest-box approval process, and Transcontinental Bluebird Trail.

www.nabluebirdsociety.org

North Carolina Bluebird Society

This organization is dedicated to preserving Eastern Bluebirds in North Carolina, encouraging people to maintain bluebird nest-box trails, conserving bluebird habitat, and educating people about bluebirds and how to help them.

Its website has sections for the January bluebird season, nesting surveys, nesting schedule for North Carolina, and how you can help.

www2.coastalnet.com/~k4y5k4ws/ncbs.htm

Ohio Bluebird Society

The objective of this organization is to return and perpetuate the Eastern Bluebird in the state of Ohio, and work to save its habitat. The organization's website has sections for reference, join the OBS, and links to bluebird and other birding sites.

www.obsbluebirds.com

Prescott Western Bluebird Recovery Project

This Western Bluebird recovery project is located in the Lower Willamette Valley of Oregon. Several nest-box trails are now operating there.

Its website has sections for the project, the Western Bluebird, bird boxes, monitoring boxes, what you can do, frequently asked questions, map of the project territory, what's new, Western Bluebird: The Comeback Bird, bluebird stories and anecdotes, nesting and banding data, and links to other bluebird sites.

home.pacifier.com/~bluebird/

Virginia Bluebird Society

This organization's objective is to promote Eastern Bluebird conservation in Virginia by using bluebird nest boxes, nest-box trails, and protection of bluebird habitat.

Its website has sections for news, trail management, join VBS, photos, nest box and guards, and links to other birding organizations.

www.geocities.com/virginiabluebirds/

Company Addresses

Contact information for companies referred to in the text is offered here. Suppliers of purple martin houses and bluebird boxes are found in appendix 5.

Agfa Corp.
100 Challenger Rd.
Ridgefield Park NJ 07660
201-440-2500
Fax 201-440-5733
www.agfa.com

Arundale Products
P.O. Box 4637
St. Louis MO 63108
314-367-8030
Fax 314-367-8030

Avian Aquatics, Inc.
P.O. Box 295
Nassau DE 19969
800-788-6478

B & H Photo-Video-Pro Audio
420 9th Ave.
New York NY 10001
800-947-6933

Bird Co.
P.O. Box 296
Appleton WI 54912-0296

Blue Jay Bookshop, Nature Saskatchewan
Room 206, 1860 Lorne St.
Regina SK
Canada S4P 2L7
306-780-9273
Fax 306-780-9263
Nature.Sask@ucomnet.unibase.com

Bogen Photo Corp.
565 East Crescent Ave.
P.O. Box 506
Ramsey NJ 07446-0506
201-818-9500
Fax 201-818-9177
www.bogenphoto.com

Bushnell Sports Optics
9200 Cody
Overland Park KS 66214
800-423-3537 or
913-752-3400
Fax 913-752-3550
www.bushnell.com

C & S Products Co., Inc.
P.O. Box 848
Fort Dodge IA 50501
515-955-5605
csprod@frontiernet.net

Canon U.S.A., Inc.
www.usa.canon.com

Celestron International
2835 Columbia St.
Torrance CA 90503
310-328-9560
Fax 310-212-5835
www.celestron.com

Contax
www.contaxcameras.com

Country Ecology
P.O. Box 59
Center Sandwich NH 03227
603-539-2139
mwv.org/birdman

Coveside Conservation Products
202 U.S. Route One, Box 374
Falmouth ME 04105
800-774-7606
Fax 207-774-7613

Dover Publications, Inc.
31 East 2nd St.
Mineola NY 11501-3882
www.doverpublications.com

Droll Yankees, Inc.
27 Mill Rd.
Foster RI 02825-1366
800-352-9164
Fax 401-647-7620
custserv@drollyankees.com
www.drollyankees.com

Duncraft Bird Feeders
P.O. Box 9020
Penacock NH 03303-9020
800-593-5656
info@duncraft.com
www.duncraft.com

Epson America, Inc.
3840 Kilroy Airport Way
Long Beach CA 90840
562-981-3840
www.epson.com

Five Islands Products, Inc.
P.O. Box 2095
Scarborough ME 04070-2095
800-269-0559

Fuji
P.O. Box 7828
Edison NJ 08818-7828
800-800-3854
Fax 732-857-3487
www.fujifilm.com

Gitzo (see Bogen)

Hasselblad USA, Inc.
10 Madison Rd.
Fairfield NJ 07004
973-227-7320
Fax 973-227-4216
www.hasselbladusa.com

Woodstream Corp. (Havahart Traps)
P.O. Box 327
Lititz PA 17543
800-800-1819

Heath Manufacturing Co.
140 Mill St.
P.O. Box 105
Coopersville MI 49404-0105
800-678-8183
Fax 616-837-9491
wildbrd@heathmfg.com
www.heathmfg.com

Hitachi
800-Hitachi (800-448-2244)
www.hitachi.com

Hyde's Birdfeeder, Inc.
33 Elm St.
Merrimack NH 03054
888-247-3830
www.hydebirdfeeder.com

Ideaform, Inc.
908 East Briggs Ave.
Fairfield IA 52556
800-779-7256
www.birdwatching.com

Invisible Fence Co., Inc.
355 Phoenixville Pike
Malvern PA 19355
610-651-0999
Fax 610-651-0986

JVC Americas Corp.
1700 Valley Rd.
Wayne NJ 07470
800-526-5308
www.jvc.com

Eastman Kodak Co.
343 State St.
Rochester NY 14650-0205
800-242-2424
www.kodak.com

Kowa Optimed, Inc.
20001 S. Vermont Ave.
Torrance CA 90502
310-327-1913
Fax 310-327-4177
www.kowascope.com

Leica Camera, Inc.
156 Ludlow Ave.
Northvale NJ 07647
201-767-7500
Fax 201-767-8666
www.leica-camera.com

Mamiya America Corp.
8 Westchester Plaza
Elmsford NY 10523
914-347-3300
Fax 914-347-3309
www.mamiya.com

Marantz America, Inc.
440 Medinah Rd.
Roselle IL 60712
800-270-4533
630-307-3100
Fax 630-307-2687

Saul Mineroff Electronics, Inc.
574 Meacham Ave.
Elmont NY 11003
516-775-1370
Fax 516-775-1371
www.mineroff.com

Mirador Optical Corp.
P.O. Box 11614
Marina Del Rey CA 90295
310-821-5587
Fax 310-305-0386

NAGRA USA, Inc.
240 Great Circle Rd., Suite 326
Nashville TN 37228
615-726-5191
Fax 615-726-5189
www.nagra.com

Natural Technology Industries
P.O. Box 582
Youngstown OH 44501
330-629-7583

Nelson Manufacturing Co.
3049 12th Street SW
Cedar Rapids IA 52404
319-363-2607
Fax 319-363-3601

Nikon Sports Optics
1300 Walt Whitman Rd.
Melville NY 11747-3064
www.nikonusa.com

Olympus
www.olympusamerica.com

Panasonic USA
www.panasonic.com

Pentax Corp.
35 Inverness Dr. E.
Englewood CO 80112
800-709-2020

Perky-Pet Products Co.
2201 South Wabash St.
Denver CO 80231
303-751-9000
Fax 303-368-9616
wings@perky-pet.com
www.perky-pet.com

Plasticraft Manufacturing Co., Inc.
115 Plasticraft Dr.
Albertville AL 35951
800-239-4105
Fax 256-891-1177

PrintFile, Inc.
P.O. Box 607638
Orlando FL 32860-7638
407-886-3100
Fax 407-886-0008
www.printfile.com

Questar Corp.
6204 Ingham Rd.
New Hope PA 18938
215-862-5277
Fax 215-862-0512

Ramphastos, LLC
P.O. Box 310
Dover NH 03821
888-221-2473
www.ramphastos.com

Rollei USA
40 Sea View Dr.
Secaucus NJ 07094
888-8Rollei (888-876-5534)
Fax 201-902-9342
www.rolleifoto.com

SANYO North America Corp.
2055 Sanyo Ave.
San Diego CA 92154
www.sanyo.com

Sennheiser Electronic Corp.
1 Enterprise Dr.
Old Lyme CT 06371
860-434-9190
Fax 860-434-1759
www.sennheiserusa.com

Sharp Electronics Corp.
Sharp Plaza
Mahwah NJ 07430-2135
www.sharpelectronics.com

Sigma Corp. of America
15 Fleetwood Court
Ronkonkoma NY 11779
631-585-1144
Fax 631-585-1895
www.sigmaphoto.com

Sony Corp. of America
www.sony.com

Stonewood Manufacturing
P.O. Box 426
Roanoke IN 46783
800-593-8303
Stonewood@birdmagnet.com
www.birdmagnet.com

Swarovski Optik North America, Ltd.
1 Wholesale Way
Cranston RI 02920
800-426-3089
Fax 401-946-2587
www.swarovskioptik.com

Swift Instruments, Inc.
952 Dorchester Ave.
Boston MA 02125
800-446-1116
Fax 617-436-3232

Thayer Birding Software
www.birding.com

Treehouse Bed & Breakfast
1305 Westwood Dr.
Henderson TX 75654
903-655-1210
www.bestinns.net/usa/tx/treehouse.html

Victor Emanuel Nature Tours
P.O. Box 33008
Austin TX 78764
800-328-8368
Fax 512-328-2919
VENTBIRD@aol.com
www.VENTBIRD.com

Water Resources Design, Inc.
551 Teton Trail
Indianapolis IN 46217
317-786-7529
oskay@surf-ici.com

Whispering Pines Enterprises
P.O. Box 8568
Moscow ID 83843
208-882-8344
Fax 208-883-8446
sales@wpines.com
www.wpines.com

Wild Bird Centers of America, Inc.
7370 MacArthur Blvd.
Glen Echo MD 20812
301-229-9585
Fax 301-320-6154
www.wildbirdcenter.com
This chain has stores nationwide. Contact the local store near you.

Wild Birds Unlimited, Inc.
888-302-2473
Fax 317-571-7110
www.wbu.com
This chain has stores nationwide. Contact the local store near you.

Yashica
www.yashica.com/site.html

Carl Zeiss, Inc.
1 Zeiss Dr.
Thornwood NY 10594

APPENDIX 5

Suppliers of Purple Martin Houses and Bluebird Boxes

As discussed in chapter 7, Purple Martins and bluebirds have special housing requirements, thus a separate appendix for suppliers of this specialized equipment. Several companies manufacture Purple Martin gourds or apartment houses. Houses vary in dimensions, design, and construction materials. Products made by the companies included here are used widely by Purple Martin landlords and conservationists.

All bluebird nest-box manufacturers and retailers on this list were approved by the North American Bluebird Society after satisfying its rigorous examination of each product. I strongly suggest that birdwatchers only purchase bluebird nest boxes approved and certified by the NABS.

PURPLE MARTIN GOURDS AND HOUSES

Bird Abodes
506 Erie St.
Edinboro PA 16440

Birds' Paradise
Route 3, Box 72
Conneautville PA 16406
814-587-3879

Carroll Industries
P.O. Box 577
Madison MS 39110
800-356-2062

Coates Manufacturing Co.
3805 McCoy Dr.
Bossier City LA 71111
800-869-2828

Heath Manufacturing Co.
P.O. Box 105
140 Mill St.
Coopersville MI 49404
800-678-8183

Lone Star Purple Martin Houses
109 Echo Ln.
Seguin TX 78155
830-401-4442

Nature House, Inc.
Purple Martin Junction
Griggsville IL 62340
800-255-2692

NATURELine/Plasticraft Manufacturing Co., Inc.
115 Plasticraft Dr.
Albertville AL 35951
800-239-4105

Trendsetter Purple Martin Houses
93 E. 3rd B Rd.
Nappanee IN 46550

BLUEBIRD NEST BOXES

Ahlgren Construction
12989 Otchipwe Ave. N.
Stillwater MN 55082
612-430-0031

Backyard Birds, Inc.
2437 S. 132 St.
Omaha NE 68144

Backyard Enhancements by R and R Creations
P.O. Box 1804
Rockville MD
20849-1804
301-738-0277
rrc@erols.com

Backyard Nature Products
Bird Stuff/Wood Country
410 Fulton St.
Chilton WI 53014
800-817-8833
Fax 920-849-4415

Bird House
2183 Sadler Rd.
Amelia Island FL 32034
904-321-1233

Bird House
701 Boyd Rd.
Azle TX 76020

Birdhouses by Walker
120 High Oaks Dr.
Double Oak TX 75077

Bluebird Society of Pennsylvania
P.O. Box 267
Enola PA 17025

Cedar Creek
15225 Industrial Rd. #8
P.O. Box 122
Bennington NE 68007

Cedar Works
19 Cedar Dr.
Peebles OH 45660

Country Ecology
P.O. Box 59
Center Sandwich NH 03227

Coveside Conservation Products
202 U.S. Route 1
Box 374
Falmouth ME 04105
800-326-2807
Fax 207-774-7613

Cranes & Crows
400-E San Felipe NW
Old Town
Albuquerque NM 87104

Duncraft Bird Feeders
102 Fisherville Rd.
Concord NH 03303

Everything for the Birds
175 Weaverville Highway,
Ste. W
Ashville NC 28804

Fruit Basket Flowerland
765 28th St. SW
Wyoming MI 49509

Garden Gate
87 Southside Dr.
Newville PA 17241

Garr's Wholesale
11620 Lebanon Rd.
Mount Juliet TN 37122
605-754-9613
Fax 605-754-9633

Gilbertson Nest Box Co.
HC5, Box 31
Aitkin MN 56431

Jenna Bird
P.O. Box 328
Whiteford MD 21160

Kooistra Woodworks
2363 Port Sheldon Ct.
Jenison KY 49428
616-669-1110
Fax 616-669-1365
kenkw@iserv.net

Little Log Co., Inc.
500 N. Highway 183
P.O. Box 457
Sargent NE 68874
308-527-2987
Fax 308-527-3988

David Long
3 Beachwood Ln.
Yardley PA 19067

Looker Products
Olin Looker Route
Route 1 N., Box 29
Milford IL 60953
815-889-5555
Fax 805-889-5550

Lucky Penny
2795 Long Oak Dr.
Germantown TN 38138
901-755-6842
Fax 901-751-6528
bjohnson@magibox.net
www.luckypenny.com

Manufacturing Source
5662 Fieldspring Ave.
New Port Richey FL 34655

Purple Martin Conservation Association
Edinboro University
of Pennsylvania
Edinboro PA 16444

Robin's Wood
2000 Riverside Dr.
Asheville NC 28804
704-281-0201
Fax 704-281-0207
robinswood@
mindspring.com
www.robinswood.com

Rustic Bird House
210 Hickory Hollow
Talledega IA 35160

Sawyer Bluebird Box
313 Bluebird Rd.
Ringgold GA 30736

Schieren Associates, Ltd.
P.O. Box 4000
Pottersville NJ 07979
908-439-2120
Fax 908-439-2113

Stapley Feed Center
6447 Transit Rd.
Depew NY 14043

Stoneware Manufacturing
192 S. Main St.
Roanoke IN 46783

Sturgeon River Pottery and Wild Bird Supply
3031 Charlevoix Ave.
Petosky MI 49770

Sunrise Wildbird Supplies
P.O. Box 133
Fortson GA 31808
706-323-BIRD

Tennessee Trading Co.
P.O. Box 733
Goodlettsville TN 37070

Floyd VanErt
39755 Highway 92
Carson IA 51525

Vari-Crafts
210 Kings Highway
Landing NJ 07850

Watershed Wooden Birdfeeders
191 Loomis St.
Burlington VT 05401

Wild Bird–Adventures
4300 Paces Ferry Rd.,
Suite 236
Atlanta GA 30339

Wild Bird Centers (all retail stores)
Nationwide in the United States.

Wild Bird Habitat Store
4306 Bryant Ave. S.
Minneapolis MN 55409

Wild Bird Marketplace
205 West Main St.
Brighton MI 48116

Wild Bird Marketplace
939 Highway K
O'Fallen MO 63366

Wild Bird Marketplace
NorthCross Shopping Center
9719 Sam Furr Rd.,
Ste. E
Huntersville NC 28078

Wild Birds Unlimited (all retail stores)
Nationwide in the United States.

Wilderness Feeds
1100 Gorham St., Unit 22
Newmarket ON
Canada L3Y 7V1
905-853-7373
Fax 905-853-3226

Wildlife's Choice
8025 Penny Rd.
Pleasant Hill OH 45359

Wildlight
189 Butternut Tr.
Wells ME 04090

Wooden Ewe, Inc.
3528 Valeview Dr.
Oakton VA 22124-2244

Woodlink
1500 Woodlink Dr.
Mount Ayr IA 50854
515-464-3905
Fax 515-464-2122

Yalcot Mountain Wood Works
P.O. Box 241
Florala AL 36442
334-858-4006
Fax 334-858-4006
and
P.O. Box 86
Yacolt WA 98675
360-686-3669
Fax 360-686-8041

APPENDIX 6

Further Reading

The titles listed here are important sources of information for backyard birdwatchers. Also listed and briefly described are major birding publications that backyard birdwatchers may find interesting.

BOOKS

Alden, Peter, and Brian Cassie. *National Audubon Society Field Guide to New England.* New York: Alfred A. Knopf, 1998.

Alden, Peter, and Brian Cassie. *National Audubon Society Field Guide to the Mid-Atlantic States.* New York: Alfred A. Knopf, 1999.

Alden, Peter, Rick Cech, and Gil Nelson. *National Audubon Society Field Guide to Florida.* New York: Alfred A. Knopf, 1998.

Alden, Peter, and Peter Friederici. *National Audubon Society Field Guide to the Southwestern States.* New York: Alfred A. Knopf, 1999.

Alden, Peter, and John Grassy. *National Audubon Society Field Guide to the Rocky Mountain States.* New York: Alfred A. Knopf, 1998.

Alden, Peter, and Fred Heath. *National Audubon Society Field Guide to California.* New York: Alfred A. Knopf, 1998.

Alden, Peter, and Dennis Paulson. *National Audubon Society Field Guide to the Pacific Northwest.* New York: Alfred A. Knopf, 1998.

American Bird Conservancy. *All the Birds of North America.* New York: HarperPerennial, 1997.

American Birding Association. *The ABA Checklist: Birds of the Continental United States and Canada.* 5th ed. Colorado Springs: American Birding Association, 1996.

American Ornithologists' Union. *Check-List of North American Birds.* 5th ed. Washington DC: American Ornithologists' Union, 1957.

American Ornithologists' Union. *Check-List of North American Birds: The Species of Birds of North America from the Arctic through Panama, Including the West Indies and Hawaiian Islands.* 6th ed. Washington DC: American Ornithologists' Union, 1983.

American Ornithologists' Union. *Check-List of North American Birds: The Species of Birds of North America from the Arctic through Panama, Including the West Indies and Hawaiian Islands.* 7th ed. Washington DC: American Ornithologists' Union, 1998.

Audubon, John James. *The Original Water-Color Paintings by John James Audubon for The Birds of America.* 2 vols. New York: American Heritage, 1966.

Bent, Arthur Cleveland. *Life Histories of North American Birds.* Washington DC: Smithsonian Institution, 1919–68.

Brewer, T. M. *Wilson's American Ornithology, with Notes by Jardine: To which Is Added A Synopsis of American Birds, Including Those Described by Bonaparte, Audubon, Nuttall, and Richardson.* New York: Charles L. Cornish, 1839.

Bull, John, and John Farrand Jr. *National Audubon Society Field Guide to North American Birds: Eastern Region.* 2nd ed. New York: Alfred A. Knopf, 1998.

Carson, Rachel. *Silent Spring.* Boston: Houghton Mifflin, 1962.

Choate, Ernest A., and Raymond A. Paynter Jr. *The Dictionary of American Bird Names.* Rev. ed. by Raymond A. Paynter Jr. Boston: Harvard Common Press, 1985.

Clements, James. *Birds of the World: A Checklist.* 5th ed. Vista CA: Ibis Publishing, 2000.

Coombes, Allen J. *Eyewitness Handbooks: Trees.* New York: DK Publishing, 1992.

Cruickshank, Allan D., and Helen G. Cruickshank. *The Birds of Brevard County, Florida.* Orlando: Florida Press, 1980.

Damude, Noreen, and Kelly Conrad Bender. *Texas Wildscapes: Gardening for Wildlife.* Austin: Texas Parks and Wildlife Press, 1999.

Dennis, John V. *A Complete Guide to Bird Feeding.* New York: Alfred A. Knopf, 1975.

Dirr, Michael A. *Dirr's Hardy Trees and Shrubs: An Illustrated Encyclopedia.* Portland OR: Timber Press, 1997.

Dorst, Jean. *The Migrations of Birds.* Boston: Houghton Mifflin, 1962.

Dunn, Jon L. *National Geographic Field Guide to the Birds of North America: Revised and Updated.* 3rd ed. Washington: National Geographic Society, 1999.

Farrand, John, Jr. *Eastern Birds: An Audubon Handbook.* New York: McGraw-Hill, 1988.

Farrand, John, Jr. *Western Birds: An Audubon Handbook.* New York: McGraw-Hill, 1988.

Farrand, John, Jr. *How to Identify Birds: An Audubon Handbook.* New York: McGraw-Hill, 1988.

Goodnight, Julie, and Sara Vickerman. *Oregon Wildlife Viewing Guide.* Lake Oswego OR: Defenders of Wildlife, 1988.

Harrison, George H. *The Backyard Bird Watcher.* New York: Simon & Schuster, 1979.

Harrison, Hal H. *A Field Guide to Birds' Nests.* Boston: Houghton Mifflin, 1975.

Heintzelman, Donald S. *A Manual for Birdwatching in the Americas.* New York: Universe Books, 1979.

Heintzelman, Donald S. *The Migrations of Hawks.* Bloomington: Indiana University Press, 1986.

Kress, Stephen W. *The Audubon Society Handbook for Birders.* New York: Charles Scribner's Sons, 1981.

Lincoln, Frederick C., and Steven R. Peterson. *Migration of Birds.* Circular 16. Rev. ed. Washington: U.S. Fish and Wildlife Service, 1979.

Martin, Alexander C., Herbert S. Zim, and Arnold L. Nelson. *American Wildlife and Plants: A Guide to Wildlife Food Habits.* New York: McGraw-Hill, 1951.

Mycio-Mommers, Luba, and Susan Fisher. *Backyard Habitat for Canada's Wildlife.* Ottawa: Canadian Wildlife Federation, 1997.

Peterson, Roger Tory. *A Field Guide to the Birds of Texas.* Boston: Houghton Mifflin, 1960.

Peterson, Roger Tory. *A Field Guide to the Birds: A Completely New Guide to All the Birds of Eastern and Central North America.* 4th ed., completely revised and enlarged. Boston: Houghton Mifflin, 1980.

Peterson, Roger Tory. *Peterson First Guide to Birds of North America.* Boston: Houghton Mifflin, 1986.

Peterson, Roger Tory. *A Field Guide to Western Birds: A Completely New Guide to All Species Found in North America West of the 100th Meridian and North of Mexico.* 3rd ed., completely revised and enlarged. Boston: Houghton Mifflin, 1990.

Ritter, Francis. *Eyewitness Garden Handbooks: Garden Trees.* New York: DK Publishing, 1996.

Robbins, Chandler S., Bertal Bruun, and Herbert S. Zim. *A Guide to Field Identification: Birds of North America.* New York: Golden Press, 1983.

Rudd, Robert L. *Pesticides and the Living Landscape.* Madison: University of Wisconsin Press, 1964.

Sanders, Jack. *Internet Guide to Birds and Birding: The Ultimate Directory to the Best Sites Online.* Camden ME: Ragged Mountain Press, 2000.

Scalise, Karyn. *Wildlife Gardening in Saskatchewan: Building Backyard Biodiversity.* Regina: Saskatchewan Environment and Resource Management, 1996.

Stokes, Donald W., and Lillian Q. Stokes. *A Guide to Bird Behavior.* Vols. 1–3. Boston: Little, Brown, 1979–89.

Stokes, Donald W., and Lillian Q. Stokes. *The Hummingbird Book.* Boston: Little, Brown, 1989.

Stokes, Donald, and Lillian Stokes. *Stokes Field Guide to Birds: Eastern Region.* Boston: Little, Brown, 1996.

Stokes, Donald, and Lillian Stokes. *Stokes Field Guide to Birds: Western Region.* Boston: Little, Brown, 1996.

Stokes, Donald, Lillian Stokes, and J. L. Brown. *Stokes Purple Martin Book: The Complete Guide to Attracting and Managing Purple Martins.* Boston: Little, Brown, 1997.

Tanner, James T. *The Ivory-Billed Woodpecker.* New York: National Audubon Society, 1942.

Terres, John K. *The Audubon Society Encyclopedia of North American Birds.* New York: Alfred A. Knopf, 1980.

Terres, John K. *Songbirds in Your Garden.* 5th rev. ed. Carrboro NC: Algonquin Books, 1994.

Tufts, Craig, and Peter Loewer. *The National Wildlife Federation's Guide to Gardening for Wildlife: How to Create a Beautiful Backyard Habitat for Birds, Butterflies and Other Wildlife.* Emmaus PA: Rodale, 1995.

Udvardy, Miklos D. G., and John Farrand Jr. *National Audubon Society Field Guide to North American Birds: Western Region.* New York: Alfred A. Knopf, 1994.

Uhrich, William D., ed. *A Century of Bird Life in Berks County, Pennsylvania.* Reading PA: Reading Public Museum, 1997.

Wauer, Roland H., and Mark A. Elwonger. *Birding Texas.* Helena MT: Falcon Press, 1998.

Weidensaul, Scott. *Living on the Wind: Across the Hemisphere with Migratory Birds.* New York: North Point Press, 1999.

Wilson, Alexander. *American Ornithology.* 9 vols. Philadelphia: Bradford and Inskeep, 1808–14.

Yuskavitch, James A. *Oregon Wildlife Viewing Guide.* Rev. ed. Helena MT: Falcon Press, 1994.

Zeleny, Lawrence. *The Bluebird: How You Can Help Its Fight for Survival.* Bloomington: Indiana University Press, 1976.

Zickefoose, Julie. *Enjoying Bluebirds More: The Bluebird Landlord's Handbook.* Marietta OH: Bird Watcher's Digest Press, 1993.

PERIODICALS

Birder's World
Kalmbach Publishing Co.
P.O. Box 1612
Waukesha WI 53187-1612
800-446-5489
customerservice@kalmbach.com

This popular and accessible magazine runs the gamut of birding topics. It is illustrated with excellent color photography and bird and wildlife art.

Birding
American Birding Association
P.O. Box 6599
Colorado Springs CO 80934
800-634-7736
www.americanbirding.org/

The ABA publishes *Birding*, a very informative but sometimes quite technical magazine, which is a benefit of ABA membership. It contains articles dealing with identification, bird finding, and bird listing. Serious birders enjoy this magazine, which is well illustrated with color photographs and the occasional painting.

Birds and Blooms
P.O. Box 991
Greendale WI 53129-0991
800-344-6913
www.reimanpub.com

This bimonthly magazine is aimed at backyard birdwatchers who enjoy wildlife gardening.

Bird Watcher's Digest
P.O. Box 110
Marietta OH 45750
800-879-2473
www.birdwatchersdigest.com

This digest-size magazine, published bimonthly, contains color photographs and original illustrations. Articles cover feeding, housing, identification skills, behavior, and habitat in an entertaining style. The publishers of *Bird Watcher's Digest* also publish *Backyard Bird News*, a bimonthly newsletter covering topics such as wildlife gardening and bird feeding.

Living Bird
Cornell Laboratory of Ornithology
159 Sapsucker Woods Rd.
Ithaca NY 14850-1999
607-254-2410

The Cornell Laboratory of Ornithology publishes an excellent magazine, *Living Bird*, which contains informative bird and birding articles. The magazine is illustrated with excellent color photographs and occasional paintings. It's sent to members as part of their membership benefits. Serious birdwatchers enjoy reading this publication.

WildBird
P.O. Box 6040
Mission Viejo CA 92690
949-855-8822
www.animalnetwork.com/wildbird/default.asp

WildBird, another large-format birding magazine, covers a wide range of birding topics with clear writing and excellent color photography.

ADVANCED BIRDING/ORNITHOLOGY

A handful of journals offer information for more advanced birders.

Auk, pica.wru.umt.edu/AUK/AUKLET.HTML
Condor, www.cooper.org/
Journal of Field Ornithology, www.afonet.org/journal.html
North American Birds, americanbirding.org/publications/nabgen.htm
Wilson Bulletin, www.ummz.Lsa.umich.edu/birds/wos.html

Index

Numbers in **bold** refer to pages with illustrations

ABOUT THE AUTHOR

Donald S. Heintzelman has served as Associate Curator of Natural Science at the William Penn Memorial Museum (The State Museum of Pennsylvania) and Curator of Ornithology at the New Jersey State Museum. Later, he was ornithologist on board the ecotourism ship M.S. *Lindblad Explorer* on expeditions to Amazonia, the Antarctic, and the Galapagos. He cofounded the Wildlife Information Center, Inc., and until recently was its president. A wildlife consultant, writer, and photographer, Heintzelman has traveled widely in North America, the West Indies, South America, the Falkland and Galapagos Islands, East Africa, and the Antarctic photographing and studying wildlife. He has published sixteen books, among them *Autumn Hawk Flights*, *A Guide to Hawk Watching in North America*, *The Migrations of Hawks*, and *Guide to Owl Watching in North America*. Heintzelman's scientific articles have been published in leading ornithology and conservation magazines, and his nontechnical articles and photography have been published in leading national magazines, including *Audubon*, *Defenders*, *National Wildlife*, *Organic Gardening*, and *Ranger Rick's Nature Magazine*. He writes a nature column for several Pennsylvania newspapers.